Data Warehousing

OLAP and Data Mining

Data Warehousing

OLAP and Data Mining

S. Nagabhushana

PUBLISHING FOR ONE WORLD

NEW AGE INTERNATIONAL (P) LIMITED, PUBLISHERS

New Delhi • Bangalore • Chennai • Cochin • Guwahati • Hyderabad
Jalandhar • Kolkata • Lucknow • Mumbai • Ranchi

Visit us at **www.newagepublishers.com**

Published by New Age International (P) Ltd., Publishers
First Edition: 2006
Reprint: 2008

Branches:

- 36, Malikarjuna Temple Street, Opp. ICWA, Basavanagudi, **Bangalore**. ✆ (080) 26677815
- 26, Damodaran Street, T. Nagar, **Chennai**. ✆ (044) 24353401
- Hemsen Complex, Mohd. Shah Road, Paltan Bazar, Near Starline Hotel, **Guwahati**. ✆ (0361) 2543669
- No. 105, 1st Floor, Madhiray Kaveri Tower, 3-2-19, Azam Jahi Road, Nimboliadda, **Hyderabad**. ✆ (040) 246524
- RDB Chambers (Formerly Lotus Cinema) 106A, Ist Floor, S.N. Banerjee Road, **Kolkata**. ✆ (033) 22275247
- 18, Madan Mohan Malviya Marg, **Lucknow**. ✆ (0522) 2209578
- 142C, Victor House, Ground Floor, N.M. Joshi Marg, Lower Parel, **Mumbai**. ✆ (022) 24927869
- 22, Golden House, Daryaganj, **New Delhi**. ✆ (011) 23262370, 23262368

ISBN (10): 81-224-1764-7

ISBN (13): 978-81-224-1764-7

Rs. 175.00

C-08-07-2737

Printed in India at Sanjeev Offset, Delhi.
Typeset at Kalyani Computer Services, Delhi.

PUBLISHING FOR ONE WORLD
NEW AGE INTERNATIONAL (P) LIMITED, PUBLISHERS
4835/24, Ansari Road, Daryaganj, New Delhi-110002
Visit us at **www.newagepublishers.com**

Dedicated

To

Beloved Friends

PREFACE

This book is intended for Information Technology (IT) professionals who have been hearing about or have been tasked to evaluate, learn or implement data warehousing technologies. This book also aims at providing fundamental techniques of KDD and Data Mining as well as issues in practical use of Mining tools.

Far from being just a passing fad, data warehousing technology has grown much in scale and reputation in the past few years, as evidenced by the increasing number of products, vendors, organizations, and yes, even books, devoted to the subject. Enterprises that have successfully implemented data warehouses find it strategic and often wonder how they ever managed to survive without it in the past. Also Knowledge Discovery and Data Mining (KDD) has emerged as a rapidly growing interdisciplinary field that merges together databases, statistics, machine learning and related areas in order to extract valuable information and knowledge in large volumes of data.

Volume-I is intended for IT professionals, who have been tasked with planning, managing, designing, implementing, supporting, maintaining and analyzing the organization's data warehouse.

The first section introduces the Enterprise Architecture and Data Warehouse concepts, the basis of the reasons for writing this book.

The second section focuses on three of the key People in any data warehousing initiative: the Project Sponsor, the CIO, and the Project Manager. This section is devoted to addressing the primary concerns of these individuals.

The third section presents a Process for planning and implementing a data warehouse and provides guidelines that will prove extremely helpful for both first-time and experienced warehouse developers.

The fourth section focuses on the Technology aspect of data warehousing. It lends order to the dizzying array of technology components that you may use to build your data warehouse.

The fifth section opens a window to the future of data warehousing.

The sixth section deals with On-Line Analytical Processing (OLAP), by providing different features to select the tools from different vendors.

Volume-II shows how to achieve success in understanding and exploiting large databases by uncovering valuable information hidden in data; learn what data has real meaning and what data simply takes up space; examining which data methods and tools are most effective for the practical needs; and how to analyze and evaluate obtained results.

S. NAGABHUSHANA

ACKNOWLEDGEMENTS

My sincere thanks to Prof. P. Rama Murthy, Principal, Intell Engineering College, Anantapur, for his able guidance and valuable suggestions - in fact, it was he who brought my attention to the writing of this book. I am grateful to Smt. G. Hampamma, Lecturer in English, Intell Engineering College, Anantapur and her whole family for their constant support and assistance while writing the book. Prof. Jeffrey D. Ullman, Department of Computer Science, Stanford University, U.S.A., deserves my special thanks for providing all the necessary resources. I am also thankful to Mr. R. Venkat, Senior Technical Associate at Virtusa, Hyderabad, for going through the script and encouraging me.

Last but not least, I thank Mr. Saumya Gupta, Managing Director, New Age International (P) Limited, Publishers. New Delhi, for their interest in the publication of the book.

CONTENTS

VOLUME I: DATA WAREHOUSING IMPLEMENTATION AND OLAP

PART I : INTRODUCTION

PART II : PEOPLE

PART III : PROCESS

PART IV : TECHNOLOGY

VOLUME II: DATA MINING

VOLUME I

DATA WAREHOUSING IMPLEMENTATION AND OLAP

PART I : INTRODUCTION

The term *Enterprise Architecture* refers to a collection of technology components and their interrelationships, which are integrated to meet the information requirements of an enterprise. This section introduces the concept of Enterprise IT Architectures with the intention of providing a framework for the various types of technologies used to meet an enterprise's computing needs.

Data warehousing technologies belong to just one of the many components in IT architecture. This chapter aims to define how data warehousing fits within the overall IT architecture, in the hope that IT professionals will be better positioned to use and integrate data warehousing technologies with the other IT components used by the enterprise.

CHAPTER 1

THE ENTERPRISE IT ARCHITECTURE

This chapter begins with a brief look at the changing business requirements and how, over time influenced the evolution of Enterprise Architectures. The Info*Motion* ("Information in Motion") Enterprise Architecture is introduced to provide IT professionals with a framework with which to classify the various technologies currently available.

1.1 THE PAST: EVOLUTION OF ENTERPRISE ARCHITECTURES

The IT architecture of an enterprise at a given time depends on three main factors:

- the business requirements of the enterprise;
- the available technology at that time; and
- the accumulated investments of the enterprise from earlier technology generations.

The business requirements of an enterprise are constantly changing, and the changes are coming at an exponential rate. Business requirements have, over the years, evolved from the day-to-day clerical recording of transactions to the automation of business processes. Exception reporting has shifted from tracking and correcting daily transactions that have gone astray to the development of self-adjusting business processes.

Technology has likewise advanced by delivering exponential increases in computing power and communications capabilities. However, for all these advances in computing hardware, a significant lag exists in the realms of software development and architecture definition. Enterprise Architectures thus far have displayed a general inability to gracefully evolve in line with business requirements, without either compromising on prior technology investments or seriously limiting their own ability to evolve further.

In hindsight, the evolution of the typical Enterprise Architecture reflects the continuous, piecemeal efforts of IT professionals to take advantage of the latest technology to improve the support of business operations. Unfortunately, this piecemeal effort has often resulted in a morass of incompatible components.

1.2 THE PRESENT: THE IT PROFESSIONAL'S RESPONSIBILITY

Today, the IT professional continues to have a two-fold responsibility: Meet business requirements through Information Technology and integrate new technology into the existing Enterprise Architecture.

Meet Business Requirements

The IT professional must ensure that the enterprise IT infrastructure properly supports a myriad set of requirements from different business users, each of whom has different and constantly changing needs, as illustrated in Figure 1.1.

Figure 1.1. Different Business Needs

Take Advantage of Technology Advancements

At the same time, the IT professional must also constantly learn new buzzwords, review new methodologies, evaluate new tools, and maintain ties with technology partners. Not all the latest technologies are useful; the IT professional must first sift through the technology jigsaw puzzle (see Figure 1.2) to find the pieces that meet the needs of the enterprise, then integrate the newer pieces with the existing ones to form a coherent whole.

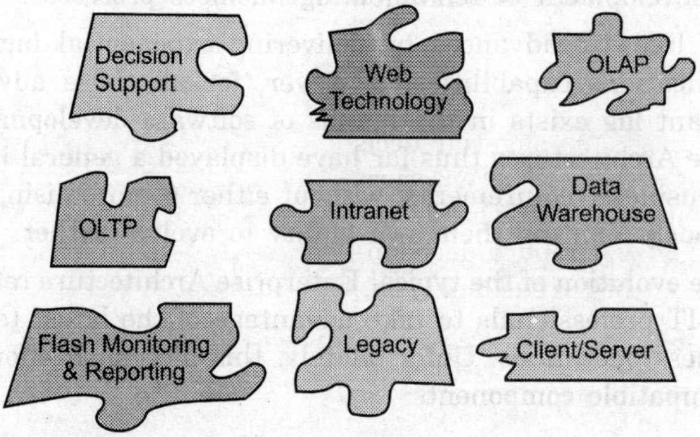

Figure 1.2. The Technology Jigsaw Puzzle

One of the key constraints the IT professional faces today is the current Enterprise IT Architecture itself. At this point, therefore, it is prudent to step back, assess the current state of affairs and identify the distinct but related components of modern Enterprise Architectures.

The two orthogonal perspectives of business and technology are merged to form one unified framework, as shown in Figure 1.3.

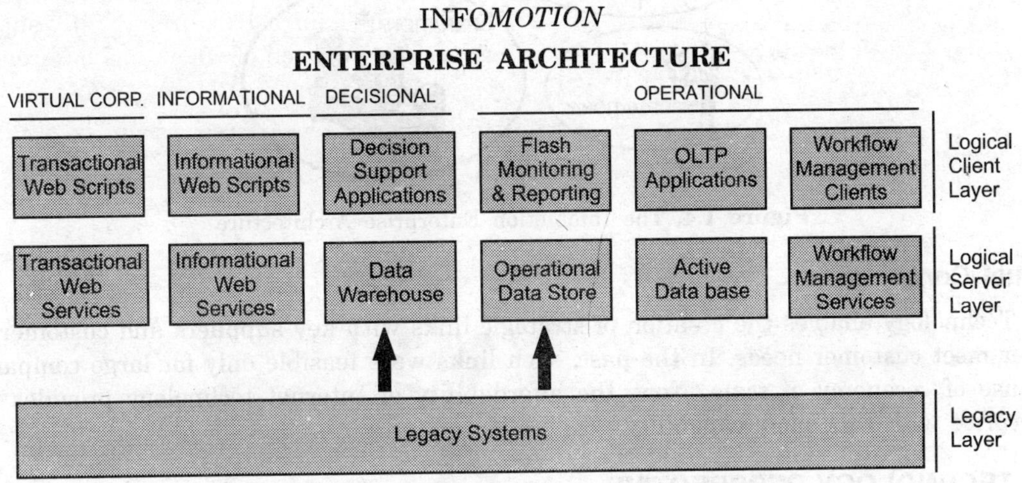

Figure 1.3. The InfoMotion Enterprise Architecture

1.3 BUSINESS PERSPECTIVE

From the business perspective, the requirements of the enterprise fall into categories illustrated in Figure 1.4 and described below.

Operational

Technology supports the smooth execution and continuous improvement of day-to-day operations, the identification and correction of errors through exception reporting and workflow management, and the overall monitoring of operations. Information retrieved about the business from an operational viewpoint is used to either complete or optimize the execution of a business process.

Decisional

Technology supports managerial decision-making and long-term planning. Decision-makers are provided with views of enterprise data from multiple dimensions and in varying levels of detail. Historical patterns in sales and other customer behavior are analyzed. Decisional systems also support decision-making and planning through scenario-based modeling, what-if analysis, trend analysis, and rule discovery.

Informational

Technology makes current, relatively static information widely and readily available to as many people as need access to it. Examples include company policies, product and service information, organizational setup, office location. corporate forms, training materials and company profiles.

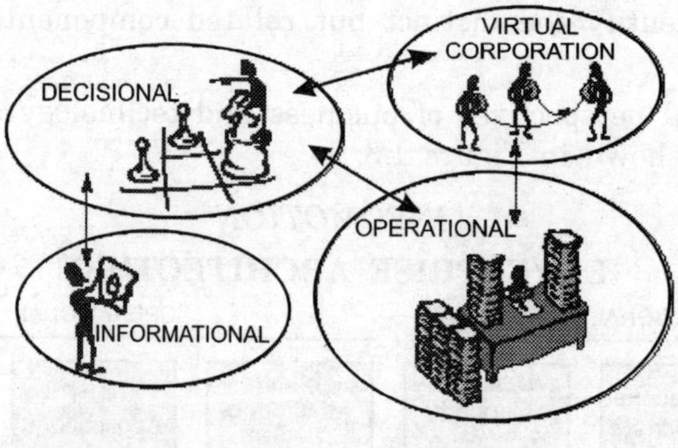

Figure 1.4. The InfoMotion Enterprise Architecture

Virtual Corporation

Technology enables the creation of strategic links with key suppliers and customers to better meet customer needs. In the past, such links were feasible only for large companies because of economy of scale. Now, the affordability of Internet technology provides any enterprise with this same capability.

1.4 TECHNOLOGY PERSPECTIVE

This section presents each architectural component from a technology standpoint and highlights the business need that each is best suited to support.

Operational Needs

Legacy Systems

The term *legacy system* refers to any information system currently in use that was built using previous technology generations. Most legacy systems are operational in nature, largely because the automation of transaction-oriented business processes had long been the priority of Information Technology projects.

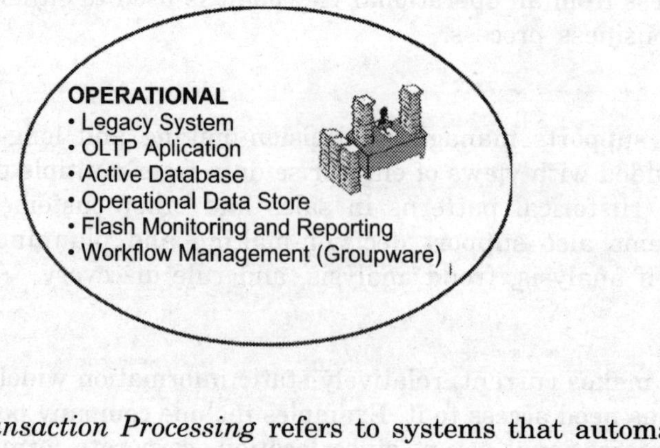

OLTP Applications

The term *Online Transaction Processing* refers to systems that automate and capture business transactions through the use of computer systems. In addition, these applications traditionally produce reports that allow business users to track the status of transactions. OLTP applications and their related active databases compose the majority of client/server systems today.

Active Databases

Databases store the data produced by Online Transaction Processing applications. These databases were traditionally passive repositories of data manipulated by business applications. It is not unusual to find legacy systems with processing logic and business rules contained entirely in the user interface or randomly interspersed in procedural code.

With the advent of client/server architecture, distributed systems, and advances in database technology, databases began to take on a more active role through database programming (e.g., stored procedures) and event management. IT professionals are now able to bullet-proof the application by placing processing logic in the database itself. This contrasts with the still-popular practice of replicating processing logic (sometimes in an inconsistent manner) across the different parts of a client application or across different client applications that update the same database. Through active databases, applications are more robust and conducive to evolution.

Operational Data Stores

An Operational Data Store or ODS is a collection of integrated databases designed to support the monitoring of operations. Unlike the databases of OLTP applications (that are function oriented), the Operational Data Store contains subject-oriented, volatile, and current enterprise-wide detailed information; it serves as a system of record that provides comprehensive views of data in operational systems.

Data are transformed and integrated into a consistent, unified whole as they are obtained from legacy and other operational systems to provide business users with an integrated and current view of operations (see Figure 1.5). Data in the Operational Data Store are constantly refreshed so that the resulting image reflects the latest state of operations.

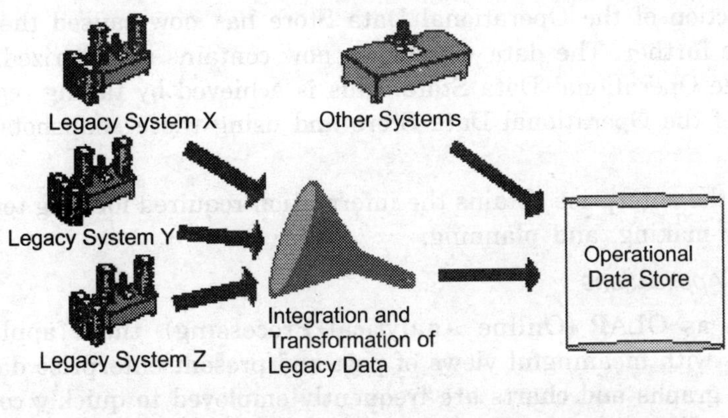

Figure 1.5. Legacy Systems and the Operational Data Store

Flash Monitoring and Reporting

These tools provide business users with a dashboard-meaningful online information on the operational status of the enterprise by making use of the data in the Operational Data

Store. The business user obtains a constantly refreshed, enterprise-wide view of operations without creating unwanted interruptions or additional load on transaction processing systems.

Workflow Management and Groupware

Workflow management systems are tools that allow groups to communicate and coordinate their work. Early incarnations of this technology supported group scheduling, e-mail, online discussions, and resource sharing. More advanced implementations of this technology are integrated with OLTP applications to support the execution of business processes.

Decisional Needs

Data Warehouse

The data warehouse concept developed as IT professionals increasingly realized that the structure of data required for transaction reporting was significantly different from the structure required to analyze data.

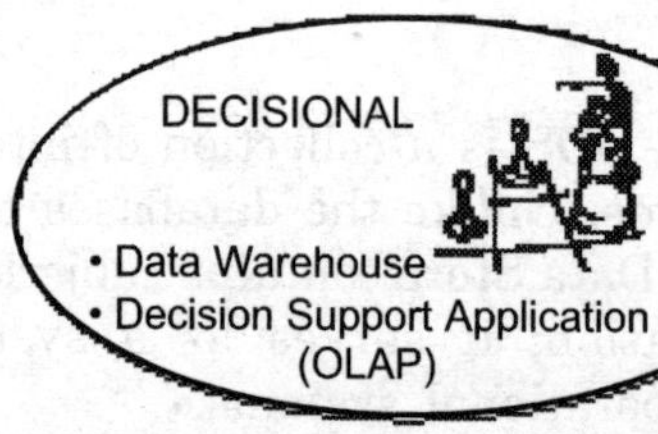

The data warehouse was originally envisioned as a separate architectural component that converted and integrated masses of raw data from legacy and other operational systems and from external sources. It was designed to contain summarized, historical views of data in production systems. This collection provides business users and decision-makers with a cross functional, integrated, subject-oriented view of the enterprise.

The introduction of the Operational Data Store has now caused the data warehouse concept to evolve further. The data warehouse now contains summarized, historical views of the data in the Operational Data Store. This is achieved by taking regular "snapshots" of the contents of the Operational Data Store and using these snapshots as the basis for warehouse loads.

In doing so, the enterprise obtains the information required for long term and historical analysis, decision-making, and planning.

Decision Support Applications

Also known as OLAP (Online Analytical Processing), these applications provide managerial users with meaningful views of past and present enterprise data. User-friendly formats, such as graphs and charts are frequently employed to quickly convey meaningful data relationships.

Decision support processing typically does not involve the update of data; however, some OLAP software allows users to enter data for budgeting, forecasting, and "what-if" analysis.

Informational Needs

Informational Web Services and Scripts

Web browsers provide their users with a universal tool or front-end for accessing information from web servers. They provide users with a new ability to both explore and publish information with relative ease. Unlike other technologies, web technology makes any user an instant publisher by enabling the distribution of knowledge and expertise, with no more effort than it takes to record the information in the first place.

By its very nature, this technology supports a paperless distribution process. Maintenance and update of information is straightforward since the information is stored on the web server.

Virtual Corporation Needs

Transactional Web Services and Scripts

Several factors now make Internet technology and electronic commerce a realistic option for enterprises that wish to use the Internet for business transactions.

- **Cost.** The increasing affordability of Internet access allows businesses to establish cost-effective and strategic links with business partners. This option was originally open only to large enterprises through expensive, dedicated wide-area networks or metropolitan area networks.
- **Security.** Improved security and encryption for sensitive data now provide customers with the confidence to transact over the Internet. At the same time, improvements in security provide the enterprise with the confidence to link corporate computing environments to the Internet.
- **User-friendliness.** Improved user-friendliness and navigability from web technology make Internet technology and its use within the enterprise increasingly popular.

Figure 1.6 recapitulates the architectural components for the different types of business needs. The majority of the architectural components support the enterprise at the operational level. However, separate components are now clearly defined for decisional and information purposes, and the virtual corporation becomes possible through Internet technologies.

Other Components

Other architectural components are so pervasive that most enterprises have begun to take their presence for granted. One example is the group of applications collectively known as office productivity tools (such as Microsoft Office or Lotus SmartSuite). Components of this type can and should be used across the various layers of the Enterprise Architecture and, therefore, are not described here as a separate item.

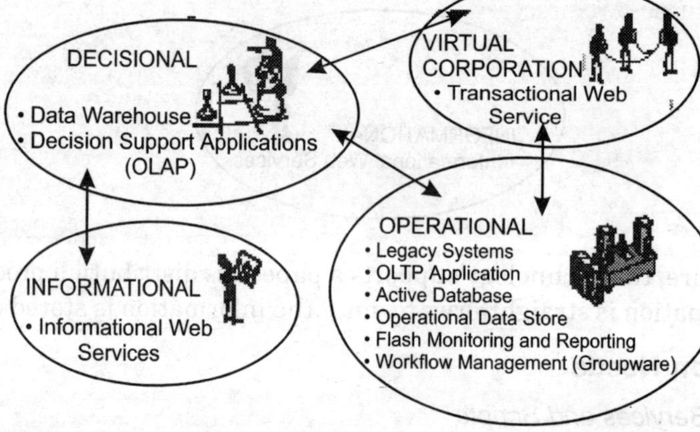

Figure 1.6. InfoMotion Enterprise Architecture Components (Applicability to Business Needs)

1.5 ARCHITECTURE MIGRATION SCENARIOS

Given the typical path that most Enterprise Architectures have followed, an enterprise will find itself in need of one or more of the following six migration scenarios. Which are recommended for fulfilling those needs.

Legacy Integration

The Need

The integration of new and legacy systems is a constant challenge because of the architectural templates upon which legacy systems were built. Legacy systems often attempt to meet all types of information requirements through a single architectural component; consequently, these systems are brittle and resistant to evolution.

Despite attempts to replace them with new applications, many legacy systems remain in use because they continue to meet a set of business requirements: they represent significant investments that the enterprise cannot afford to scrap, or their massive replacement would result in unacceptable levels of disruption to business operations.

The Recommended Approach

The integration of legacy systems with the rest of the architecture is best achieved through the Operational Data Store and/or the data warehouse. Figure 1.7 modifies Figure 1.5 to show the integration of legacy systems.

Legacy programs that produce and maintain summary information are migrated to the data warehouse. Historical data are likewise migrated to the data warehouse. Reporting functionality in legacy systems is moved either to the flash reporting and monitoring tools (for operational concerns), or to decision support applications (for long-term planning and decision-making). Data required for operational monitoring are moved to the Operational Data Store. Table 1.1 summarizes the migration avenues.

The Operational Data Store and the data warehouse present IT professionals with a natural migration path for legacy migration. By migrating legacy systems to these two components, enterprises can gain a measure of independence from legacy components that were designed with old, possibly obsolete, technology. Figure 1.8 highlights how this approach fits into the Enterprise Architecture.

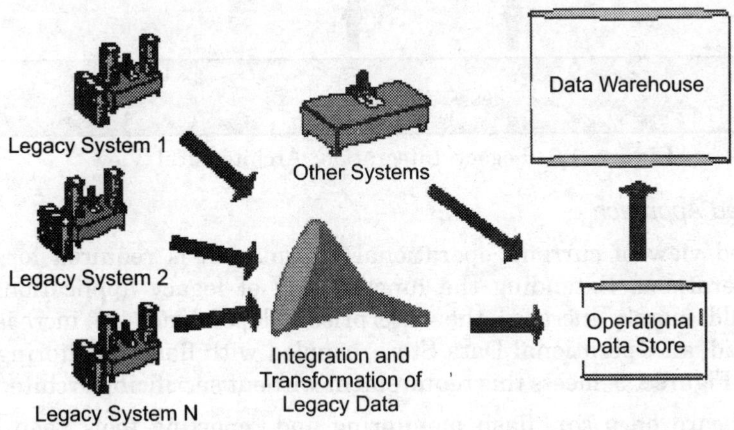

Figure 1.7. Legacy Integration

Operational Monitoring

The Need

Today's typical legacy systems are not suitable for supporting the operational monitoring needs of an enterprise. Legacy systems are typically structured around functional or organizational areas, in contrast to the cross-functional view required by operations monitoring. Different and potentially incompatible technology platforms may have been used for different systems. Data may be available in legacy databases but are not extracted in the format required by business users. Or data may be available but may be too raw to be of use for operational decision-making (further summarization, calculation, or conversion is required). And lastly, several systems may contain data about the same item but may examine the data from different viewpoints or at different time frames, therefore requiring reconciliation.

Table 1.1. Migration of Legacy Functionality to the Appropriate Architectural Component

Functionality in Legacy Systems	*Should be Migrated to . . .*
Summary Information	Data Warehouse
Historical Data	Data Warehouse
Operational Reporting	Flash Monitoring and Reporting Tools
Data for Operational	Monitoring Operational Data Store
Decisional Reporting	Decision Support Applications

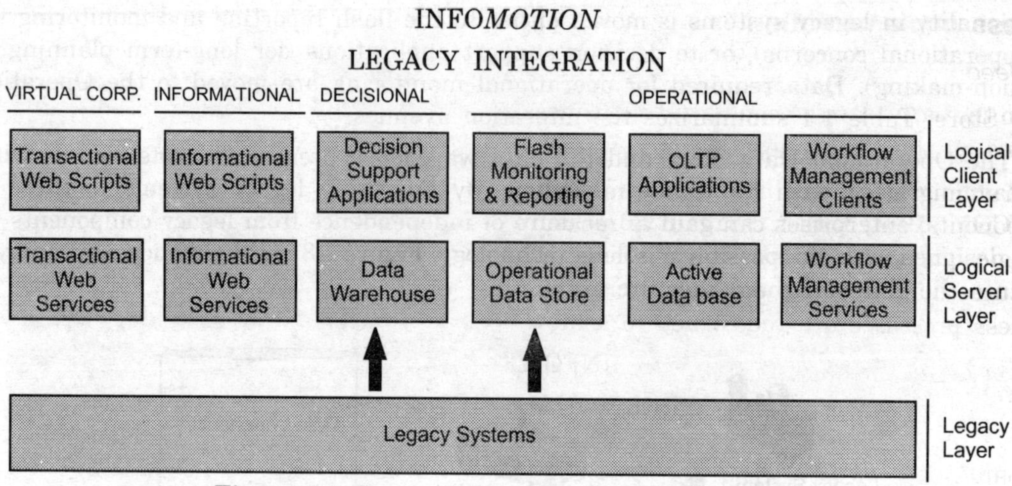

Figure 1.8. Legacy Integration: Architectural View

The Recommended Approach

An integrated view of current, operational information is required for the successful monitoring of operations. Extending the functionality of legacy applications to meet this requirement would merely increase the enterprise's dependence on increasingly obsolete technology. Instead, an Operational Data Store, coupled with flash monitoring and reporting tools, as shown in Figure 1.9, meets this requirement without sacrificing architectural integrity.

Like a dashboard on a car, flash monitoring and reporting tools keep business users apprised of the latest cross-functional status of operations. These tools obtain data from the Operational Data Store, which is regularly refreshed with the latest information from legacy and other operational systems.

Business users are consequently able to step in and correct problems in operations while they are still smaller or better, to prevent problems from occurring altogether. Once alerted of a potential problem, the business user can manually intervene or make use of automated tools (i.e., control panel mechanisms) to fine-tune operational processes. Figure 1.10 highlights how this approach fits into the Enterprise Architecture.

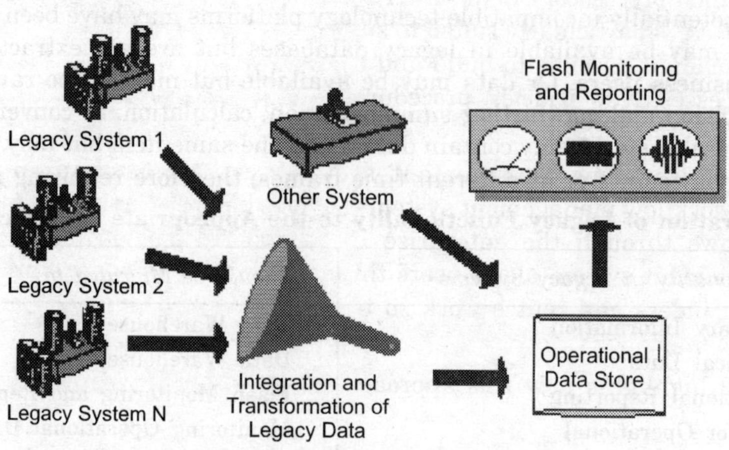

Figure 1.9. Operational Monitoring

Process Implementation

The Need

In the early 90s, the popularity of business process reengineering (BPR) caused businesses to focus on the implementation of new and redefined business processes.

Raymond Manganelli and Mark Klein, in their book *The Reengineering Handbook* (AMACOM, 1994, ISBN: 0-8144-0236-4) define BPR as "the rapid and radical redesign of *strategic, value-added business processes*–and the systems, policies, and organizational structures that support them–to optimize the work flow and productivity in an organization." Business processes are redesigned to achieve desired results in an optimum manner.

INFO*MOTION*

OPERATIONAL MONITORING

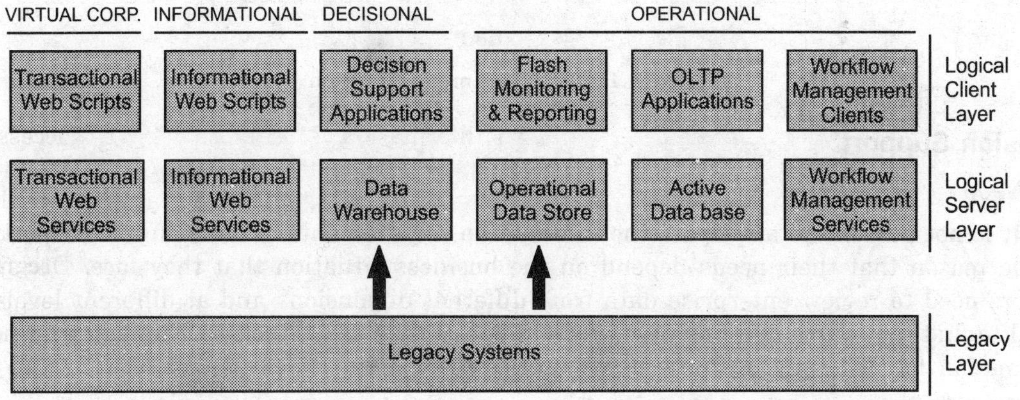

Figure 1.10. Operational Monitoring: Architectural View

The Recommended Approach

With BPR, the role of Information Technology shifted from simple automation to enabling radically redesigned processes. Client/server technology, such as OLTP applications serviced by active databases, is particularly suited to supporting this type of business need. Technology advances have made it possible to build and modify systems quickly in response to changes in business processes. New policies, procedures and controls are supported and enforced by the systems.

In addition, workflow management systems can be used to supplement OLTP applications. A workflow management system converts business activities into a goal-directed process that flows through the enterprise in an orderly fashion (see Figure 1.11). The workflow management system alerts users through the automatic generation of notification messages or reminders and routes work so that the desired business result is achieved in an expedited manner.

Figure 1.12 highlights how this approach fits into the Enterprise Architecture.

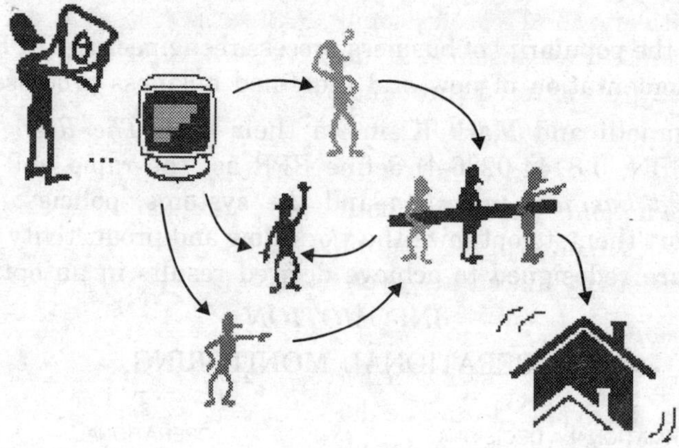

Figure 1.11. Process Implementation

Decision Support

The Need

It is not possible to anticipate the information requirements of decision makers for the simple reason that their needs depend on the business situation that they face. Decision-makers need to review enterprise data from different dimensions and at different levels of detail to find the source of a business problem before they can attack it. They likewise need information for detecting business opportunities to exploit.

Decision-makers also need to analyze trends in the performance of the enterprise. Rather than waiting for problems to present themselves, decision-makers need to proactively mobilize the resources of the enterprise in anticipation of a business situation.

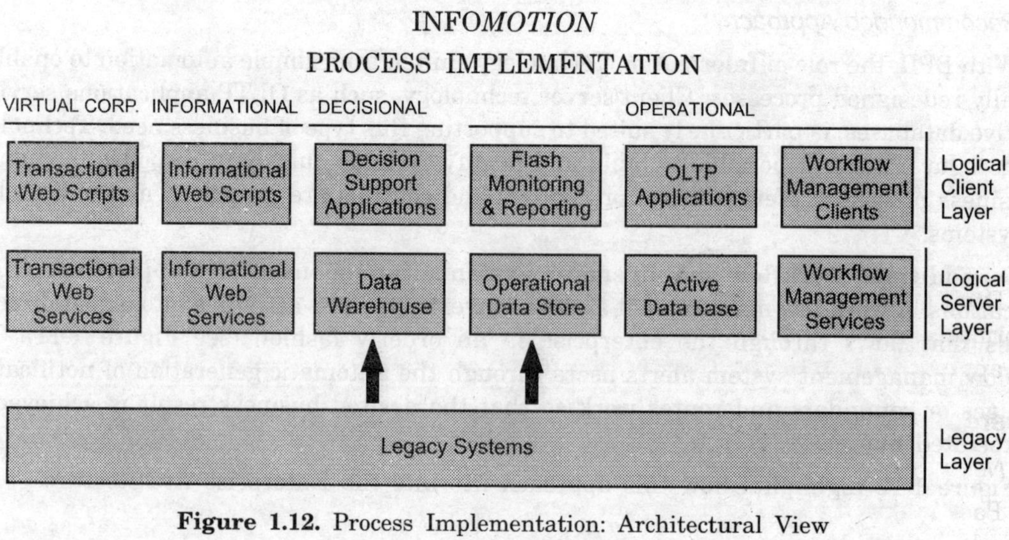

Figure 1.12. Process Implementation: Architectural View

Since these information requirements cannot be anticipated, the decision maker often resorts to reviewing pre-designed inquiries or reports in an attempt to find or derive needed information. Alternatively, the IT professional is pressured to produce an ad hoc report from legacy systems as quickly as possible. If unlucky, the IT professional will find the data needed for the report are scattered throughout different legacy systems. An even unluckier may find that the processing required to produce the report will have a toll on the operations of the enterprise.

These delays are not only frustrating both for the decision-maker and the IT professional, but also dangerous for the enterprise. The information that eventually reaches the decision-maker may be inconsistent, inaccurate, worse, or obsolete.

The Recommended Approach

Decision support applications (or OLAP) that obtain data from the data warehouse are recommended for this particular need. The data warehouse holds transformed and integrated enterprise-wide operational data appropriate for strategic decision-making, as shown in Figure 1.13. The data warehouse also contains data obtained from external-sources, whenever this data is relevant to decision-making.

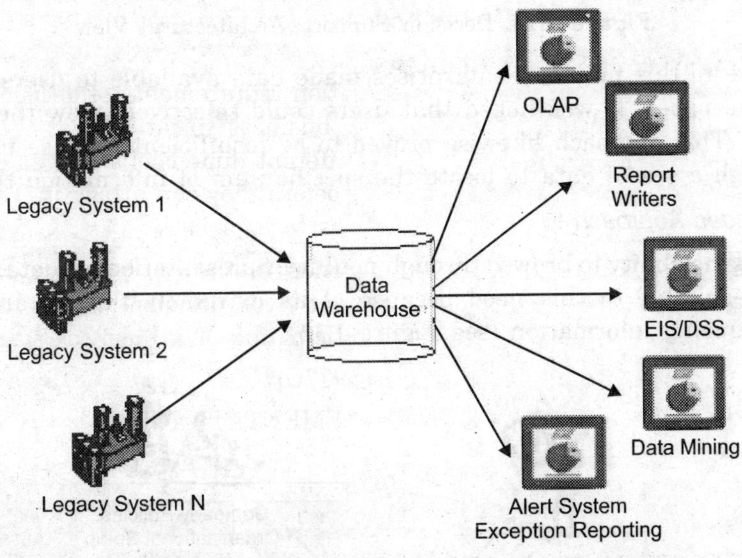

Figure 1.13. Decision Support

Decision support applications analyze and make data warehouse information available in formats that are readily understandable by decision-makers. Figure 1.14 highlights how this approach fits into the Enterprise Architecture.

Hyperdata Distribution

The Need

Past informational requirements were met by making data available in physical form through reports, memos, and company manuals. This practice resulted in an overflow of documents providing much data and not enough information.

Paper-based documents also have the disadvantage of becoming dated. Enterprises encountered problems in keeping different versions of related items synchronized. There was a constant need to update, republish and redistribute documents.

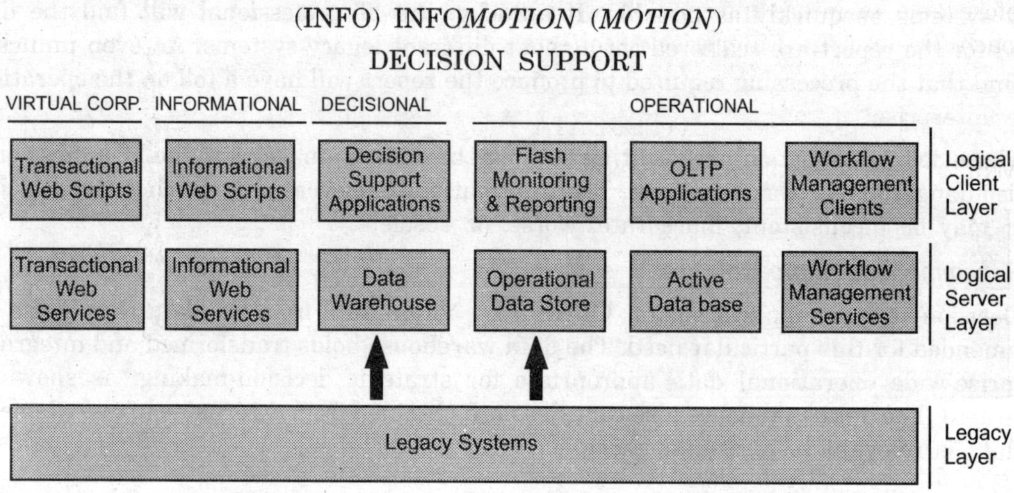

Figure 1.14. Decision Support: Architectural View

In response to this problem, enterprises made data available to users over a network to eliminate the paper. It was hoped that users could selectively view the data whenever they needed it. This approach likewise proved to be insufficient because users still had to navigate through a sea of data to locate the specific item of information that was needed.

The Recommended Approach

Users need the ability to browse through nonlinear presentations of data. Web technology is particularly suitable to this need because of its extremely flexible and highly visual method of organizing information (see Figure 1.15).

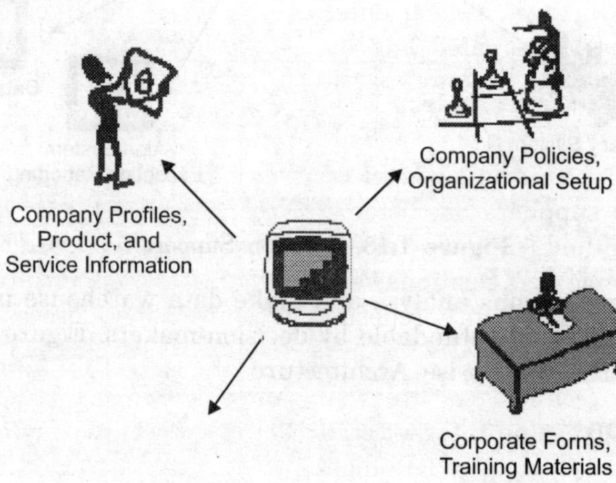

Figure 1.15. Hyperdata Distribution

Web technology allows users to display charts and figures; navigate through large amounts of data; visualize the contents of database files; seamlessly navigate across charts, data, and annotation; and organize charts and figures in a hierarchical manner. Users are therefore able to locate information with relative ease. Figure 1.16 highlights how this approach fits into the Enterprise Architecture.

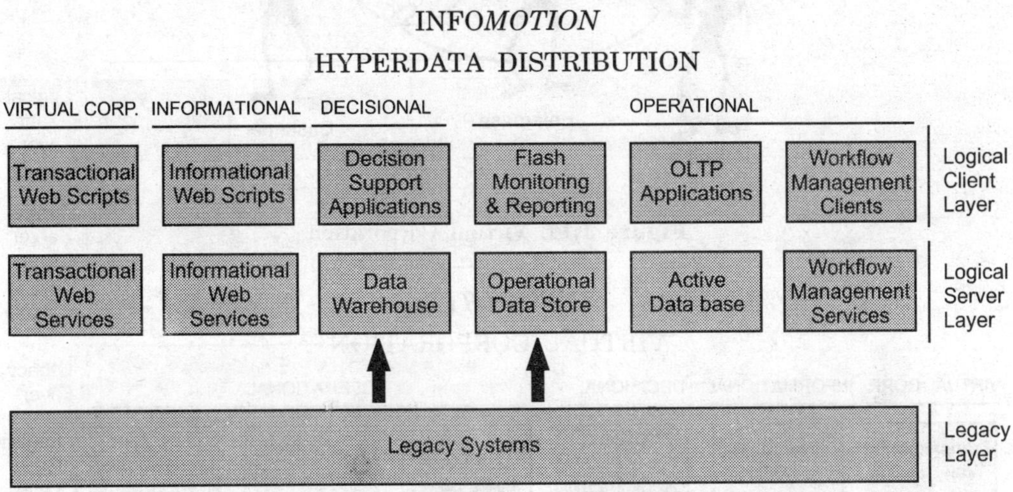

Figure 1.16. Hyperdata Distribution: Architectural View

Virtual Corporation

The Need

A virtual corporation is an enterprise that has extended its business processes to encompass both its key customers and suppliers. Its business processes are newly redesigned; its product development or service delivery is accelerated to better meet customer needs and preferences; its management practices promote new alignments between management and labor, as well as new linkages among enterprise, supplier and customer. A new level of cooperation and openness is created and encouraged between the enterprise and its key business partners.

The Recommended Approach

Partnerships at the enterprise level translate into technological links between the enterprise and its key suppliers or customers (see Figure 1.17). Information required by each party is identified, and steps are taken to ensure that this data crosses organizational boundaries properly. Some organizations seek to establish a higher level of cooperation with their key business partners by jointly redesigning their business processes to provide greater value to the customer.

Internet and web technologies are well suited to support redesigned, transactional processes. Thanks to decreasing Internet costs, improved security measures, improved user-friendliness, and navigability. Figure 1.18 highlights how this approach fits into the Enterprise Architecture.

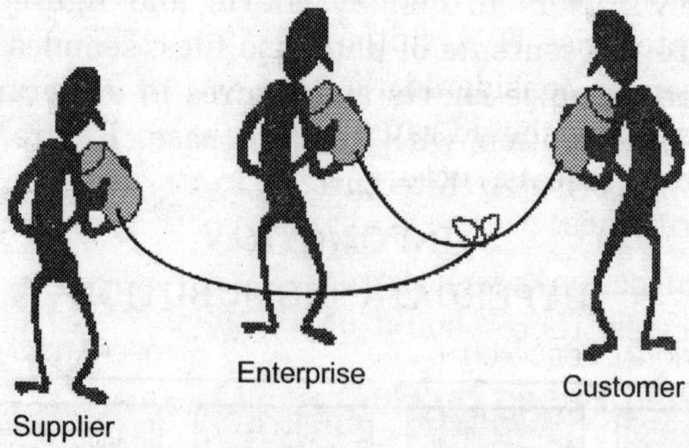

Figure 1.17. Virtual Corporation

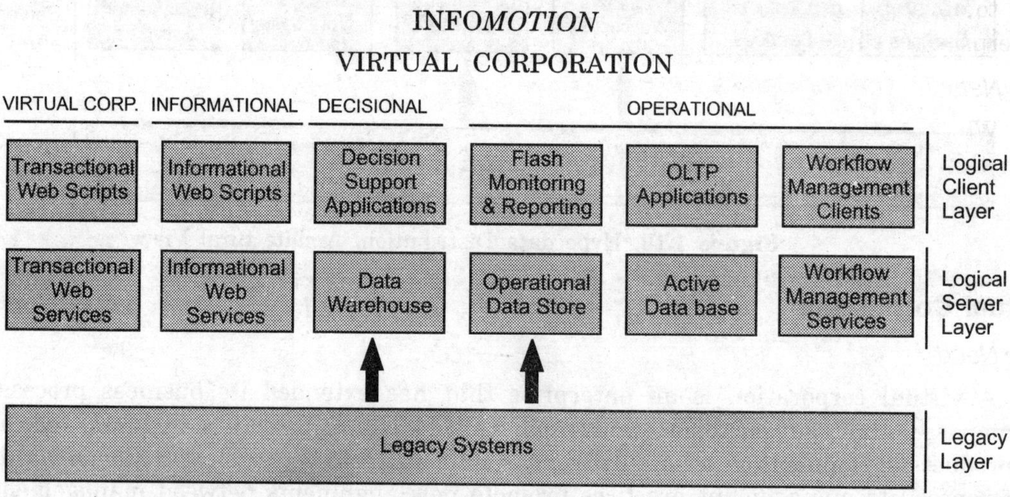

Figure 1.18. Virtual Corporation: Architectural View

1.6 MIGRATION STRATEGY: HOW DO WE MOVE FORWARD?

The strategies presented in the previous section enable organizations to move from their current technology architectures into the Info*Motion* Enterprise Architecture. This section describes the tasks for any migration effort.

Review the Current Enterprise Architecture

As simple as this may sound, the starting point is a review of the current Enterprise Architecture. It is important to have an idea of whatever that is already available before planning for further achievements.

The IT department or division should have this information readily available, although it may not necessarily be expressed in terms of the architectural components identified above. A short and simple exercise of mapping the current architecture of an enterprise to the architecture described above should quickly highlight any gaps in the current architecture.

Identify Information Architecture Requirements

Knowing that the Enterprise IT Architecture has gaps is not sufficient. It is important to know whether these can be considered real gaps when viewed within the context of the enterprise's requirements. Gaps should cause concern only if the absence of an architectural component prevents the IT infrastructure from meeting present requirements or from supporting long-term strategies.

For example, if transactional web scripts are not critical to an enterprise given its current needs and strategies, there should be no cause for concern.

Develop a Migration Plan Based on Requirements

It is not advisable for an enterprise to use this list of architectural gaps to justify a dramatic overhaul of its IT infrastructure; such an undertaking would be expensive and would cause unnecessary disruption of business operations. Instead, the enterprise would do well to develop a migration plan that consciously maps coming IT projects to the Info*Motion* Enterprise Architecture.

The Natural Migration Path

While developing the migration plan, the enterprise should consider the natural migration path that the Info*Motion* architecture implies, as illustrated in Figure 1.19.

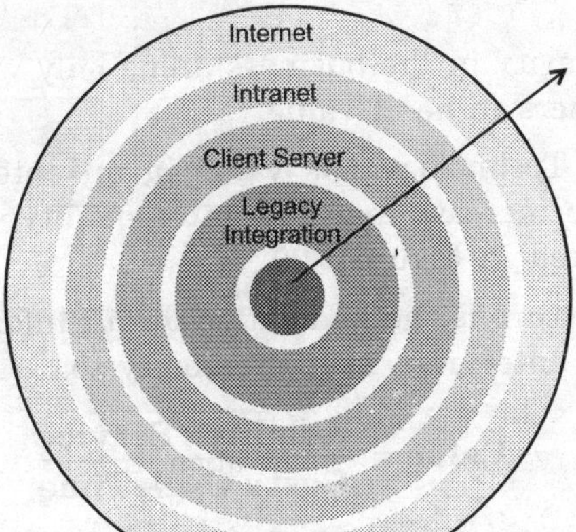

Figure 1.19. Natural Migration Roadmap

- The legacy layer at the very core of the Enterprise Architecture. For most companies, this core layer is where the majority of technology investments have been made. It should also be the starting point of any architecture migration effort, i.e., the enterprise should start from this core technology before focusing its attention on newer forms or layers of technology.
- The Legacy Integration layer insulates the rest of the Enterprise Architecture from the growing obsolescence of the Legacy layer. It also provides the succeeding technology layers with a more stable foundation for future evolution.
- Each of the succeeding technology layers (i.e., Client/Server, Intranet, Internet) builds upon its predecessors.
- At the outermost layer, the public Internet infrastructure itself supports the operations of the enterprise.

The Customized Migration Path

Depending on the priorities and needs of the enterprise, one or more of the migration scenarios described in the previous section will be helpful starting points. The scenarios provide generic roadmaps that address typical architectural needs.

The migration plan, however, must be customized to address the specific needs of the enterprise. Each project defined in the plan must individually contribute to the enterprise in the short term, while laying the groundwork for achieving long-term enterprise and IT objectives.

By incrementally migrating its IT infrastructure (one component and one project at a time), the enterprise will find itself slowly but surely moving towards a modern, resilient Enterprise Architecture, with minimal and acceptable levels of disruption in operations.

Monitor and Update the Migration Plan

The migration plan must be monitored, and the progress of the different projects fed back into the planning task. One must not lose sight of the fact that a modern Enterprise Architecture is a moving target; inevitable new technology renders continuous evolution of the Enterprise Architecture.

IN Summary

An enterprise has longevity in the business arena only when its products and services are perceived by its customers to be of value.

Likewise, Information Technology has value in an enterprise only when its cost is outweighed by its ability to increase and guarantee quality, improve service, cut costs or reduce cycle time, as depicted in Figure 1.20.

The Enterprise Architecture is the foundation for all Information Technology efforts. It therefore must provide the enterprise with the ability to:

$$\textbf{Value} = \frac{\textbf{Quality} \times \textbf{Service}}{\textbf{Cost} \times \textbf{CycleTime}}$$

Figure 1.20. The Value Equation

- distill information of value from the data which surrounds it, which it continuously generates (information/data); and
- get that information to the right people and processes at the right time (motion).

These requirements form the basis for the Info*Motion* equation, shown in Figure 1.21.

$$\textbf{Info}\boldsymbol{Motion} = \frac{\textbf{Information}}{\textbf{Data} \times \textbf{Motion}}$$

Figure 1.21. The Info*Motion* Equation

By identifying distinct architectural components and their interrelationships, the Info*Motion* Enterprise Architecture increases the capability of the IT infrastructure to meet present business requirements while positioning the enterprise to leverage emerging trends, such as data warehousing, in both business and technology. Figure 1.22 shows the Info*Motion* Enterprise Architecture, the elements of which we have discussed.

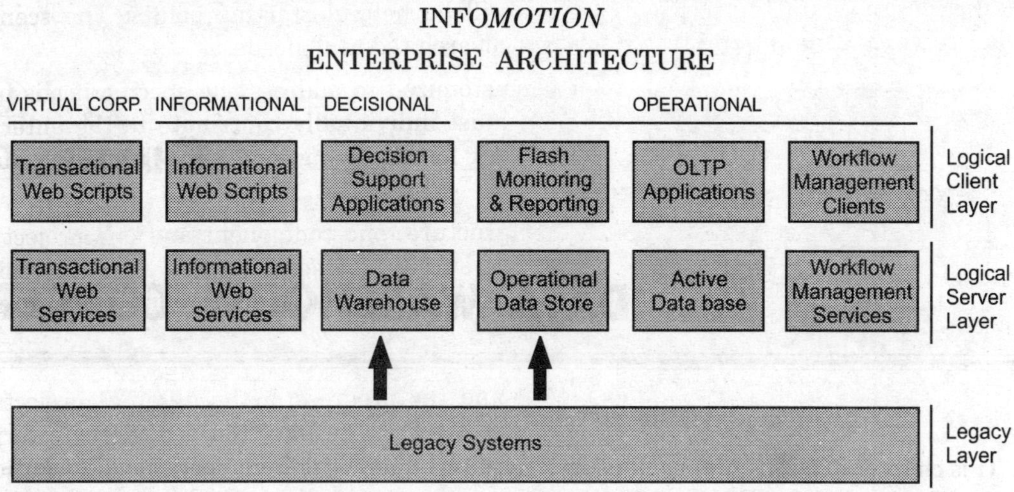

Figure 1.22. The Info*Motion* Architecture

CHAPTER 2

DATA WAREHOUSE CONCEPTS

This chapter explains how computing has changed its focus from operational to decisional concerns. It also defines data warehousing concepts and cites the typical reasons for building data warehouses.

2.1 GRADUAL CHANGES IN COMPUTING FOCUS

In retrospect, it is easy to see how computing has shifted its focus from operational to decisional concerns. The differences in operational and decisional information requirements presented new challenges that old computing practices could not meet. Below, we elaborate on how this change in computing focus became the impetus for the development of data warehousing technologies.

Early Computing Focused on Operational Requirements

The Business Cycle (depicted in Figure 2.1) shows that any enterprise must operate at three levels: operational (i.e., the day-to-day running of the business), tactical (i.e., the definition of policy and the monitoring of operations) and strategic (i.e., the definition of organization's vision, goals and objectives).

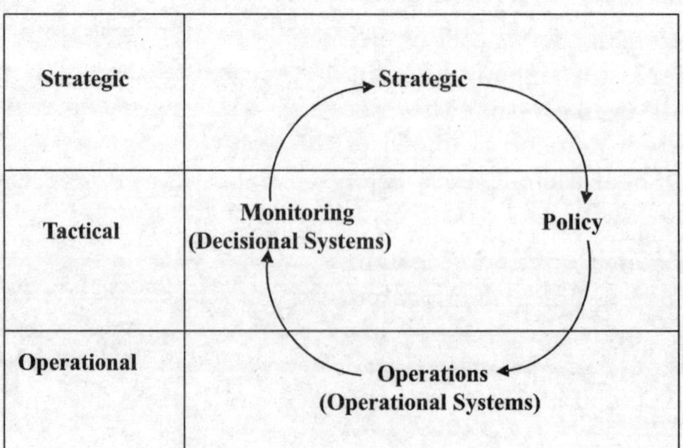

Figure 2.1. The Business Cycle

In Chapter 1, it is noted that much of the effort and money in computing has been focused on meeting the operational business requirements of enterprises. After all, without the OLTP applications that records thousands, even millions of discrete transactions each day, it would not be possible for any enterprise to meet customer needs while enforcing business policies consistently. Nor would it be possible for an enterprise to grow without significantly expanding its manpower base.

With operational systems deployed and day-to-day information needs being met by the OLTP systems, the focus of computing has over the recent years shifted naturally to meeting the decisional business requirements of an enterprise. Figure 2.1 illustrates the business cycle as it is viewed today.

Decisional Requirements Cannot be Fully Anticipated

Unfortunately, it is not possible for IT professionals to anticipate the information requirements of an enterprise's decision-makers, for the simple reason that their information needs and report requirements change as the business situation changes.

Decision-makers themselves cannot be expected to know their information requirements ahead of time; they review enterprise data from different perspectives and at different levels of detail to find and address business problems as the problems arise. Decision-makers also need to look through business data to identify opportunities that can be exploited. They examine performance trends to identify business situations that can provide competitive advantage, improve profits, or reduce costs. They analyze market data and make the tactical as well as strategic decisions that determine the course of the enterprise.

Operational Systems Fail to Provide Decisional Information

Since these information requirements cannot be anticipated, operational systems (which correctly focus on recording and completing different types of business transactions) are unable to provide decision-makers with the information they need. As a result, business managers fall back on the time-consuming, and often frustrating process of going through operational inquiries or reports already supported by operational systems in an attempt to find or derive the information they really need. Alternatively, IT professionals are pressured to produce an adhoc report from the operational systems as quickly as possible.

It will not be unusual for the IT professional to find that the data needed to produce the report are scattered throughout different operational systems and must first be carefully integrated. Worse, it is likely that the processing required to extract the data from each operational system will demand so much of the system resources that the IT professional must wait until non-operational hours before running the queries required to produce the report.

Those delays are not only time-consuming and frustrating both for the IT professionals and the decision-makers, but also dangerous for the enterprise. When the report is finally produced, the data may be inconsistent, inaccurate, or obsolete. There is also the very real possibility that this new report will trigger the request for another adhoc report.

Decisional Systems have Evolved to Meet Decisional Requirements

Over the years, decisional systems have been developed and implemented in the hope of meeting these information needs. Some enterprises have actually succeeded in developing and deploying data warehouses within their respective organizations, long before the term data warehouse became fashionable.

Most decisional systems, however, have failed to deliver on their promises. This book introduces data warehousing technologies and shares lessons learnt from the success and failures of those who have been on the "bleeding edge."

2.2 DATA WAREHOUSE CHARACTERISTICS AND DEFINITION

A data warehouse can be viewed as an information system with the following attributes:

- It is a database designed for analytical tasks, using data from multiple applications.
- It supports a relatively small number of users with relatively long interactions.
- Its usage is read-intensive.
- Its content is periodically updated (mostly additions).
- It contains current and historical data to provide a historical perspective of information.
- It contains a few large tables.

Each query frequently results in a large results set and involves frequent full table scan and multi-table joins.

What is a data warehouse? William H. Inmon in Building the Data Warehouse (QED Technical Publishing Group, 1992 ISBN: 0-89435-404-3) defines a data warehouse as "a collection of integrated subject-oriented databases designed to supply the information required for decision-making."

A more thorough look at the above definition yields the following observations.

Integrated

A data warehouse contains data extracted from the many operational systems of the enterprise, possibly supplemented by external data. For example, a typical banking data warehouse will require the integration of data drawn from the deposit systems, loan systems, and the general ledger.

Each of these operational systems records different types of business transactions and enforces the policies of the enterprise regarding these transactions. If each of the operational systems has been custom built or an integrated system is not implemented as a solution, then it is unlikely that these systems are integrated. Thus, Customer A in the deposit system and Customer B in the loan system may be one and the same person, but there is no automated way for anyone in the bank to know this. Customer relationships are managed informally through relationships with bank officers.

A data warehouse brings together data from the various operational systems to provide an integrated view of the customer and the full scope of his or her relationship with the bank.

Subject Oriented

Traditional operational systems focus on the data requirements of a department or division, producing the much-criticized "stovepipe" systems of model enterprises. With the advent of business process reengineering, enterprises began espousing process-centered teams and case workers. Modern operational systems, in turn, have shifted their focus to the operational requirements of an entire business process and aim to support the execution of the business process from start to finish.

A data warehouse goes beyond traditional information views by focusing on enterprise-wide subjects such as customers, sales, and profits. These subjects span both organizational and process boundaries and require information from multiple sources to provide a complete picture.

Databases

Although the term data warehousing technologies is used to refer to the gamut of technology components that are required to plan, develop, manage, implement, and use a data warehouse, the term data warehouse itself refers to a large, read-only repository of data.

At the very heart of every data warehouse lie the large databases that store the integrated data of the enterprise, obtained from both internal and external data sources. The term internal data refers to all data that are extracted from the operational systems of the enterprise. External data are data provided by third-party organizations, including business partners, customers, government bodies, and organizations that choose to make a profit by selling their data (e.g., credit bureaus).

Also stored in the databases are the metadata that describe the contents of the data warehouse. A more thorough discussion on metadata and their role in data warehousing is provided in Chapter 3.

Required for Decision-Making

Unlike the databases of operational systems, which are often normalized to preserve and maintain data integrity, a data warehouse is designed and structured in a demoralized manner to better support the usability of the data warehouse. Users are better able to examine, derive, summarize, and analyze data at various levels of detail, over different periods of time, when using a demoralized data structure.

The database is demoralized to mimic a business user's dimensional view of the business. For example, while a finance manager is interested in the profitability of the various products of a company, a product manager will be more interested in the sales of the product in the various sales regions. In data warehousing parlance, users need to "slice and dice" through different areas of the database at different levels of detail to obtain the information they need. In this manner, a decision-maker can start with a high-level view of the business, then drill down to get more detail on the areas that require his attention, or vice versa.

Each Unit of Data is Relevant to a Point in Time

Every data warehouse will inevitably have a Time dimension; each data item {also called facts or measures) in the data warehouse is time-stamped to support queries or reports that require the comparison of figures from prior months or years.

The time-stamping of each fact also makes it possible for decision-makers to recognize trends and patterns in customer or market behavior over time.

A Data Warehouse Contains both Atomic and Summarized Data

Data warehouses hold data at different levels of detail. Data at the most detailed level, i.e., the atomic level, are used to derive the summarized aggregated values. Aggregates (presummarized data) are stored in the warehouse to speed up responses to queries at higher levels of granularity.

If the data warehouse stores data only at summarized levels, its users will not be able to drill down on data items to get more detailed information. However, the storage of very detailed data results in larger space requirements.

2.3 THE DYNAMIC, AD HOC REPORT

The most ideal scenario for enterprise decision-makers (and for IT professionals) is to have a repository of data and a set of tools that will allow decision-makers to create their own set of dynamic reports. The term dynamic report refers to a report that can be quickly modified by its user to present either greater or lesser detail, without any additional programming required. Dynamic reports are the only kind of reports that provide true, ad-hoc reporting capabilities. Figure 2.2 presents an example of a dynamic report.

For Current Year, 2Q

Sales Region	Targets ('000s)	Actuals ('000s)
Asia	24,000	25,550
Europe	10,000	12,200
North America	**8,000**	**2,000**
Africa	5,600	6,200
...	...	...

Figure 2.2. The Dynamic Report–Summary View

A decision-maker should be able to start with a short report that summarizes the performance of the enterprise. When the summary calls attention to an area that bears closer inspecting, the decision-maker should be able to point to that portion of the report, then obtain greater detail on it dynamically, on an as-needed basis, with no further programming. Figure 2.3 presents a detailed view of the summary shown in Figure 2.2,

For Current Year, 2Q

Sales Region	Country	Targets ('000s)	Actuals ('000s)
Asia	Philippines	14,000	15,050
	Hong Kong	10,000	10,500
Europe	France	4,000	4,050
	Italy	6,000	8,150
North America	United States	1,000	1,500
	Canada	**7,000**	**500**
Africa	Egypt	5,600	6,200

Figure 2.3. The Dynamic Report–Detailed View

By providing business users with the ability to dynamically view more or less of the data on an ad hoc, as needed basis, the data warehouse eliminates delays in getting information and removes the IT professional from the report-creation loop.

2.4 THE PURPOSES OF A DATA WAREHOUSE

At this point, it is helpful to summarize the typical reasons, the enterprises undertake data warehousing initiatives.

To Provide Business Users with Access to Data

The data warehouse provides access to integrated enterprise data previously locked away in unfriendly, difficult-to-access environments. Business users can now establish, with minimal effort, a secured connection to the warehouse through their desktop PC. Security is enforced either by the warehouse front-end application, or by the server database, or by the both.

Because of its integrated nature, a data warehouse spares business users from the need to learn, understand, or access operational data in their native environments and data structures.

To Provide One Version of the Truth

The data in the data warehouse are consistent and quality assured before being released to business users. Since a common source of information is now used, the data warehouse puts to rest all debates about the veracity of data used or cited in meetings. The data warehouse becomes the common information resource for decisional purposes throughout the organization.

Note that "one version of the truth" is often possible only after much discussion and debate about the terms used within the organization. For example, the term customer can have different meanings to different people—it is not unusual for some people to refer to prospective clients as "customers," while others in the same organization may use the term "customers" to mean only actual, current clients.

While these differences may seem trivial at the first glance, the subtle nuances that exist depending on the context may result in misleading numbers and ill-informed decisions. For example, when the Western Region sales manager asks for the number of customers, he probably means the "number of customers from the Western Region," not the "number of customers served by the entire company."

To Record the Past Accurately

Many of the figures arid numbers that managers receive have little meaning unless compared to historical figures. For example, reports that compare the company's present performance with that of the last year's are quite common. Reports that show the company's performance for the same month over the past three years are likewise of interest to decision-makers.

The operational systems will not be able to meet this kind of information need for a good reason. A data warehouse should be used to record the past accurately, leaving the OLTP systems free to focus on recording current transactions and balances. Actual historical values are neither stored on the operational system nor derived by adding or subtracting transaction values against the latest balance. Instead, historical data are loaded and integrated with other data in the warehouse for quick access.

To Slice and Dice Through Data

As stated earlier in this chapter, dynamic reports allow users to view warehouse data from different angles, at different levels of detail business users with the means and the ability to slice and dice through warehouse data can actively meet their own information needs.

The ready availability of different data views also improves business analysis by reducing the time and effort required to collect, format, and distill information from data.

To Separate Analytical and Operational Processing

Decisional processing and operational information processing have totally divergent architectural requirements. Attempts to meet both decisional and operational information needs through the same system or through the same system architecture merely increase the brittleness of the IT architecture and will create system maintenance nightmares.

Data warehousing disentangles analytical from operational processing by providing a separate system architecture for decisional implementations. This makes the overall IT architecture of the enterprise more resilient to changing requirements.

To Support the Reengineering of Decisional Processes

At the end of each BPR initiative come the projects required to establish the technological and organizational systems to support the newly reengineered business process.

Although reengineering projects have traditionally focused on operational processes, data warehousing technologies make it possible to reengineer decisional business processes as well. Data warehouses, with their focus on meeting decisional business requirements, are the ideal systems for supporting reengineered decisional business processes.

2.5 DATA MARTS

A discussion of data warehouses is not complete without a note on data marts. The concept of the data mart is causing a lot of excitement and attracts much attention in the data warehouse industry. Mostly, data marts are presented as an inexpensive alternative to a data warehouse that takes significantly less time and money to build. However, the term data mart means different things to different people. A rigorous definition of this term is a data store that is subsidiary to a data warehouse of integrated data. The data mart is directed at a partition of data (often called a subject area) that is created for the use of a dedicated group of users. A data mart might, in fact, be a set of denormalized, summarized, or aggregated data. Sometimes, such a set could be placed on the data warehouse database rather than a physically separate store of data. In most instances, however, the data mart is a physically separate store of data and is normally resident on a separate database server, often on the local area enterprises relational OLAP technology which creates highly denormalized star schema relational designs or hypercubes of data for analysis by groups of users with a common interest in a limited portion of the database. In other cases, the data warehouse architecture may incorporate data mining tools that extract sets of data for a particular type of analysis. All these type of data marts, called dependent data marts because their data content is sourced from the data warehouse, have a high value because no matter how many are deployed and no matter how many different enabling technologies are used, the different users are all accessing the information views derived from the same single integrated version of the data.

Unfortunately, the misleading statements about the simplicity and low cost of data marts sometimes result in organizations or vendors incorrectly positioning them as an alternative to the data warehouse. This viewpoint defines independent data marts that in fact represent fragmented point solutions to a range of business problems in the enterprise. This type of implementation should rarely be deployed in the context of an overall technology of applications architecture. Indeed, it is missing the ingredient that is at the heart of the data warehousing concept: data integration. Each independent data mart makes its own assumptions about how to consolidate the data, and the data across several data marts may not be consistent.

Moreover, the concept of an independent data mart is dangerous – as soon as the first data mart is created, other organizations, groups, and subject areas within the enterprise embark on the task of building their own data marts. As a result, an environment is created in which multiple operational systems feed multiple non-integrated data marts that are often overlapping in data content, job scheduling, connectivity, and management. In other words, a complex many-to-one problem of building a data warehouse is transformed from operational and external data sources to a many-to-many sourcing and management nightmare.

Another consideration against independent data marts is related to the potential scalability problem: the first simple and inexpensive data mart was most probably designed without any serious consideration about the scalability (for example, an expensive parallel computing platform for an "inexpensive" and "small" data mart would not be considered). But, as usage begets usage, the initial small data mart needs to grow (i.e., in data sizes and the number of concurrent users), without any ability to do so in a scalable fashion.

It is clear that the point-solution-independent data mart is not necessarily a bad thing, and it is often a necessary and valid solution to a pressing business problem, thus achieving the goal of rapid delivery of enhanced decision support functionality to end users. The business drivers underlying such developments include:

- Extremely urgent user requirements.
- The absence of a budget for a full data warehouse strategy.
- The absence of a sponsor for an enterprise wide decision support strategy.
- The decentralization of business units.
- The attraction of easy-to-use tools and a mind-sized project.

To address data integration issues associated with data marts, the recommended approach proposed by Ralph Kimball is as follows. For any two data mart in an enterprise, the common dimensions must conform to the equality and roll-up rule, which states that these dimensions are either the same or that one is a strict roll-up of another.

Thus, in a retail store chain, if the purchase orders database is one data mart and the sales database is another data mart, the two data marts will form a coherent part of an overall enterprise data warehouse if their common dimensions (e.g., time and product) conform. The time dimensions from both data marts might be at the individual day level, or, conversely, one time dimension is at the day level but the other is at the week level. Because days roll up to weeks, the two time dimensions are conformed. The time dimensions would not be conformed if one time dimension were weeks and the other time dimension, a fiscal quarter. The resulting data marts could not usefully coexist in the same application.

In summary, data marts present two problems: (1) scalability in situations where in initial small data mart grows quickly in multiple dimensions and (2) data integration. Therefore, when designing data marts, the organizations should pay close attention to system scalability, data consistency, and manageability issues. The key to a successful data mart strategy is the development of overall scalable data warehouse architecture; and key step in that architecture is identifying and implementing the common dimensions.

A number of misconceptions exist about data marts and their relationships to data warehouses discuss two of those misconceptions below.

MISCONCEPTION

Data Warehouses and Data Marts cannot Coexist

There are parties who strongly advocate the deployment of data marts as opposed to the deployment of data warehouses. They correctly point out the difficulties of building an enterprise wide data warehouse in one large project and lead unsuspecting organizations down the "data mart vs. data warehouse" path.

What many do not immediately realize is that data warehouses and data marts can coexist within the same organization; the correct approach is "data mart and data warehouse." This is discussed more thoroughly in the "Warehousing Architectures" section of Chapter 5.

Data Marts can be Built Independently of One Another

Some enterprises find it easier to deploy multiple data marts independently of one another. At the first glance, such an approach is indeed easier since there are no integration issues. Different groups of users are involved with each data mart, which implies fewer conflicts about the use of terms and about business rules. Each data mart is free to exist within its own isolated world, and all the users are happy.

Unfortunately, that enterprises fail to realize until much later is that by deploying one isolated data mart after another, the enterprise has actually created new islands of automation. While at the onset those data marts are certainly easier to develop, the task of maintaining many unrelated data marts is exceedingly complex and will create data management, synchronization, and consistency issues. Each data mart presents its own version of "the truth" and will quite naturally provide information that conflicts with the reports from other data marts.

Multiple data marts are definitely appropriate within an organization, but these should be implemented only under the integrating framework of an enterprise-wide data warehouse. Each data mart is developed as an extension of the data warehouse and is fed by the data warehouse. The data warehouses enforces a consistent set of business rules and ensures the consistent use of terms and definitions.

2.6 OPERATIONAL DATA STORES

Data warehouse discussions will also naturally lead to Operational Data Stores, which at the first glance may appear no different from data warehouses.

Although both technologies support decisional information needs of enterprise decision-makers, the two are distinctly different and are deployed to meet different types of decisional information needs.

Definition of Operational Data Stores

In Building the Operational Data Store (John Wiley & Sons, 1996, ISBN: 0-471-12822-8), W.H. Inmon, C. Imhoff, and G. Battas define an Operational Data Store as "the architectural construct where collective integrated operational data is stored." ODS can also be defined as a collection of integrated databases designed to support operational monitoring. Unlike the databases of OLTP applications (that are operational or function oriented), the Operational Data Store contains subject-oriented, enterprise-wide data. However, unlike data warehouses, the data in Operational Data Stores are volatile, current and detailed.

However, some significant challenges of the ODS still remain. Among them are

- Location of the appropriate sources of data
- Transformation of the source data to satisfy the ODS data model requirements.
- Complexity of near-real-time propagation of changes from the operational systems to the ODS (including tasks to recognize, obtain, synchronize, and move changes from a multitude of disparate systems.)
- A DBMS that combines effective query processing with transactional processing capabilities that ensure the ACID transaction properties.

Table 2.1. Compares the Data Warehouse with the Operational Data Store

	Data Warehouse	*Operational Data Stores*
Purpose:	Strategic Decision Support	Operational Monitoring
Similarities:	Integrated Data	Integrated Data
	Subject-Oriented	Subject-Oriented
Differences:	Static Data	Volatile Data
	Historical Data	Current Data
	Summarized Data	More Detailed

The ODS provides an integrated view of the data in the operational systems. Data are transformed and integrated into a consistent, unified whole as they are obtained from legacy and other operational systems to provide business users with an integrated and current view of operations. Data in the Operational Data Store are constantly refreshed so that the resulting image reflects the latest state of operations.

Flash Monitoring and Reporting Tools

As mentioned in Chapter 1, flash monitoring and reporting tools are like a dashboard that provides meaningful online information on the operational status of the enterprise. This service is achieved by the use of ODS data as inputs to the flash monitoring and reporting tools, to provide business users with a constantly refreshed, enterprise-wide view of operations without creating unwanted interruptions or additional load on transaction-processing systems. Figure 2.4 diagrams how this scheme works.

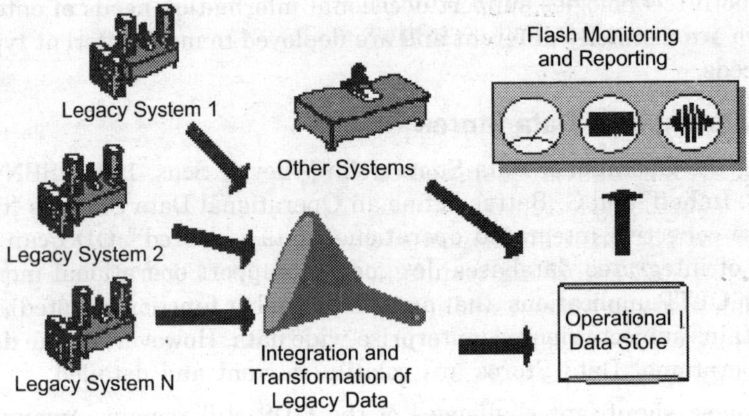

Figure 2.4. Operational Monitoring

Relationship of Operational Data Stores to Data Warehouse

Enterprises with Operational Data Stores find themselves in the enviable position of being able to deploy data warehouses with considerable ease. Since operational data stores are integrated, many of the issues related to extracting, transforming, and transporting data from legacy systems have been addressed by the ODS, as illustrated in Figure 2.5.

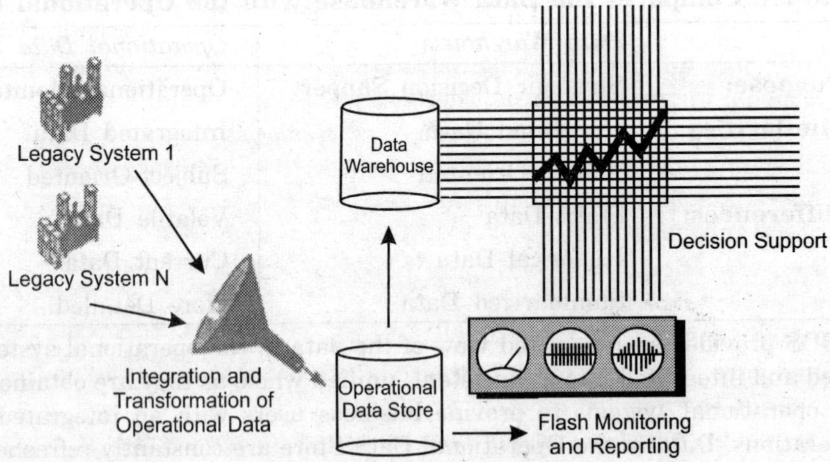

Figure 2.5. The Operational Data Store Feeds the Data Warehouse

The data warehouse is populated by means of regular snapshots of the data in the Operational Data Store. However, unlike 'the ODS, the data warehouse maintains the historical snapshots of the data for comparisons across different time frames. The ODS is free to focus only on the current state of operations and is constantly updated in real time.

2.7 DATA WAREHOUSE COST-BENEFIT ANALYSIS/RETURN ON INVESTMENT

Senior management typically requires a cost-benefit analysis (CBA) or a study of return on investment (ROI) prior to embarking on a data warehousing initiative. Although the task of calculating ROI for data warehousing initiatives is unique to each enterprise, it is possible to classify the type of benefits and costs that are associated with data warehousing.

Benefits

Data warehousing benefits can be expected from the following areas:

- **Redeployment of staff assigned to old decisional systems.** The cost of producing today's management reports is typically undocumented and unknown within an enterprise. The quantification of such costs in terms of staff hours and erroneous data may yield surprising results. Benefits of this nature, however, are typically minimal, since warehouse maintenance and enhancements require staff as well. At best, staff will be redeployed to more productive tasks.
- **Improved productivity of analytical staff due to availability of data.** Analysts go through several steps in their day-to-day work: locating data, retrieving data, analyzing data to yield information, presenting information, and recommending a course of action. Unfortunately, much of the time (sometimes up to 40 percent) spent by enterprise analysts on a typical day is devoted to locating and retrieving data. The availability of integrated, readily accessible data (in the data warehouse) should significantly reduce the time that analysts spend with data collection tasks and increase the time available to actually analyze the data they have collected. This leads either to shorter decision cycle times or improvements in the quality of the analysis.
- **Business improvements resulting from analysis of warehouse data.** The most significant business improvements in warehousing result from the analysis of warehouse data, especially if the easy availability of information yields insights here before unknown to the enterprise. The goal of the data warehouse is to meet decisional information needs, therefore it follows naturally the greatest benefits of warehousing that are obtained when decisional information needs are actually met and sound business decisions are made both at the tactical and strategic level. Understandably, such benefits are more significant and therefore, more difficult to project and quantify.

Costs

Data warehousing costs typically fall into one of the four categories. These are:

- **Hardware.** This item refers to the costs associated with setting up the hardware and operating environment required by the data warehouse. In many instances, this setup may require the acquisition of new equipment or the upgrade of existing equipment. Larger warehouse implementations naturally imply higher hardware costs.
- **Software.** This item refers to the costs of purchasing the licenses to use software products that automate the extraction, cleansing, loading, retrieval, and presentation of warehouse data.
- **Services.** This item refers to services provided by systems integrators, consultants, and trainers during the course of a data warehouse project. Enterprises typically

rely more on the services of third parties in early warehousing implementations, when the technology is quite new to the enterprise.

- **Internal staff costs.** This item refers to costs incurred by assigning internal staff to the data warehousing effort, as well as to costs associated with training internal staff on new technologies and techniques.

ROI Considerations

The costs and benefits associated with data warehousing vary significantly from one enterprise to another. The differences are chiefly influenced by

- The current state of technology within the enterprise;
- The culture of the organization in terms of decision-making styles and attitudes towards technology and
- The company's position in its chosen market vs. its competitors.

The effect of data warehousing on the tactical and strategic management of an enterprise is often likened to cleaning the muddy windshield of a car. It is difficult to quantify the value of driving a car with a cleaner windshield. Similarly, it is difficult to quantify the value of managing an organization with better information and insight.

Lastly, it is important to note that data warehouse justification is often complicated by the fact that much of the benefit may take sometime to realize and therefore is difficult to quantify in advance.

In Summary

Data warehousing technologies have evolved as a result of the unsatisfied decisional information needs of enterprises. With the increased stability of operational systems, information technology professionals have increasingly turned their attention to meeting the decisional requirements of the enterprise.

A data warehouse, according to Bill Inmon, is a collection of integrated, subject-oriented databases designed to supply the information required for decision-making. Each data item in the data warehouse is relevant to some moment in time.

A data mart has traditionally been defined as a subset of the enterprise-wide data warehouse. Many enterprises, upon realizing the complexity involved in deploying a data warehouse, will opt to deploy data marts instead. Although data marts are able to meet the immediate needs of a targeted group of users, the enterprise should shy away from deploying multiple, unrelated data marts. The presence of such islands of information will only result in data management and synchronization problems.

Like data warehouses, Operational Data Stores are integrated and subject-oriented. However, an ODS is always current and is constantly updated (ideally in real time). The Operational Data Store is the ideal data source for a data warehouse, since it already contains integrated operational data as of a given point in time.

Although data warehouses have proven to have significant returns on investment, particularly when they are meeting a specific, targeted business need, it is extremely difficult to quantify the expected benefits of a data warehouse. The costs are easier to calculate, as these break down simply into hardware, software, services, and in-house staffing costs.

PART II : PEOPLE

Although a number of people are involved in a single data warehousing project, there are three key roles that carry enormous responsibilities. Negligence in carrying out any of these three roles can easily derail a well-planned data warehousing initiative. This section of the book therefore focuses on the Project Sponsor, the Chief Information Officer, and the Project Manager and seeks to answer the questions frequently asked by individuals who have accepted the responsibilities that come with these roles.

- **Project Sponsor.** Every data warehouse initiative has a Project Sponsor-a high-level executive who provides strategic guidance, support, and direction to the data warehousing project. The Project Sponsor ensures that project objectives are aligned with enterprise objectives, resolves organizational issues, and usually obtains funding for the project.
- **Chief Information Officer (CIO).** The CIO is responsible for the effective deployment of information technology resources and staff to meet the strategic, decisional, and operational information requirements of the enterprise. Data warehousing, with its accompanying array of new technology and its dependence on operational systems, naturally makes strong demands on the physical and human resources under the jurisdiction of the CIO, not only during design and development but also during maintenance and subsequent evolution.
- **Project Manager.** The warehouse Project Manager is responsible for all technical activities related to implementing a data warehouse. Ideally, an IT professional from the enterprise fulfills this critical role. It is not unusual, however, for this role to be outsourced for early or pilot projects, because of the newness of warehousing technologies and techniques.

CHAPTER 3

THE PROJECT SPONSOR

Before the Project Sponsor becomes comfortable with the data warehousing effort, quite a number of his or her questions and concerns will have to be addressed. This chapter attempts to provide answers to questions frequently asked by Project Sponsors.

3.1 HOW DOES A DATA WAREHOUSE AFFECT DECISION-MAKING PROCESSES?

It is naive to expect an immediate change to the decision-making processes in an organization when a data warehouse first goes into production. End users will initially be occupied more with learning how to use the data warehouse than with changing the way they obtain information and make decisions. It is also likely that the first set of predefined reports and queries supported by the data warehouse will differ little from existing reports.

Decision-makers will experience varying levels of initial difficulty with the use of the data warehouse; proper usage assumes a level of desktop computing skills, data knowledge, and business knowledge.

Desktop Computing Skills

Not all business users are familiar and comfortable with the desktop computers, and it is unrealistic to expect all the business users in an organization to make direct, personal use of the front-end warehouse tools. On the other hand, there are power users within the organization who enjoy using computers, love spreadsheets, and will quickly push the tools to the limit with their queries and reporting requirements.

Data Knowledge

It is critical that business users be familiar with the contents of the data warehouse before they make use of it. In many cases, this requirement entails extensive communication on two levels. First, the scope of the warehouse must be clearly communicated to property manage user expectations about the type of information they can retrieve, particularly in the earlier rollouts of the warehouse. Second, business users who will have direct access to the data warehouse must be trained on the use of the selected front-end tools and on the meaning of the warehouse contents.

Business Knowledge

Warehouse users must have a good understanding of the nature of their business and of the types of business issues that they need to address. The answers that the warehouse will provide are only as good as the questions that are directed to it.

As end users gain confidence both in their own skills and in the veracity of the warehouse contents, data warehouse usage and overall support of the warehousing initiative will increase. Users will begin to "outgrow" the canned reports and will move to a more ad hoc, analytical style when using the data warehouse.

As the data scope of the warehouse increases and additional standard reports are produced from the warehouse data, decision-makers will start feeling overwhelmed by the number of standard reports that they receive. Decision-makers either gradually want to lessen their dependence on the regular reports or want to start relying on exception reporting or highlighting, and alert systems.

Exception Reporting or Highlighting

Instead of scanning regular reports one line item at a time, decision-makers want to receive exception reports that enumerate only the items that meet their definition of "exceptions". For example, instead of receiving sales reports per region for all regions within the company, a sales executive may instead prefer to receive sales reports for areas where actual sales figures are either 10 percent more or less than the budgeted figures.

Alert Systems

Alert systems also follow the same principle, that of highlighting or bringing to the fore areas or items that require managerial attention and action. However, instead of reports, decision-makers will receive notification of exceptions through other means, for example, an e-mail message.

As the warehouse gains acceptance, decision-making styles will evolve from the current practice of waiting for regular reports from IT or MIS to using the data warehouse to understand the current status of operations and, further, to using the data warehouse as the basis for strategic decision-making. At the most sophisticated level of usage, a data warehouse will allow senior management to understand and drive the business changes needed by the enterprise.

3.2 HOW DOES A DATA WAREHOUSE IMPROVE FINANCIAL PROCESSES? MARKETING? OPERATIONS?

A successful enterprise-wide data warehouse effort will improve financial, marketing and operational processes through the simple availability of integrated data views. Previously unavailable perspectives of the enterprise will increase understanding of cross-functional operations. The integration of enterprise data results in standardized terms across organizational units (e.g., a uniform definition of customer and profit). A common set of metrics for measuring performance will emerge from the data warehousing effort. Communication among these different groups will also improve.

Financial Processes

Consolidated financial reports, profitability analysis, and risk monitoring improve the financial processes of an enterprise, particularly in financial service institutions, such as banks. The very process of consolidation requires the use of a common vocabulary and increased understanding of operations across different groups in the organization.

While financial processes will improve because of the newly available information, it is important to note that the warehouse can provide information based only on available data. For example, one of the most popular banking applications for data warehousing is profitability analysis. Unfortunately, enterprises may encounter a rude shock when it becomes apparent that revenues and costs are not tracked at the same level of detail within the organization. Banks frequently track their expenses at the level of branches or organization units but wish to compute profitability on a per customer basis. With profit figures at the customer level and costs at the branch level, there is no direct way to compute profit. As a result, enterprises may resort to formulas that allow them to compute or derive cost and revenue figures at the same level for comparison purposes.

Marketing

Data warehousing supports marketing organizations by providing a comprehensive view of each customer and his many relationships with the enterprise. Over the years, marketing efforts have shifted in focus. Customers are no longer viewed as individual accounts but instead are viewed as individuals with multiple accounts. This change in perspective provides the enterprise with cross-selling opportunities.

The notion of customers as individuals also makes possible the segmentation and profiling of customers to improve target-marketing efforts. The availability of historical data makes it possible to identify trends in customer behavior, hopefully with positive results in revenue.

Operations

By providing enterprise management with decisional information, data warehouses have the potential of greatly affecting the operations of an enterprise by highlighting both problems and opportunities that here before went undetected.

Strategic or tactical decisions based on warehouse data will naturally affect the operations of the enterprise. It is in this area that the greatest return on investment and, therefore, greatest improvement can be found.

3.3 WHEN IS A DATA WAREHOUSE PROJECT JUSTIFIED?

As mentioned in Chapter 2, return on investment (ROI) from data warehousing projects varies from organization to organization and is quite difficult to quantify prior to a warehousing initiative.

However, a common list of problems encountered by enterprises can be identified as a result of unintegrated customer data and lack of historical data. A properly deployed data warehouse can solve the problems, as discussed below.

Lack of Information Sharing

- Divisions or departments have the same customers but do not share information with each other.
- As a result, cross-selling opportunities are missed, and improved customer understanding is lost. Customers are annoyed by requests for the same information by different units within the same enterprise.

Solving this problem results in the following benefits: better customer management decisions can be made, customers are treated as individuals; new business opportunities can be explored.

Different Groups Produce Conflicting Reports

- Data in different operational systems provide different information on the same subject. The inconsistent use of terms results in different business rules for the same item.
- Thus, facts and figures are inconsistently interpreted, and different versions of the "truth" exist within the enterprise. Decision-makers have to rely on conflicting data and may lose credibility with customers, suppliers, or partners.
- Solving this problem results in the following benefits: a consistent view of enterprise operations becomes available; better informed decisions can be made.

Tedious Report Creation Process

- Critical reports take too long a time to be produced. Data gathering is ad hoc, inconsistent, and manually performed. There are no formal rules to govern the creation of these reports.
- As a result, business decisions based on these reports may be bad decisions. Business analysts within the organization spend more time collecting data instead of analyzing data. Competitors with more sophisticated means of producing similar reports have a considerable advantage.
- Solving this problem results in the following benefits: the report creation process is dramatically streamlined, and the time required to produce the same reports is significantly reduced. More time can be spent on analyzing the data, and decision-makers do not have to work with " old data".

Reports are not Dynamic, and do not Support an ad hoc Usage Style

- Managerial reports are not dynamic and often do not support the ability to drill down for further detail.
- As a result, when a report highlights interesting or alarming figures, the decision-maker is unable to zoom in and get more detail.
- When this problem is solved, decision-makers can obtain more detail as needed. Analysis for trends and causal relationships are possible.

Reports that Require Historical Data are Difficult to Produce

- Customer, product, and financial histories are not stored in operational systems data structures.
- As a result, decision-makers are unable to analyze trends over time. The enterprise is unable to anticipate events and behave proactively or aggressively. Customer demands come as a surprise, and the enterprise must scramble to react.
- Decision-makers can increase or strengthen relationships with current customers. Marketing campaigns can be predictive in nature, based on historical data.

Apart from solving the problems above, other reasons commonly used to justify a data warehouse initiative are the following:

Support of Enterprise Strategy

The data warehouse is a key supporting factor in the successful execution of one or more parts of the enterprise's strategy, including enhanced revenue or cost control initiatives.

Enterprise Emphasis on Customer and Product Profitability

Increase the focus and efficiency of the enterprise by gaining a better understanding of its customers and products.

Perceived Need Outside the IT Group

Data warehousing is sought and supported by business users who demand integrated data for decision-making. A true business does not need technological experimentation, but drives the initiative.

Integrated Data

The enterprise lacks a repository of integrated and historical data that are required for decision-making.

Cost of Current Efforts

The current cost of producing standard, regular managerial reports is typically hidden within an organization. A study of these costs can yield unexpected results that help justify the data warehouse initiative.

The Competition does it

Just because competitors are going into data warehousing, it does not mean that an enterprise should plunge headlong into it. However, the fact that the competition is applying data warehousing technology should make any manager stop and see whether data warehousing is something that his own organization needs.

3.4 WHAT EXPENSES ARE INVOLVED?

The costs associated with developing and implementing a data warehouse typically fall into the categories described below:

Hardware

Warehousing hardware can easily account for up to 50 percent of the costs in a data warehouse pilot project. A separate machine or server is often recommended for data warehousing so as not to burden operational IT environments. The operational and decisional environments may be connected via the enterprise's network, especially if automated tools have been scheduled to extract data from operational systems or if replication technology is used to create copies of operational data.

Enterprises heavily dependent on mainframes for their operational systems can look to powerful client/server platforms for their data warehouse solutions.

Hardware costs are generally higher at the start of the data warehousing initiative due to the purchase of new hardware. However, data warehouses grow quickly, and subsequent extensions to the warehouse may quickly require hardware upgrades.

A good way to cut down on the early hardware costs is to invest in server technology that is highly scalable. As the warehouse grows both in volume and in scope, subsequent investments in hardware can be made as needed.

Software

Software refers to all the tools required to create, set up, configure, populate, manage, use, and maintain the data warehouse. The data warehousing tools currently available from a variety of vendors are staggering in their features and price range (Chapter 11 provides an overview of these tools).

Each enterprise will be best served by a combination of tools, the choice of which is determined or influenced not only by the features of the software but also by the current computing environment of the operational system, as well as the intended computing environment of the warehouse.

Services

Services from consultants or system integrators are often required to manage and integrate the disparate components of the data warehouse. The use of system integrators, in particular, is appealing to enterprises that prefer to use the "best of breed" of hardware and software products and have no wish to assume the responsibility for integrating the various components.

The use of consultants is also popular, particularly with early warehousing implementations, when the enterprise is just learning about data warehousing technologies and techniques.

Service-related costs can account for roughly 30 percent to 35 percent of the overall cost of a pilot project but may drop as the enterprise decreases its dependence on external resources.

Internal Staff

Internal staff costs refer to costs incurred as a result of assigning enterprise staff to the warehousing project. The staff could otherwise have been assigned to other activities.

The heaviest demands are on the time of the IT staff who have the task of planning, designing, building, populating, and managing the warehouse. The participation of end users, typically analysts and managers, is also crucial to a successful warehousing effort.

The Project Sponsor, the CIO, and the Project manager will also be heavily involved because of the nature of their roles in the warehousing initiative.

Summary of Typical Costs

The external costs of a typical data warehouse pilot project of three to six months can range anywhere from US$ 0.8M to US$ 2M, depending on the combination of hardware, software, and services required.

Table 3.1 provides an indicative breakdown of the external costs of a warehousing pilot project where new hardware is purchased.

Table 3.1. Typical External Cost Breakdown for a Data Warehouse Pilot (Amounts Expressed in US$)

Item	*Min*	*Min. as% of Total*	*Max*	*Max. as % of Total*
Hardware	400,000	49.26	1,000,000	51.81
Software	132,000	16.26	330,000	17.10
Services	280,000	34.48	600,000	31.09
Totals	812,000		1,930,000	

Note that the costs listed above do not yet consider any infrastructure improvements or upgrades (e.g., network cabling or upgrades) that may be required to properly integrate the warehousing environment into the rest of the enterprise IT architecture.

3.5 WHAT ARE THE RISKS?

The typical risks encountered on data warehousing projects fall into the following categories:

- Organizational: These risks relate either to the project team structure and composition or to the culture of the enterprise.
- Technological: These risks relate to the planning, selection, and use of warehousing technologies. Technological risks also arise from the existing computing environment, as well as the manner by which warehousing technologies are integrated into the existing enterprise IT architecture.
- Project management: These risks are true of most technology projects but are particularly dangerous in data warehousing because of the scale and scope of warehousing projects.
- Data warehouse design: Data warehousing requires a new set of design techniques that differ significantly from the well-accepted practices in OLTP system development.

Organizational

Wrong Project Sponsor

The Project sponsor must be a business executive, not an IT executive. Considering its scope and scale, the warehousing initiative should be business driven; otherwise, the organization will view the entire effort as a technology experiment.

A strong Project Sponsor is required to address and resolve organizational issues before these have a choice to derail the project (e.g., lack of user participation, disagreements regarding definition of data, political disputes). The Project Sponsor must be someone who will be a user of the warehouse, someone who can publicly assume responsibility for the warehousing initiative, and someone with sufficient clout.

This role cannot be delegated to a committee. Unfortunately, many an organization chooses to establish a data warehouse steering committee to take on the collective responsibility of this role. If such a committee is established, the head of the committee may by default become the Project Sponsor.

End-User Community Not Involved

The end-user community provides the data warehouse implementation team with the detailed business requirements. Unlike OLTP business requirements, which tend to be exact and transaction based, data warehousing requirements are moving targets and are subject to constant change.

Despite this, the intended warehouse end-users should be interviewed to provide an understanding of the types of queries and reports (query profiles) they require. By talking to the different users, the warehousing team also gains a better understanding of the IT literacy of the users (user profiles) they will be serving and will better understand the types of data access and retrieval tools that each user will be more likely to use. The end-user community also provides the team with the security requirements (access profiles) of the warehouse.

These business requirements are critical inputs to the design of the data warehouse.

Senior Management Expectations Not Managed

Because of the costs, data warehousing always requires a go-signal from senior management, often obtained after a long, protracted ROI presentation.

In their bid to obtain senior management support, warehousing supporters must be careful not to overstate the benefits of the data warehouse, particularly during requests for budgets and business case presentations. Raising senior management expectations beyond manageable levels is one sure way to court extremely embarrassing and highly visible disasters.

End-User Community Expectations not Managed

Apart from managing senior management expectations, the warehousing team must, in the same manner, manage the expectations of their end users.

Warehouse analysts must bear in mind that the expectations of end users are immediately raised when their requirements are first discussed. The warehousing team must constantly manage these expectations by emphasizing the phased nature of data warehouse implementation projects and by clearly identifying the intended scope of each data warehouse rollout.

End users should also be reminded that the reports they will get from the warehouse are heavily dependent on the availability and quality of the data in the enterprise's operational systems.

Political Issues

Attempts to produce integrated views of enterprise data are likely to raise political issues. For example, different units have been known to wrestle for "ownership" of the warehouse, especially in organizations where access to information is associated with political power. In other enterprises, the various units want to have as little to do with warehousing as possible, for fear of having warehousing costs allocated to their units.

Understandably, the unique combination of culture and politics within each enterprise will exert its own positive and negative influences on the warehousing effort.

Logistical Overhead

A number of tasks in data warehousing require coordination with multiple parties, not only within the enterprise, but with external suppliers and service providers as well. A number of factors increase the logistical overhead in data warehousing. A few among are:

- **Formality.** Highly formal organizations generally have higher logistical overhead because of the need to comply with pre-established methods for getting things done.
- **Organizational hierarchies.** Elaborate chains of command likewise may cause delays or may require greater coordination efforts to achieve a given result.
- **Geographical dispersion.** Logistical delays also arise from geographical distribution, as in the case of multi-branch banks, nationwide operations or international corporations. Multiple, stand-alone applications with no centralized data store have the same effect. Moving data from one location to another without the benefit of a network or a transparent connection is difficult and will add to logistical overhead.

Technological

Inappropriate Use of Warehousing Technology

A data warehouse is an inappropriate solution for enterprises that need operational integration on a real-time, online basis. An ODS is the ideal solution to needs of the nature.

Multiple unrelated data marts are likewise not the appropriate architecture for meeting enterprise decisional information needs. All data warehouse and data mart projects should remain under a single architectural framework.

Poor Data Quality of Operational Systems

When the data quality of the operational systems is suspect, the team will, by necessity, devote much of its time and effort to data scrubbing and data quality checking. Poor data quality also adds to the difficulties of extracting, transforming, and loading data into the warehouse.

The importance of data quality cannot be overstated. Warehouse end users will not make use of the warehouse if the information they retrieve is wrong or of dubious quality. The perception of lack of data quality, whether such a perception is true or not, is all that is required to derail a data warehousing initiative.

Inappropriate End-user Tools

The wide range of end-user tools provides data warehouse users with different levels of functionality and requires different levels of IT sophistication from the user community.

Providing senior management users with the inappropriate tools is one of the quickest ways to kill enthusiasm for the data warehouse effort. Likewise, power users will quickly become disenchanted with simple data access and retrieval tools.

Over Dependence on Tools to Solve Data Warehousing Problems

The data warehouse solution should not be built around tools or sets of tools. Most of the warehousing tools (e.g., extraction, transformation, migration, data quality, and metadata from mature at this point.

Unfortunately, enterprises are frequently on the receiving end of sales pitches that promise to solve all the various problems (data quality/extraction /replication/loading) that plague warehousing efforts through the selection of the right tool or, even, hardware platform.

What enterprises soon realize in their first warehousing project is that much of the effort in a warehousing project still cannot be automated.

Manual Data Capture and Conversion Requirements

The extraction process is highly dependent on the extent to which data are available in the appropriate electronic format. In cases where the required data simply do not exist in any of the operational systems, a warehousing team may find itself resorting to the strongly discouraged practice of using data capture screens to obtain data through manual encoding operations. Unfortunately, a data warehouse quite simply cannot be filled up through manual data that will be available in the warehouse.

Technical Architecture and Networking

Study and monitor the impact of the data warehouse development and usage on the network infrastructure. Assumptions about batch windows, middleware, extract mechanisms, etc.. should be verified to avoid nasty surprises midway into the project.

Project Management

Defining Project Scope Inappropriately

The mantra for data warehousing should be start small and build incrementally. Organizations that prefer the big-bang approach quickly find themselves on the path to certain failure. Monolithic projects are unwieldy and difficult to mange, especially when the warehousing team is new to the technology and techniques.

In contrast, the phased, iterative approach has consistently proven itself to be effective, not only in data warehousing but also in most information technology initiatives. Each phase has a manageable scope, requires a smaller team, and lends itself well to a coaching and learning environment. The lessons learned by the team on each phase are a form of direct feedback into subsequent phases.

Underestimating Project Time Frame

Estimates in data warehousing projects often fail to devote sufficient time to the extraction, integration, and transformation tasks. Unfortunately, it is not unusual for this area of the project to consume anywhere between 60 percent to 80 percent of a team's time and effort. Figure 3.1 illustrates the distribution of efforts.

The project team should therefore work on stabilizing the back-end of the warehouse as quickly as possible. The front-end tools are useless if the warehouse itself is not yet ready for use.

Underestimating Project Overhead

Time estimates in data warehousing projects often fail to consider delays due to logistics. Keep an eye on the lead time for hardware delivery, especially if the machine is yet to be imported into the city or country. Quickly determine the acquisition time for middleware or warehousing tools. Watch out for logistical overhead.

Allocate sufficient time for team orientation and training prior to and during the course of the project to ensure that everyone remains aligned. Devote sufficient time and effort to creating and promoting effective communication within the team.

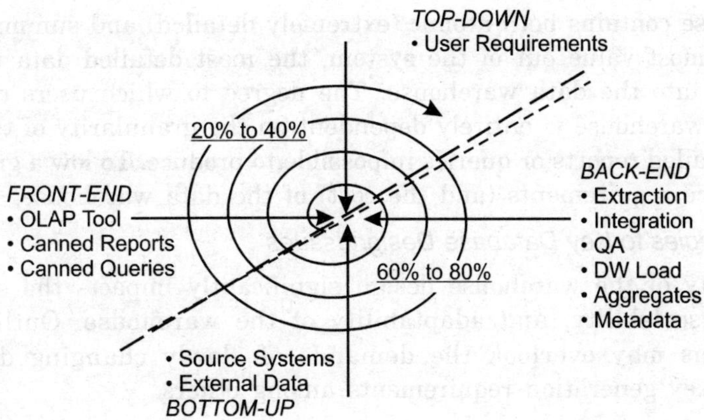

Figure 3.1. Typical Effort Distribution on a Warehousing Project

Losing Focus

The data warehousing effort should be focused entirely on delivering the essential minimal characteristics (EMCs) of each phase of the implementation. It is easy for the team to be distracted by requests for nonessential or low-priority features (i.e., nice-to have data or functionality.) These should be ruthlessly deferred to a later phase; otherwise, valuable project time and effort will be frittered away on nonessential features, to the detriment of the warehouse scope or schedule.

Not Looking Beyond the First Data Warehouse Rollout

A data warehouse needs to be strongly supported and nurtured (also known as "care and feeding") for at least a year after its initial launch. End users will need continuous training and support, especially new users are gradually granted access to the warehouse. Collect warehouse usage and query statistics to get an idea of warehouse acceptance and to obtain inputs for database optimization and tuning. Plan subsequent phases or rollouts of the warehouse, taking into account the lessons learned from the first rollout. Allocate, acquire, or train the appropriate resources for support activities.

Data Warehouse Design

Using OLTP Database Design Strategies for the Data Warehouse

Enterprises that venture into data warehousing for the first time may make the mistake of applying OLTP database design techniques to their data warehouse. Unfortunately, data warehousing requires design strategies that are very different from the design strategies for transactional, operation systems.

For example, OLTP database are fully normalized and are designed to consistently store operational data, one transaction at a time. In direct contrast, a data warehouse requires database designs that even business users find directly usable. Dimensional or star schemas with highly denormalized dimension tables on relational technology require different design techniques and different indexing strategies. Data warehousing may also require the use of hypercubes or multidimensional database technology for certain functions and users.

Choosing the Wrong Level of Granularity

The warehouse contains both atomic (extremely detailed) and summarized (high-level) data. To get the most value out of the system, the most detailed data required by users should be loaded into the data warehouse. The degree to which users can slice and dice through the data warehouse is entirely dependent on the granularity of the facts. Too high a grain makes detailed reports or queries impossible to produce. To low a grain unnecessarily increases the space requirements (and the cost) of the data warehouse.

Not Defining Strategies to Key Database Design Issues

The suitability of the warehouse design significantly impacts the size, performance, integrity, future scalability, and adaptability of the warehouse. Outline(or high-level) warehouse designs may overlook the demands of slowly changing dimensions, large dimensions, and key generation requirements among others.

3.6 RISK-MITIGATING APPROACHES

The above risks are best addressed through the people and mechanisms described below:

- **The right project sponsor and project manager.** Having the appropriate leaders setting the tone, scope, and direction of a data warehousing initiative can spell the difference between failure and success.
- **Appropriate architecture.** The enterprise must verify that a data warehouse is the appropriate solution to its needs. If the need is for operational integration, then an Operational Data Store is more appropriate.
- **Phased approach.** The entire data warehousing effort must be phased so that the warehouse can be iteratively extended in a cost-justified and prioritized manner. A number of prioritized areas should be delivered first; subsequent areas are implemented in incremental steps. Work on no urgent components is deferred.
- **Cyclical refinement.** Obtain feedback from users as each rollout or phase is completed, and as users make use of the data warehouse and the front-end tools. Any feedback should serve as inputs to subsequent rollouts. With each new rollout, users are expected to specify additional requirements and gain a better understanding of the types of queries that are now available to them.
- **Evolutionary life cycle.** Each phase of the project should be conducted in a manner that promotes evolution, adaptability, and scalability. An overall data warehouse architecture should be defined when a high-level understanding of user needs has been obtained and the phased implementation path has been studied.
- **Completeness of data warehouse design.** The data warehouse design must address slowly changing dimensions, aggregation, key generalization, heterogeneous facts and dimensions, and minidimensions. These dimensional modeling concerns are addressed in Chapter 12.

3.7 IS THE ORGANIZATION READY FOR A DATA WAREHOUSE?

Although there are no hard-and-fast rules for determining when your organization is ready to launch a data warehouse initiative, the following positive signs are good clues:

Decision-Makers Feel the Need for Change

A successful data warehouse implementation will have a significant impact on the enterprise's decision-making processes, which in turn will have significant impact on the operations of the enterprise. The performance measures and reward mechanisms are likely to change, and they bring about corresponding changes to the processes and the culture of the organization.

Individuals who have an interest in preserving the status quo are likely to resist the data warehousing initiative, once it becomes apparent that such technologies enable organizational change.

Users Clamor for Integrated Decisional Data

A data warehouse is likely to get strong support from both the IT and user community if there is a strong and unsatisfied demand for integrated decisional data (as opposed to integrated operational data). It will be foolish to try using data warehousing technologies to meet operational information needs.

IT professionals will benefit from a long-term, architected solution to users' information needs, and users will benefit from having information at their fingertips.

The Operational Systems are Fairly Stable

An IT department, division, or unit that continuously fights fires on unstable operational systems will quickly deprioritize the data warehousing effort. Organizations will almost always defer the warehousing effort in favor of operational concerns–after all, the enterprise has survived without a data warehouse for year; another few months will not hurt.

When the operational systems are up in production and are fairly stable, there are internal data sources for the warehouse and a data warehouse initiative will be given higher priority.

There is Adequate Funding

A data warehouse project cannot afford to fizzle out in the middle of the effort due to a shortage of funds. Be aware of long-term funding requirements beyond the first data warehouse rollout before starting on the pilot project.

3.8 HOW THE RESULTS ARE MEASURED?

Data warehousing results come in different forms and can, therefore, be measured in one or more of the following ways:

New Reports/Queries Support

Results are seen clearly in the new reports and queries that are now readily available but would have been difficult to obtain without the data warehouse.

The extent to which these reports and queries actually contribute to more informed decisions and the translation of these informed decisions to bottom line benefits may not be easy to trace, however.

Turnaround Time

Now, Results are also evident in the lesser time that it takes to obtain information on the subjects covered by the warehouse. Senior managers can also get the information they need directly, thus improving the security and confidentiality of such information.

Turnaround time for decision-making is dramatically reduced. In the past, decision-makers in meetings either had to make an uninformed decision or table a discussion item because they lacked information. The ability of the data warehouse to quickly provide needed information speeds up the decision-making process.

Timely Alerts and Exception Reporting

The data warehouse proves its worth each time it sounds an alert or highlights an exception in enterprise operations. Early detection makes it possible to avert or correct potentially major problems and allows decision-makers to exploit business situations with small or immediate windows of opportunity.

Number of Active Users

The number of active users provides a concrete measure for the usage and acceptance of the warehouse.

Frequency of Use

The number of times a user actually logs on to the data warehouse within a given time period (e.g., weekly) shows how often the warehouse is used by any given users. Frequent usage is a strong indication of warehouse acceptance and usability. An increase in usage indicates that users are asking questions more frequently. Tracking the time of day when the data warehouse is frequently used will also indicate peak usage hours.

Session Times

The length of time a user spends each time he logs on to the data warehouse shows how much the data warehouse contributes to his job.

Query Profiles

The number and types of queries users make provide an idea how sophisticated the users have become. As the queries become more sophisticated, users will most likely request additional functionality or increased data scope.

This metric also provides the Warehouse Database Administrator (DBA) with valuable insight as to the types of stored aggregates or summaries that can further optimize query performance. It also indicates which tables in the warehouse are frequently accessed. Conversely, it also allows the warehouse DBA to identify tables that are hardly used and therefore are candidates for purging.

Change Requests

An analysis of users change requests can provide insight into how well users are applying the data warehouse technology. Unlike most IT projects, a high number of data warehouse change requests is a good sign; it implies that users are discovering more and more how warehousing can contribute to their jobs.

Business Changes

The immediate results of data warehousing are fairly easy to quantify. However; true warehousing ROI comes from business changes and decisions that have been made possible by information obtained from the warehouse. These, unfortunately, are not as easy to quantify and measure.

In Summary

The importance of the Project Sponsor in a data warehousing initiative cannot be overstated. The project sponsor is the highest-level business representative of the warehousing team and therefore must be a visionary, respected, and decisive leader.

At the end of the day, the Project Sponsor is responsible for the success of the data warehousing initiative within the enterprise.

CHAPTER 4

THE CIO

The Chief Information Officer (CIO) is responsible for the effective deployment of information technology resources and staff to meet the strategic, decisional, and operational information requirements of the enterprise.

Data warehousing, with its accompanying array of new technologies and its dependence on operational systems, naturally makes strong demands on the technical and human resources under the jurisdiction of the CIO.

For this reason, it is natural for the CIO to be strongly involved in any data warehousing effort. This chapter attempts to answer the typical questions of CIOs who participate in data warehousing initiatives.

4.1 HOW IS THE DATA WAREHOUSE SUPPORTED?

After the data warehouse goes into production, different support services are required to ensure that the implementation is not derailed. These support services fall into the categories described below.

Regular Warehouse Load

The data warehouse needs to be constantly loaded with additional data. The amount of work required to load data into the warehouse on a regular basis depends on the extent to which the extraction, transformation, and loading processes have been automated, as well as the load frequency required by the warehouse.

The frequency of the load depends on the user requirements, as determined during the data warehouse design activity. The most frequent load possible with a data warehouse is once a day, although it is not unusual to find organizations that load their warehouses once a week, or even once a month.

The regular loading activities fall under the responsibilities of the warehouse support team, who almost invariably report directly or indirectly to the CIO.

Applications

After the data warehouse and related data marts have been deployed, the IT department of division may turn its attention to the development and deployment of executive systems or custom applications that run directly against the data warehouse or the data marts. These applications are developed or targeted to meet the needs of specific user groups.

Any in-house application development will likely be handled by internal IT staff; otherwise, such projects should be outsourced under the watchful eye of the CIO.

Warehouse DB Optimization

Apart from the day-to-day database administration support of production systems, the warehouse DBA must also collect and monitor new sets of query statistics with each rollout or phase of the data warehouse.

The data structure of the warehouse is then refined or optimized on the basis of these usage statistics, particularly in the area of stored aggregates and table indexing strategies.

User Assistance or Help Desk

As with any information system in the enterprise, a user assistance desk or help desk can provide users with general information, assistance, and support. An analysis of the help requests received by the help desk provides insight on possible subjects for follow-on training with end users.

In addition, the help desk is an ideal site for publicizing the status of the system after every successful load.

Training

Provide more training as more end users gain access to the data warehouse. Apart from covering the standard capabilities, applications, and tools that are available to the users, the warehouse training should also clearly convey what data are available in the warehouse.

Advanced training topics may be appropriate for more advanced users. Specialized work groups or one-on-one training may be appropriate as follow-on training, depending on the type of questions and help requests that the help desk receives.

Preparation for Subsequent Rollouts

All internal preparatory work for subsequent rollouts must be performed while support activities for prior rollouts are underway. This activity may create resource contention and therefore should be carefully managed.

4.2 HOW DOES DATA WAREHOUSE EVOLVE?

One of the toughest decisions any data warehouse planner has to make is to decide when to evolve the system with new data and when to wait for the user base, IT organization, and business to catch up with the latest release of the warehouse.

Warehouse evolution is not only a technical and management issue, it is also a political issue. The IT organization must continually either:

- Market or sell the warehouse for continued funding and support of existing capabilities; or
- Attempt to control the demand for new capabilities.

Each new extension of the data warehouse results in increased complexity in terms of data scope, data management, and warehouse optimization. In addition, each rollout of the warehouse is likely to be in different stages and therefore they have different support needs.

For example, an enterprise may find itself busy with the planning and design of the third phase of the warehouse, while deployment and training activities are underway for the second phase, and help desk support is available for the first phase. The CIO will undoubtedly face the unwelcome task of making critical decisions regarding resource assignments.

In general, data warehouse evolution takes place in one or more of the following areas:

Data

Evolution in this area typically results in an increase in scope (although a decrease is not impossible). The extraction subsystem will require modification in cases where the source systems are modified or new operational systems are deployed.

Users

New users will be given access to the data warehouse, or existing users will be trained on advanced features. This implies new or additional training requirements, the definition of new users and access profiles, and the collection of new usage statistics. New security measures may also be required.

IT Organization

New skill sets are required to build, manage, and support the data warehouse. New types of support activities will be needed.

Business

Changes in the business result in changes in the operations, monitoring needs, and performance measures used by the organization. The business requirements that drive the data warehouse change as the business changes.

Application Functionality

New functionality can be added to existing OLAP tools, or new tools can be deployed to meet end-user needs.

4.3 WHO SHOULD BE INVOLVED IN A DATA WAREHOUSE PROJECT?

Every data warehouse project has a team of people with diverse skills and roles. The involvement of internal staff during the warehouse development is critical to the warehouse maintenance and support tasks once the data warehouse is in production. Not all the roles in a data warehouse project can be outsourced to third parties; of the typical roles listed below, internal enterprise staff should fulfill the roles listed below:

- Steering Committee
- User Reference Group
- Warehouse Driver
- Warehouse Project Manager
- Business Analysts

- Warehouse Data Architect
- Metadata Administrator
- Warehouse DBA
- Source System DBA and System Administrator
- Project Sponsor (see Chapter 3)

Every data warehouse project has a team of people with diverse skills and roles. Below is a list of typical roles in a data warehouse project. Note that the same person may play more than one role.

Steering Committee

The steering committee is composed of high-level executives representing each major type of user requiring access to the data warehouse. The project sponsor is a member of the committee. In most cases, the sponsor heads the committee. The steering committee should already be formed by the time data warehouse implementation starts; however, the existence of a steering committee is not a prerequisite for data warehouse planning. During implementation, the steering committee receives regular status reports from the project team and intervenes to redirect project efforts whenever appropriate.

User Reference Group

Representatives from the user community (typically middle-level managers and analysts) provide critical inputs to data warehousing projects by specifying detailed data requirements, business rules, predefined queries, and report layouts. User representatives also test the outputs of the data warehousing effort.

It is not unusual for end-user representatives to spend up to 80 percent of their time on the project, particularly during the requirements analysis and data warehouse design activities. Toward the end of a rollout, up to 80 percent of the representatives time may be required again for testing the usability and correctness of warehouse data.

End users also participate in regular meetings or interviews with the warehousing team throughout the life of each rollout (up to 50 percent involvement).

Warehouse Driver

The warehouse driver reports to the steering committee, ensures that the project is moving in the right direction, and is responsible for meeting project deadlines.

The warehouse driver is a business manager, but is a business manager responsible for defining the data warehouse strategy (with the assistance of the warehouse project manager) and for planning and managing the data warehouse implementation from the business side of operations.

The warehouse driver also communicates the warehouse objectives to other areas of the enterprise this individual normally serves as the coordinator in cases where the implementation team has cross-functional team members. It is therefore not unusual for the warehouse driver to be the liaison to the user reference group.

Warehouse Project Manager

The project manager is usually an individual who is very well versed in technology and in managing technology projects. This person's technical skills strongly complement the business acumen of the warehouse driver.

The project manager normally reports to the warehouse driver and jointly defines the data warehouse strategy. It is not unusual, however to find organizations where the warehouse driver and project manager jointly manage the project. In such cases, the project manager is actually a technical manager.

The project manager is responsible for implementing the project plans and acts as coordinator and the technology side of the project, particularly when the project involves several vendors. The warehouse project manager keeps the warehouse driver updated on the technical aspects of the project but isolates the warehouse driver from the technical details.

Business Analyst(s)

The analysts act as liaisons between the user reference group and the more technical members of the project team. Through interviews with members of the user reference group, the analysts identify, document, and model the current business requirements and usage scenarios.

Analysts play a critical role in managing end-user expectations, since most of the contact between the user reference group and the warehousing team takes place through the analysts. Analysts represent the interests of the end users in the project and therefore have the responsibility of ensuring that the resulting implementation will meet end-user needs.

Warehouse Data Architect

The warehouse data architect develops and maintains the warehouse's enterprise-wide view of the data. This individual analyzes the information requirements specified by the user community and designs the data structures of the data warehouse accordingly.

The workload of the architect is heavier at the start of each rollout, when most of the design decisions are made. The workload tapers off as the rollout gets underway.

The warehouse data architect has an increasingly critical role as the warehouse evolves. Each successive rollout that extends the warehouse must respect an overall integrating architecture–and the responsibility for the integrating architecture falls squarely on the warehouse data architect. Data mart deployments that are fed by the warehouse should likewise be considered part of the architecture to avoid the data administration problems created by multiple, unrelated data marts.

Metadata Administrator

The metadata administrator defines metadata standards and manages the metadata repository of the warehouse. The workload of the metadata administrator is quite high both at the start and toward the end of each warehouse rollout. Workload is high at the start primarily due to metadata definition and setup work. Workload toward the end of a rollout increases as the schema, the aggregate strategy, and the metadata repository contents are finalized.

Metadata plays important role in data warehousing projects and therefore requires a separate discussion in Chapter 13.

Warehouse DBA

The warehouse database administrator works closely with the warehouse data architect. The workload of the warehouse DBA is typically heavy throughout a data warehouse project. Much of this individuals time will be devoted to setting up the warehouse schema at the start of each rollout. As the rollout gets underway, the warehouse DBA takes on the responsibility of loading the data, monitoring the performance of the warehouse, refining the initial schema, and creating dummy data for testing the decision support front-end tools. Toward the end of the rollout, the warehouse DBA will be busy with database optimization tasks as well as aggregate table creation and population.

As expected, the warehouse DBA and the metadata administrator work closely together. The warehouse DBA is responsible for creating and populating metadata tables within the warehouse in compliance with the standards that have been defined by the metadata administrator.

Source System Database Administrators (DBAs) and System Administrators (SAs)

These IT professionals play extremely critical roles in the data warehousing effort. Among their typical responsibilities are:

- **Identify best extraction mechanisms.** Given their familiarity with the current computing environment, source system DBAs and SAs are often asked to identify the data transfer and extraction mechanisms best suited for their respective operational systems.
- **Contribute to source-to-target field mapping.** These individuals are familiar with the data structures of the operational systems and are therefore the most qualified to contribute to or finalize the mapping of source system fields to warehouse fields.
- **Data quality assessment.** In the course of their day-to-day operations, the DBAs and SAs encounter data quality problems and are therefore in a position to highlight areas that require special attention during data cleansing and transformation.

  Depending on the status of the operational systems, these individuals may spend the majority of their time on the above activities during the course of a rollout.

Conversion and Extraction Programmer(s)

The programmers write the extraction and conversion programs that pull data from the operational databases. They also write programs that integrate, convert, and summarize the data into the format required by the data warehouse. Their primary resource persons for the extraction programs will be the source system DBAs and SAs.

If data extraction, transformation, and transportation tools are used, these individuals are responsible for setting up and configuring the selected tools and ensuring that the correct data records are retrieved for loading into the warehouse.

Technical and Network Architect

The technical and network architect ensures that the technical architecture defined for the data warehouse rollout is suitable for meeting the stated requirements. This individual also ensures that the technical and network architecture of the data warehouse is consistent with the existing enterprise infrastructure.

The network architect coordinates with the project team on the extensions to the enterprise's network infrastructure required to support the data warehouse and constantly monitors the warehouse's impact on network capacity and throughput.

Trainer

The trainer develops all required training materials and conducts the training courses for the data warehousing project. The warehouse project team will require some data warehousing training, particularly during early or pilot projects. Toward the end of each rollout, end users of the data warehouse will also require training on the warehouse contents and on the tools that will be used for analysis and reporting.

4.4 WHAT IS THE TEAM STRUCTURE LIKE?

Figure 4.1 illustrates a typical project team structure for a data warehouse project. Note that there are many other viable alternative team structures. Also, unless the team is quite large and involves many contracted parties, a formal team structure may not even be necessary.

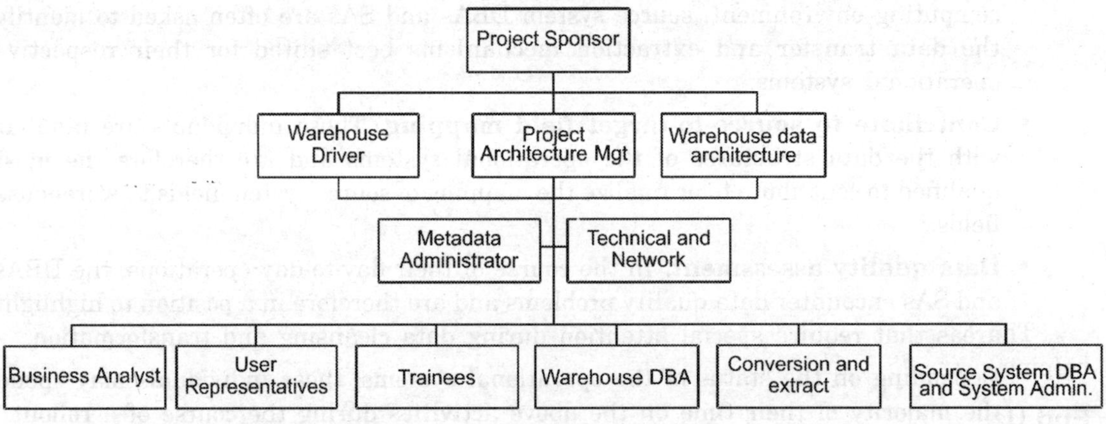

Figure 4.1. Typical Project Team Structure for Development

The team structure will evolve once the project has been completed. Day-to-day maintenance and support of the data warehouse will call for a different organizational structure–sometimes one that is more permanent.

Resource contention will arise when a new rollout is underway and resources are required for both warehouse development and support.

4.5 WHAT NEW SKILLS WILL PEOPLE NEED?

IT professionals and end-users will both require new but different skill sets, as described below:

IT Professionals

Data warehousing places new demands on the IT professionals of an enterprise. New skill sets are required, particularly in the following areas:

- **New database design skills.** Traditional database design principles do not work well with a data warehouse. Dimensional modeling concepts break many of the OLTP design rules. Also, the large size of warehouse tables requires database optimization and indexing techniques that are appropriate for very large database (VLDB) implementations.
- **Technical capabilities.** New technical skills are required, especially in enterprises where new hardware or software is purchased (e.g., new hardware platform, new RDBMS, etc.). System architecture skills are required for warehouse evolution, and networking management and design skills are required to ensure the availability of network bandwidth for warehousing requirements.
- **Familiarity with tools.** In many cases, data warehousing works better when tools are purchased and integrated into one solution. IT professionals must become familiar with the various warehousing tools that are available and must be able to separate the wheat from the chaff. IT professionals must also learn to use, and learn to work around, the limitations of the tools they select.
- **Knowledge of the business.** Thorough understanding of the business and of how the business will utilize data are critical in a data warehouse effort. IT professionals cannot afford to focus on technology only. Business analysts, in particular, have to understand the business well enough to properly represent the interests of end users. Business terms have to be standardized, and the corresponding data items in the operational systems have to be found or derived.
- **End-user support**. Although IT professionals have constantly provided end-user support to the rest of the enterprise, data warehousing puts the IT professional in direct contact with a special kind of end user: senior management. Their successful day-to-day use of the data warehouse (and the resulting success of the warehousing effort) depends greatly on the end-user support that they receive.

The IT professional's focus changes from meeting operational user requirements to helping users satisfy their own information needs.

End Users

Gone are the days when end users had to wait for the IT department to release printouts or reports or to respond to requests for information. End users can now directly access the data warehouse and can tap it for required information, looking up data themselves.

The advance assumes that end users have acquired the following skills:

- **Desktop computing.** End users must be able to use OLAP tools (under a graphical user interface environment) to gain direct access to the warehouse. Without desktop computing skills, end users will always rely on other parties to obtain the information they require.
- **Business knowledge.** The answers that the data warehouse provides are only as good as the questions that it receives. End users will not be able to formulate the correct questions or queries without a sufficient understanding of their own business environment.

- **Data knowledge.** End users must understand the data that is available in the warehouse and must be able to relate the warehouse data to their knowledge of the business.

Apart from the above skills, data warehousing is more likely to succeed if end users are willing to make the warehouse an integral part of the management and decision-making process of the organization. The warehouse support team must help end users overcome a natural tendency to revert to "business as usual" after the warehouse is rolled out.

4.6 HOW DOES DATA WAREHOUSING FIT INTO IT ARCHITECTURE?

As discussed in Chapter 1, the data warehouse is an entirely separate architectural component, distinct from the operational systems. Each time a new architectural component is added or introduced, the enterprise architect must consciously study its impact on the rest of the IT architecture and ensure that

- The IT architecture does not become brittle as a result of this new component; and
- The new architectural components are isolated from the obsolescence of legacy applications.

A data warehouse places new demands on the technical infrastructure of the enterprise. The following factors determine the technical environment required.

- **User requirements.** The user requirements largely determine the scope of the warehouse, i.e., the requirements are the basis for identifying the source systems and the required data items.
- **Location of the source systems and the warehouse.** If the source systems and the data warehouse are not in the same location, the extraction of data from operational systems into the warehouse may present difficulties with regard to logistics or network communications. In actual practice, the initial extraction is rarely 100 percent correct–some fine-tuning will be required because of errors in the source-to-target field mapping, misunderstood requirements, or changes in requirements. Easy, immediate access to both the source systems and the warehouse make it easier to modify and correct the data extraction, transformation, and loading processes. The availability of easy access to both types of computing environments depends on the current technical architecture of the enterprise.
- **Number and location of warehouse users.** The number of users that may access the warehouse concurrently implies a certain level of network traffic. The location of each user will also be a factor in determining how users will be granted access to the warehouse data. For example, if the warehouse users are dispersed over several remote locations, the enterprise may decide to use secure connections through the public internet infrastructure to deliver the warehouse data.
- **Existing enterprise IT architecture.** The existing enterprise IT architecture defines or sets the limits on what is technically feasible and practical for the data warehouse team.
- **Budget allocated to the data warehousing effort.** The budget for the warehousing effort determines how much can be done to upgrade or improve the current technical infrastructure in preparation for the data warehouse.

It is always prudent to first study and plan the technical architecture (as part of defining the data warehouse strategy) before the start of any warehouse implementation project.

4.7 HOW MANY VENDORS ARE NEEDED TO TALK TO?

A warehousing project, like any IT project, will require a combination of hardware, software, and services, which may not be available in all from one vendor. Some enterprises choose to isolate themselves from the vendor selection and liaison process by hiring a systems integrator, who subcontracts work to other vendors. Other enterprises prefer to deal with each vendor directly, and therefore assume the responsibility of integrating the various tools and services they acquire.

Vendor Categories

Although some vendors have products or services that allow them to fit in more than one of the vendor categories below, most if not all vendors are particularly strong in only one of the categories discussed below:

- **Hardware or operating system vendors.** Data warehouses require powerful server platforms to store the data and to make these data available to multiple users. All the major hardware vendors offer computing environments that can be used for data warehousing.
- **Middleware/data extraction and transformation tool vendors.** These vendors provide software products that facilitate or automate the extraction, transportation, and transformation of operational data into the format required for the data warehouse.
- **RDBMS vendors.** These vendors provide the relational database management systems that are capable of storing up to terabytes of data for warehousing purposes. These vendors have been introducing more and more features (e.g., advanced indexing features) that support VLDB implementations.
- **Consultancy and integration services supplier.** These vendors provide services either by taking on the responsibility of integrating all components of the warehousing solution on behalf of the enterprise, by offering technical assistance on specific areas of expertise, or by accepting outsourcing work for the data warehouse development or maintenance.
- **Front-end/OLAP/decision support/data access and retrieval tool vendors.** These vendors offer products that access, retrieve, and present warehouse data in meaningful and attractive formats. Data mining tools, which actively search for previously unrecognized patterns in the data, also fall into this category.

Enterprise Options

The number of vendors that an enterprise will work with depends on the approach the enterprise wishes to take. There are three main alternatives to build a data warehouse. An enterprise can:

- **Build its own.** The enterprise can build the data warehouse, using a custom architecture. A "best of breed" policy is applied to the selection of warehouse components and vendors. The data warehouse team accepts responsibility for integrating all the distinct selected products from multiple vendors.

- **Use a framework.** Nearly all data warehousing vendors present a warehousing framework to influence and guide the data warehouse market. Most of these frameworks are similar in scope and substance, with differences greatly influenced by the vendor's core technology or product. Vendors have also opportunistically established alliances with one another and are offering their product combinations as the closest thing to an "off the shelf" warehousing solution.
- **Use an anchor supplier (hardware, software, or service vendor).** Enterprises may also select a supplier for a product or service as its key or anchor vendor. The anchor supplier's products or services are then used to influence the selection of other warehousing products and services.

4.8 WHAT SHOULD BE LOOKED FOR IN A DATA WAREHOUSE VENDOR?

The following sections provide evaluation criteria for the different components that make up a data warehouse solution. Different weighting should be applied to each criterion, depending on its importance to the organization.

Solution Framework

The following evaluation criteria can be applied to the overall warehousing solution:

- **Relational data warehouse.** The data warehouse resides on a relational DBMS. (Multidimensional databases are not an appropriate platform for an enterprise data warehouse, although they may be used for data marts with power-user requirements.)
- **Scalability.** The warehouse solution can scale up in terms of disk space, processing power, and warehouse design as the warehouse scope increases. This scalability is particularly important if the warehouse is expected to grow at a rapid rate.
- **Front-end independence.** The design of the data warehouse is independent of any particular front-end tool. This independence leaves the warehouse team free to mix and match different front-end tools according to the needs and skills of warehouse users. Enterprises can easily add more sophisticated front-ends (such as data mining tools) at a later time.
- **Architectural integrity.** The proposed solution does not make the overall system architecture of the enterprise brittle; rather, it contributes to the long-term resiliency of the IT architecture.
- **Preservation of prior investments.** The solution leverages as much as possible prior software and hardware investments and existing skill sets within the organization.

Project and Integration Consultancy Services

The following evaluation criteria can be applied to consultants and system integrators:

- **Star join schema.** Warehouse designers use a dimensional modeling approach based on a star join schema. This form of modeling results in database designs that are navigable by business users and are resilient to evolving business requirements.

- **Source data audit.** A thorough physical and logical data audit is performed prior to implementation, to identify data quality issues within source systems and propose remedial steps. Source system quality issues are the number-one cause of data warehouse project delays. The data audit also serves as a reality check to determine if the required data are available in the operational systems of the enterprise.
- **Decisional requirements analysis.** Perform a through decisional requirements analysis activity with the appropriate end-user representatives prior to implementation to identify detailed decisional requirements and their priorities. This analysis must serve as the basis for key warehouse design decisions.
- **Methodology.** The consultant team specializes in data warehousing and uses a data warehousing methodology based on the current state-of-the-art. Avoid consultants who apply unsuitable OLTP methodologies to the development of data warehouses.
- **Appropriate fact record granularity.** The fact records are stored at the lowest granularity necessary to meet current decisional requirements without precluding likely future requirements. The wrong choice of grain can dramatically reduce the usefulness of the warehouse by limiting the degree to which users can slice and dice through data.
- **Operational data store.** The consultant team capable of implementing on operational data store layer beneath the data warehouse if one is necessary for operational integrity. The consultant team is cognizant of the key differences between operational data store and warehousing design issues, and it designs the solution accordingly.
- **Knowledge transfer.** The consultant team views knowledge transfer as a key component of a data warehousing initiative. The project environment encourages coaching and learning for both IT staff and end users. Business users are encouraged to share their in-depth understanding and knowledge of the business with the rest of the warehousing team.
- **Incremental rollouts.** The overall project approach is driven by risks and rewards, with clearly defined phases (rollouts) that incrementally extend the scope of the warehouse. The scope of each rollout is strictly managed to prevent schedule slippage.

Front-End/OLAP/Decision Support/ Data Access and Retrieval Tools

The following evaluation criteria can be applied to front-end/OLAP/decision support/ data access and retrieval tools:

- **Multidimensional views.** The tool supports pivoting, drill-up and drill-down and displays query results as spreadsheets, graphs, and charts.
- **Usability.** The tool works under the GUI environment and has features that make it user-friendly (e.g., the ability to open and run an existing report with one or two clicks of the mouse).
- **Star schema aware.** It is applicable only to relational OLAP tools. The tool recognizes a star schema database and takes advantage of the schema design.
- **Tool sophistication.** The tool is appropriate for the intended user. Not all users are comfortable with desktop computing, and relational OLAP tools can meet most

user requirements. Multidimensional databases are highly sophisticated and are more appropriate for power users.

- **Delivery lead time.** The product vendor can deliver the product within the required time frame.
- **Planned functionality for future releases.** Since this area of data warehousing technologies is constantly evolving and maturing, it is helpful to know the enhancements or features that the tool will eventually have in its future releases. The planned functionality should be consistent with the above evaluation criteria.

Middleware/Data Extraction and Transformation Tools

The following evaluation criteria can be applied to middleware and extraction and transformation tools:

- **Price/Performance.** The product performs well in a price/performance/maintenance comparison with other vendors of similar products.
- **Extraction and transformation steps supported.** The tool supports or automates one or more of the basic steps to extracting and transforming data. These steps are reading source data, transporting source data, remapping keys, creating load images, generating or creating stored aggregates, logging load exceptions, generating indexes, quality assurance checking, alert generation, and backup and recovery.
- **Delivery load time.** The product vendor can deliver the product within the required time frame.

Most tools in this category are very expensive. Seriously consider writing in-house versions of these tools as an alternative, especially if source and target environments are homogeneous.

Relational Database Management Systems

The following evaluation criteria can be applied to an RDBMS:

- **Preservation of prior investments.** The warehouse solution larges as much as possible prior software and hardware investments and existing skill sets within the organization. However, data warehousing does enquire additional database management techniques because of the size and scale of the database.
- **Financial stability.** The product vendor has proven to be a strong and visible player in the relational database market, and its financial performance indicates growth or stability.
- **Data warehousing features.** The product has or will have features that support data warehousing requirements (e.g., bit-mapped indexes for large tables, aggregate navigation).
- **Star schema aware.** The product's query optimizer recognizes the star schema and optimizes the query accordingly. Note that most query optimizers strongly support only OLTP-type queries. Unfortunately, although these optimizers are appropriate for transactional environments, they may actually slow down the performance on decisional queries.
- **Warehouse metadata.** The tool for the use of warehouse metadata for aggregate navigation, query statistics collection, etc.

- **Price/Performance.** The product performs well in a price/performance comparison with other vendors of similar products.

Hardware or Operating System Platforms

The following evaluation criteria can be applied to hardware and operating system platforms:

- **Scalability.** The warehouse solution can scale up in terms of space and processing power. This scalability is particularly important if the warehouse is projected to grow at a rapid rate.
- **Financial stability.** The product vendor has proven to be a strong and visible player in the hardware segment, and its financial performance indicates growth or stability.
- **Price/Performance.** The product performs well in a price/performance comparison with other vendors of similar products.
- **Delivery lead time.** The product vendor can deliver the hardware or an equivalent service unit within the required time frame. If the unit is not readily available within the same country, there may be delays due to importation logistics.
- **Reference sites.** The hardware vendor has a reference site that is using a similar unit for the same purpose. The warehousing team can either arrange a site visit or interview representatives from the site visit. Alternatively, an onsite test of the unit can be conducted, especially if no reference is available.
- **Availability of support.** Support for the hardware and its operating system is available, and support response times and within the acceptable down time for the warehouse.

4.9 HOW DOES DATA WAREHOUSING AFFECT EXISTING SYSTEMS?

Existing operational systems are the source of internal warehouse data. Extractions can take place only during the batch windows of the operational systems, typically after office hours. If batch windows are sufficiently large, warehouse-related activities will have little or no disruptive effects on normal, day-to-day operations.

Improvement Areas in Operational Systems

Data warehousing, however, highlight areas in existing systems where improvements can be made to operational systems, particularly in two areas:

- **Missing data items.** Decisional information needs always require the collection of data that are currently outside the scope of the existing systems. If possible, the existing systems are extended to support the collection of such data. The team will have to study alternatives to data collection if the operational systems cannot be modified (for example, if the operational system is an application package whose warranties will be void if modifications are made).
- **Insufficient data quality.** The data warehouse efforts may also identify areas where the data quality of the operational systems can be improved. This is especially true for data items that are used to uniquely identify customers, such as social security numbers.

The data warehouse implementation team should continuously provide constructive feedback regarding the operational systems. Easy improvements can be quickly implemented, and improvements that require significant effort and resources can be prioritized during IT planning.

By ensuring that each rollout of a data warehouse phase is always accompanied by a review of the existing systems, the warehousing team can provide valuable inputs to plans for enhancing operational systems.

4.10 DATA WAREHOUSING AND ITS IMPACT ON OTHER ENTERPRISE INITIATIVES

By its enterprise-wide nature, a data warehousing initiative will naturally have an impact on other enterprise initiatives, two of which are discussed below.

How Does Data Warehousing Tie in with BPR?

Data warehousing refers to the gamut of activities that support the decisional information requirements of the enterprise. BPR is "the radical redesign of strategic and value-added processes and the systems, policies, and organizational structures that support them to optimize the work flows and productivity in an organization."

Most BPR projects have focused on the optimization of operational business processes. Data warehousing, on the other hand, focuses on optimizing the decisional (or decision-making) processes within the enterprise. It can be said that data warehousing is the technology enabler for reengineering decisional processes.

The ready availability of integrated data for corporate decision-making also has implications for the organizational structure of the enterprise. Most organizations are structured or designed to collect, summarize, report, and direct the status of operations (i.e., there is an operational monitoring purpose). The availability of integrated data different levels of detail may encourage a flattening of the organization structure.

Data warehouses also provide the enterprise with the measures for gauging competitive standing. The use of the warehouse leads to insights as to what drives the enterprise. These insights may quickly lead to business process reengineering initiatives in the operational areas.

How Does Data Warehousing Tie in with Intranets?

The term intranet refers to the use of internet technologies for internal corporate networks. Intranets have been touched as cost-effective, client/server solutions to enterprise computing needs. Intranets are also popular due to the universal, easy-to-learn, easy-to-use front-end, i.e., the web browser.

A data warehouse with a web-enabled front-end therefore provides enterprises with interesting options for intranet based solutions.

With the introduction of technologies that enable secure connections over the public internet infrastructure, enterprises now also have a cost-effective way of distributing delivering warehouse data to users in multiple locations.

4.11 WHEN IS A DATA WAREHOUSE NOT APPROPRIATE?

Not all organizations are ready for a data warehousing initiative. Below are two instances when a data warehouse is simply inappropriate.

When the Operational Systems are not Ready

The data warehouse is populated with information primarily from the operational systems of the enterprise. A good indicator of operational system readiness is the amount of IT effort focused on operational systems.

A number of telltale signs indicate a lack of readiness. These include the following:

- **Many new operational systems are planned for development or are in the process of being deployed.** Much of the enterprise's IT resources will be assigned to this effort and will therefore not be available for data warehousing projects.
- **Many of the operational systems are legacy applications that require much fire fighting.** The source systems are brittle or unstable candidates for replacement. IT resources are also directed at fighting operational system fires.
- **Many of the operational systems require major enhancements and must be overhauled.** If the operational systems require major enhancements, many choices for these systems do not sufficiently support the day-to-day operations of the enterprise. Again, IT resources will be directed to enhancement or replacement efforts. Furthermore, deficient operational systems always fall to capture all the data required to meet the decisional information needs of business managers.

Regardless of the reason for a lack of operational system readiness, the bottom line is simple: an enterprise-wide data warehouse is out of the question due to the lack of adequate source systems. However, this does not preclude a phased data warehousing initiative, as illustrated in Figure 4.2.

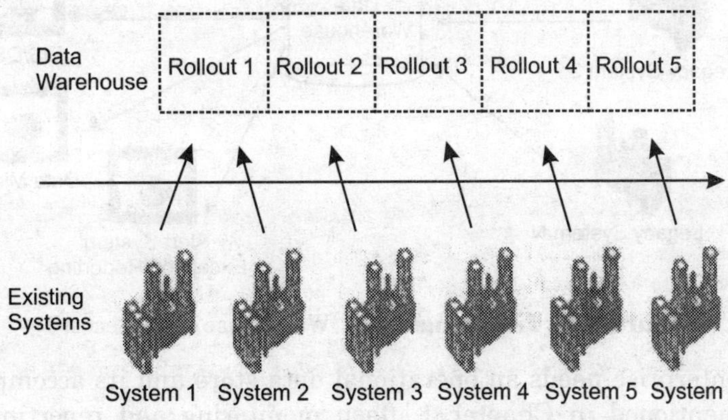

Figure 4.2. Data Warehouse Rollout Strategy

The enterprise may opt for an interleaved deployment of systems. A series of projects can be conducted, where a project to deploy an operational system is followed by a project that extends the scope of the data warehouse to encompass the newly stabilized operational system.

The main focus of the majority of IT staff remains on deploying the operational systems. However, a data warehouse scope extension project is initiated as each operational system stabilizes. This project extends the data warehouse scope with data from each new operational system.

However, this approach may create unrealistic end-user expectations, particularly during earlier rollouts. The scope and strategy should therefore be communicated clearly and consistently to all users. Most, if not all, business users will understand that enterprise-wide views of data are not possible while most of the operational systems are not feeding the warehouse.

When Does the Operational Integration Needed?

Despite its ability to provide integrated data for decisional information needs, a data warehouse does not in any way contribute to meeting the operational information needs of the enterprise. Data warehouses are refreshed at best on a daily basis. They do not integrate data quickly enough or often enough for operational management purposes.

If the enterprise needs operational integration, then the typical data warehouse deployment (as shown in Figure 4.3) is insufficient.

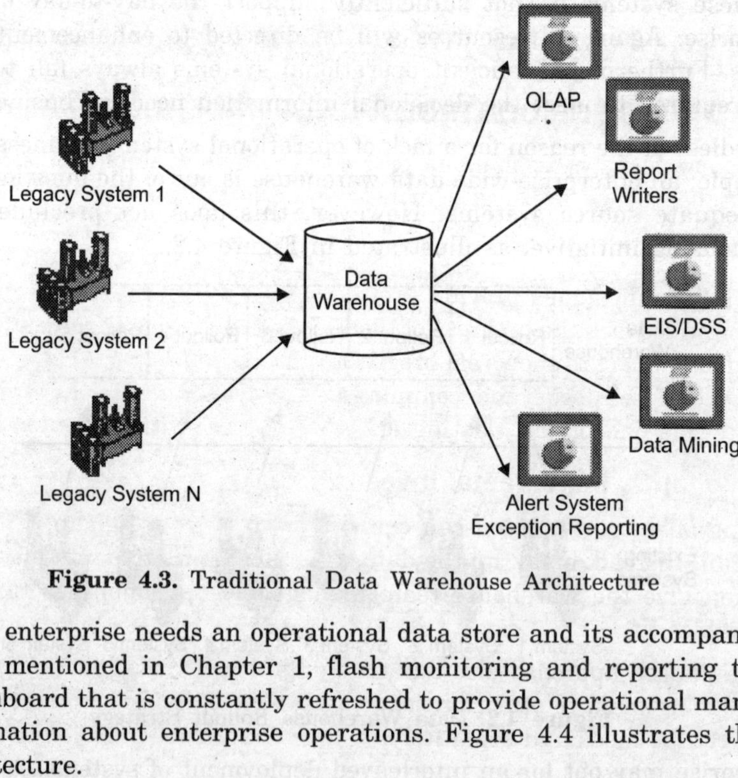

Figure 4.3. Traditional Data Warehouse Architecture

Instead, the enterprise needs an operational data store and its accompanying front-end applications. As mentioned in Chapter 1, flash monitoring and reporting tools are often likened to a dashboard that is constantly refreshed to provide operational management with the latest information about enterprise operations. Figure 4.4 illustrates the operational data store architecture.

When the intended users of the system are operational managers and when the requirements are for an integrated view of constantly refreshed operational data, an operational data store is the appropriate solution.

Enterprises that have implemented operational data stores will find it natural to use the operational data store as one of the primary source systems for their data warehouse. Thus, the data warehouse contains a series (i.e., layer upon layer) of ODS snapshots, where each layer corresponds to data as of a specific point in time.

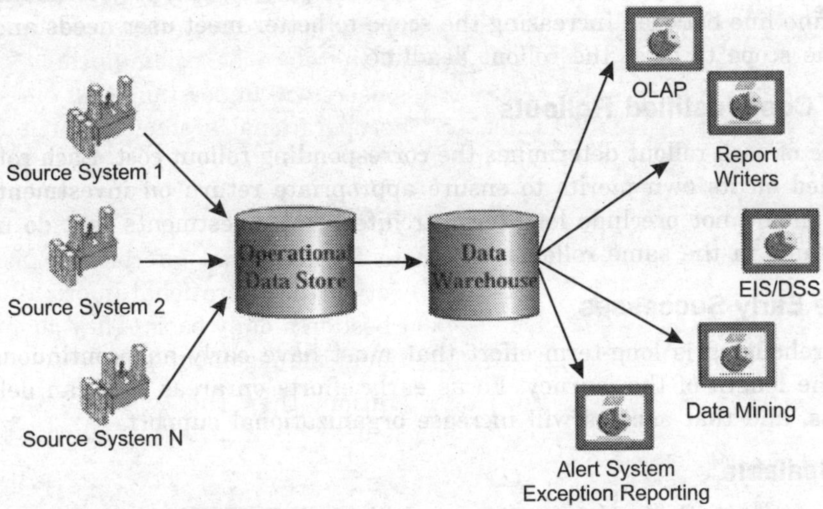

Figure 4.4. The Data Warehouse and the Operational Data Store

4.12 HOW TO MANAGE OR CONTROL A DATA WAREHOUSE INITIATIVE?

There are several ways to manage or control a data warehouse project. Most of the techniques described below are useful in any technology project.

Milestones

Clearly defined milestones provide project management and the project sponsor with regular checkpoints to track the progress of the data warehouse development effort. Milestones should be far enough apart to show real progress, but not so far apart that senior management becomes uneasy or loses focus and commitment. In general, one data warehouse rollout should be treated as one project, lasting anywhere between three to six months.

Incremental Rollouts, Incremental Investments

Avoid biting off more than you can chew; projects that are gigantic leaps forward are more likely to fail. Instead, break up the data warehouse initiative into incremental rollouts. By doing so, you give the warehouse team manageable but ambitious targets and clearly defined deliverables.

Applying a phased approach also has the added benefit of allowing the project sponsor and the warehousing team to set priorities and manage end-user expectations. The benefits of each rollout can be measured separately; and the data warehouse is justified on a phase-per-phase basis.

A phased approach, however, requires an overall architect so that each phase also lays the foundation for subsequent warehousing efforts; and earlier investments remain intact.

Clearly Defined Rollout Scopes

To the maximum extent possible, clearly define the scope of each rollout to set the expectations of both senior management and warehouse end-users. Each rollout should deliver useful functionality. As in most development project, the project manager will be walking the fine line between increasing the scope to better meet user needs and ruthlessly controlling the scope to meet the rollout deadline.

Individually Cost-Justified Rollouts

The scope of each rollout determines the corresponding rollout cost. Each rollout should be cost-justified on its own merits to ensure appropriate return on investment. However, this practice should not preclude long-term architectural investments that do not have an immediate return in the same rollout.

Plan to have Early Successes

Data warehousing is long-term effort that must have early and continuous successes that justify the length of the journey. Focus early efforts on areas that can deliver highly visible success, and that success will increase organizational support.

Plan to be Scalable

Initial successes with the data warehouse will result in a sudden demand for increased data scope, increased functionality, or both! The warehousing environment and design must both be scalable to deal with increased demand as needed.

Reward your Team

Data warehousing is a hard work, and teams need to know their work is appreciated. A motivated team is always an asset in long-term initiatives.

In Summary

The Chief Information Officer (CIO) has the unenviable task of juggling the limited IT resources of the enterprise. He or she makes the resource assignment decisions that determine the skill sets of the various IT project teams.

Unfortunately, data warehousing is just one of the many projects on the CIO's plate. If the enterprise is still in the process of deploying operational system, data warehousing will naturally be at a lower priority.

CIOs also have the difficult responsibility of evolving the enterprise's IT architecture. They must ensure that the addition of each new system, and the extension of each existing system, contributes to the stability and resiliency of the overall IT architecture.

Fortunately, data warehouse and operational data store technologies allow CIOs to migrate reporting and analytical functionality from legacy or operational environments, thereby creating a more robust and stable computing environment for the enterprise.

CHAPTER 5

THE PROJECT MANAGER

The warehouse Project Manager is responsible for any and all technical activities related to planning, designing, and building a data warehouse. Under ideal circumstances, this role is fulfilled by internal IT staff. It is not unusual, however, for this role to be outsourced, especially for early or pilot projects, because warehousing technologies and techniques are so new.

5.1 HOW TO ROLL OUT A DATA WAREHOUSE INITIATIVE?

To start a data warehouse initiative, there are three main things to be kept in mind. Always start with a planning activity. Always implement a pilot project as your "proof of concept." And, always extend the functionality of the warehouse in an iterative manner.

Start with a Data Warehouse Planning Activity

The scope of a data warehouse varies from one enterprise to another. The desired scope and scale are typically determined by the information requirements that drive the warehouse design and development. These requirements, in turn, are driven by the business context of the enterprise–the industry, the fierceness of competition, and the state of the art in industry practices.

Regardless of the industry, however, it is advisable to start a data warehouse initiative with a short planning activity. The Project Manager should launch and manage the activities listed below.

Decisional Requirements Analysis

Start with an analysis of the decision support needs of the organization. The warehousing team must understand the user requirements and attempt to map these to the data sources available. The team also designs potential queries or reports that can meet the stated information requirements.

Unlike system development projects for OLTP applications, the information needs of decisional users cannot be pinned down and are frequently changing. The requirements analysis team should therefore gain enough of an understanding of the business to be able to anticipate likely changes to end-user requirements.

Decisional Source System Audit

Conduct an audit of all potential sources of data. This crucial and very detailed task verifies that data sources exist to meet the decisional information needs identified during requirements analysis. There is no point in designing a warehouse schema that cannot be populated because of a lack of source data.

Similarly, there is no point in designing reports or queries when data are not available to generate them. Log all data items that are currently not supported or provided by the operational systems and submit these to the CIO as inputs for IT planning.

Logical and Physical Warehouse Schema Design (Preliminary)

The results of requirements analysis and source system audit serve as inputs to the design of the warehouse schema. The schema details all fact and dimension tables and fields, as well as the data sources for each warehouse field. The preliminary schema produced as part of the warehousing planning activity will be progressively refined with each rollout of the data warehouse.

The goal of the team is to design a data structure that will be resilient enough to meet the constantly changing information requirements of warehouse end-users.

Other Concerns

The three tasks described above should also provide the warehousing team with an understanding of.

- The required warehouse architecture.
- The appropriate phasing and rollout strategy; and
- The ideal scope for a pilot implementation.

The data warehouse plan must also evaluate the need for an ODS layer between the operational systems and the data warehouse.

Additional information on the above activities is available in part III. Process.

Implement a Proof-of-Concept Pilot

Start with a pilot implementation as the first rollout for data warehousing. Pilot projects have the advantage of being small and manageable, thereby providing the organization with a data warehouse "proof of concept" that has a good chance of success.

Determine the functional scope of a pilot implementation based on two factors:

- **The degree of risk the enterprise is willing to take.** The project difficulty increases as the number of source systems, users, and locations increases. Politically sensitive areas of the enterprise are also very high risk.
- **The potential for leveraging the pilot project.** Avoid constructing a "throwaway" prototype for the pilot project. The pilot warehouse must have actual value to the enterprise. Figure 5.1 is a matrix for assessing the pilot project.

Avoid high-risk projects with very low reward possibilities. Ideally, the pilot project has low or manageable risk factors but has a highly visible impact on the way decisions are made in the enterprise. An early and high profile success will increase the grassroots support of the warehousing initiative.

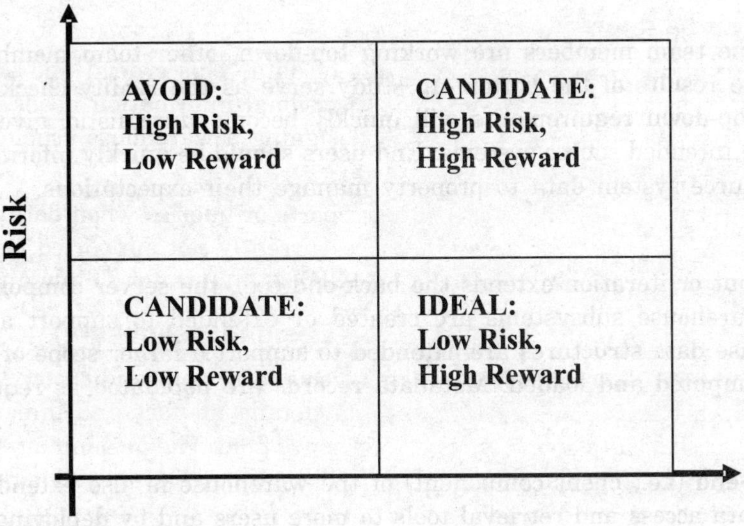

Figure 5.1. Selecting a Pilot Project: Risks vs Reward

Extend Functionality Iteratively

Once the warehouse pilot is in place and is stable, implement subsequent rollouts of the data warehouse to continuously layer new functionality or extend existing warehousing functionality on a cost-justifiable, prioritized basis, illustrated by the diagram in Figure 5.2.

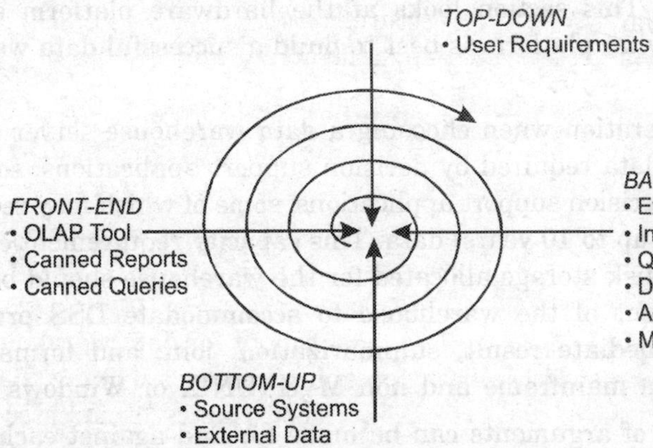

Figure 5.2. Iterative Extension of Functionality, i.e., Evolution

Top-down

Drive all rollouts by a top-down study of user requirements. Decisional requirements are subject to constant change; the team will never be able to fully document and understand the requirements, simply because the requirements change as the business situation changes. Don't fall into the trap of wanting to analyze everything to extreme detail (i.e., analysis paralysis).

Bottom-up

While some team members are working top-down, other team members are working bottom-up. The results of the bottom-up study serve as the reality check for the rollout–some of the top-down requirements will quickly become unrealistic, given the state and contents of the intended source systems. End users should be quickly informed of limitations imposed by source system data to property manage their expectations.

Back-end

Each rollout or iteration extends the back-end (i.e., the server component) of the data warehouse. Warehouse subsystems are created or extended to support a larger scope of data. Warehouse data structures are extended to support a larger scope of data. Aggregate records are computed and loaded. Metadata records are populated as required.

Front-end

The front-end (i.e., client component) of the warehouse is also extended by deploying the existing data access and retrieval tools to more users and by deploying new tools (e.g., data mining tools, new decision support applications) to warehouse users. The availability of more data implies that new reports and new queries can be defined.

5.2 HOW IMPORTANT IS THE HARDWARE PLATFORM?

Since many data warehouse implementations are developed into already existing environments, many organizations tend to leverage the existing platforms and skill base to build a data warehouse. This section looks at the hardware platform selection from an architectural viewpoint: what platform is best to build a successful data warehouse from the ground up.

An important consideration when choosing a data warehouse server is its capacity for handling the volumes of data required by decision support applications, some of which may require data required by decision support applications, some of which may require a significant amount of historical (e.g., up to 10 years) data. This capacity requirement can be quite large. For example, in general, disk storage allocated for the warehouse should be 2 to 3 times the size of the data component of the warehouse to accommodate DSS processing, such as sorting, storing of intermediate result, summarization, join, and formatting. Often, the platform choice between a mainframe and non MVS (UNIX or Windows NT) server.

Of course, a number of arguments can be made for and against each of these choices. For example, a mainframe is based on a proven technology; has large data and throughput capacity; is reliable, available, and serviceable; and may support the legacy databases that are used as sources for the data warehouse. The data warehouse residing on the mainframe is best suited for situations in which large amounts of legacy data need to be stored in the data warehouse. A mainframe system, however, is not as open and flexible as a contemporary client/server systems, and is not optimized for ad hoc query processing. A modern server (non-mainframe) can also support large data volumes and a large number of flexible GUI-based end-user tools, and can relieve the mainframe from ad hoc query processing. However, in general, non-MVS servers are not as reliable as mainframes, are more difficult to manage and integrate into the existing environment, and may require new skills and even new organizational structures.

From the architectural viewpoint, however, the data warehouse server has to be specialized for the tasks associated with the data warehouse, and a mainframe scan be well suited to be a data warehouse server. Let's look at the hardware features that make a server-whether it is mainframe, UNIX or NT-based–an appropriate technical solution for the data warehouse.

To begin with, the data warehouse server has to be able to support large data volumes and complex query processing. In addition, it has to be scalable, since the data warehouse is never finished, as new user requirements, new data sources, and more historical data are continuously incorporated into the warehouse, and as the user population of the data warehouse continues to grow. Therefore, a clear requirement for the data warehouse server is the scalable high performance for data loading and ad hoc query processing as well as the ability to support large databases in a reliable, efficient fashion. Chapter 4 briefly touched on various design points to enable server specialization for scalability in performance, throughput, user support, and very large database (VLDB) processing.

Balanced Approach

An important design point when selecting a scalable computing platform is the right balance between all computing components, for example, between the number of processors in a multiprocessor system and the I/O bandwidth. Remember that the lack of balance in a system inevitably results in bottleneck!

Typically, when a hardware platform is sized to accommodate the data warehouse, this sizing is frequently focused on the number and size of disks. A typical disk configuration includes 2.5 to 3 times the amount of raw data. An important consideration–disk throughput comes from the actual number of disks, and not the total disk space. Thus, the number of disks has direct impact on data parallelism. To balance the system, it is very important to allocate a correct number of processors to efficiently handle all disk I/O operations. If this allocation is not balanced, an expensive data warehouse platform can rapidly become CPU-bound. Indeed, since various processors have widely different performance ratings and thus can support a different number of disks per CPU, data warehouse designers should carefully analyze the disk I/O rates and processor capabilities to derive an efficient system configuration. For example, if it takes a CPU rated warehouse designers should carefully analyze the disk I/O rates and processor capabilities to derive an efficient system configuration. For example, if it takes a CPU rated at 10 SPEC to efficiently handle one 3-Gbyte disk drive, then a single 30 SPEC into processor in a multiprocessor system can handle three disk drivers. Knowing how much data needs to be processed should give you an idea of how big the multiprocessor system should be. Another consideration is related to disk controllers. A disk controller can support a certain amount of data throughput (e.g., 20 Mbytes/s). Knowing the per-disk throughput ratio and the total number of disks can tell you how many controllers of a given type should be configured in the system.

The idea of a balanced approach can (and should) be carefully extended to all system components. The resulting system configuration will easily handle known workloads and provide a balanced and scalable computing platform for future growth.

Optimal Hardware Architecture for Parallel Query Scalability

An important consideration when selecting a hardware platform for a data warehouse is that of scalability. Therefore, a frequent approach to system selection is to take advantage of hardware parallelism that comes in the form of shared-memory symmetric multiprocessors (SMPs), massively multi processing (MPPs) and clusters explained in Chapter 10. The scalability of these systems can be seriously affected by the system-architecture-induced data skew. This architecture-induced data skew is more severe in the low-density asymmetric connection architectures e.g., daisy-chained, 2-D and 3-D mesh), and is virtually nonexistent in symmetric connection architectures (e.g., cross-bar switch). Thus, when selecting a hardware platform for a data warehouse, take into account the fact that the system-architecture-induced data skew can overpower even the best data layout for parallel query execution, and can force and expensive parallel computing system to process queries serially.

The choice between SMP and MPP is influenced by a number of factors, including the complexity of the query environment, the price/performance ratio, the proven processing capacity of the hardware platform with the target RDBMS, the anticipated warehouse applications, and the foreseen increases in warehouse size and users.

For example, complex queries that involve multiple table joins might realize better performance with an MPP configuration. MPPs though, are generally more expensive. Clustered SMPs may provide a highly scalable implementation with better price/performance benefits.

5.3 WHAT ARE THE TECHNOLOGIES INVOLVED?

Several types of technologies are used to make data warehousing possible. These technology types are enumerated briefly below. More information is available in Part 4, Technology.

- **Source systems.** The operational systems of the enterprise are the most likely source systems for a data warehouse. The warehouse may also make use of external data sources from third parties.
- **Middleware, extraction, transportation and transformation technologies.** These tools extract and reorganize data from the various source systems. These tools vary greatly in terms of complexity, features, and price. The ideal tools for the enterprise are heavily dependent on the computing environment of the source systems and the intended computing environment of the data warehouse.
- **Data quality tools.** These tools identify or correct data quality errors that exist in the raw source data. Most tools of this type are used to call the warehouse team's attention to potential quality problems. Unfortunately, much of the data cleansing process is still manual; it is also tedious due to the volume of data involved.
- **Warehouse storage.** Database management systems (DBMS) are used to store the warehouse data. DBMS products are generally classified as relational (e.g., Oracle, Informix, Sybase) or multidimensional (e.g., Essbase, BrioQuery, Express Server).
- **Metadata management.** These tools create, store, and manage the warehouse metadata.

- **Data access and retrieval tools.** These are tools used by warehouse end users to access, format, and disseminate warehouse data in the form of reports, query results, charts, and graphs. Other data access and retrieval tools actively search the data warehouse for patterns in the data (i.e., data mining tools). Decision Support Systems and Executive Information Systems also fall into this category.
- **Data modeling tools.** These tools are used to prepare and maintain an information model of both the source databases and the warehouse database.
- **Warehouse management tools.** These tools are used by warehouse administrators to create and maintain the warehouse (e.g., create and modify warehouse data structures, generate indexes).
- **Data warehouse hardware.** This refers to the data warehouse server platforms and their related operating systems.

Figure 5.3 depicts the typical warehouse software components and their relationships to one another.

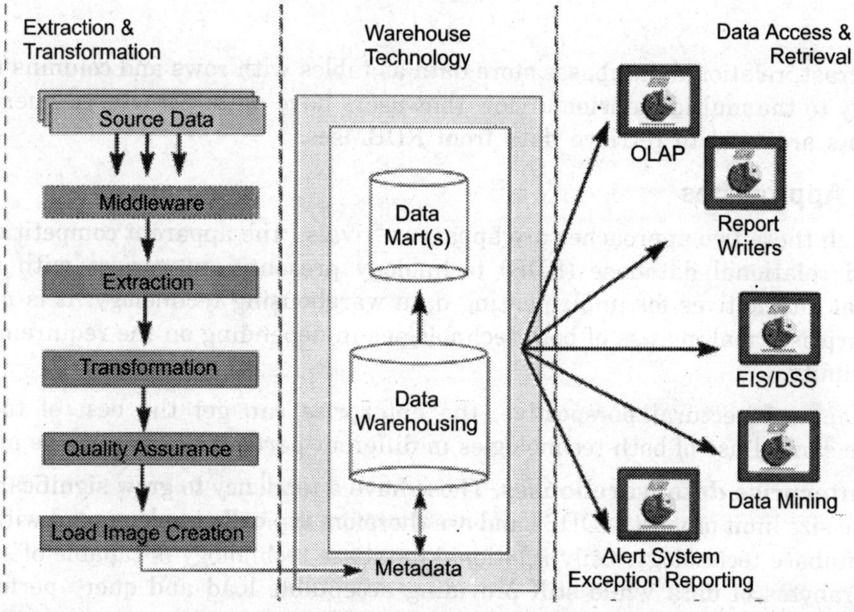

Figure 5.3. Data Warehouse Components

5.4 ARE THE RELATIONAL DATABASES STILL USED FOR DATA WAREHOUSING?

Although there were initial doubts about the use of relational database technology in data warehousing, experience has shown that there is actually no other appropriate database management system for an enterprise-wide data warehouse.

MDDBs

The confusion about relational databases arises from the proliferation of OLAP products that make use of a multidimensional database (MDDB). MDDBs store data in a "hypercube" i.e., a multidimensional array that is paged in and out of memory as needed, as illustrated in Figure 5.4.

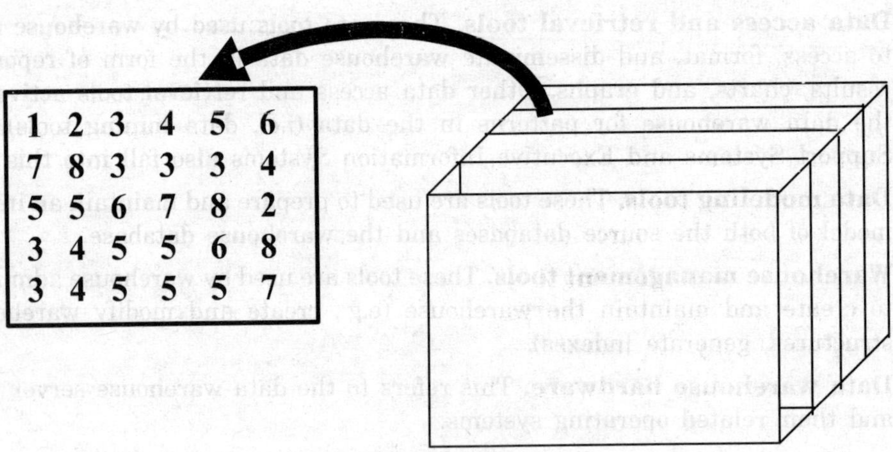

Figure 5.4. MDDB Data Structures

RDBMS

In contrast, relational databases store data as tables with rows and columns that do not map directly to the multidimensional view that users have data. Structured query language (SQL) scripts are used to retrieve data from RDBMses.

Two Rival Approaches

Although these two approaches are apparent "rivals," the apparent competition between MDDB and relational database (RDB) technology presents enterprises with interesting architectural alternatives for implementing data warehousing technology. It is not unusual to find enterprises making use of both technologies in depending on the requirements of the user community.

From an architectural perspective, the enterprise can get the best of tooth worlds through the careful use of both technologies in different parts of the warehouse architecture.

- **Enterprise data warehouses.** These have a tendency to grow significantly beyond the size limit of most MDDBs and are therefore typically implemented with relational database technology. Only relational database technology is capable of storing upto terabytes of data while still providing acceptable load and query performance.
- **Data marts.** A data mart is typically a subset of the enterprise data warehouse. These subsets are determined either by geography (i.e., one data mart per location) or by user group. Data marts, due to their smaller size, may take advantage of multidimensional databases for better reporting and analysis performance.

Warehousing Architectures

How the relational and multi-dimensional database technologies can be used together for data warehouse and data mart implementation is presented below.

RDBMSes in Warehousing Architectures

Data warehouses are built on relational database technology. Online analytical processing (OLAP) tools are then used to interact directly with the relational data warehouse or with a relational data mart (see Figure 5.5). Relational OLAP (ROLAP) tools recognize the relational nature of the database but still present their users with multidimensional views of the data.

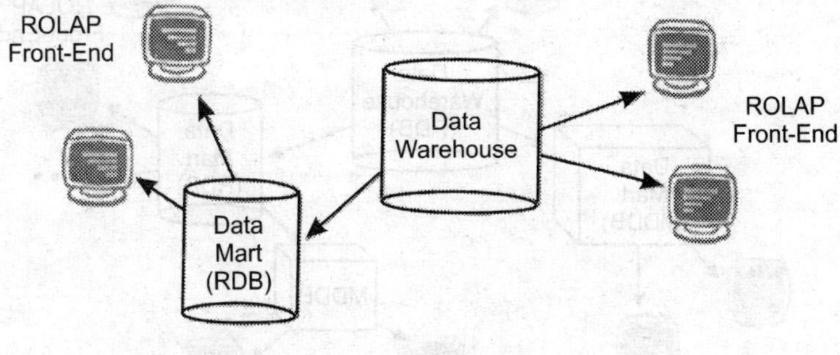

Figure 5.5. Relational Databases

MDDBs in Warehousing Architectures

Alternatively data is extracted from the relational data warehouse and placed in multidimensional data structures to reflect the multidimensional nature of the data (see Figure 5.6). Multidimensional OLAP (MOLAP) tools run against the multidimensional server, rather than against the data warehouse.

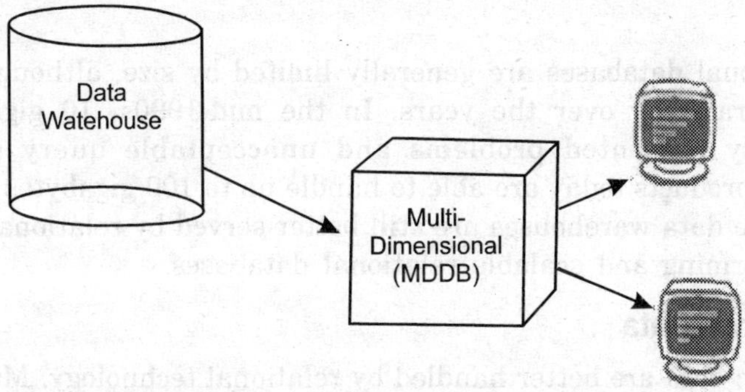

Figure 5.6. Multidimensional Databases

Tiered Data Warehousing Architectures

The enterprise is free to mix and match these two database technologies, depending on the scale and size of the data warehouse, as illustrated in Figure 5.7.

It is not unusual to find an enterprise with the following tiered data warehousing architecture:

- ROLAP tools, which run directly against relational databases, are used whenever the queries are fairly simple and when the administration overhead that comes with multidimensional tools is not justified for a particular user base.
- Multidimensional databases are used for data marts, and specific multidimensional front-end applications query the contents of the MDDB. Data marts may also use relational database technology, in which case, users make use of ROLAP front-ends.

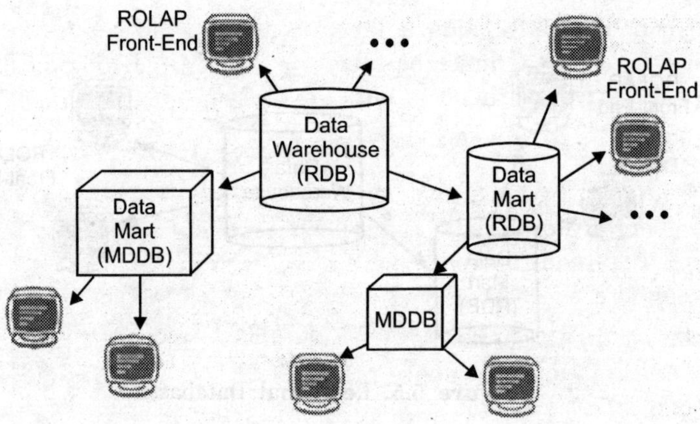

Figure 5.7. Tiered Data Warehousing Architecture

Trade-Offs: MDDB vs. RDBMS

Consider the following factors while choosing between the multidimensional and relational approaches:

Size

Multidimensional databases are generally limited by size, although the size limit has been increasing gradually over the years. In the mid-1990s, 10 gigabytes of data in a hypercube already presented problems and unacceptable query performance. Some multidimensional products today are able to handle up to 100 gigabytes of data. Despite this improvement, large data warehouses are still better served by relational front-ends running against high performing and scalable relational databases.

Volatility of Source Data

Highly volatile data are better handled by relational technology. Multidimensional data in hypercubes generally take long to load and update. Thus the time required to constantly load and update the multidimensional data structure may prevent the enterprise from loading new data as often as desired.

Aggregate Strategy

Multidimensional hypercubes support aggregations better, although this advantage will disappear as relational databases improve their support of aggregate navigation. Drilling up and down on RDBMSes generally take longer than on MDDBs as well. However, due to their size limitation, MDDBS will not be suited to warehouses or data marts with very detailed data.

Investment Protection

Most enterprises have already made significant investments in relational technology (e.g., RDBMS assets) and skill sets. The continued use of these tools and skills for another purpose provides additional return on investment and lowers the technical risk for the data warehousing effort.

Ability to Manage Complexity

A multidimensional DBMS adds a layer to the overall systems architecture of the warehouse. Sufficient resources must be allocated to administer and maintain the MDDB layer. If the administrative overhead is not or cannot be justified, and MDDB will not be appropriate.

Type of Users

Power users generally prefer the range of functionality available in multidimensional OLAP tools. Users that require broad views of enterprise data require access to the data warehouse and therefore are best served by a relational OLAP tool.

Recently, many of the large database vendors have announced plans to integrate their multidimensional and relational database products. In this scenario, end-users make use of the multidimensional front-end tools or all their queries. If the query requires data that are not available in the MDDB, the tools will retrieve the required data from the larger relational database. Subbed as a "drill-through" feature, this innovation will certainly introduce new data warehousing.

5.5 HOW LONG DOES A DATA WAREHOUSING PROJECT LAST?

Data warehousing is a long, daunting task; it requires significant, prolonged effort on the part of the enterprise and may have the unpleasant side effect of highlighting problem areas in operational systems. Like any task of great magnitude, the data warehousing effort must be partitioned into manageable chunks, where each piece is managed as an individual project or rollout.

Data warehouse rollouts after the pilot warehouse must fit together within an overall strategy. Define the strategy at the start of the data warehousing effort. Constantly update (at least once a year) the data warehouse strategy as new requirements are understood, new operational systems are installed, and new tools become available.

In cases where the enterprise also has an operational data store initiative, the ODS and warehousing projects must be synchronized. The data warehouse should take advantage of the ODS as a source system as soon as possible. Figure 5.8 depicts how the entire decisional systems effort can be interleaved.

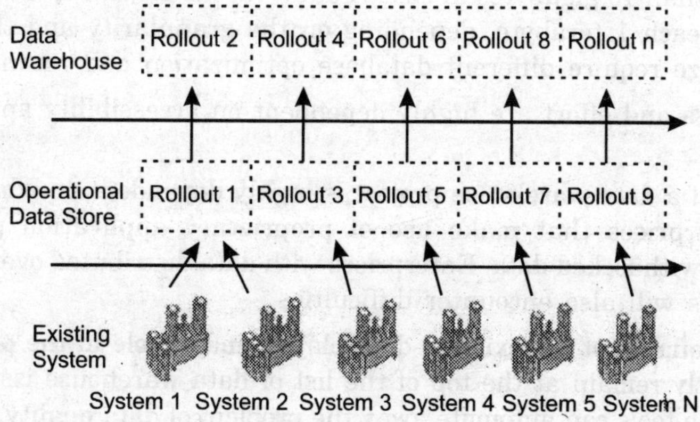

Figure 5.8. Interleaved Operational, ODS, and Warehouse Projects

Each data warehouse rollout should be scoped to last anywhere between three to six months, with a team of about 6 to 12 people working on it full time. Part-time team members can easily bring the total number of participants to more than 20. Sufficient resources must be allocated to support each rollout.

5.6 HOW IS A DATA WAREHOUSE DIFFERENT FROM OTHER IT PROJECTS?

Since much of computing has focused on meeting operational information needs, IT professionals have a natural tendency to apply the same methodologies, approaches or techniques to data warehousing projects. Unfortunately, data warehousing projects differ from other IT projects in a number of ways, as discussed below.

A Data Warehouse Project is not a Package Implementation Project

A data warehouse project requires a number of tools and software utilities that are available from multiple vendors. At present, there is still no single suite of tools that can automate the entire data warehousing effort.

Most of the major warehouse vendors, however, are now attempting to provide off-the-shelf solutions for warehousing projects by bundling their warehousing products with that of other warehousing partners. This solution limits the potential tool integration problems of the warehousing team.

A Data Warehouse Never Stops Evolving; it Changes with the Business

Unlike OLTP systems that are subject only to changes related to the process or area of the business they support, a data warehouse is subject to changes to the decisional information requirements of decision-makers. In other words, it is subject to any changes in the business context of the enterprise.

Also unlike OLTP systems, a successful data warehouse will result in more questions from business users. Change requests for the data warehouse are a positive indication that the warehouse is being used.

Data Warehouses are Huge

Without exaggeration, enterprise-wide data warehouses are huge. A pilot data warehouse can easily be more than 10 gigabytes in size. A data warehouse in production for a little over a year can easily reach 1 terabyte, depending on the granularity and the volume of data. Database of this size require different database optimization and tuning techniques.

Project progress and effort are highly dependent on accessibility and quality of source system data.

The progress of a data warehouse project is highly dependent on where the operational data resides. Enterprises that make use of proprietary application packages will find themselves dealing with locked data. Enterprises with data distributed over different locations with no easy access will also encounter difficulties.

Similarly, the quality of the existing data plays a major role in the project. Data quality problems consistently remain at the top of the list of data warehouse issues. Unfortunately, none of the available tools can automate away the problem of data quality. Although tools can help identify problem areas, these problems can only be resolved manually.

5.7 WHAT ARE THE CRITICAL SUCCESS FACTORS OF A DATA WAREHOUSING PROJECT?

A number of factors influence the progress and success of data warehousing projects. While the list below does not claim to be complete, it highlights areas of the warehousing project that the project manager is in a position to actively control or influence.

- **Proper planning.** Define a warehousing strategy and expect to review it after each warehouse rollout. Bear in mind that IT resources are still required to manage and administer the warehouse once it is in production. Stay coordinated with any scheduled maintenance work on the warehouse source systems.
- **Iterative development and change management.** Stay away from the big-bang approach. Divide the warehouse initiative into manageable rollouts, each to last anywhere between three to six months. Constantly collect feedback from users. Identify lessons learnt at the end of each project and feed these into the next iteration.
- **Access to and involvement of key players.** The Project Sponsor, the CIO, and the Project Manager must all be actively involved in setting the direction of the warehousing project. Work together to resolve the business and technical issues that will arise on the project. Choose the project team members carefully, taking care to ensure that the project team roles that must be performed by internal resources are staffed accordingly.
- **Training and communication.** If data warehousing is new to the enterprise or if new team members are joining the warehousing initiative, set aside enough time for training the team members. The roles of each team member must be communicated clearly to set role expectations.
- **Vigilant issue management.** Keep a close watch on project issues and ensure their speedy resolution. The Project Manager should be quick to identify the negative consequences on the project schedule if issues are left unresolved. The Project Sponsor should intervene and ensure the proper resolution of issues, especially if these are clearly causing delays, or deal with highly politicized areas of the business.
- **Warehousing approach.** One of the worst things a Project Manager can do is to apply OLTP development approaches to a warehousing project. Apply a system development approach that is tailored to data warehousing; avoid OLTP development approaches that have simply been repackaged into warehousing terms.
- **Demonstration with a pilot project.** The ideal pilot project is a high-impact, low-risk area of the enterprise. Use the pilot as a proof-of-concept to gain champions within the enterprise and to refute the opposition.
- **Focus on essential minimal characteristics.** The scope of each project or rollout should be ruthlessly managed to deliver the essential minimal characteristics for that rollout. Don't get carried away by spending time on the bells and whistles, especially with the front-end tools.

In Summary

The Project Manager is responsible for all technical aspects of the project on a day-to-day basis. Since upto 80 percent of any data warehousing project can be devoted to the back-end of the warehouse, the role of Project Manager can easily be one of the busiest on the project.

Despite the fact that business users now drive the warehouse development, a huge part of any data warehouse project is still technology centered. The critical success factors of typical technology projects therefore still apply to data warehousing projects. Bear in mind, however, that data warehousing projects are more susceptible to organizational and logistical issues than the typical technology project.

PART III : PROCESS

Although there have been attempts to use traditional software development methodologies from the OLTP arena for data warehouse development, warehousing practitioners generally agree that an iterative development approach is more suited to warehouse development than are traditional waterfall approaches.

This section of the book presents an iterative warehousing approach for enterprises about to embark on a data warehousing initiative. The approach begins with the definition of a data warehouse strategy, then proceeds to define the way to set up warehouse management and support processes.

The latter part of the approach focuses on the tasks required to plan and implement one rollout (i.e., one phases) of the tasks required to plan and implement one rollout (i.e., one phase) of the warehouse. These tasks are repeated for each phase of the warehouse development.

CHAPTER 6

WAREHOUSING STRATEGY

Defines the warehouse strategy as part of the information technology strategy of the enterprise. The traditional Information Strategy Plan (ISP) addresses operational computing needs thoroughly but may not give sufficient attention to decisional information requirements. A data warehouse strategy remedies this by focusing on the decisional needs of the enterprise.

We start this chapter by presenting the components of a Data Warehousing strategy. We follow with a discussion of the tasks required to define a strategy for an enterprise.

6.1 STRATEGY COMPONENTS

At a minimum, the data warehouse strategy should include the following elements:

Preliminary Data Warehouse Rollout Plan

Not all of the user requirements can be met in one data warehouse project—such a project would necessarily be large, and dangerously unmanageable. It is more realistic to prioritize the different user requirements and assign them to different warehouse rollouts. Doing so allows the enterprise to divide the warehouse development into phased, successive rollouts, where each rollout focuses on meeting an agreed set of requirements.

The iterative nature of such an approach allows the warehousing temp to extend the functionality of the warehouse in a manageable manner. The phased approach lowers the overall risk of the data warehouse project, while delivering increasing functionality to the users.

Preliminary Data Warehouse Architecture

Define the overall data warehouse architecture for the pilot and subsequent warehouse rollouts to ensure the scalability of the warehouse. Whenever possible, define the initial technical architecture of each rollout.

By consciously thinking through the data warehouse architecture, warehouse planners can determine the various technology components (e.g., MDDB. RDBMS, tools) those are required for each rollout.

Short-listed Data Warehouse Environment and Tools

There are a number of tools and warehousing environments from which to be chosen. Create a short - list for the tools and environments that appear to meet a warehousing needs. A standard set of tools will lessen tool integration problems and will minimize the learning required for both the warehousing team and the warehouse users.

Below are the tasks required to create the enterprise's warehousing strategy. Note that the tasks described below can typically be completed in three to five weeks, depending on the availability of resource persons and the size of the enterprise.

6.2 DETERMINE ORGANIZATIONAL CONTEXT

An understanding of the organization helps to establish the context of the project and may highlight aspects of the corporate culture that my ease or complicate the warehousing project. Answers to organizational background questions are typically obtained from the Project Sponsor, the CIO, or the Project Manager assigned to the warehousing effort.

Typical organizational background questions include:

- **Who is the Project Sponsor for this project?**

  The Project Sponsor sets the scope of the warehousing project. He or she also plays a crucial role in establishing the working relationship among warehousing team members, especially if third parties are involved. Easy access to warehousing data may also be limited to the organizational scope that is within the control or authority of the Project Sponsor.

- **What are the IS or IT groups in the organization, which are involved in the data warehousing effort?**

  Since data warehousing is very much a technology-based endeavor, the IS or IT groups within the organization will always be involved in any warehousing effort. It is often insightful to understand the bulk of the work currently performed within the IS or IT departments. If the IS or IT groups are often fighting fires or are very busy deploying operational systems, data warehousing is unlikely to be high on the list of IT priorities.

- **What are the roles and responsibilities of the individuals who have been assigned to this effort?**

  It is helpful to define the roles and responsibilities of the various individuals involved in the data warehousing project. This practice sets common, realistic expectations and improves understanding and communication within the team. In cases where the team is composed of external parties (especially where several vendors are involved), a clear definition of roles becomes critical.

6.3 CONDUCT PRELIMINARY SURVEY OF REQUIREMENTS

Obtain an inventory of the requirements of business users through individual and group interview with the enduser community. Whenever possible, obtain layouts of the current management reports (and their planned enhancements).

The requirements inventory represents the breadth of information that the warehouse is expected to eventually provide. While it is important to get a clear picture of the extent of requirements, it is not necessary to detail all the requirements in depth at this point. The objective is to understand the user needs enough to prioritize the requirements. This is a critical input for identifying the scope of each data warehouse rollout.

Interview Categories and Sample Questions

The following questions, arranged by category, should be useful as a starting point for the interview with intended end users of the warehouse:

- **Functions.** What is the mission of your group or unit? How do you go about fulfilling this mission? How do you know if you've been successful with your mission? What are the key performance indicators and critical success factors?
- **Customers.** How do you group or classify your customers? Do these groupings change over time? Does your grouping affect how you treat your customers? What kind of information do you track for each type of client? What demographic information do you use, if any? Do you need to track customer data for each customer?
- **Profit.** At what level do you measure profitability in your group? Per agent? Per customer? Per product? Per region? At what level of detail are costs and revenues tracked in your organization? How do you track costs and revenues now? What kind of profitability reports do you use or produce now?
- **Systems.** What systems do you use as part of your job? What systems are you aware of in other groups that contain information you require? What kind of manual data transformations do you have to perform when data are unavailable?
- **Time.** How many months or years of data you need to track? Do you analyze performance across years? At what level of detail do you need to see figures? Daily? Weekly? Monthly? Quarterly? Yearly? Do you need to see figures? How soon do you need to see data (e.g., do you need yesterday's data today?) How soon after week-end, month-end, quarter-end, and year-end do you need to see the previous period figures?
- **Queries and reports.** What reports do you use now? What information do you actually use in each of the reports you now receive? Can we obtain samples, of these reports? How often are these reports produced? Do you get them soon enough, frequently enough? Who makes these reports for you? What reports do you produce for other people?
- **Product.** What products do you sell, and how do you classify them? Do you have a product hierarchy? Do you analyze data for all products at the same time, or do you analyze one product type at a time? How do you handle changes in product hierarchy and product description?
- **Geography.** Does your company operate in more than one location? Do you divide your market into geographical areas? Do you track sales per geographic region?

Interviewing Tips

Many of the interviewing tips enumerated below may seem like common sense. Nevertheless, interviewers are encouraged to keep the following points in mind:

- **Avoid making commitments about warehouse scope.** It will not be surprising to find that some of the queries and reports requested by interviewes cannot be supported by the data that currently reside in the operational databases. Interviewers should keep this in mind and communicate this potential limitation to their interviewees. The interviewers cannot afford to make commitments regarding the warehouse scope at this time.
- **Keep the interview objective in mind.** The objective of these interviews is to create an inventory of requirements. There is no need to get a detailed understanding of the requirements at this point.
- **Don't overwhelm the interviewees.** The interviewing team should be small; two people are the ideal number—one to ask questions, another to take notes. Interviewees may be intimidated if a large group of interviewers shows up.
- **Record the session if the interviewee lets you.** Most interviewees will not mind if interviewers bring along a tape recorder to record the session. Transcripts of the session may later prove helpful.
- **Change the interviewing style depending on the interviewee.** Middle-Managers more likely to deal with actual reports and detailed information requirements. Senior executives are more likely to dwell on strategic information needs. Change the interviewing style as needed by adapting the type of questions to the type of interviewee.
- **Listen carefully.** Listen to what the interviewee has to say. The sample interview questions are merely a starting point—follow-up questions have the potential of yielding interesting and critical of yielding interesting and critical information. Take note of the terms that the interviewee uses. Popular business terms such as "profit" may have different meanings or connotations within the enterprise.
- **Obtain copies of reports, whenever possible.** The reports will give the warehouse team valuable information about source systems (which system produced the report), as well as business rules and terms. If a person manually makes the reports, the team may benefit from talking to this person.

6.4 CONDUCT PRELIMINARY SOURCE SYSTEM AUDIT

Obtain an inventory of potential warehouse data sources through individual and group interview with key personnel in the IT organization. While the CIO no doubt has a broad, high-level view of the systems in the enterprise, the best resource persons for the source system audit are the DBAs and system administrators who maintain the operational systems.

Typical background interview questions, arranged by categories, for the IT department include:

- **Current architecture.** What is the current technology architecture of the organization? What kind of systems, hardware, DBMS, network, end-user tools, development tools, and data access tools are currently in use?
- **Source system relationships.** Are the source systems related in any way? Does one system provide information to another? Are the systems integrated in any manner? In cases where multiple systems have customer and product records, which one serves as the "master" copy?

- **Network facilities.** Is it possible to use a single terminal or PC to access the different operational systems, from all locations?
- **Data quality.** How much cleaning, scrubbing, de-duplication, and integration do you suppose will be required? What areas (tables or fields) in the source systems are currently known to have poor data quality?
- **Documentation.** How much documentation is available for the source systems? How accurate and up-to-date are these manuals and reference materials? Try to obtain the following information whenever possible: copies of manuals and reference documents, database size, batch window, planned enhancements, typical backup size, backup scope and backup medium, data scope of the system (e.g., important tables and fields), system codes and their meanings, and keys generation schemes.
- **Possible extraction mechanisms.** What extraction mechanisms are possible with this system? What extraction mechanisms have you used before with this system? What extraction mechanisms will not work?

6.5 IDENTIFY EXTERNAL DATA SOURCES (IF APPLICABLE)

The enterprise may also make use of external data sources to augment the data from internal source systems. Example of external data that can be used are:

- Data from credit agencies.
- Zip code or mail code data.
- Statistical or census data.
- Data from industry organizations.
- Data from publications and news agencies.

Although the use of external data presents opportunities for enriching the data warehouse, it may also present difficulties because of difference in granularity. For example, the external data may not be readily available at the level of detail required by the data warehouse and may require some transformation or summarization.

6.6 DEFINE WAREHOUSE ROLLOUTS (PHASED IMPLEMENTATION)

Divide the data warehouse development into phased, successive rollout. Note that the scope of each rollout will have to be finalized as part of the planning for that rollout. The availability and quality of source data will play a critical role in finalizing that scope.

As stated earlier, applying a phased approach for delivering the warehouse should lower the overall risk of the data warehouse project while delivering increasing functionality and data to more users. It also helps manage user expectations through the clear definition of scope for each rollout.

Figure 6.1 is a sample table listing all requirements identified during the initial round of interviews with end users. Each requirement is assigned a priority level. An initial complexity assessment is made, based on the estimated number of source systems, early data quality assessments, and the computing environments of the source systems. The intended user group is also identified.

No.	Requirement	Priority	Complexity	Users	Rollout No.
1	Customer Profitability	High	High	Customer Service	1
2	Product Market Share	High	Medium	Product Manager	1
3	Weekly Sales Trends	Medium	Low	VP, Sales	2
—	—	—	—	—	—

Figure 6.1. Sample Rollout Definition

More factors can be listed to help determine the appropriate rollout number for each requirement. The rollout definition is finalized only when it is approved by the Project Sponsor.

6.7 DEFINE PRELIMINARY DATA WAREHOUSE ARCHITECTURE

Define the preliminary architecture of each rollout based on the approved rollout scope. Explore the possibility of using a mix of relational and multidimensional databases and tools, as illustrated in Figure 6.2.

At a minimum, the preliminary architecture should indicate the following:

- **Data warehouses and data mart.** Define the intended deployment of data warehouses and data marts for each rollout. Indicate how the different databases are related (i.e., how the databases feed one another). The warehouse architecture must ensure that the different data marts are not deployed in isolation.

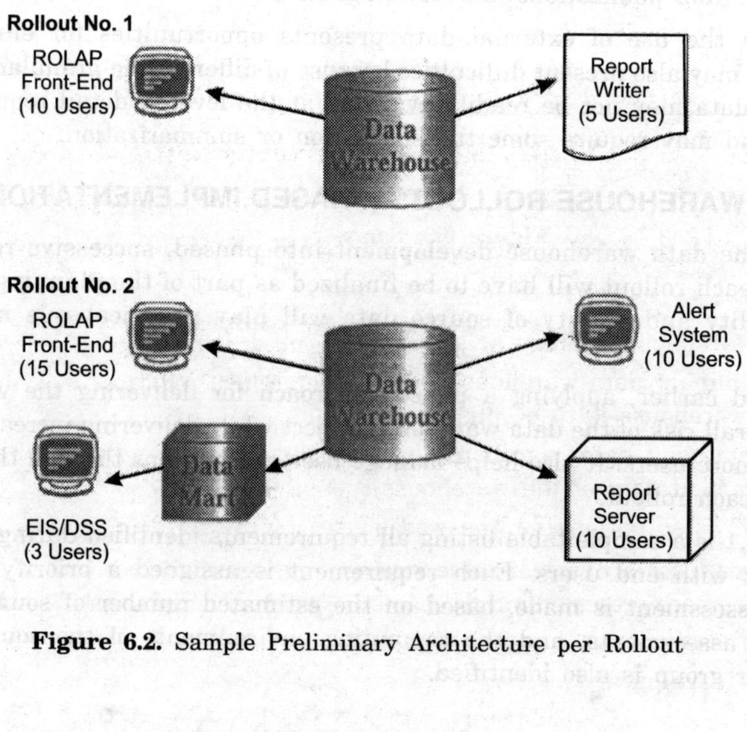

Figure 6.2. Sample Preliminary Architecture per Rollout

- **Number of users.** Specify the intended number of users for each data access and retrieval tool (or front-end) for each rollout.
- **Location.** Specify the location of the data warehouse, the data marts, and the intended users for each rollout. This has implications on the technical architecture requirements of the warehousing project.

6.8 EVALUATE DEVELOPMENT AND PRODUCTION ENVIRONMENT AND TOOLS

Enterprises can choose from several environments and tools for the data warehouse initiative, select the combination of tools that best meets the needs of the enterprise. At present, no single vendor provides an integrated suite of warehousing tools. There are, however, clear leaders for each tool category.

Eliminate all unsuitable tools, and produce a short-list from which each rollout or project will choose its tool set (see Figure 6.3). Alternatively, select and standardize on a set of tools for all warehouse rollouts.

No.	Tool Category	Short-listed Tools	Evaluation Criteria	Weights (%)	Preliminary Scores
1	Data Access	Tool A	Criterion 1	30%	
	and Retrieval		Criterion 2	30%	78%
			Criterion 3	40%	
		Tool B	Criterion 1	30%	
			Criterion 2	30%	82%
			Criterion 3	40%	
		Tool C	Criterion 1	30%	
			Criterion 2	30%	84%
			Criterion 3	40%	
2	RDBMS				

Figure 6.3. Sample Tool Short-List

In Summary

A data warehouse strategy at a minimum contains:

- Preliminary data warehouse rollout plan, which indicates how the development of the warehouse is to be phased:
- Preliminary data warehouse architecture, which indicates the likely physical implementation of the warehouse rollout; and
- Short-listed options for the warehouse environment and tools.

The approach for arriving at these strategy components may vary from one enterprise to another, the approach presented in this chapter is one that has consistently proven to be effective.

Expect the data warehousing strategy to be updated annually. Each warehouse rollout provides new learning and as new tools and technologies become available.

CHAPTER 7

WAREHOUSE MANAGEMENT AND SUPPORT PROCESSES

Warehouse Management and Support Processes are designed to address aspects of planning and managing a data warehouse project that are critical to the successful implementation and subsequent extension of the data warehouse. Unfortunately, these aspects are all too often overlooked in initial warehousing deployments.

These processes are defined to assist the project manager and warehouse driver during warehouse development projects.

7.1 DEFINE ISSUE TRACKING AND RESOLUTION PROCESS

During the course of a project, it is inevitable that a number of business and technical issues will surface. The project will quickly be delayed by unresolved issues if an issue tracking and resolution process is not in place. Of particular importance are business issues that involve more than one group of users. These issues typically include disputes over the definition of business terms and the financial formulas that govern the transformation of data.

An individual on the project should be designated to track and follow up the resolution of each issue as it arises. Extremely urgent issues (i.e., issues that may cause project delay if left unresolved) or issues with strong political overtones can be brought to the attention of the Project Sponsor, who must use his or her clout to expedite the resolution process.

Figure 7.1 shows a sample issue logs that tracks all the issues that arise during the course of the project.

The following issue tracking guidelines will prove helpful:

- **Issue description.** State the issue briefly in two to three sentences. Provide a more detailed description of the issue as a separate paragraph. If there are possible resolutions to the issue, include these .in the issue description. Identify the consequences of leaving this issue open, particularly and impact on the project schedule.

No.	Issue Description	Urgency	Raised By	Assigned To	Date Opened	Date Closed	Resolved By	Resolution Description
1	Conflict over definition of "Customer"	High	MWH	MCD	Feb 03	Feb 05	CEO	Use CorPlan's definition
2	Currency exchange rates are not tracked in GL	High	MCD	RGT	Feb 04			

Figure 7.1. Sample Issue Log

- **Urgency.** Indicate the priority level of the issue: high, medium, or low. Low-priority issues that are left unresolved may later become high priority. The team may have agreed on a resolution rate depending on the urgency of the issue. For example, the team can agree to resolve high-priority issues within three days, medium-priority issues within a week, and low-priority issues within two weeks.
- **Raised by.** Identify the person who raised the issue. If the team is large or does not meet on a regular basis, provide information on how to contact the person (e.g., telephone number, e-mail address). The people who are resolving the issue may require additional information or details that only the issue originator can provide.
- **Assigned to.** Identify the person on the team who is responsible for resolving the issue. Note that this person does not necessarily have answer. However, he or she is responsible for tracking down the person who can actually resolve the issue. He or she also follows up on issues that have been left unresolved.
- **Date opened.** This is the date when the issue was first logged.
- **Date closed.** This is the date when the issue was finally resolved.
- **Resolved by.** The person who resolves the issue must have the required authority within the organization. User representatives typically resolve business issues. The CIO or designated representatives typically resolve technical issues, and the project sponsor typically resolves issues related project scope.
- **Resolution description.** State briefly the resolution of this issue in two or three sentences. Provide a more detailed description of the resolution in a separate paragraph. If subsequent actions are required to implement the resolution, these should be stated clearly and resources should be assigned to implement them. Identify target dates for implementation.

Issue logs formalize the issue resolution process. They also serve as a formal record of key decisions made throughout the project.

In some cases, the team may opt to augment the log with yet another form–one form for each issue. This typically happens when the issue descriptions and resolution descriptions are quite long. In this case, only the brief issue statement and brief resolution descriptions are recorded in the issue log.

7.2 PERFORM CAPACITY PLANNING

Warehouse capacity requirements come in the following forms: space required, machine processing power, network bandwidth, and number of concurrent users. These requirements increase with each rollout of the data warehouse.

During the stage of defining the warehouse strategy, the team will not have the exact information for these requirements. However, as the warehouse rollout scopes are finalized, the capacity requirements will likewise become more defined.

Review the following capacity planning requirements basing your review on the scope of each rollout.

There are several aspects to the data warehouse environment that make capacity planning for the data warehouse a unique exercise. The first factor is that the workload for the data warehouse environment is very variable. In many ways trying to anticipate the DSS workload requires imagination. Unlike the operational workload that has an air of regularity to it, the data warehouse DSS workload is much less predictable. This factor, in and of itself, makes capacity planning for the data warehouse a chancy exercise.

A second factor making capacity planning for the data warehouse a risky business is that the data warehouse normally entails much more data than was ever encountered in the operational environment. The amount of data found in the data warehouse is directly related to the design of the data warehouse environment. The designer determines the granularity of data that in turn determines how much data there will be in the warehouse. The finer the degree of granularity, the more data there is. The coarser the degree of granularity, the less data there is. And the volume of data not only affects the actual disk storage required, but the volume of data affects the machine resources required to manipulate the data. In very few environments is the capacity of a system so closely linked to the design of the system.

A third factor making capacity planning for the data warehouse environment a nontraditional exercise is that the data warehouse environment and the operational environments do not mix under the stress of a workload of any size at all. This imbalance of environments must be understood by all parties involved-the capacity planner, the systems programmer, management, and the designer of the data warehouse environment.

Consider the patterns of hardware utilization as shown by Figure 7.2.

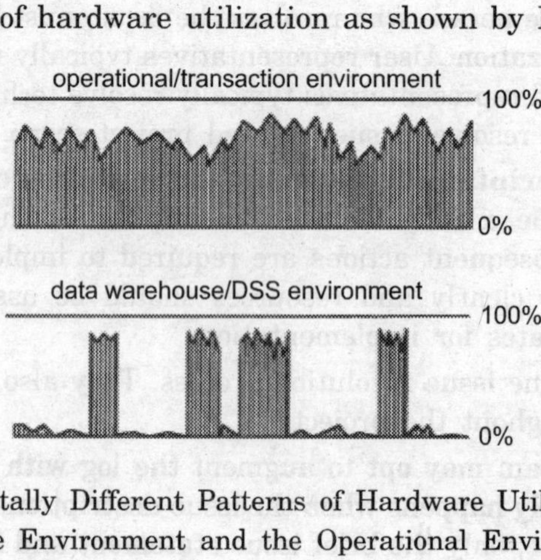

Figure 7.2. The Fundamentally Different Patterns of Hardware Utilization between the Data Warehouse Environment and the Operational Environment

In Figure 7.2 it is seen that the operational environment uses hardware in a static fashion. There are peaks and valleys in the operational environment, but at the end of the day hardware utilization is predictable and fairly constant. Contrast the pattern of hardware utilization found in the operational environment with the hardware utilization found in the data warehouse/DSS environment.

In the data warehouse, hardware is used in a binary fashion. Either the hardware is being used constantly or the hardware is not being used at all. Furthermore, the pattern is such that it is unpredictable. One day much processing occurs at 8:30 a.m. The next day the bulk of processing occurs at 11:15 a.m. and so forth.

There are then, very different and incompatible patterns of hardware utilization associated with the operational and the data warehouse environment. These patterns apply to all types of hardware CPU, channels, memory, disk storage, etc.

Trying to mix the different patterns of hardware leads to some basic difficulties. Figure 7.3 shows what happens when the two types of patterns of utilization are mixed in the same machine at the same time.

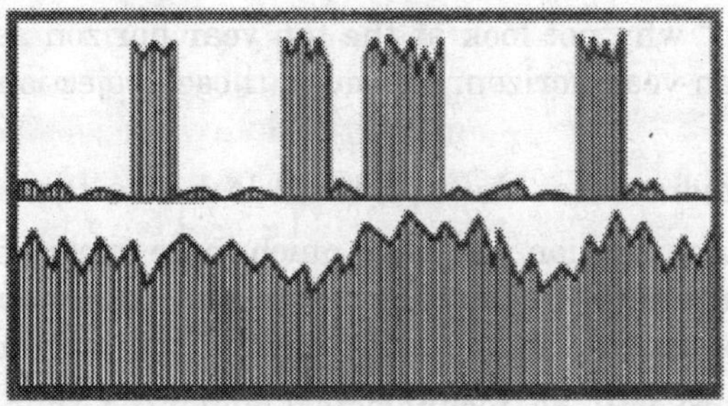

Figure 7.3. Trying to Mix the Two Fundamentally Different Patterns of the Execution in the Same Machine at the Same Time Leads to Some Very Basic Conflicts

The patterns are simply incompatible. Either you get good response time and a low rate of machine utilization (at which point the financial manager is unhappy), or you get high machine utilization and poor response time (at which point the user is unhappy.) The need to split the two environments is important to the data warehouse capacity planner because the capacity planner needs to be aware of circumstances in which the patterns of access are mixed. In other words, when doing capacity planning, there is a need to separate the two environments. Trying to do capacity planning for a machine or complex of machines where there is a mixing of the two environments is a nonsensical task. Despite these difficulties with capacity planning, planning for machine resources in the data warehouse environment is a worthwhile endeavor.

Time Horizons

As a rule there are two time horizons, the capacity planner should aim for–the one-year time horizon and the five-year time horizon. Figure 7.4 shows these time horizons.

The one-year time horizon is important in that it is on the immediate requirements list for the designer. In other words, at the rate that the data warehouse becomes designed and populated, the decisions made about resources for the one year time horizon will have to be lived with. Hardware, and possibly software acquisitions will have to be made. A certain amount of "burn-in" will have to be tolerated. A learning curve for all parties will have to be survived, all on the one-year horizon. The five-year horizon is of importance as well. It is where the massive volume of data will show up. And it is where the maturity of the data warehouse will occur.

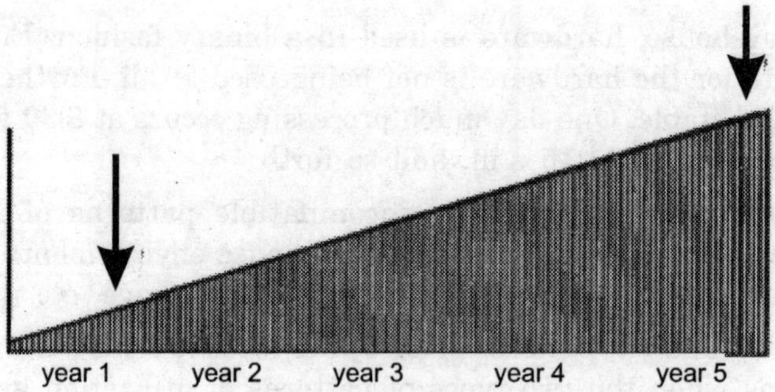

Figure 7.4. Projecting Hardware Requirements out to Year 1 and Year 5

An interesting question is – " why not look at the ten year horizon as well?" Certainly projections can be made to the ten-year horizon. However, those projections are not usually made because:

- It is very difficult to predict what the world will look like ten years from now,
- It is assumed that the organization will have much more experience handling data warehouses five years in the future, so that design and data management will not pose the same problems they do in the early days of the warehouse, and
- It is assumed that there will be technological advances that will change the considerations of building and managing a data warehouse environment.

DBMS Considerations

One major factor affecting the data warehouse capacity planning is what portion of the data warehouse will be managed on disk storage and what portion will be managed on alternative storage. This very important distinction must be made, at least in broad terms, prior to the commencement of the data warehouse capacity planning effort.

Once the distinction is made, the next consideration is that of the technology underlying the data warehouse. The most interesting underlying technology is that of the Data Base Management System-DBMs. The components of the DBMs that are of interest to the capacity planner are shown in Figure 7.5.

The capacity planner is interested in the access to the data warehouse, the DBMs capabilities and efficiencies, the indexing of the data warehouse, and the efficiency and operations of storage. Each of these aspects plays a large role in the throughput and operations of the data warehouse.

Some of the relevant issues in regards to the data warehouse data base management system are:

- How much data can the DBMs handle? (**Note:** There is always a discrepancy between the theoretical limits of the volume of data handled by a data base management system and the practical limits.)

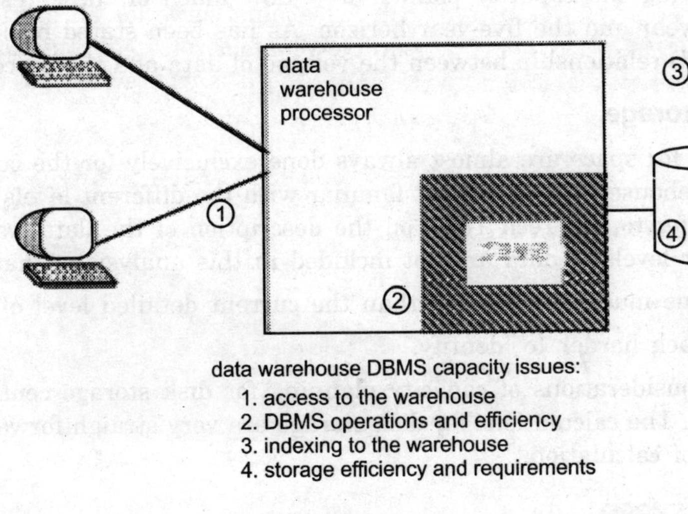

Figure 7.5

- How can the data be stored? Compressed? Indexed? Encoded? How are null values handled?
- Can locking be suppressed?
- Can requests be monitored and suppressed based on resource utilization?
- Can data be physically denormalized?
- What support is there for metadata as needed in the data warehouse? and so forth. Of course the operating system and any teleprocessing monitoring must be factored in as well.

Disk Storage and Processing Resources

The two most important parameters of capacity management are the measurement of disk storage and processing resources. Figure 7.6 shows those resources.

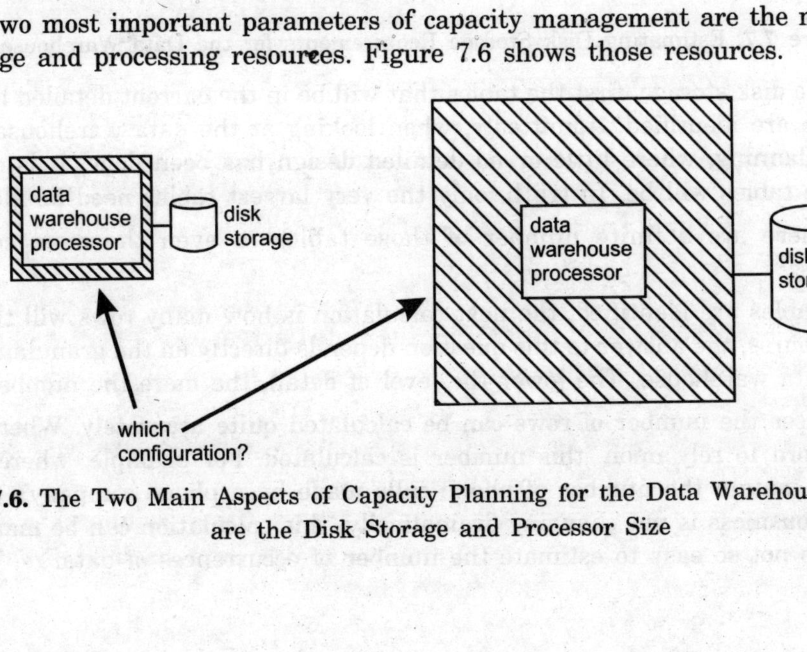

Figure 7.6. The Two Main Aspects of Capacity Planning for the Data Warehouse Environment are the Disk Storage and Processor Size

The question facing the capacity planner is – how much of these resources will be required on the one-year and the five-year horizon. As has been stated before, there is an indirect (yet very real) relationship between the volume of data and the processor required.

Calculating Disk Storage

The calculations for space are almost always done exclusively for the current detailed data in the data warehouse. (If you are not familiar with the different levels of data in the warehouse, please refer to the Tech Topic on the description of the data warehouse.) The reason why the other levels of data are not included in this analysis is that:

- They consume much less storage than the current detailed level of data, and
- They are much harder to identify.

Therefore, the considerations of capacity planning for disk storage center around the current detailed level. The calculations for disk storage are very straightforward. Figure 7.7 shows the elements of calculation.

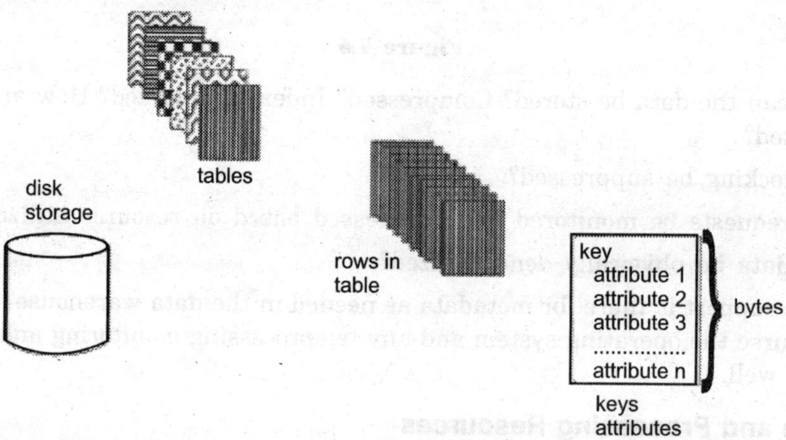

Figure 7.7. Estimating Disk Storage Requirements for the Data Warehouse

To calculate disk storage, first the tables that will be in the current detailed level of the data warehouse are identified. Admittedly, when looking at the data warehouse from the standpoint of planning, where little or no detailed design has been done, it is difficult to divise what the tables will be. In truth, only the very largest tables need be identified.

Usually there are a finite number of those tables in even the most complex of environments.

Once the tables are identified, the next calculation is how many rows will there be in each table. Of course, the answer to this question depends directly on the granularity of data found in the data warehouse. The lower the level of detail, the more the number of rows.

In some cases the number of rows can be calculated quite accurately. Where there is a historical record to rely upon, this number is calculated. For example, where the data warehouse will contain the number of phone calls made by a phone company's customers and where the business is not changing dramatically, this calculation can be made. But in other cases it is not so easy to estimate the number of occurrences of data.

One approach is to look across the industry and see what other companies have experienced. This approach is quite effective if you can find out information that other companies are willing to share and if the company has a similar profile. Unfortunately, often times a comparative company is hard to find.

A third approach is to estimate the number of occurrences based on business plans, economic forecasts, and using the advice of specialized industry consultants. This is the least accurate method and the most expensive, but sometimes it is the only choice.

The number of occurrences of data is a function of more than just the business. The other factors are:

- The level of detail the data will be kept at, and
- The length of time the data will be kept.

After the number of rows are divised, the next step is to calculate the size of each row. This is done by estimating the contents of each row–the keys and the attributes. Once the contents of the row are taken into consideration, the indexes that are needed are factored in.

As a matter of practice, very little if any free space is left in the data warehouse because data is not updated in the warehouse. In most circumstances, any free space in a data warehouse is wasted. The total disk requirements then are calculated by adding all the requirements mentioned.

Processor Requirements

In order to make sense of the estimation of the processor requirements for the data warehouse, the work passing through the data warehouse processor must be divided into one of three categories—background processing, predictable DSS processing, and unpredictable DSS processing. Figure 7.8 shows these three categories.

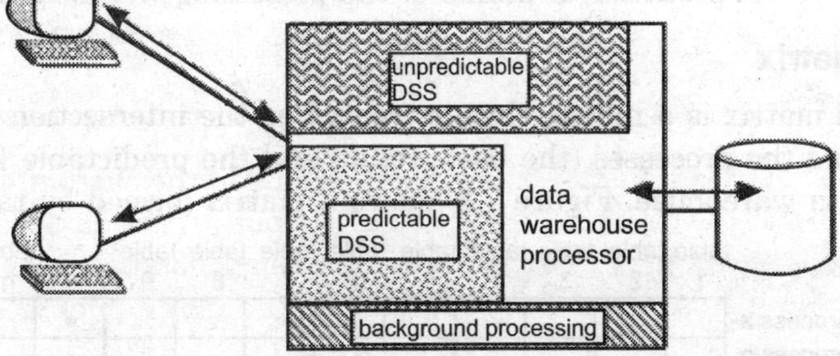

Figure 7.8. The Three Types of Processing that Occur in the Data Warehouse

Background processing is that processing that is done on a predictable, (usually) batch basis. Typical of background processing is extract processing, data warehouse loads, monitors, sorts/merges, restructuring, index creations, etc. Background processing is that utilitarian processing necessary to the data warehouse but not directly associated with a query or an analysis of data warehouse data.

Background processing can be run at off peak times and can be spread evenly throughout the day. There is seldom much of a time constraint for background processing.

Predictable DSS processing is that processing that is regularly done, usually on a query or transaction basis. Predictable DSS processing may be modeled after DSS processing done today but not in the data warehouse environment. Or predictable DSS processing may be projected, as are other parts of the data warehouse workload.

The parameters of interest for the data warehouse designer (for both the background processing and the predictable DSS processing) are:

- The number of times the process will be run,
- The number of I/Os the process will use,
- Whether there is an arrival peak to the processing,
- The expected response time.

These metrics can be arrived at by examining the pattern of calls made to the DBMS and the interaction with data managed under the DBMS.

The third category of process of interest to the data warehouse capacity planner is that of the unpredictable DSS analysis. The unpredictable process by its very nature is much less manageable than either background processing or predictable DSS processing.

However, certain characteristics about the unpredictable process can be projected (even for the worst behaving process.) For the unpredictable processes, the:

- Expected response time (in minutes, hours, or days) can be outlined,
- Total amount of I/O can be predicted, and
- Whether the system can be quiesced during the running of the request can be projected.

Once the workload of the data warehouse has been broken into these categories, the estimate of processor resources is prepared to continue. The next decision to be made is whether the eight-hour daily window will be the critical processing point or whether overnight processing will be the critical point. Usually the eight-hour day from 8:00 a.m. to 5:00 p.m. as the data warehouse is being used is the critical point. Assuming that the eight-hour window is the critical point in the usage of the processor, a profile of the processing workload is created.

The Workload Matrix

The workload matrix is a matrix that is created as the intersection of the tables in the data warehouse and the processes (the background and the predictable DSS processes) that will run in the data warehouse. Figure 7.9 shows a matrix formed by tables and processes.

	table 1	table 2	table 3	table 4	table 5	table 6	table 7	table 8	table 9	.....	table n
process a										•	
process b										•	
process c										•	
process d										•	
process e										•	
....	•	•	•	•	•	•	•	•	•	•	•
process z										•	

Figure 7.9. A Matrix Approach Helps to Organize the Activities

The workload matrix is then filled in. The first pass at filling in the matrix involves putting the number of calls and the resulting I/O from the calls the process would do if the process were executed exactly once during the eight hour window. Figure 7-10 shows a simple form of a matrix that has been filled in for the first step.

	table 1	table 2	table 3	table 4	table 5	table 6	table 7	table 8	table 9	.....	table n
process a	2/5			2/10		5/15				•	3/9
process b	1/3		3/9						1/2	•	
process c		5/25					4/12		1/5	•	2/5
process d	1/6		4/8		1/2	3/9		3/9		•	1/2
process e	1/5		3/4		2/2	6/12		6/12		•	
....	•	•	•	•	•	•	•	•	•	•	•
process z	1/5	5/25	4/8		1/2				5/15	•	5/15

number of calls I/O's per access

Figure 7.10. The Simplest Form of a Matrix is to Profile a Individual Transactions in Terms of Calls and I/O's.

For example, in Figure 7.10 the first cell in the matrix–the cell for process **a** and table 1- contains a "2/5". The 2/5 indicates that upon execution process **a** has two calls to the table and uses a total of 5 I/Os for the calls. The next cell–the cell for process **a** and table 2 - indicates that process **a** does not access table 2. The matrix is filled in for the processing profile of the workload as if each transaction were executed once and only once. Determining the number of I/Os per call can be a difficult exercise. Whether an I/O will be done depends on many factors:

- The number of rows in a block,
- Whether a block is in memory at the moment it is requested,
- The amount of buffers there are,
- The traffic through the buffers,
- The DBMS managing the buffers,
- The indexing for the data,
- The other part of the workload,
- The system parameters governing the workload, etc.

There are, in short, MANY factors affecting how many physical I/O will be used. The I/Os an be calculated manually or automatically (by software specializing in this task). After the single execution profile of the workload is identified, the next step is to create the actual workload profile. The workload profile is easy to create. Each row in the matrix is multiplied by the number of times it will execute in a day. The calculation here is a simple one. Figure 7.11 shows an example of the total I/Os used in an eight-hour day being calculated.

	table 1	table 2	table 3	table 4	table 5	table 6	table 7	table 8	table 9	.....	table n
process a	2500			5000		7500				•	4500
process b	1000		3000						666	•	
process c		2500					1200		500	•	500
process d	750		1000		250	1250		1250		•	250
process e	700		566		283			1750		•	
....	•	•	•	•	•	•	•	•	•	•	•
process z	750	3750	1000		300				2250	•	2250
total I/O	15000	85000	12250	10250	5750	27750	19500	6750	8926	•	87560

total I/Os

Figure 7.11. After the Individual Transactions are Profiled, the profile is Multiplied by the Number of Expected Executions per Day

At the bottom of the matrix the totals are calculated, to reach a total eight-hour I/O requirement. After the eight hour I/O requirement is calculated, the next step is to determine what the hour-by-hour requirements are. If there is no hourly requirement, then it is assumed that the queries will be arriving in the data warehouse in a flat arrival rate. However, there usually are differences in the arrival rates. Figure 7.12, shows the arrival rates adjusted for the different hours in the day.

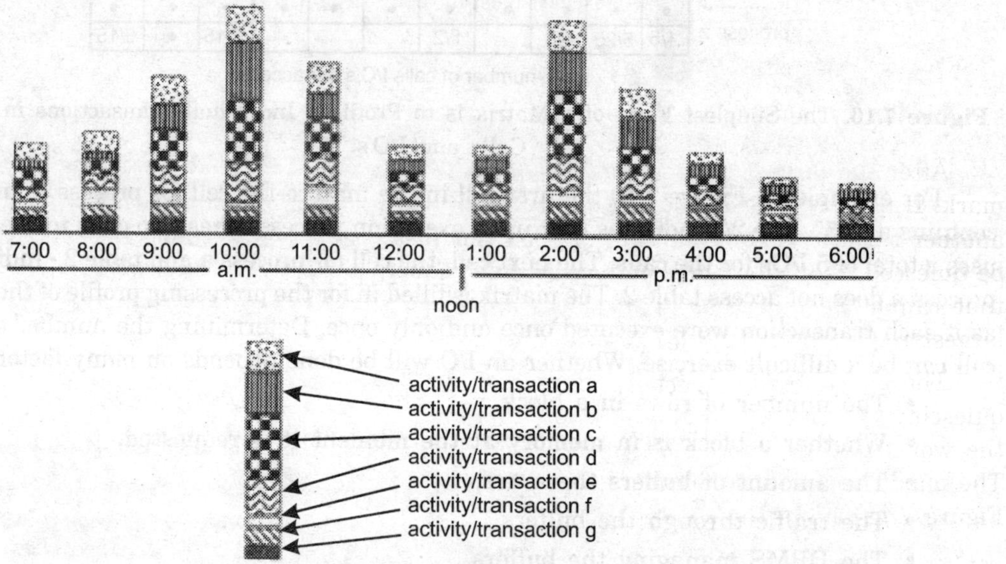

Figure 7.12. The Different Activities are Tallied at their Processing Rates for the Hours of the Day

Figure 7.12, shows that the processing required for the different identified queries is calculated on an hourly basis. After the hourly calculations are done, the next step is to identify the "high water mark. "The high water mark is that hour of the day when the most demands will be made of the machine. Figure 7.13, shows the simple identification of the high water mark.

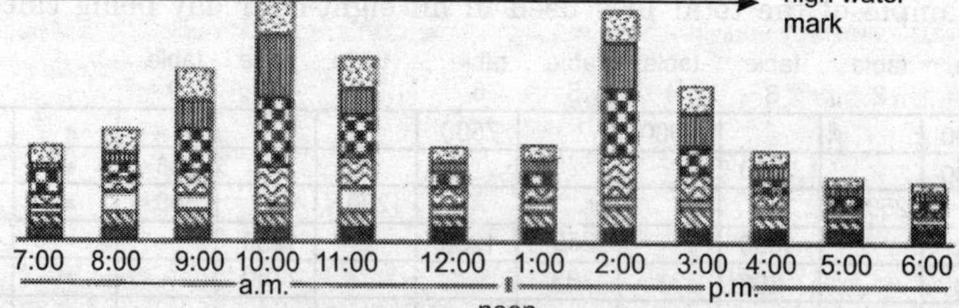

Figure 7.13. The High "Water Mark" for the Day is Determined

After the high water mark requirements are identified, the next requirement is to scope out the requirements for the largest unpredictable request. The largest unpredictable request must be parameterized by:

- How many total I/Os will be required,
- The expected response time, and
- Whether other processing may or may not be quiesced.

Figure 7.14, shows the specification of the largest unpredictable request.

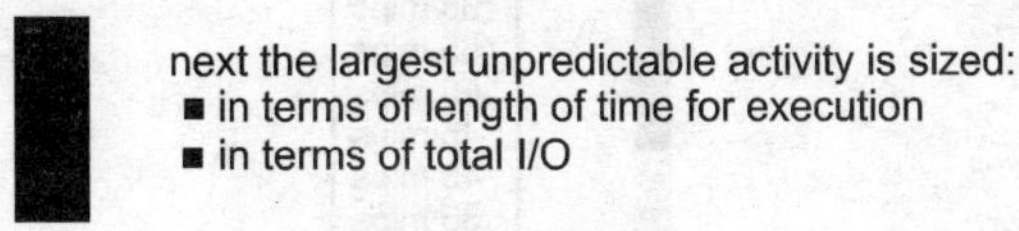

Figure 7.14

After the largest unpredictable request is identified, it is merged with the high water mark. If no quiescing is allowed, then the largest unpredictable request is simply added as another request. If some of the workload (for instance, the predictable DSS processing) can be quiesced, then the largest unpredictable request is added to the portion of the workload that cannot be quiesced. If all of the workload can be quiesced, then the unpredictable largest request is not added to anything.

The analyst then selects the larger of the two–the unpredictable largest request with quiescing (if quiescing is allowed), the unpredictable largest request added to the portion of the workload that cannot be quiesced, or the workload with no unpredictable processing. The maximum of these numbers then becomes the high water mark for all DSS processing. Figure 7.15 shows the combinations.

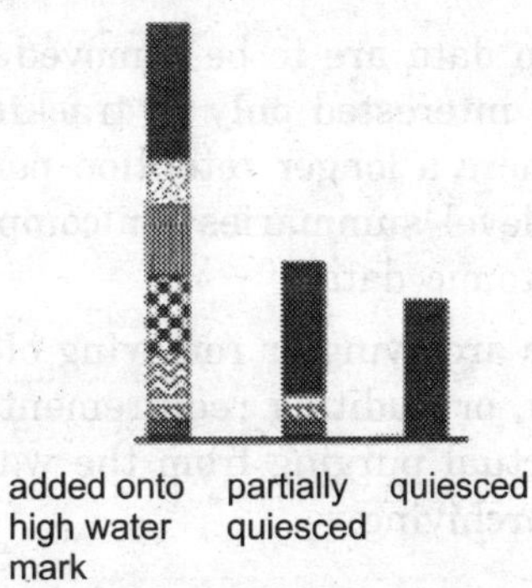

Figure 7.15. The Impact of the Largest Unpredictable Request is Estimated

The maximum number then is compared to a chart of MIPS required to support the level of processing identified, as shown in Figure 7.16.

Figure 7.16, merely shows that the processing rate identified from the workload is matched against a machine power chart.

Of course there is no slack processing factored. Many shops factor in at least ten percent. However, factoring an unused percentage may satisfy the user with better response time, but costs money in any case.

The analysis described here is a general plan for the planning of the capacity needs of a data warehouse. It must be pointed out that the planning is usually done on an iterative basis. In other words, after the first planning effort is done, another more refined version soon follows. In all cases it must be recognized that the capacity planning effort is an estimate.

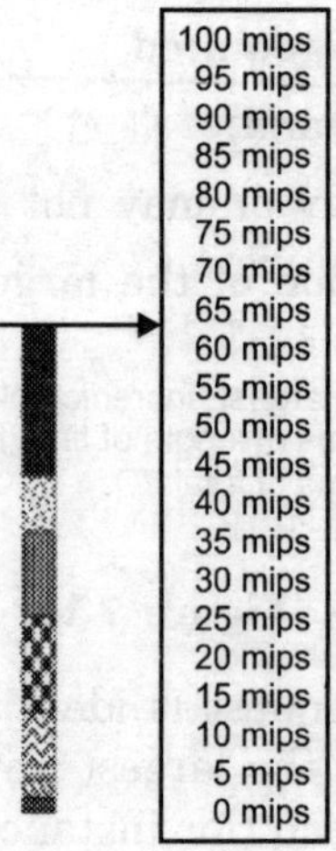

Figure 7.16. Matching the High Water Mark for all Processing Against the Required MIPS

Network Bandwidth

The network bandwidth must not be allowed to slow down the warehouse extraction and warehouse performance. Verify all assumptions about the network bandwidth before proceeding with each rollout.

7.3 DEFINE WAREHOUSE PURGING RULES

Purging rules specify when data are to be removed from the data warehouse. Keep in mind that most companies are interested only in tracking their performance over the last three to five years. In cases where a longer retention period is required, the end users will quite likely require only high-level summaries for comparison purposes. They will not be interested in the detailed or atomic data.

Define the mechanisms for archiving or removing older data from the data warehouse. Check for any legal, regulatory, or auditing requirements that may warrant the storage of data in other media prior to actual purging from the warehouse. Acquire the software and devices that are required for archiving.

7.4 DEFINE SECURITY MANAGEMENT

Keep the data warehouse secure to prevent the loss of competitive information either to unforeseen disasters or to unauthorized users. Define the security measures for the data warehouse, taking into consideration both physical security (i.e., where the data warehouse is physically located), as well as user-access security.

Security management deals with how system integrity is maintained amid possible man-made threats and risks, intentional or unintentional. Intentional man-made threats include espionage, hacks, computer viruses, etc. Unintentional threats include those due to accidents or user ignorance of the effects of their actions. Security management ranges from identification of risks to determination of security measures and controls, detection of violations, and analysis of security violations. This section describes the process steps involved in security management, and discusses factors critical to the success of security management.

Determine and Evaluate of IT Assets

Three types of assets must be identified:

- **Physical.** Computer hardware and software resources, building facilities, and resources used to house sensitive assets or process sensitive information;
- **Information.** Sensitive data pertaining to the company's operations, plans, and strategies. Examples are marketing and sales plans, detailed financial data, trade secrets, personnel information, IT infrastructure data, user profiles and passwords, sensitive office correspondence, minutes of meetings, etc. Lately, there is also concern about protecting company logos and materials posted on the public Internet; and
- **People.** Vital individuals holding key roles, whose incapacity or absence will impact the business in one way or another.

After you identify company assets, the next step is to determine their security level. Depending on the company's requirements, assets may be classified into two, three, or more levels of security, depending on the value of the asset being protected. We recommend having only two levels for organizations with minimal security threats: public and confidential. A three-level security classification scheme can be implemented if security needs are greater: public, confidential, and restricted.

Beware of having too many security levels, as this tends to dilute their importance in the eyes of the user. A large multinational IT vendor used to have four levels of security: public, internal use only, confidential, confidential restricted, and registered confidential. Today, they have cut it down to three: public, internal use only, and confidential. Employees were getting confused as to the differences between the secured levels, and the procedures associated with each one. Having too many security levels proved expensive in terms of employee education, security facilities, and office practices - the costs were often greater than the potential losses from a security violation.

Analyze Risk

Every effective security management system reflects a careful evaluation of how much security is needed. Too little security means the system can easily be compromised intentionally or unintentionally. Too much security can make the system hard to use or degrade its performance unacceptably. Security is inversely proportional to utility - if you want the system to be 100 percent secure, don't let anybody use it. There will always be risks to systems, but often these risks are accepted if they make the system more powerful or easier to use.

Sources of risks to assets can be *intentional* (criminals, hackers, or terrorists; competitors; disgruntled employees; or self-serving employees) or *unintentional* (careless employees; poorly trained users and system operators; vendors and suppliers).

Acceptance of risk is central to good security management. You will never have enough resources to secure assets 100 percent; in fact, this is virtually impossible even with unlimited resources. Therefore, identify all risks to the system, then choose which risks to accept and which to address via security measures. Here are a few reasons why some risks are acceptable:

- The threat is minimal;
- The possibility of compromise is unlikely;

- The value of the asset is low;
- The cost to secure the asset is greater than the value of the asset;
- The threat will soon go away; and
- Security violations can easily be detected and immediately corrected.

After the risks are identified, the next step is to determine the impact to the business if the asset is lost or compromised. By doing this, you get a good idea of how many resources should be assigned to protecting the asset. One user workstation almost certainly deserves fewer resources than the company's servers.

The risks you choose to accept should be documented and signed by all parties, not only to protect the IT organization, but also to make everybody aware that unsecured company assets do exist.

Define Security Practices

Define in detail the following key areas of security management:

- **Asset classification practices**. Guidelines for specifying security levels as discussed above;
- **Risk assessment and acceptance**. As above;
- **Asset ownership.** Assignment of roles for handling sensitive assets;
- **Asset handling responsibilities.** The different tasks and procedures to be followed by the different entities handling the asset, as identified above;
- **Policies regarding mishandling of security assets;**
- **How security violations are reported and responded to;**
- **Security awareness practices.** Education programs, labeling of assets; and
- **Security audits.** Unannounced checks of security measures put in place to find out whether they are functioning.

Implement Security Practices

At this phase, implement the security measures defined in the preceding step. You can do this in stages to make it easier for everybody to adapt to the new working environment. Expect many problems at the start, especially with respect to user resistance to their security tasks, such as using passwords. Staged implementation can be performed:

- **By department,** starting with the most sensitive assets. The natural first choice would be the IT department.
- **By business function or activity,** starting with those that depends upon (or create) the most sensitive assets. You might begin with all Business Planning activities, followed by Marketing, Human Resources, etc.
- **By location**, especially if prioritized sensitive assets are mostly physical. This approach is easiest to implement. However, its effectiveness is doubtful for information assets residing in networked computer systems. You might start with the IT data center, then gradually widen the secured area to encompass the entire business facility.
- **By people,** starting with key members of the organization.

Monitor for Violations and Take Corresponding Actions

An effective security management discipline depends on adequate compliance monitoring. Violations of security practices, whether intentional or unintentional, become more frequent and serious if not detected and acted upon. A computer hacker who gets away with the first system penetration will return repeatedly if he knows no one can detect his activities. Users who get away with leaving confidential documents on their desks will get into bad habits if not corrected quickly.

There are two major activities here: *detecting* security violations and *responding* to them. With respect to sensitive assets, it is important to know:

- Who has the right to handle the assets (user names);
- How to authenticate those asset users (password, IDs, etc.);
- Who has tried to gain access to them;
- How to restrict access to allowed activities; and
- Who has tried to perform actions beyond those that are allowed.

Document the response to security violations, and follow up immediately after a violation is detected. The IT organization should have a Computer Emergency Response Team to deal with security violations. Members of this team should have access to senior management so that severe situations can easily be escalated.

Responses can be built into your security tools or facilities to ensure that the response to a violation is immediate. For example, a password checking utility may be designed to lock out a user name immediately after three invalid password entries. Alarms can be installed around the data center facility so that if any window or door is forced open, security guards or police are immediately notified.

A critical part of this activity is the generation of reports for management that discuss significant security violations and trends of minor incidences. The objective is to spot potential major security violations before they cause serious damage.

Re-evaluate IT Assets and Risks

Security management is a discipline that never rests. Some major changes that would require a reassessment of the security management practice are:

- Security violations are rampant
- Organizational structure or composition changes
- Business environment changes
- Technology changes
- Budget allocation decreases

Additional precautions are required if either the warehouse data or warehouse reports are available to users through an intranet or over the public Internet infrastructure.

7.5 DEFINE BACKUP AND RECOVERY STRATEGY

Define the backup and recovery strategy for the warehouse, taking into consideration the following factors:

- **Data to be backed up.** Identify the data that must be backed up on a regular basis. This gives an indication of the regular backup size. Aside from warehouse data and metadata, the team might also want to back up the contents of the staging or de-duplication areas of the warehouse.
- **Batch window of the warehouse.** Backup mechanisms are now available to support the backup of data even when the system is online, although these are expensive. If the warehouse does not need to be online 24 hours a day, 7 days a week, determine the maximum allowable down time for the warehouse (i.e., determine its batch window). Part of that batch window is allocated to the regular warehouse load and, possibly, to report generation and other similar batch jobs. Determine the maximum time period available for regular backups and backup verification.
- **Maximum acceptable time for recovery.** In case of disasters that result in the loss of warehouse data, the backups will have to be restored in the quickest way possible. Different backup mechanisms imply different time frames for recovery. Determine the maximum acceptable length of time for the warehouse data and metadata to be restored, quality assured, and brought online.
- **Acceptable costs for backup and recovery.** Different backup mechanisms imply different costs. The enterprise may have budgetary constraints that limit its backup and recovery options.

Also consider the following when selecting the backup mechanism:

- **Archive format.** Use a standard archiving format to eliminate potential recovery problems.
- **Automatic backup devices.** Without these, the backup media (e.g., tapes) will have to be changed by hand each time the warehouse is backed up.
- **Parallel data streams.** Commercially available backup and recovery systems now support the backup and recovery of databases through parallel streams of data into and from multiple removable storage devices. This technology is especially helpful for the large databases typically found in data warehouse implementations.
- **Incremental backups.** Some backup and recovery systems also support incremental backups to reduce the time required to back up daily. Incremental backups archive only new and updated data.
- **Offsite backups.** Remember to maintain offsite backups to prevent the loss of data due to site disasters such as fires.
- **Backup and recovery procedures.** Formally define and document the backup and recovery procedures. Perform recovery practice runs to ensure that the procedures are clearly understood.

7.6 SET UP COLLECTION OF WAREHOUSE USAGE STATISTICS

Warehouse usage statistics are collected to provide the data warehouse designer with inputs for further refining the data warehouse design and to track general usage and acceptance of the warehouse.

Define the mechanism for collecting these statistics, and assign resources to monitor and review these regularly.

In Summary

The capacity planning process and the issue tracking and resolution process are critical to the successful development and deployment of data warehouses, especially during early implementations.

The other management and support processes become increasingly important as the warehousing initiative progress further.

CHAPTER 8

DATA WAREHOUSE PLANNING

The data warehouse planning approach presented in this chapter describes the activities related to planning one rollout of the data warehouse. The activities discussed below build on the results of the warehouse strategy formulation described in Chapter 6.

Data warehouse planning further details the preliminary scope of one warehouse rollout by obtaining detailed user requirements for queries and reports, creating a preliminary warehouse schema design to meet the user requirements, and mapping source system fields to the warehouse schema fields. By so doing, the team gains a thorough understanding of the effort required to implement that one rollout.

A planning project typically lasts between five to eight weeks, depending on the scope of the rollout. The progress of the team varies, depending (among other things) on the participation of enterprise resource persons, the availability and quality of source system documentation, and the rate at which project issues are resolved.

Upon completion of the planning effort, the team moves into data warehouse implementation for the planned rollout. The activities for data warehouse implementation are discussed in Chapter 9.

8.1 ASSEMBLE AND ORIENT TEAM

Identify all parties who will be involved in the data warehouse implementation and brief them about the project. Distribute copies of the warehouse strategy as background material for the planning activity.

Define the team setup if a formal project team structure is required. Take the time and effort to orient the team members on the rollout scope, and explain the role of each member of the team. This approach allows the project team members to set realistic expectations about skill sets, project workload, and project scope.

Assign project team members to specific roles, taking care to match skill sets to role responsibilities. When all assignments have been completed, check for unavoidable training requirements due to skill-role mismatches (i.e., the team member does not possess the appropriate skill sets to properly fulfill his or her assigned role).

If required, conduct training for the team members to ensure a common understanding of data warehousing concepts. It is easier for everyone to work together if all have a common goal and an agreed approach for attaining it. Describe the schedule of the planning project to the team. Identify milestones or checkpoints along the planning project timeline. Clearly explain dependencies between the various planning tasks.

Considering the short time frame for most planning projects, conduct status meetings at least once a week with the team and with the project sponsor. Clearly set objectives for each week. Use the status meeting as the venue for raising and resolving issues.

8.2 CONDUCT DECISIONAL REQUIREMENTS ANALYSIS

Decisional Requirements Analysis is one of two activities that can be conducted in parallel during Data Warehouse Planning; the other activity being Decisional Source System Audit (described in the next section). The object of Decisional Requirements Analysis is to gain a thorough understanding of the information needs of decision-makers.

Decisional Requirements Analysis is Working Top-Down

Decisional requirements analysis represents the top-down aspect of data warehousing. Use the warehouse strategy results as the starting point of the decisional requirements analysis; a preliminary analysis should have been conducted as part of the warehouse strategy formulation.

Review the intended scope of this warehouse rollout as documented in the warehouse strategy document. Finalize this scope by further detailing the preliminary decisional requirements analysis. It will be necessary to revisit the user representatives. The rollout scope is typically expressed in terms of the queries or reports that are to be supported by the warehouse by the end of this rollout. The project sponsor must review and approve the scope to ensure that management expectations are set properly.

Document any known limitations about the source systems (e.g., poor data quality, missing data items). Provide this information to source system auditors for their confirmation. Verified limitations in source system data are used as inputs to finalizing the scope of the rollout—if the data are not available, they cannot be loaded into the warehouse.

Take note that the scope strongly influences the implementation time frame for this rollout. Too large a scope will make the project unmanageable. As a general rule, limit the scope of each project or rollout so that it can be delivered in three to six months by a full-time team of 6 to 12 team members.

Conducting Warehouse Planning Without a Warehouse Strategy

It is not unusual for enterprises to go directly into warehouse planning without previously formulating a warehouse strategy. This typically happens when a group of users is clearly driving the warehouse initiative and are more than ready to participate in the initial rollout as user representatives. More often than not, these users have already taken the initiative to list and prioritize their information requirements.

In this type of situation, a number of tasks from the strategy formulation will have to be conducted as part of the planning for the first warehouse rollout. These tasks are as follows:

- **Determine organizational context.** An understanding of the organization is always helpful in any warehousing project, especially since organizational issues may completely derail the warehouse initiative.
- **Define data warehouse rollouts.** Although business users may have already predefined the scope of the first rollout, it helps the warehouse architect to know what lies ahead in subsequent rollouts.
- **Define data warehouse architecture.** Define the data warehouse architecture for the current rollout (and if possible, for subsequent rollouts).
- **Evaluate development and production environment and tools.** The strategy formulation was expected to produce a short-list of tools and computing environments for the warehouse. This evaluation will be finalized during planning by the actual selection of both environments and tools.

8.3 CONDUCT DECISIONAL SOURCE SYSTEM AUDIT

The decisional source system audit is a survey of all information systems that are current or potential sources of data for the data warehouse.

A preliminary source system audit during warehouse strategy formulation should provide a complete inventory of data sources. Identify all possible source systems for the warehouse if this information is currently unavailable.

Data Sources can be Internal or External

Data sources are primarily internal. The most obvious candidates are the operational systems that automate the day-to-day business transactions of the enterprise. Note that aside from transactional or operational processing systems, one often-used data source in the enterprise general ledger, especially if the reports or queries focus on profitability measurements.

If external data sources are also available, these may be integrated into the warehouse.

DBAs and IT Support Staff are the Best Resource Persons

The best resource persons for a decisional source system audit of internal systems are the database administrators (DBAs), system administrators and other IT staff who support each internal system that is a potential source of data. With their intimate knowledge of the systems, they are in the best position to gauge the suitability of each system as a warehouse data source.

These individuals are also more likely to be familiar with any data quality problems that exist in the source systems. Clearly document any known data quality problems, as these have a bearing on the data extraction and cleansing processes that the warehouse must support. Known data quality problems also provide some indication of the magnitude of the data cleanup task.

In organizations where the production of managerial reports has already been automated (but not through an architected data warehouse), the DBAs and IT support staff can provide very valuable insight about the data that are presently collected. These staff members can also provide the team with a good idea of the business rules that are used to transform the raw data into management reports.

Conduct individual and group interviews with the IT organization to understand the data sources that are currently available. Review all available documentation on the candidate source systems. This is without doubt one of the most time-consuming and detailed tasks in data warehouse planning, especially if up-to-data documentation of the existing systems is not readily available.

As a consequence, the whole-hearted support of the IT organization greatly facilitates this entire activity.

Obtain the following documents and information if these have not yet been collected as part of the data warehouse strategy definition:

- **Enterprise IT architecture documentation.** This refers to all documentation that provides a bird's eye view of the IT architecture of the enterprise, including but not limited to:
  - System architecture diagrams and documentation—A model of all the information systems in the enterprise and their relationships to one another.
  - Enterprise data model—A model of all data that currently stored or maintained by the enterprise. This may also indicate which systems support which data item.
  - Network architecture—A diagram showing the layout and bandwidth of the enterprise network, especially for the locations of the project team and the user representatives participating in this rollout.
- **User and technical manuals of each source system.** This refers to data models and schemas for all existing information systems that are candidate's data sources.

If extraction programs are used for ad hoc reporting, obtain documentation of these extraction programs as well. Obtain copies of all other available system documentation, whenever possible.

- **Database sizing.** For each source system, identify the type of database used, the typical backup size, as well as the backup format and medium. It is helpful also to know what data are actually backed up on a regular basis. This is particularly important if historical data are required in the warehouse and such data are available only in backups.
- **Batch window.** Determine the batch windows for each of the operational systems. Identify all batch jobs that are already performed during the batch window. Any data extraction jobs required to feed the data warehouse must be completed within the batch windows of each source system without affecting any of the existing batch jobs already scheduled. Under no circumstances will the team want to disrupt normal operations on the source systems.
- **Future enhancements.** What application development projects, enhancements, or acquisition plans have been defined or approved for implementation in the next 6 to 12 months, for each of the source systems? Changes to the data structure will affect the mapping of source system fields to data warehouse fields. Changes to the operational systems may also result in the availability of new data items or the loss of existing ones.
- **Data scope.** Identify the most important tables of each source system. This information is ideally available in the system documentation. However, if definitions of these tables are not documented, the DBAs are in the best position to provide that information. Also required are business descriptions or definitions of each field in each important table, for all source systems.
- **System codes and keys.** Each of the source systems no doubt uses a set of codes for the system will be implementing key generation routines as well. If these are not documented, ask the DBAs to provide a list of all valid codes and a textual description for each of the system codes that are used. If the system codes have changed over time, ask the DBAs to provide all system code definitions for the relevant time frame. All key generation routines should likewise be documented. These include rules for assigning customer numbers, product numbers, order numbers, invoice numbers, etc. check whether the keys are reused (or recycled) for new records over the years. Reused keys may cause errors during reduplication and must therefore be thoroughly understood.
- **Extraction mechanisms.** Check if data can be extracted or read directly from the production databases. Relational databases such as oracle or Sybase are open and should be readily accessible. Application packages with proprietary database management software, however, may present problems, especially if the data structures are not documented. Determine how changes made to the database are tracked, perhaps through an audit log. Determine also if there is a way to identify data that have been changed or updated. These are important inputs to the data extraction process.

8.4 DESIGN LOGICAL AND PHYSICAL WAREHOUSE SCHEMA

Design the data warehouse schema that can best meet the information requirements of this rollout. Two main schema design techniques are available:

- **Normalization.** The database schema is designed using the normalization techniques traditionally used for OLTP applications;
- **Dimensional modeling.** This technique produces demoralized, star schema designs consisting of fact and dimension tables. A variation of the dimensional star schema also exists (i.e., snowflake schema).

There are ongoing debates regarding the applicability or suitability of both these modeling techniques for data warehouse projects, although dimensional modeling has certainly been gaining popularity in recent years. Dimensional modeling has been used successfully in larger data warehousing implementations across multiple industries. The popularity of this modeling technique is also evident from the number of databases and front-end tools that now support optimized performance with star schema designs (e.g., Oracle RDBMS 8, R/olap XL).

A discussion of dimensional modeling techniques is provided in Chapter 12.

8.5 PRODUCE SOURCE-TO-TARGET FIELD MAPPING

The Source-To-Target Field Mapping documents how fields in the operational (source) systems are transformed into data warehouse fields. Under no circumstances should this mapping be left vague or open to misinterpretation, especially for financial data. The mapping allows non-team members to audit the data transformations implemented by the warehouse.

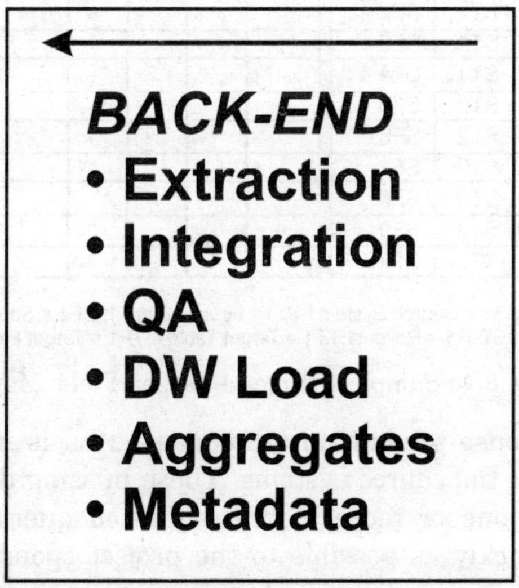

Many-to-Many Mappings

A single field in the data warehouse may be populated by data from more than one source system. This is a natural consequence of the data warehouse's role of integrating data from multiple sources.

The classic examples are customer name and product name. Each operational system will typically have its own customer and product records. A data warehouse field called customer name or product name will therefore be populated by data from more than one systems.

Conversely, a single field in the operational systems may need to be split into several fields in the warehouse. There are operational systems that still record addresses as lines of text, with field names like address line 1, address line^2, etc. these can be split into multiple address fields such as street name, city, country and Mail/Zip code. Other examples are numeric figures or balances that have to be allocated correctly to two or more different fields.

To eliminate any confusion as to how data are transformed as the data items are moved from the source systems to the warehouse database, create a source-to-target field mapping that maps each source field in each source system to the appropriate target field in the data warehouse schema. Also, clearly document all business rules that govern how data values are integrated or split up. This is required for each field in the source-to-target field mapping.

The source-to-target field mapping is critical to the successful development and maintenance of the data warehouse. This mapping serves as the basis for the data extraction and transformation subsystems. Figure 8.1 shows an example of this mapping.

			TARGET No.	1	2	3	4	5	6	7
SOURCE			Schema	R1	R1	R1	R1	R1	R1	R1
			Table	TT1	TT1	TT1	TT2	TT2	TT2	TT2
No.	System	Table	Fields	TF1	TF2	TF3	TF4	TF5	TF6	TF7
1	SS1	ST1	SF1							
2	SS1	ST1	SF2							
3	SS1	ST1	SF3							
4	SS1	ST1	SF4							
5	SS1	ST2	SF5							
6	SS1	ST2	SF6							
7	SS2	ST2	SF7							
8	SS2	ST3	SF8							
9	Ss2	ST3	SF9							
10	SS2	ST3	SF10							
...	...	...	...	...	...	...	...	...	...	...

SOURCE: SS1 = Source System1.ST1= Source Table 1. SF1 = Source Field 1
TARGET: R1 = Rollout1.TT1 = Target Table1. TF1 = Target Field 1

Figure 8.1. Sample Source-to-Target Field Mapping.

Revise the data warehouse schema on an as-needed basis if the field-to-field mapping yields missing data items in the source systems. These missing data items may prevent the warehouse from producing one or more of the requested queries or reports. Raise these types of scope issues as quickly as possible to the project sponsors.

Historical Data and Evolving Data Structures

If users require the loading of historical data into the data warehouse, two things must be determined quickly:

- **Changes in schema.** Determine if the schemas of all source systems have changed over the relevant time period. For example, if the retention period of the data warehouse is two years and data from the past two years have to be loaded into the warehouse, the team must check for possible changes in source system schemas over the past two years. If the schemas have changed over time, the task of extracting the data immediately becomes more complicated. Each different schema may require a different source-to-target field mapping.

- **Availability of historical data.** Determine also if historical data are available for loading into the warehouse. Backups during the relevant time period may not contain the required data item. Verify assumptions about the availability and suitability of backups for historical data loads.

These two tedious tasks will be more difficult to complete if documentation is out of data or insufficient and if none of the IT professionals in the enterprise today are familiar with the old schemas.

8.6 SELECT DEVELOPMENT AND PRODUCTION ENVIRONMENT AND TOOLS

Finalize the computing environment and tool set for this rollout based on the results of the development and production environment and tools study during the data warehouse strategy definition. If an exhaustive study and selection had been performed during the strategy definition stage, this activity becomes optional.

If, on the other hand, the warehouse strategy was not formulated, the enterprise must now evaluate and select the computing environment and tools that will be purchased for the warehousing initiative. This activity may take some time, especially if the evaluation process requires extensive vendor presentations and demonstrations, as well as site visits. This activity is therefore best performed early on to allow for sufficient time to study and select the tools. Sufficient lead times are also required for the delivery (especially if importation is required) of the selected equipment and tools.

8.7 CREATE PROTOTYPE FOR THIS ROLLOUT

Using the short-listed or final tools and production environment, create a prototype of the data warehouse.

A prototype is typically created and presented for one or more of the following reasons:

- **To assists in the selection of front-end tools.** It is sometimes possible to ask warehousing vendors to present a prototype to the evaluators as part of the selection process. However, such prototypes will naturally not be very specific to the actual data and reporting requirements of the rollout.

- **To verify the correctness of the schema design.** The team is better served by creating a prototype using the logical and physical warehouse schema for this rollout. If possible, use actual data from the operational systems for the prototype queries and reports. If the user requirements (in terms of queries and reports) can be created using the schema, then the team has concretely verified the correctness of the schema design.
- **To verify the usability of the selected front-end tools.** The warehousing team can invite representatives from the user community to actually use the prototype to verity the usability of the selected front-end tools.
- **To obtain feedback from user representatives.** The prototype is often the first concrete output of the planning effort. It provides users with something that they can see and touch. It allows users to experience for the first time the kind of computing environment they will have when the warehouse is up. Such an experience typically triggers a lot of feedback (both positive and negative) from users. It may even cause users to articulate previously unstated requirements.

  Regardless of the type of feedback, however, it is always good to hear what the users have to say as early as possible. This provides the team more time to adjust the approach or the design accordingly.

  During the prototype presentation meeting, the following should be made clear to the business users who will be viewing or using the prototype:

- **Objective of the prototype meeting.** State the objectives of the meeting clearly to properly orient all participants. If the objective is to select a tool set, then the attention and focus of users should be directed accordingly.
- **Nature of data used.** If actual data from the operational systems are used with the prototype, make clear to all business users that the data have not yet been quality assured. If dummy or test data are used, then this should be clearly communicated as well. Users who are concerned with the correctness of the prototype data have unfortunately sidetracked many prototype presentations.
- **Prototype scope.** If the prototype does not yet mimic all the requirements identified for this rollout, then say so. Don't wait for the users to explicitly ask whether the team has considered (or forgotten!) the requirements they had specified in earlier meetings or interviews.

8.8 CREATE IMPLEMENTATION PLAN OF THIS ROLLOUT

With the scope now fully defined and the source-to-target field mapping fully specified, it is now possible to draft an implementation plan for this rollout. Consider the following factors when creating the implementation plan:

- **Number of source systems, and their related extraction mechanisms and logistics.** The more source systems there are, the more complex the extraction and integration processes will be. Also, source systems with open computing environments present fewer complications with the extraction process than do proprietary systems.

- **Number of decisional business processes supported.** The larger the number of decisional business processes supported by this rollout, the more users there are who will want to have a say about the data warehouse contents, the definition of terms, and the business rules that must be respected.
- **Number of subject areas involved.** This is a strong indicator of the rollout size. The more subject areas there are, the more fact tables will be required. This implies more warehouse fields to map to source systems and, of course, a larger rollout scope.
- **Estimated database size.** The estimated warehouse size provides an early indication of the loading, indexing, and capacity challenges of the warehousing effort. The database size allows the team to estimate the length of time it takes to load the warehouse regularly (given the number of records and the average length of time it takes to load and index each record).
- **Availability and quality of source system documentation.** A lot of the team's time will be wasted on searching for or misunderstanding the data that are available in the source systems. The availability of good-quality documentation will significantly improve the productivity of source system auditors and technical analysts.
- **Data quality issues and their impact on the schedule.** Unfortunately, there is no direct way to estimate the impact of data quality problems on the project schedule. Any attempts to estimate the delays often produce unrealistically low figures, much to the concentration of warehouse project managers. Early knowledge and documentation of data quality issues will help the team to anticipate problems. Also, data quality is very much a user responsibility that cannot be left to IT to solve. Without sufficient user support, data quality problems will continually be a thorn in the side of the warehouse team.
- **Required warehouse load rate.** A number of factors external to the warehousing team (particularly batch windows of the operational systems and the average size of each warehouse load) will affect the design and approach used by the warehouse implementation team.
- **Required warehouse availability.** The warehouse itself will also have batch windows. The maximum allowed down time for the warehouse also influences the design and approach of the warehousing team. A fully available warehouse (24 hours × 7 days) requires an architecture that is completely different from that required by a warehouse that is available only 12 hours a day, 5 days a week. These different architectural requirements naturally result in differences in cost and implementation time frame.
- **Lead time for delivery and setup of selected tools, development, and production environment.** Project schedules sometimes fail to consider the length of time required to setup the development and production environments of the warehousing project. While some warehouse implementation tasks can proceed while the computing environments and tools are on their way, significant progress cannot be made until the correct environment and tool sets are available.

- **Time frame required for IT infrastructure upgrades.** Some IT infrastructure upgrades (e.g., network upgrade or extension) may be required or assumed by the warehousing project. These dependencies should be clearly marked on the project schedule. The warehouse Project Manager must coordinate with the infrastructure Project Manager to ensure that sufficient communication exists between all concerned teams.
- **Business sponsor support and user participation.** There is no way to overemphasize the importance of Project Sponsor support and end user participation. No amount of planning by the warehouse Project Manager (and no amount of effort by the warehouse project team) can make up for the lack of participation by these two parties.
- **IT support and participation.** Similarly, the support and participation of the database administrators and system administrators will make a tremendous difference to the overall productivity of the warehousing team.
- **Required vs. existing skill sets.** The match (or mismatch) of personnel skill sets and role assignments will likewise affect the productivity of the team. If this is an early or pilot project, then training on various aspects of warehousing will most likely be required. These training sessions should be factored into the implementation schedule as well and, ideally, should take place before the actual skills are required.

8.9 WAREHOUSE PLANNING TIPS AND CAVEATS

The actual data warehouse planning activity will rarely be a straightforward exercise. Before conducting your planning activity, read through this section for planning tips and caveats.

Follow the Data Trail

In the absence of true decision support systems, enterprises have, over the years, been forced to find stopgap or interim solutions for producing the managerial or decisional reports that decision-makers require. Some of these solutions require only simple extraction programs that are regularly run to produce the required reports. Other solutions require a complex series of steps that combine manual data manipulation, extraction programs, conversion formulas, and spreadsheet macros.

In the absence of a data warehouse, many of the managerial reporting requirements are classified as ad hoc reports. As a result, most of these report generation programs and processes are largely undocumented and are known only by the people who actually produce the reports. This naturally leads to a lack of standards (i.e., different people may apply different formulas and rules to the same data item), and possible inconsistencies each time the process is executed. Fortunately, the warehouse project team will be in a position to introduce standards and consistent ways of manipulating data.

Following the data trail (see Figure 8.2) from the current management reports, back to their respective data sources can prove to be a very enlightening exercise for data warehouse planners.

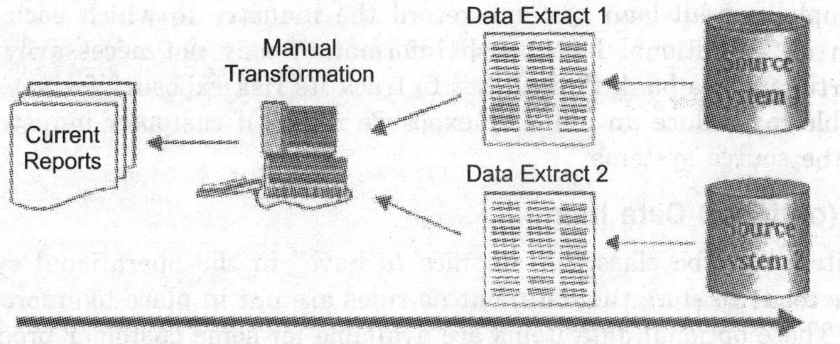

Figure 8.2. Follow the Data Trail

Through this exercise, the data warehouse planner will find:

- **All data sources currently used for decisional reporting.** At the very least, these data sources should also be included in the decisional source system audit. The team has the added benefit of knowing before hand which fields in these systems are considered important.
- **All current extraction programs.** The current extraction programs are a rich input for the source-to-target field mapping. Also, if these programs manipulate or transform or convert the data in any way, the transformation rules and formulas may also prove helpful to the warehousing effort.
- **All undocumented manual steps to transform the data.** After the raw data have been extracted from the operational systems, a number of manual steps may be performed to further transform the data into the reports that enterprise managers. Interviews with the appropriate persons should provide the team with an understanding of these manual conversion and transformation steps (if any).

Apart from the above items, it is also likely that the data warehouse planner will find subtle flaws in the way reports are produced today. It is not unusual to find inconsistent use of business terms formulas, and business rules, depending on the person who creates and reads the reports. This lack of standard terms and rules contributes directly to the existence of conflicting reports from different groups in the same enterprise, i.e., the existence of "different versions of the truth".

Limitations Imposed by Currently Available Data

Each data item that is required to produce the reports required by decision-makers comes from one or more of the source systems available to the enterprise. Understandably, there will be data items that are not readily supported by the source systems.

Data limitations generally fall into one of the following types.

Missing Data Items

A data item is considered missing, if no provisions were made to collect or store this data item in any of the source systems. This omission particularly occurs with data items that may have no bearing on the day-to-day operations of the enterprise but will have tactical or managerial implications.

For example, not all loan systems record the industry to which each loan customer belongs; from an operational level, such information may not necessarily be considered critical. Unfortunately, a bank that wishes to track its risk exposure for any given industry will not be able to produce an industry exposure report if customer industry data are not available at the source systems.

Incomplete (optional) Data Items

A data item may be classified as "nice to have" in the operational systems, and so provisions are made to store the data, but no rules are put in place to enforce the collection of such data. These optional data items are available for some customer products, accounts, or orders but may be unavailable for others.

Returning to the above example, a loan system may have a field called customer industry, but the application developers may have made the field optional, in recognition of the fact that data about a customers industry are not ready available in cases such as this, only customers with actual data can be classified meaningfully in the report.

Wrong Data

Errors occur when data are stored in one or more source systems but are not accurate. There are many potential reasons or causes for this, including the following ones:

- **Data entry error.** A genuine error is made during data entry. The wrong data are stored in the database.
- **Data item is mandatory but unavailable.** A data item may be defined as mandatory but it may not be readily available, and the random substitution of other information has no direct impact on the day-to-day operations of the enterprise. This implies that any data can be entered without adversely affecting the operation processes.

Returning to the above example, if customer industry was a mandatory customer data item and the person creating the customer record does not know the industry to which the customer belongs, he is likely to select, at random, any of the industry codes that are recognized by the system. Only by so doing will he or she be able to create the customer record.

Another data item that can be randomly substituted is the social security number, especially if these numbers are stored for reference purposes only, and not for actual processing. Data entry personnel remain focused on the immediate task of creating the customer record which the system refuses to do without all the mandatory data items. Data entry personnel are rarely in a position to see the consequences to recording the wrong data.

Improvements to Source Systems

From the above examples, it is easy to see how the scope of a data warehousing initiative can be severely compromised by data limitations in the source systems. Most pilot data warehouse projects are thus limited only to the data that are available. However, improvements can be made to the source systems in parallel with the warehousing projects. The team should therefore properly document any source system limitations that are encountered. These documents can be used as inputs to upcoming maintenance projects on the operational systems.

A decisional source system audit report may have a source system review section that covers the following topics:

- **Overview of operational systems.** This section lists all operational systems covered by the audit. A general description of the functionality and data of each operational system is provided. A list of major tables and fields may be included as an appendix. Current users of each of the operational systems are optionally documented.
- **Missing data items.** List all the data items that are required by the data warehouse but are currently not available in the source systems. Explain why each item is important (e.g., cite reports or queries where these data items are required). For each data item, identify the source system where the data item is best stored.
- **Data quality improvement areas.** For each operational system, list all areas where the data quality can be improved. Suggestions as to how the data quality improvement can be achieved can also be provided.
- **Resource and effort estimate.** For each operational system, it might be possible to provide an estimate or the cost and length of time required to either add the data item or improve the data quality for that data item.

In Summary

Data warehouse planning is conducted to clearly define the scope of one data warehouse rollout. The combination of the top-down and bottom-up tracks gives the planning process the best of both worlds—a requirements-driven approach that is grounded on available data.

The clear separation of the front-end and back-end tracks encourages the development of warehouse subsystems for extracting, transporting, cleaning, and loading warehouse data independently of the front-end tools that will be used to access the warehouse.

The four tracks converge when a prototype of the warehouse is created and when actual warehouse implementation takes place.

Each rollout repeatedly executes the four tracks (top-down, bottom-up, back-end), and the scope of the data warehouse is iteratively extended as a result Figure 8.3 illustrates the concept.

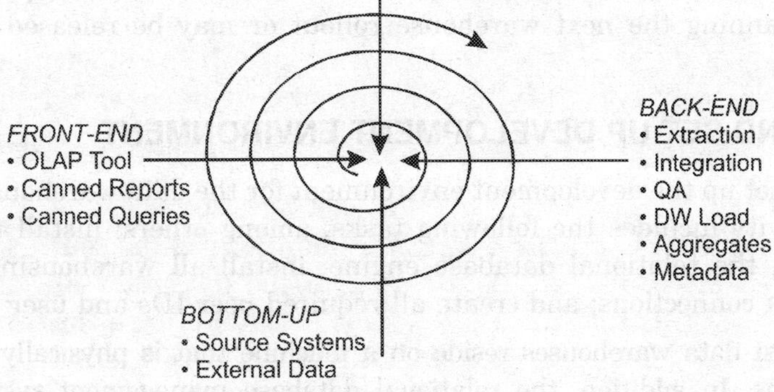

Fig. 8.3

CHAPTER 9

DATA WAREHOUSE IMPLEMENTATION

The data Warehouse implementation approach presented in this chapter describes the activities related to implementing one rollout of the date warehouse. The activities discussed here are built on the results of the data warehouse planning described in the previous chapter.

The data warehouse implementation team builds or extends an existing warehouse schema based on the final logical schema design produced during planning. The team also builds the warehouse subsystems that ensure a steady, regular flow of clean data from the operational systems into the data warehouse. Other team members install and configure the selected front-end tools to provide users with access to warehouses data.

An implementation project should be scoped to last between three to six months. The progress of the team varies, depending (among other things) on the quality of the warehouse design, the quality of the implementation plan, the availability and participation of enterprise resource persons, and the rate at which project issues are resolved.

User training and warehouse testing activities take place towards the end of the implementation project, just prior to the deployment to users. Once the warehouse has been deployed, the day-to-day warehouse management, maintenance, and optimization tasks begin. Some members of the implementation team may be asked to stay on and assist with the maintenance activities to ensure continuity. The other members of the project team may be asked to start planning the next warehouse rollout or may be released to work on other projects.

9.1 ACQUIRE AND SET UP DEVELOPMENT ENVIRONMENT

Acquire and set up the development environment for the data warehouse implementation project. This activity includes the following tasks, among others: install the hardware, the operating system, the relational database engine; install all warehousing tools; create all necessary network connections; and create all required user IDs and user access definitions.

Note that most data warehouses reside on a machine that is physically separate from the operational systems. In addition, the relational database management system used for data warehousing need not be the same database management system used by the operational systems.

At the end of this task, the development environment is set up, the project team members are trained on the (new) development environment, and all technology components have been purchased and installed.

9.2 OBTAIN COPIES OF OPERATIONAL TABLES

There may be instances where the team has no direct access to the operational source systems from the warehouse development environment. This is especially possible for pilot projects, where the network connection to the warehouse development environment may be available.

Regardless of the reason for the lack of access, the warehousing team must establish and document a consistent, reliable, and easy-to-follow procedure for obtaining copies of the relevant tables from the operational systems. Copies of these tables are made available to the warehousing team on another medium (most likely tape) and are restored on the warehouse server. The creation of copies can also be automated through the use of replication technology.

The warehousing team must have a mechanism for verifying the correctness and completeness of the data that are loaded onto the warehouse server. One of the most effective completeness checks is meaningful business counts (e.g., number of customers, number of accounts, number of transactions) that are computed and compared to ensure data completeness. Data quality utilities can help assess the correctness of the data.

The use of copied tables as described above implies additional space requirements on the warehouse server. This should not be a problem during the pilot project.

9.3 FINALIZE PHYSICAL WAREHOUSE SCHEMA DESIGN

Translate the detailed logical and physical warehouse design from the warehouse planning stage into a final physical warehouse design, taking into consideration the specific, selected database management system.

The key considerations are :

- **Schema design.** Finalize the physical design of the fact and dimension tables and their respective fields. The warehouse database administrator (DBA) may opt to divide one logical dimension (e.g., customer) into two or more separate ones (e.g., a customer dimension and a customer demographic dimension) to save on space and improve query performance.
- **Indexes.** Identify the appropriate indexing method to use on the warehouse tables and fields, based on the expected data volume and the anticipated nature of warehouse queries. Verify initial assumptions made about the space required by indexes to ensure that sufficient space has been allocated.
- **Partitioning.** The warehouse DBA may opt to partition fact and dimension tables, depending on their size and on the partitioning features that are supported by the database engine. The warehouses DBA who decides to implement partitioned views must consider the trade-offs between degradation in query performance and improvements in warehouse manageability and space requirements.

9.4 BUILD OR CONFIGURE EXTRACTION AND TRANSFORMATION SUBSYSTEMS

Easily 60 percent to 80 percent of a warehouse implementation project is devoted to the back-end of the warehouse. The back-end subsystems must extract, transform, clean, and load the operational data into the data warehouse. Understandably, the back-end subsystems vary significantly from one enterprise to another due to differences in the computing environments, source systems, and business requirements. For this reason, much of the warehousing effort cannot simply be automated away by warehousing tools.

Extraction Subsystem

The first among the many subsystems on the back-end of the warehouse is the data extraction subsystem. The term extraction refers to the process of retrieving the required data from the operational system tables, which may be the actual tables or simply copies that have been loaded into the warehouse server.

Actual extraction can be achieved through a wide variety of mechanisms, ranging from sophisticated third-party tools to custom-written extraction scripts or programs developed by in house IT staff. Third-party extraction tools are typically able to connect to mainframe, midrange and UNIX environments, thus freeing their users from the nightmare of handling heterogeneous data sources. These tools also allow users to document the extraction process (i.e., they have provisions for storing metadata about the extraction).

These tools, unfortunately, are expensive. For this reason, organizations may also turn to writing their own extraction programs. This is a particularly viable alternative if the source systems are on a uniform or homogenous computing environment (e.g., all data reside on the same RDBMS, and they make use of the same operating system). Custom-written extraction programs, however, may be difficult to maintain, especially if these programs are not well documented. Considering how quickly business requirements will change in the warehousing environment, ease of maintenance is an important factor to consider.

Transformation Subsystem

The transformation subsystem literally transforms the data in accordance with the business rules and standards that have been established for the data warehouse.

Several types of transformations are typically implemented in data warehousing.

- **Format changes.** Each of the data fields in the operational systems may store data in different formats and data types. These individual data items are modified during the transformation process to respect a standard set of formats. For example, all data formats may be changed to respect a standard format, or a standard data type is used for character fields such as names, addresses.
- **De-duplication.** Records from multiple sources are compared to identify duplicate records based on matching field values. Duplicates are merged to create a single record of a customer; a product, an employee, or a transaction, Potential duplicates are logged as exceptions that are manually resolved. Duplicate records with conflicting data values are also logged for manual correction if there is no system of record to provide the “master” or “correct” value.

- **Splitting up fields.** A data item in the source system may need to be split up into one or more fields in the warehouse. One of the most commonly encountered problems of this nature deals with customer addresses that have simply been stored as several lines of text. These textual values may be split up into distinct fields; street number, street name, building name, city, mail or zip code, country, etc.
- **Integrating fields.** The opposite of splitting up fields is integration. Two or more fields in the operational systems may be integrated to populate one warehouse field.
- **Replacement of values.** Values that are used in operational systems may not be comprehensible to warehouse users. For example, system codes that have specific meanings in operational systems are meaningless to decision-makers. The transformation subsystem replaces the original with new values that have a business meaning to warehouse users.
- **Derived values.** Balances, ratios, and other derived values can be computed using agreed formulas. By pre-computing and loading these values into the warehouse, the possibility of miscomputation by individual users is reduced. A typical example of a pre-computed value is the average daily balance of bank accounts. This figure is computed using the base data and is loaded as it is into the warehouse.
- **Aggregates.** Aggregates can also be pre-computed for loading into the warehouse. This is an alternative to loading only atomic (base-level) data in the warehouse and creating in the warehouse the aggregate records based on the atomic warehouse data.

The extraction and transformation subsystems (see Figure 9.1) create load images, i.e., tables and fields populated with the data that are to be loaded into the warehouse. The load images are typically stored in tables that have the same schema as the warehouse itself. By doing so, the extraction and transformation subsystems greatly simplify the load process.

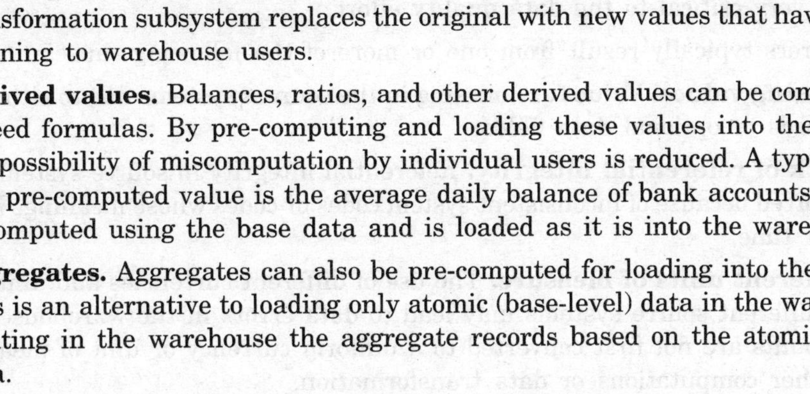

Figure 9.1. Extraction and Transformation Subsystems

9.5 BUILD OR CONFIGURE DATA QUALITY SUBSYSTEM

Data quality problems are not always apparent at the start of the implementation project, when the team is concerned more about moving massive amounts of data rather than the actual individual data values that are being moved. However, data quality (or to be more precise, the lack of it) will quickly become a major, show-stopping problem if it is not addressed directly.

One of the quickest ways to inhibit user acceptance is to have poor data quality in the warehouse. Furthermore, the perception of data quality is in some ways just as important as the actual quality of the data warehouse. Data warehouse users will make use of the warehouse, only if they believe that the information they will retrieve from it is correct. Without user confidence in the data quality, a warehouse initiative will soon lose support and eventually die off.

A data quality subsystem on the back-end of the warehouse therefore is critical component of the overall warehouse architecture.

Causes of Data Errors

An understanding of the causes of data errors makes these errors easier to find. Since most data errors originate from the source systems, source system database administrators and system administrators, with their day-to-day experiences working with the sources systems are very critical to the data quality effort.

Data errors typically result from one or more of the following causes:

- **Missing values.** Values are missing in the sources systems due to either incomplete records or optional data fields.
- **Lack of referential integrity.** Referential integrity in source systems may not be enforced because of inconsistent system codes or codes whose meanings have changed over time.
- **Different units of measure.** The use of different currencies and units of measure in different source systems may lead to data errors in the warehouse if figures or amounts are not first converted to a uniform currency or unit of measure prior to further computations or data transformation.
- **Duplicates.** De-duplication is performed on source system data prior to the warehouse load. However, the de-duplication process depends on comparison of data values to find matches. If the data are not available to start with, the quality of the de-duplication may be compromised. Duplicate records may therefore be loaded into the warehouse.
- **Fields to be split up.** As mentioned earlier, there are times when a single field in the sources system has to be split up to populate multiple warehouse fields. Unfortunately, it is not possible to manually split up the fields one at a time because of the volume of the data. The team often resorts to some automated form of field splitting, which may not be 100 percent correct.
- **Multiple hierarchies.** Many warehouse dimensions will have multiple hierarchies for analysis purposes. For example, the time dimension typically has day-month-quarter-year hierarchy. This same time dimension may also have a day-week hierarchy and a day-fiscal, month-fiscal, quarter-fiscal year hierarchy. Lack of understanding of these multiple hierarchies in the different dimensions may result in erroneous warehouse loads.
- **Conflicting or inconsistent terms and rules.** The conflicting or inconsistent use of business terms and business rules may mislead warehouse planners into loading two distinctly different data items into the same warehouse field, or vice versa. Inconsistent business rules may also cause the misuse of formulas during data transformation.

Data Quality Improvement Approach

Below is an approach for improving the overall data quality of the enterprise.

- **Assess current level of data quality.** Determine the current data quality level of each of the warehouse sources systems. While the enterprise may have a data quality initiative that is independent of the warehousing project, it is best to focus the data quality efforts on warehouse sources systems—these systems obviously contains data that are of interest to enterprise decision—makers.
- **Identify key data items.** Set the priorities of the data quality team by identifying the key data items in each of the warehouse source systems. Key data items, by definition, are the data items that must achieve and maintain a high level of data quality. By prioritizing data items in this manner, the team can target its efforts on the more critical data areas and therefore provides greater value to the enterprise.
- **Define cleansing tactics for key data items.** For each key data item with poor data quality, define an approach or tactic for cleaning or raising the quality of that data item. Whenever possible, the cleansing approach should target the source systems first, so that errors are corrected at the source and not propagated to other systems.
- **Define error-prevention tactics for key data items.** The enterprise should not stop at error-correction activities. The best way to eliminate data errors is to prevent them from happening in the first place. If error-producing operational processes are not corrected, they will continue to populate enterprise databases with erroneous data. Operational and data-entry staff must be made aware of the cost of poor data quality. Reward mechanisms within the organization may have to be modified to create a working environment that focuses on preventing data errors at the source.
- **Implement quality improvement and error-prevention processes.** Obtain the resources and tools to execute the quality improvement and error-prevention procession. After some time, another assessment may be conducted, and a new set of key data items may be targeted for quality improvement.

Data Quality Assessment and Improvements

Data quality assessments can be conducted at any time at different points along the warehouse back-end. As shown in Figure 9.2, assessments can be conducted on the data while it is in the source systems, in warehouse loads images or in the data warehouse itself.

Note that while data quality products assist in the assessment and improvement of data quality, it is unrealistic to expect any single program or data quality product to find and correct all data quality errors in the operational systems or in the data warehouse. Nor is it realistic to expect data quality improvements to be completed in a matter of months. It is unlikely that an enterprise will ever bring its databases to a state that is 100 percent error free.

Despite the long-term nature of the effort, however, the absolute worst thing that any warehouse Project Manager can do is to ignore the data quality problem in the vain hope that it will disappear. The enterprise must be willing and prepared to devote time and effort to the tedious task of cleaning up data errors rather than sweeping the problem under the rug.

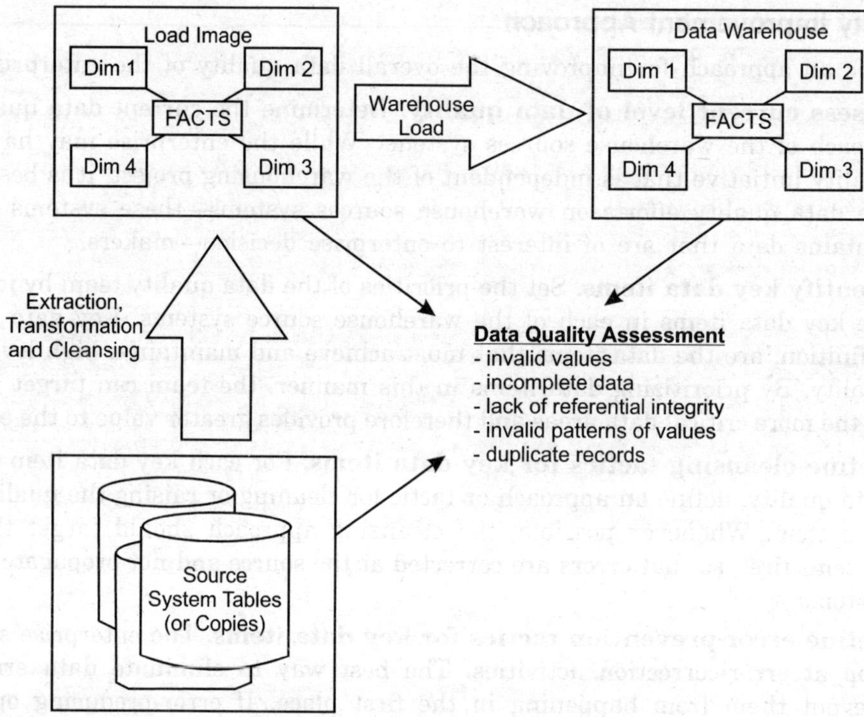

Figure 9.2. Data Quality Assessments at the Warehouse Back-End

Correcting Data Errors at the Source

All data errors found are, under ideal circumstances, corrected at the source, i.e., the operational system database is updated with the correct values. This practice ensures that subsequent data users at both the operational and decisional levels will benefit from clean data.

Experience has shown, however, that correcting data at the source may prove difficult to implement for the following reasons:

- **Operational responsibility.** The responsibility for updating the source system data will naturally fall into the hands of operational staff, who may not be so inclined to accept the additional responsibility of tracking down and correcting past data-entry errors.
- **Correct data are unknown.** Even if the people in operations know that the data in a given record are wrong, there may be no easy way to determine the correct data. This is particularly true of customer data (e.g., a customer's social security number). The people in operations have no other resource but to approach the customers one at a time to obtain the correct data. This is tedious, time-consuming, and potentially irritating to customers.

Other Considerations

Many of the available warehousing tools have features that automate different areas of the warehouse extraction, transformation, and data quality subsystems.

The more data sources there are, the higher the likelihood of data quality problems. Likewise, the larger the data volume, the higher the number of data errors to correct.

The inclusion of historical data in the warehouse will also present problems due to changes (over time) in system codes, data structures, and business rules.

9.6 BUILD WAREHOUSE LOAD SUBSYSTEM

The warehouse load subsystem takes the load images created by the extraction and transformation subsystems and loads these images directly into the data warehouse. As mentioned earlier, the data to be loaded are stored in tables that have the same schema design as the warehouse itself. The load process is therefore fairly straightforward from a data standpoint.

Basic Features of a Load Subsystem

The load subsystem should be able to perform the following:

- **Drop indexes on the warehouse.** When new records are inserted into an indexed table, the relational database management system immediately updates the index of the table in response. In the context of a data warehouse load, where up to hundreds of thousands of records are inserted in rapid succession into one single table, the immediate re-indexing of the table after each insert results in a significant processing overhead. As a consequence, the load process slows down dramatically. To avoid this problem, drop the indexes on the relevant warehouse table prior to each load.
- **Load dimension records.** In the source systems each record of a customer, product, or transaction is uniquely identified through a key. Likewise, the customers, products, and transactions in the warehouse must be identifiable through a key value. Source system keys are often inappropriate as warehouse keys, and a key generation approach is therefore used during the load process. Insert new dimension records, or update existing records based on the load images.
- **Load fact records.** The primary key of a Fact table is the concatenation of the keys of its related dimension records. Each fact record therefore makes use to the generated keys of the dimension records. Dimension records are loaded prior to the fact records to allow the enforcement of referential integrity checks. The load subsystem therefore inserts new fact records or updates old records based on the load images. Since the data warehouse is essentially a time series, most of the records in the Fact table will be new records.
- **Compute aggregate records, using base fact and dimension records.** After the successful load of atomic or base level data into the warehouse, the load subsystem may now compute aggregate records by using the base-level fact and dimension records. This step is performed only if the aggregates are not pre-computed for direct loading into the warehouse.
- **Rebuild or regenerate indexes.** Once all loads have been completed, the indexes on the relevant tables are rebuilt or regenerated to improve query performance.
- **Log load perceptions.** Log all referential integrity violations during the load process as load exceptions. There are two types of referential integrity violations: (*a*) missing key values one of the key fields of the fact record does not have a value: and (*b*) wrong key values the key fields have values, but one or more of them do

not have a corresponding dimension record. In both cases, the warehousing team has option of (*a*) not loading the record until the correct key values are found or (*b*) loading the record, but replacing the missing or wrong key values with hard-coded values that users can recognize as a load exception.

The load subsystem, as described above, assumes that the load images do not yet make use of warehouse keys; i.e., the load images contain only source system keys. The warehouse keys are therefore generated as part of the load process.

Warehousing teams may opt to separate the key generation routines from the load process. In this scenario, the key generation routine is applied on the initial load images (i.e., the load images created by the extraction and transformation subsystems). The final load images (with warehouse keys) are then loaded into the warehouse.

Loading Dirty Data

There are ongoing debates about loading dirty data (i.e., data that fail referential integrity checks) into the warehouse. Some teams prefer to load only clean data into the warehouse, arguing that dirty data can mislead and misinform. Others prefer to load all data, both clean and dirty, provided that the dirty data are clearly marked as dirty. Depending on the extent of data errors, the use of only clean data in the warehouse can be equal to or more dangerous than relying on a mix of clean and dirty data. If more than 20 percent of data are dirty and only 80 percent clean data are loaded into the warehouse, the warehouse users will be making decisions based on an incomplete picture.

The use of hard-coded values to identify warehouse data with referential integrity violations on one dimension allows warehouse users to still make use of the warehouse data on clean dimensions.

Consider the example in Figure 9.3. If a Sales Fact record is dependent on Customer, Data (Time dimension) and Product and if the Customer key is missing, then a "Sales per Product" report from the warehouse will still produce the correct information.

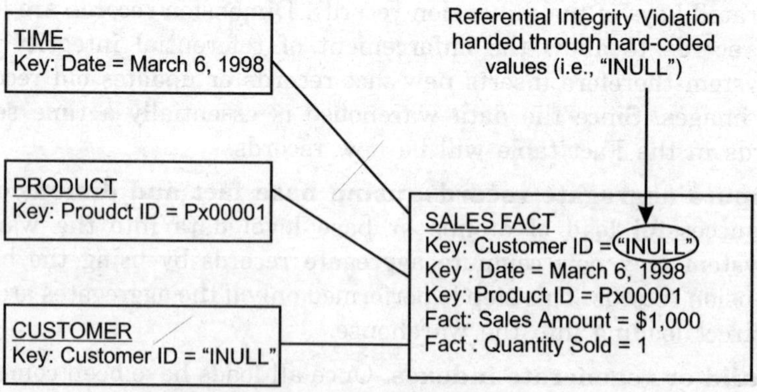

Figure 9.3. Loading Dirty Data

When a "sales per customer" report is produced (as shown in Figure 9.4), the hard-coded value that signifies a referential integrity violation will be listed as a customer ID, and the user is aware that the corresponding sales amount cannot be attributed to valid customer.

Hard-coded values clearly identify dirty data.

SALES PER CUSTOMER
Date: March 6, 1998

Customer	Sales Amount
INULL	1,000
Customer A	10,000
Customer B	8,000
...	...

Figure 9.4. Sample Report with Dirty Date Identified Through Hard-Coded Value.

By handling a referential integrity violation during warehouse loads in the manner described above. The users get full picture of the facts on clean dimensions and are clearly aware when dirty dimensions are used.

The Need for Load Optimization

The time required for a regular warehouse load is often of great concern to warehouse designers and project managers. Unless the warehouse was designed and architects to be fully available 24 hours a day, the warehouse will be offline and unavailable to its users during the load period.

Much of the challenge in building the load subsystem therefore lies in optimizing the load process to reduce the total time required. For this reason, parallel load features in later releases of relational database management systems and parallel processing capabilities in SMP and MPP machines are especially welcome in data warehousing implementations.

Test Loads

The team may like to test the accuracy and performance of the warehouse load subsystem on dummy data before attempting a real load with actual load images. The team should know as early as possible how much load optimization work is still required.

Also, by using dummy data, the warehousing team does not have to wait for the completion of the extraction and transformation subsystems to start testing the warehouse load subsystem.

Warehouse load subsystem testing of course, is possible only if the data warehouse schema is already up and available.

Set Up Data Warehouse Schema

Create the data warehouse schema in the development environment while the team is constructing or configuring the warehouse back-end subsystems (i.e., the data extraction and transformation subsystems, the data quality subsystem, and the warehouse load subsystem).

As part of the schema setup, the warehouse DBA must do the following:

- **Create warehouse tables.** Implement the physical warehouse database design by creating all base-level fact and dimension tables, core and custom tables, and aggregate tables.

- **Build Indexes.** Build the required indexes on the tables according to the physical warehouse database design.
- **Populate special referential tables and records.** The data warehouse may require special referential tables or records that are not created through regular warehouse loads. For example, if the warehouse team uses hard-coded values to handle load with referential integrity violations, the warehouse dimension tables must have records that use the appropriate hard-coded value to identify fact records that have referential integrity violations. It is usually helpful to populate the data warehouse with test data as soon as possible. This provides the front-end team with the opportunity to test the data access and retrieval tools; even while actual warehouse data are not available. Figure 9.5 presents a typical data warehouse scheme.

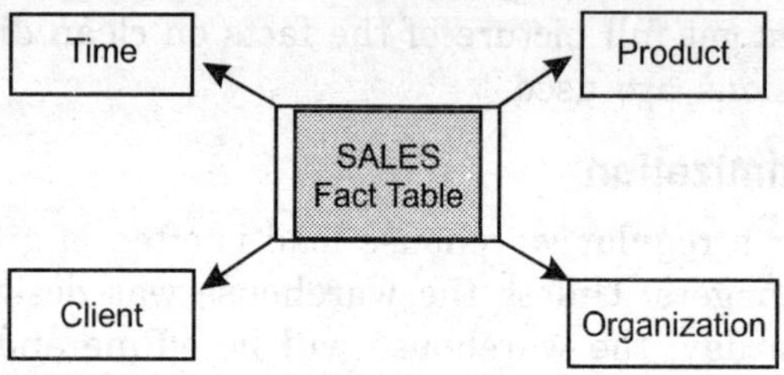

Figure 9.5. Sample Warehouse Schema

9.7 SET UP WAREHOUSE METADATA

Metadata have traditionally been defined as "data about data." While such a statement does not seem very helpful, it is actually quite appropriate as a definition-metadata describe the contents of the data warehouse, indicate where the warehouse data originally came from, and document the business rules that govern the transformation of the data.

Warehousing tools also use metadata as the basis for automating certain aspects of the warehousing project. Chapter 13 in the Technology section of this book discusses metadata in depth.

9.8 SET UP DATA ACCESS AND RETRIEVAL TOOLS

The data access and retrieval tools are equivalent to the tip of the warehousing iceberg. While they may represent as little as 10 percent of the entire warehousing effort, they all are that users of the warehouse. As a result, these tools are critical to the acceptance and usability of the warehouse.

Acquire and Install Data Access and Retrieval Tools

Acquire and install the selected data access tools in the appropriate environments and machines. The front-end team will find it prudent to first install the selected data access tools on a test machine that has access to the warehouse. The test machine should be loaded with the software typically used by the enterprise. Through this activity, the front-end team may identify unforeseen conflicts between the various software programs without causing inconvenience to anyone.

Verify that the data access and retrieval tools can establish and hold connections to the data warehouse over the corporate network. In the absence of actual warehouse data, the team may opt to use test data in the data warehouse schema to test the installation of front-end tools.

Build Predefined Reports and Queries

The prototype initially developed during warehouse planning is refined by incorporating user feedback and by building all predefined reports and queries that have been agreed on with the end-users.

Different front-end tools have different requirements for the efficient distribution of predefined reports and queries to all users. The front-end team should therefore perform the appropriate administration tasks as required by the selected front-end tools.

By building these predefined reports and queries, the data warehouse implementation team is assured that the warehouse schema meets the decisional information requirements of the users.

Support staff, who will eventually manage the warehouse Help Desk should participate in this activity, since this participation provides excellent learning opportunities.

Set Up Role or Group Profiles

Define role or group profiles on the database management system. The major database management systems provide the use of a role or a group to define the access rights of multiple users through one role definition.

The warehousing team must determine the appropriate role definitions for the warehouse. The following roles are recommended as a minimum:

- **Warehouse user.** The typical warehouse user is granted Select rights on the production warehouse tables. Updates are granted on the warehouse dimension records.
- **Warehouse administrator.** This role is assigned to users strictly for the direct update of data warehouse dimension records. *Select* and *update* rights are granted on the warehouse dimension record.
- **Warehouse developer.** This role applies to any warehouse implementation team member who works on the back-end of the warehouse. Users with this role can create development warehouse objects but cannot modify or update the structure and content of production warehouse tables.

Set Up User Profiles and Map These to Role Profiles

Define user profiles for each warehouse user and assign one or more roles to each user profile to grant the user access to the warehouse. While it is possible for multiple users to use the same user profile, this practice is greatly discouraged for the following reasons:

- **Collection of warehouse statistics.** Warehouse statistics are collected as part of the warehouse maintenance activities. The team will benefit from knowing (*a*) how many users have access to the warehouse. (*b*) which users are actually making use of the warehouse, and (*c*) how often a particular user makes use of the warehouse.
- **Warehouse security.** The warehousing team must be able to track the use of the warehouse to a specific individual, not just to a group of individuals. Users may also be less careful with Ids and passwords if they know these are shared. Unique user Ids are also required should the warehouse start restricting or granting access based on record values in warehouse tables (e.g., a branch manager can see only the records related to his or her branch).

- **Audit Trail.** If one or more users have Update access to the warehouse, distinct, users IDs will allow the warehouse team to track down the warehouse user responsible for each update.
- **Query performance complaints.** In case where a query on the warehouse server is slow or has stalled, the warehouse administrator will be better able to identify the slow or stalled query when each user has a distinct user ID.

9.9 PERFORM THE PRODUCTION WAREHOUSE LOAD

The production data warehouse load can be performed only when the load images are ready and both the warehouse schema and metadata are setup.

Prior to the actual production warehouse load, it is a good practice to conduct partial loads to get some indication of the total load time. Also, since the data warehouse schema design may require refinement, particularly when the front-end tools are first setup, it will be easier and quicker to make changes to the data warehouse schema when very little data have been loaded. Only when the end users have had a chance to provide positive feedback should large volumes of data be loaded into the warehouse.

Data warehouses are not refreshed more than once every 24 hours. If the user requirements call for up-to-the-minute information for operational monitoring purposes, then a data warehouse is not the solution; these requirements should be addressed through an Operational Data Store.

The warehouse is typically available to end-users during the working day. For this reason, warehouse loads typically take place at night or over a weekend.

If the retention period of the warehouse is several years; the warehouse team should first load the data for the current time period and verify the correctness of the load. Only when the load is successful should the team start loading historical data into the warehouse. Due to potential changes to the schemas of the sources systems over the past few years, it is natural for the warehouse team to start from the most current period and work in reverse chronological order when loading historical data.

9.10 CONDUCT USER TRAINING

The IT organization is encouraged to fully take over the responsibility of conducting user training, contrary to the popular practice of having product vendors or warehouse consultant to assist in the preparation of the first warehousing classes. Doing so will enable the warehousing team to conduct future training courses independently.

Scope of User Training

Conduct training for all intended users of this rollout of the data warehouses. Prepare training materials if required. The training should cover the following topics:

- **What is a warehouse?** Different people have different expectations of what a data warehouse is. Start the training with a warehouse definition.
- **Warehouse scope.** All users must know the contents of the warehouses. The training should therefore clearly state what is not supported by the current warehouse rollout. Trainers might need to know what functionality has been deferred to later phases, and why.
- **Use of front-end tools.** The users should learn how to use the front-end tools. Highly usable front-ends should require fairly little training. Distribute all relevant user documentation to training participants.

- **Load timing and publication.** Users should be informed of the schedule for warehouse loads (e.g., "the warehouse is loaded with sales data on a weekly basis, and a special month-end load is performed for the GL expense data"). Users should also know how the warehouse team intends to publish the results of each warehouse load.
- **Warehouse support structure.** Users should know how to get additional help from the warehousing team. Distribute Help Desk phone numbers, etc.

Who Should Attend the Training?

Training should be conducted for all intended end users of the data warehouse. Some senior managers, particularly those who do not use computers every day, may ask their assistants or secretaries to attend the training in their place. In this scenario, the senior manager should be requested to attend at least the portion of the training that deals with the warehouse scope.

Different Users Have Different Training Needs

An understanding of the users computing literacy provides insight to the type and pace of training required. If the user base is large enough, it may be helpful to divide the trainees into two groups - a basic class and an advanced class. Power users will otherwise quickly become bored in a basic class, and beginners will feel overwhelmed if they are in an advanced class. Attempting to meet the training needs of both types of users in one class may prove to be difficult and frustrating.

At the end of the training, it is a good practice to identify training participants who would require post-training follow up and support from the warehouse implementation team. Also ask participants to evaluate the warehouse training, constructive criticism will allow the trainers to deliver better training in the future.

Training as a Prerequisite to Testing

A subset of the users will be requested to test the warehouse. This user subset may have to undergo user training earlier than others, since user training is a prerequisite to user testing. Users cannot adequately test the warehouse if they do not know what is in it or how to use it.

9.11 CONDUCT USER TESTING AND ACCEPTANCE

The data warehouse, like any system, must undergo user testing and acceptance. Some considerations are discussed below:

Conduct Warehouse Trails

Representatives of the end-user community are requested to test this warehouse rollout. In general, the following aspects should be tested.

- **Support of specified queries and reports.** Users test the correctness of the queries and reports of this warehouse rollout. In many cases, this is achieved by preparing the same report manually (or through existing mechanisms) and comparing this report to the one produced by the warehouse. All discrepancies are accounted for, and the appropriate corrections are made. The team should not discount the possibility that the errors are in the manually prepared report.

- **Performance/response time.** Under the most ideal circumstances, each warehouse query will be executed in less than one or two seconds. However, this may not be realistically achievable, depending on the warehouse size (number of rows and dimensions) and the selected tools. Warehouse optimization at the hardware and database levels can be used to improve response times. The use of stored aggregates will likewise improve warehouse performance.
- **Usability of client front-end·** Training on the front-end tools is required, but the tools must be usable for the majority of the users.
- **Ability to meet report frequency requirements.** The warehouse must be able to provide the specified queries and reports at the frequency (i.e., daily, weekly, monthly, quarterly, or yearly) required by the users.

Acceptance

The rollout is considered accepted when the testing for this rollout is completed to the satisfaction of the user community. A concrete set of acceptance criteria can be developed at the start of the warehouse rollout for use later as the basis for acceptance. The acceptance criteria are helpful to users because they know exactly what to test. It is likewise helpful to the warehousing team because they know what must be delivered.

In Summary

Data warehouse implementation is without question the most challenging part of data warehousing. Not only will the team have to resolve the technical difficulties of moving, integrating, and cleaning data, they will also face the more difficult task of addressing policy issues, resolving organizational conflicts, and untangling logistical delays.

In general, the following areas present more problems during warehouse implementation and bear the more watching.

- **Dirty data.** The identification and cleanup of dirty data can easily consume more resources than the project can afford.
- **Underestimated logistics.** The logistics involved in warehousing typically require more time than originally expected. Tasks such as installing the development environment, collecting source data, transporting data, and loading data are generally beleaguered by logistical problems. The time required to learn and configure warehousing tools likewise contributes to delays.
- **Policies and political issues.** The progress of the team can slow to a crawl if a key project issue remains unresolved for too long.
- **Wrong warehouse design.** The wrong warehouse design results in unmet user requirements or inflexible implementations. It also creates rework for the schema as well as all the back-end subsystems; extraction and transformation, quality assurance, and loading.

At the end of the project, however, a successful team has the satisfaction of meeting the information needs of key decision-makers in a manner that is unprecedented in the enterprise.

PART IV : TECHNOLOGY

A quick browse through the Process section of this book makes it quite clear that a data warehouse project requires a wide array of technologies and tools. The data warehousing products market (particularly the software segment) is a rapidly growing one; new vendors continuously announce the availability of new products, while existing vendors add warehousing-specific features to their existing product lines.

Understandably, the gamut of tools makes tool selection quite confusing. This section of the book aims to lend order to the warehousing tools market by classifying these tools and technologies. The two main categories, understandably, are:

- **Hardware and Operating Systems.** These refer primarily to the warehouse servers and their related operating systems. Key issues include database size, storage options, and backup and recovery technology.
- **Software.** This refers primarily to the tools that are used to extract, clean, integrate, populate, store, access, distribute, and present warehouse data. Also included in this category are metadata repositories that document the data warehouse. The major database vendors have all jumped on the data warehousing bandwagon and have introduced, or are planning to introduce, features that allow their database products to better support data warehouse implementations.

In addition, this section of the book focuses on two key technology issues in data warehousing:

- **Warehouse Schema Design.** We present an overview of the dimensional modeling techniques, as popularized by Ralph Kimball, to produce database designs that are particularly suited for warehousing implementations.
- **Warehouse Metadata.** We provide a quick look at warehouse metadata—what it is, what it should encompass, and why it is critical in data warehousing.

CHAPTER 10

HARDWARE AND OPERATING SYSTEMS

The terms hardware and operating systems refers to the server platforms and operating systems that serve as the computing environment of the data warehouse. Warehousing environments are typically separate from the operational computing environments (i.e., a different machine is used) to avoid potential resource contentions between operational and decisional processing.

Enterprises are correctly varied of computing solutions that may compromise the performance levels of mission-critical operational systems.

The major hardware vendors have established data warehousing initiatives or partnership programs with other firms in a bid to provide comprehensive data warehousing solution. Frameworks to their customers. This is very consistent with the solution integrator role that major hardware vendors typically play on large computing projects.

10.1 PARALLEL HARDWARE TECHNOLOGY

As we mentioned, the two primary categories of parallel hardware used for data warehousing are the symmetric multiprocessing (SMP) machines and massively parallel processing (MPP) machines.

Symmetric Multiprocessing

These systems consist of from a pair to as many as 64 processors that share memory and disk I/O resources equally under the control of one copy of the operating system, as shown in Figure 10.1. Because system resources are equally shared between processors, they can be managed more effectively. SMP systems make use of extremely high-speed interconnections to allow each processor to share memory on an equal basis. These interconnections are two orders of magnitude faster than those found in MPP systems, and range from the 2.6 GB/sec interconnect on Enterprise 4000, 5000, and 6000 systems to the 12.8 GB/sec aggregate throughput of the Enterprise 10000 server with the Gigaplane-XB™ architecture.

In addition to high bandwidth, low communication latency is also important if the system is to show good scalability. This is because common data warehouse database operations such as index lookups and joins involve communication of small data packets. This system provides very low latency interconnects. At only 400 nscc. For local access, the latency of the Starfire server's Gigaplane-XB interconnects is 200 times less than the 80,000 nsec. Latency of the IBM SP2 interconnects. Of all the systems discussed in this paper, the lowest latency is on the Enterprise 6000, with a uniform latency of only 300 nsec.

When the amount of data contained in each message is small, the importance of low latencies are paramount.

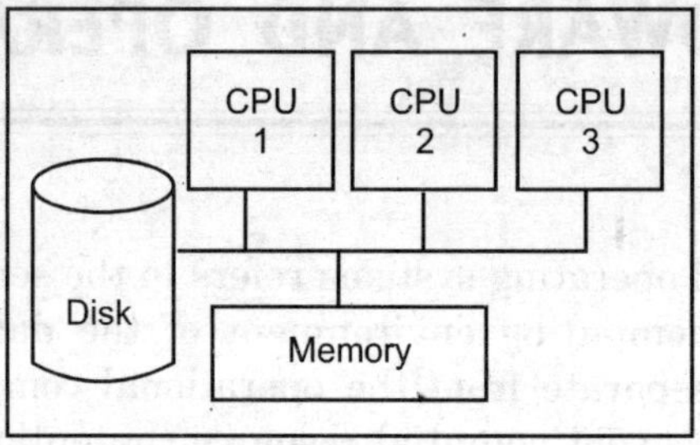

Figure 10.1. SMP Architectures Consist of Multiple Processors Sharing Memory and I/O Resources Through a High-Speed Interconnect, and Use a Single Copy of the Operating System

Massively Parallel Processor Systems

Massively parallel processor systems use a large number of nodes each accessed using an interconnect mechanism that supports message-based data transfers typically on the order of 13 to 38 MB/sec. Figure 10.2, illustrates that each node is a self-sufficient processor complex consisting of CPU, memory, and disk subsystems. In the vernacular, an MPP is considered a "shared nothing" system because memory and I/O resources are independent, with each node even supporting its own copy of the operating system. MPP systems promise unlimited scalability, with a growth path that allows as many processors as necessary to be added to a system.

MPP architectures provide excellent performance in situations where a problem can be partitioned so that all nodes can run in parallel with little or no inter-node communication. In reality, the true ad hoc queries typical of data warehouses can only rarely be so well partitioned, and thus limit the performance that MPP architectures actually deliver. When either data skew or high inter-node communication requirements prevail, the scalability of MPP architectures is severely limited. Reliability is a concern with MPP systems because the loss of a node does not merely reduce the processing power available to the whole system; it can make any database objects that are wholly or partially located on the failed node unavailable.

An interesting industry trend is for MPP vendors to augment single-processor "thin" nodes with multiprocessor "fat" nodes using many processors in an SMP configuration within each node. If the trend continues, each MPP node will have increasing numbers of processors, fewer nodes, and the architecture begins to resemble clusters of SMP systems, discussed below.

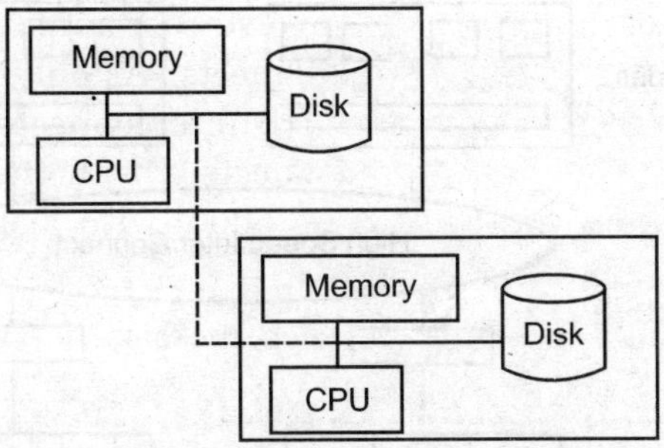

Figure 10.2. MPP Architectures Consist of a Set of Independent Shared-Nothing Nodes, Each Containing Processor, Memory, and Local Disks, Connected with a Message-Based Interconnect.

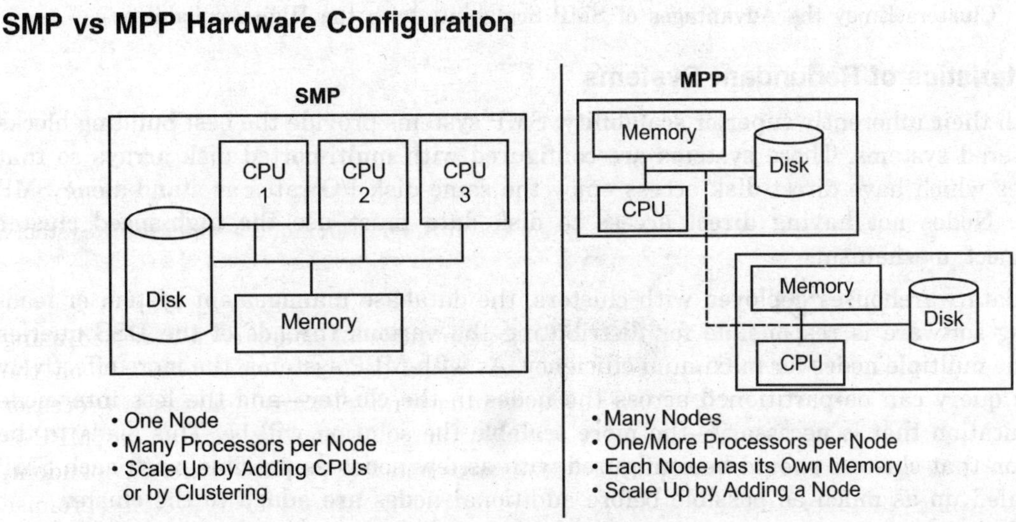

SMP is the architecture yielding the best reliability and performance, and has worked through the difficult engineering problems to develop servers that can scale nearly linearly with the incremental addition of processors. Ironically, the special shared-nothing versions of merchant database products that run on MPP systems also run with excellent performance on SMP architectures, although the reverse is not true.

Clustered Systems

When data warehouses must be scaled beyond the number of processors available in current SMP configurations, or when the high availability (HA) characteristics of a multiple-system complex are desirable, clusters provide an excellent growth path. High-availability software can enable the other nodes in a cluster to take over the functions of a failed node, ensuring around-the-clock availability of enterprise-critical data warehouses.

A cluster of four SMP servers is illustrated in Figure 10.3. The same database management software that exploits multiple processors in an SMP architecture and distinct processing nodes in MPP architecture can create query execution plans that utilize all servers in the cluster.

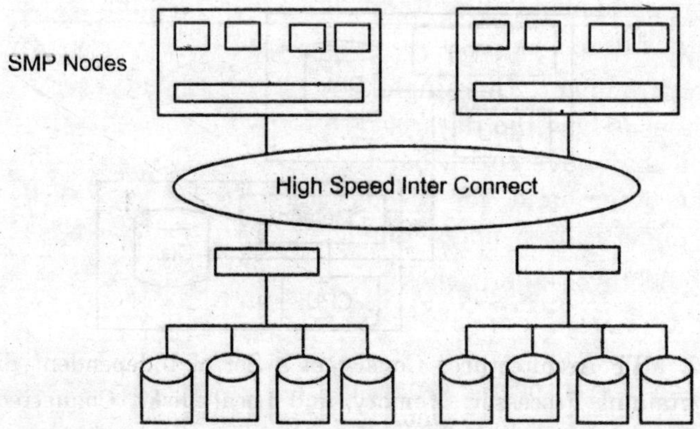

Figure 10.3. Cluster of Four SMP Systems Connected via a High Speed Interconnect Mechanism. Clusters Enjoy the Advantages of SMP Scalability with the High Availability.

Characteristics of Redundant Systems

With their inherently superior scalability, SMP systems provide the best building blocks for clustered systems. These systems are configured with multi-ported disk arrays so that the nodes which have direct disk access enjoy the same disk I/O rates as stand-alone SMP systems. Nodes not having direct access to disk data must use the high-speed cluster interconnect mechanism.

In data warehouses deployed with clusters, the database management system or load-balancing software is responsible for distributing the various threads of the DSS queries across the multiple nodes for maximum efficiency. As with MPP systems, the more effectively that the query can be partitioned across the nodes in the cluster—and the less inter-node communication that is necessary—the more scalable the solution will be. This leads to the conclusion that clusters should be configured with as few nodes as possible, with each SMP node scaled up as much as possible before additional nodes are added to the cluster.

Currently, clustering of 30-processor Enterprise 6000 platforms, with the ability to cluster 64-processor Enterprise 10000 systems available in the future.

Beware that, the larger the number of nodes in a cluster, the more the cluster looks like an MPP system, and the database administrator may need to deal with the issues of large numbers of nodes much sooner than they would with clusters of more powerful SMP systems. These are the familiar issues of non-uniformity of data access, partitioning of database tables across nodes, and the performance limits imposed by the high bandwidth interconnects. A new direction that is taking with clustered systems is to develop software that allows a single system image to be executed across a clustered architecture, increasing the ease of management far beyond that of today's clusters.

10.2 THE DATA PARTITIONING ISSUE

The range of architectural choices from MPP to SMP offers a complex decision space for organizations deploying data warehouses. Given that companies tend to make architectural choices early, and then invest up to hundreds of millions of dollars as they grow, the result of choosing architecture that presents increasingly intractable partitioning problems and the likelihood of idle nodes can have consequences that measure in the millions of dollars.

A system that scales well exploits all of its processors and makes best use of the investment in computing infrastructure.

Regardless of environment, the single largest factor influencing the scalability of a decision support system is how the data is partitioned across the disk subsystem. Systems that do not scale well may have entire batch queries waiting for a single node to complete an operation. On the other hand, for throughput environments with multiple concurrent jobs running, these underutilized nodes may be exploited to accomplish other work.

There are typically three approaches to partitioning database records:

Range Partitioning

Range partitioning places specific ranges of table entries on different disks. For example, records having "name" as a key may have names beginning with A-B in one partition, C-D in the next, and so on. Likewise, a DSS managing monthly operations might partition each month onto a different set of disks. In cases where only a portion of the data is used in a query—the C-D range, for example—the database can avoid examining the other sets of data in what is known as *partition elimination.* This can dramatically reduce the time to complete a query.

The difficulty with range partitioning is that the quantity of data may vary significantly from one partition to another, and the frequency of data access may vary as well. For example, as the data accumulates, it may turn out that a larger number of customer names fall into the M-N range than the A-B range. Likewise, mail-order catalogs find their December sales to far outweigh the sales in any other month.

Round-Robin Partitioning

Round-robin partitioning evenly distributes records across all disks that compose a logical space for the table, without regard to the data values being stored. This permits even workload distribution for subsequent table scans. Disk striping accomplishes the same result —spreading read operations across multiple spindles—but with the logical volume manager, not the DBMS, managing the striping. One difficulty with round-robin partitioning is that, if appropriate for the query, performance cannot be enhanced with partition elimination.

Hash Partitioning

Hash partitioning is a third method of distributing DBMS data evenly across the set of disk spindles. A hash function is applied to one or more database keys, and the records are distributed across the disk subsystem accordingly.

Again, a drawback of hash partitioning is that partition elimination may not be possible for those queries whose performance could be improved with this technique. For symmetric multiprocessors, the main reason for data partitioning is to avoid "hot spots" on the disks, where records on one spindle may be frequently accessed, causing the disk to become a bottleneck. These problems can usually be avoided by combinations of database partitioning and the use of disk arrays with striping. Because all processors have equal access to memory and disks, the layout of data does not significantly affect processor utilization. For massively parallel processors, improper data partitioning can degrade performance by an order of magnitude or more. Because all processors do not share memory and disk resources equally, the choice of on which node to place which data has a significant impact on query performance.

The choice of partition key is a critical, fixed decision, that has extreme consequences over the life of an MPP-based data warehouse. Each database object can be partitioned once and only once without re-distributing the data for that object. This decision determines long into the future whether MPP processors are evenly utilized, or whether many nodes sit idle while only a few are able to efficiently process database records. Unfortunately, because the very purpose of data warehouses is to answer *ad hoc* queries that have never been foreseen, a correct choice of partition key is one that is, by its very definition, impossible to make. This is a key reason why database administrators who wish to minimize risks tend to recommend SMP architectures where the choice of partition strategy and keys have significantly less impact.

Architectural Impacts on Query Performance

Three fundamental operations composing the steps of query execution plans are table scans, joins, and index lookup operations. Since decision support system performance depends on how well each of these operations are executed, it's important to consider how their performance varies between SMP and MPP architectures.

Table Scans

On MPP systems where the database records happen to be uniformly partitioned across nodes, good performance on single-user batch jobs can be achieved because each node/memory/disk combination can be fully utilized in parallel table scans, and each node has an equivalent amount of work to complete the scan. When the data is not evenly distributed, or less than the full set of data is accessed, load skew can occur, causing some nodes to finish their scanning quickly and remain idle until the processor having the largest number of records to process is finished. Because the database is statically partitioned, and the cost of eliminating data skew by moving parts of tables across the interconnect is prohibitively high, table scans may or may not equally utilize all processors depending on the uniformity of the data layout. Thus the impact of database partitioning on an MPP can allow it to perform as well as an SMP, or significantly less well, depending on the nature of the query.

On an SMP system, all processors have equal access to the database tables, so consistent performance is achieved regardless of the database partitioning. The database query coordinator simply allocates a set of processes to the table scan based on the number of processors available and the current load on the DBMS. Table scans can be parallelized by dividing up the table's records between processes and having each processor examine an equal number of records—avoiding the problems of load skew that can cripple MPP architectures.

Join Operations

Consider a database join operation in which the tables to be joined are equally distributed across the nodes in an MPP architecture. A join of this data may have very good or very poor performance depending on the relationship between the partition key and the join key:

- *If the partition key is equal to the join key,* a process on each of the MPP nodes can perform the join operation on its local data, most effectively utilizing the processor complex.
- *If the partition key is not equal to the join key,* each record on each node has the potential to join with matching records on all of the other nodes.

When the MPP hosts *N* nodes, the join operation requires each of the *N* nodes to transmit each record to the remaining *N-1* nodes, increasing communication overhead and reducing join performance. The problem gets even more complex when real-world data having an uneven distribution is analyzed. Unfortunately, with ad-hoc queries predominating in decision support systems, the case of partition key not equal to the join key can be quite common.

To make matters worse, MPP partitioning decisions become more complicated when joins among multiple tables are required. For example, consider Figure 10.4, where the DBA must decide how to physically partition three tables: Supplier, PartSupp, and Part. It is likely that queries will involve joins between Supplier and PartSupp, as well as between PartSupp and Part. If the DBA decides to partition PartSupp across MPP nodes on the Supplier key, then joins to Supplier will proceed optimally and with minimum inter-node traffic. But then joins between Part and PartSupp could require high inter-node communication, as explained above. The situation is similar if instead the DBA partitions PartSupp on the Part key.

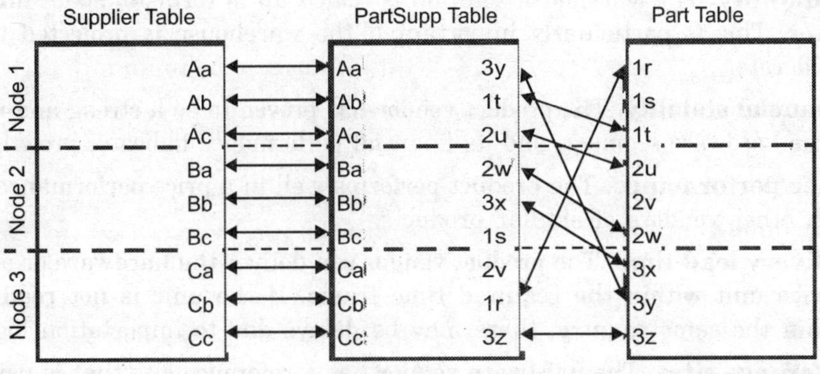

MPP: costly inter-node communication required

SMP: all communication at memory speeds

Figure 10.4. The Database Logical Schema may Make it Impossible to Partition All Tables on the Optimum Join Keys. Partitioning Causes Uneven Performance on MPP, while Performance on SMP Performance is Optimal.

For an SMP, the records selected for a join operation are communicated through the shared memory area. Each process that the query coordinator allocates to the join operation has equal access to the database records, and when communication is required between processes it is accomplished at memory speeds that are two orders of magnitude faster than MPP interconnect speeds. Again, an SMP has consistently good performance independent of database partitioning decisions.

Index Lookups

The query optimizer chooses index lookups when the number of records to retrieve is a small (significantly less than one percent) portion of the table size. During an index lookup, the table is accessed through the relevant index, thus avoiding a full table scan. In cases where the desired attributes can be found in the index itself, the query optimizer will access the index alone, perhaps through a parallel full-index scan, not needing to examine the base table at all. For example, assume that the index is partitioned evenly across all nodes of an MPP, using the same partition key as used for the data table. All nodes can be equally involved in satisfying the query to the extent that matching data rows are evenly distributed across all nodes. If a global index—one not partitioned across nodes—is used, then the workload distribution is likely to be uneven and scalability low.

On SMP architectures, performance is consistent regardless of the placement of the index. Index lookups are easily parallelized on SMPs because each processor can be assigned to access its portion of the index in a large shared memory area. All processors can be involved in every index lookup, and the higher interconnect bandwidth can cause SMPs to outperform MPPs even in the case where data is also evenly partitioned across the MPP architecture.

10.3 HARDWARE SELECTION CRITERIA

The following selection are recommended for hardware selection:

- **Scalability.** The warehouse solution is scaled up in terms of space and processing power. This is particularly important if the warehouse is projected to grow at a rapid rate.
- **Financial stability.** The product vendor has proven to be a strong and visible player in the hardware segment, and its financial performance indicates growth or stability.
- **Price/performance.** The product performs well in a price/performance comparison with other vendors of similar products.
- **Delivery lead time.** The product vendor can deliver the hardware or an equivalent service unit within the required time frame. If the unit is not readily available within the same country, there may be delays due to importation logistics.
- **Reference sites.** The hardware vendor has a reference site that is using a similar unit for the same purpose. The warehousing team can either arrange a site visit or interview representatives from the site visit. Alternatively, an onsite test of the unit can be conducted, especially if no reference is available.
- **Availability of support.** Support for the hardware and its operating system is available, and support response times are within the acceptable down time for the warehouse.

  Examples of hardware and operating system platforms are provided below for reference purposes only and are by no means an attempt to provide a complete list of companies with warehousing platforms.

  The tools are listed in alphabetical order by company name; the sequence does not imply any form of ranking.

- **Digital.** 64-bit Alpha Servers and Digital Unix or Open VMS. Both SMP and MPP configurations are available.
- **HP.** HP 9000 Enterprise Parallel Serve.
- **IBM.** RS 6000 and the AIX operating system have been positioned for data warehousing. The AS/400 has been used for data mart implementations.

- **Microsoft.** The Windows NT operating system has been positioned quite successfully for data mart deployments.
- **Sequent.** Sequent NUMA-Q and the DYNIX operating system.

In Summary

Major hardware vendors have understandably established data warehousing initiatives or partnership programs with both software vendors and consulting firms in a bid to provide comprehensive data warehousing solutions to their customers.

Due to the potential size explosion of data warehouses, and enterprise is best served by a powerful hardware platform that is scalable both in terms of processing power and disk capacity. If the warehouse achieves a mission-critical status in the enterprise, then the reliability, availability, and security of the computing platform become key evaluation criteria.

The clear separation of operational and decisional platforms also gives enterprises the opportunity to use a different computing platform for the warehouse (i.e., different from the operational systems).

CHAPTER 11

WAREHOUSING SOFTWARE

A warehousing team will require several different types of tools during the course of a warehousing project. These software products generally fall into one or more of the categories illustrated in Figure 11.1 and described below.

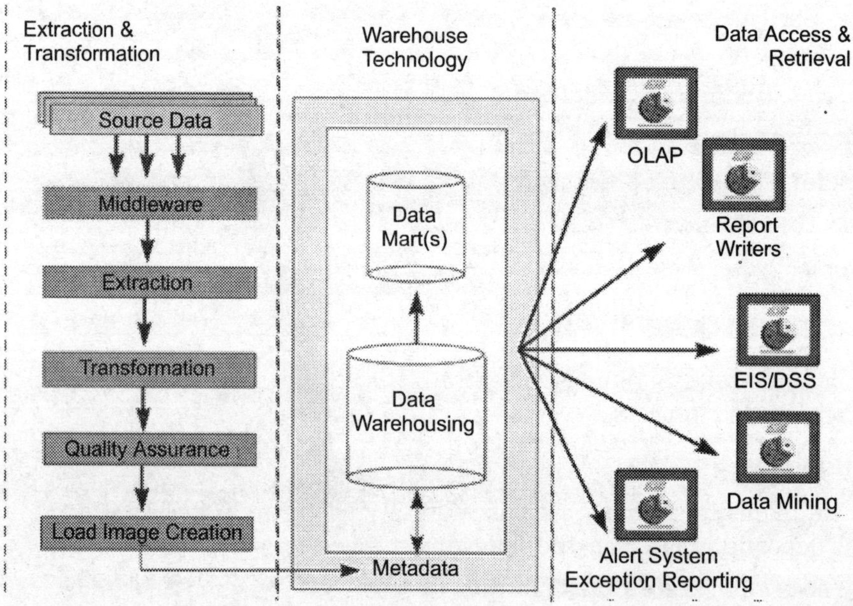

Figure 11.1. Data Warehouse Software Components

- **Extraction and transformation.** As part of the data extraction and transformation process, the warehouse team requires tools that can extract, transform, integrate, clean, and load data from source systems into one or more data warehouse databases. Middleware and gateway products may be required for warehouses that extract data from host-based source systems.

- **Warehouse storage.** Software products are also required to store warehouse data and their accompanying metadata. Relational database management systems in particular are well suited to large and growing warehouses.
- **Data access and retrieval.** Different types of software are required to access, retrieve, distribute, and present warehouse data to its end users.

Tool examples listed throughout this chapter are provided for reference purposes only and are by no means an attempt to provide a complete list of vendors and tools. The tools are listed in alphabetical order by company name; the sequence does not imply any form of ranking.

Also, many of the sample tools listed automate more than one aspect of the warehouse back-end process. Thus, a tool listed in the extraction category may also have features that fit into the transformation or data quality categories.

11.1 MIDDLEWARE AND CONNECTIVITY TOOLS

Connectivity tools provide transparent access to source systems in heterogeneous computing environments. Such tools are expensive but quite often prove to be invaluable because they provide transparent access to database of different types, residing on different platforms.

Examples of commercial middleware and connectivity tools include:

- **IBM:** Data Joiner
- **Oracle:** Transparent Gateway
- **SAS:** SAS/Connect
- **Sybase:** Enterprise Connect

11.2 EXTRACTION TOOLS

There are now quite a number of extraction tools available, making tool selection a potentially complicated process.

Tool Selection

Warehouse teams have many options when it comes to extraction tools. In general, the choice of tool depends greatly on the following factors:

- **The source system platform and database.** Extraction and transformation tools cannot access all types of data sources on all types of computing platforms. Unless the team is willing to invest in middleware, the tool options are limited to those that can work with the enterprise's source systems.
- **Built-in extraction or duplication functionality.** The source systems may have built-in extraction or duplication features, either through application code or through database technology. The availability of these built-in tools may help reduce the technical difficulties inherent in the data extraction process.
- **The batch windows of the operational systems.** Some extraction mechanisms are faster or more efficient than others. The batch windows of the operational systems determine the available time frame for the extraction process and therefore may limit the team to a certain set of tools or extraction techniques.

The enterprise may opt to use simple custom-programmed extraction scripts for open homogeneous computing environments, although without a disciplined approach to documentation, such an approach may create an extraction system that is difficult to maintain. Sophisticated extraction tools are a better choice for source systems in proprietary, heterogeneous environments, although these tools are quite expensive.

Extraction Methods

There are two primary methods for extracting data from source systems (See Figures 11.2):

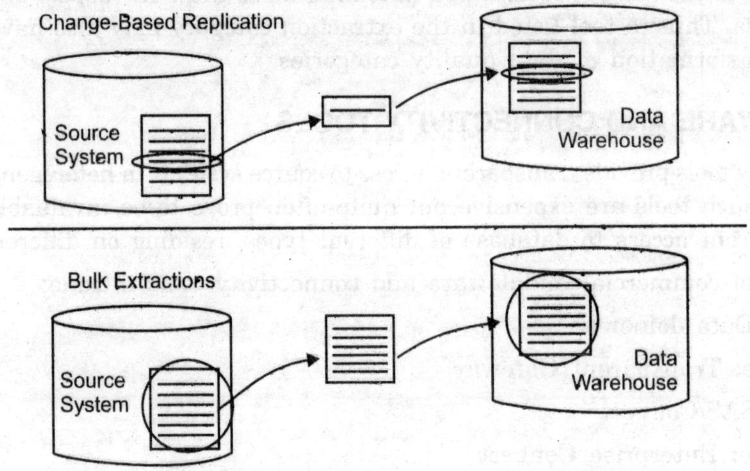

Figure 11.2. Extraction Options

- **Bulk extractions.** The entire data warehouse is refreshed periodically by extractions from the source systems. All applicable data are extracted from the source systems for loading into the warehouse. This approach heavily taxes the network connection between source and target databases, but such warehouses are easier to set up and maintain.
- **Change-based replication.** Only data that have been newly inserted or updated in the source systems are extracted and loaded into the warehouse. This approach places less stress on the network (due to the smaller volume of data to be transported) but requires more complex programming to determine when a new warehouse record must be inserted or when an existing warehouse record must be updated.

Examples of Extraction tools include:

- **Apertus Carleton:** Passport
- **Evolutionary Technologies:** ETI Extract
- **Platinum:** InfoPump

11.3 TRANSFORMATION TOOLS

Transformation tools are aptly named; they transform extracted data into the appropriate format, date structure, and values that are required by the data warehouse.

Most transformation tools provide the features illustrated in Figure 11.3 and described below.

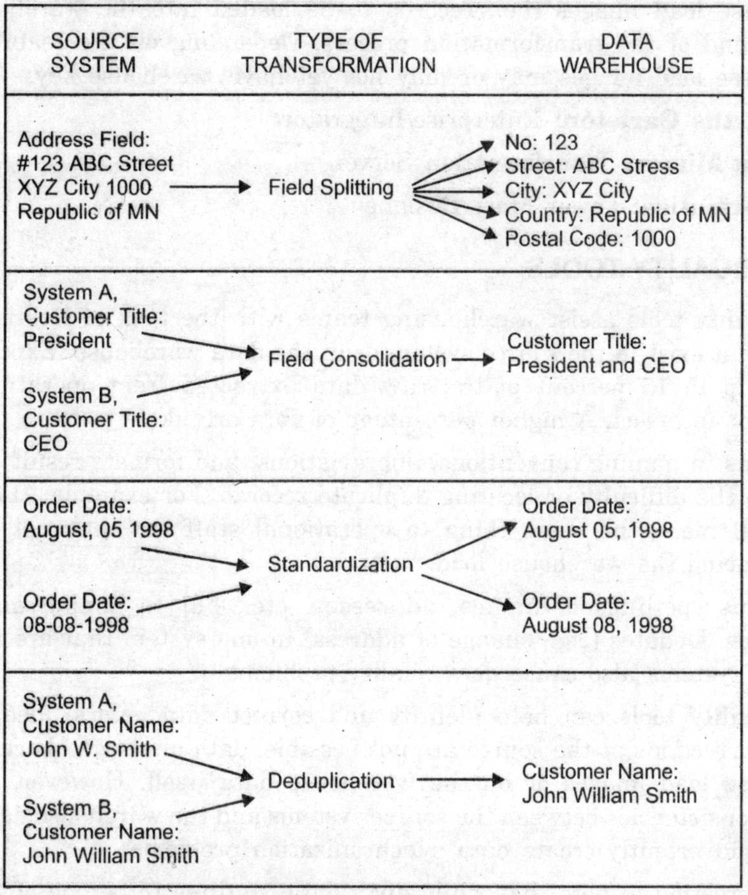

Figure 11.3. Data Transformations

- **Field splitting and consolidation.** Several logical data items may be implemented as a single physical field in the source systems, resulting in the need to split up a single source field into more than one target warehouse field. At the same time, there will be many instances when several source system fields must be consolidated and stored in one single warehouse field. This is especially true when the same field can be found in more than one source system.
- **Standardization.** Standards and conventions for abbreviations, date formats, data types, character formats, etc., are applied to individual data items to improve uniformity in both format and content. Different naming conventions for different warehouse object types are also defined and implemented as part of the transformation process.
- **De-duplication.** Rules are defined to identify duplicate stores of customers or products. In many cases, the lack of data makes it difficult to determine whether two records actually refer to the same customer or product. When a duplicate is

identified, two or more records are merged to form one warehouse record. Potential duplicates can be identified and logged for further verification.

Warehouse load images (i.e., records to be loaded into the warehouse) are created towards the end of the transformation process. Depending on the team's key generation approach, these load images may or may not yet have warehouse key.

- **Apertus Carleton:** Enterprise/Integrator
- **Data Mirror:** Transformation Server
- **Informatica:** Power Mart Designer

11.4 DATA QUALITY TOOLS

Data quality tools assist warehousing teams with the task of locating and correcting data errors that exist in the source system or in the data warehouse. Experience has shown that easily up to 15 percent of the raw data extracted from operational systems are inconsistent or incorrect. A higher percentage of data are likely to be in the wrong format.

Variations in naming conventions, abbreviations, and formats result in inconsistencies that increase the difficulty or locating duplicate records. For example, "14/F," "14th Floor," 14th Fir." All mean the same thing to operational staff but may not be recognized as equivalent during the warehouse load.

Erroneous spellings of names, addresses, etc., but to homonyms likewise cause inconsistencies. Updates (e.g., change of address) in one system that are not propagated to other source systems also cause data quality problems.

Data quality tools can help identify and correct data errors, ideally at the source systems. If corrections at the source are not possible, data quality tools can also be used on the warehouse load images or on the warehouse data itself. However, this practice will introduce inconsistencies between the source systems and the warehouse data; the warehouse team may inadvertently create data synchronization problems.

It is interesting to note that while dirty data continue to be one of the biggest issues for data warehousing initiatives, research indicates that data quality investments consistently receive but a small percentage of total warehouse spending.

Examples of data quality tools include the following:

- **Data Flux:** Data Quality Workbench
- **Pine Cone Systems:** Content Tracker
- **Prism:** Quality Manager
- **Vality Technology:** Integrity Data Reengineering

11.5 DATA LOADERS

Data loaders load transformed data (i.e., load images) into the data warehouse. If load images are available on the same RDBMS engine as the warehouse, then stored procedures can be used to handle the warehouse loading.

If the load images do not have warehouse keys, then data loaders must generate the appropriate warehouse keys as part of the load process.

11.6 DATABASE MANAGEMENT SYSTEMS

A database management system is required to store the cleansed and integrated data for easy retrieval by business users. Two flavors of database management systems are currently popular: Relational Databases and Multidimensional Databases.

Relational Database Management Systems (RDBMS)

All major relational database vendors have already announced the availability or upcoming availability of data warehousing related features in their products. These features aim to make the respective RDBMSes particularly suitable to very large databases (VLDB) implementations. Examples of such features are bit-mapped indexes and parallel query capabilities.

Examples of these products include

- **IBM:** DB2
- **Informix:** Informix RDBMS
- **Microsoft:** SQL Server
- **Oracle:** Oracle RDBMS
- **Red Brick Systems:** Red Brick Warehouse
- **Sybase:** RDBMS Engine-System II

Multidimensional Databases (MDDBs)

Multidimensional database engines store data in hypercubes, i.e., pages of numbers that are paged in and out or memory on an as-needed basis, depending on the scope and type of query. This approach is in contrast to the use of tables and fields in relational databases.

Examples of these products include:

- **Arbor:** Essbase
- **BrioQuery:** Enterprise
- **Dimensional Insight:** DI-Diver
- **Oracle:** Express Server

Convergence of RDBMSes and MDDBs

Many relational database vendors have announced plants to integrate multidimensional capabilities into their RDBMSes. This integration will be achieved by caching SQL query results on a multidimensional hypercube on the database. Such Database OLAP technology (sometimes referred to as DOLAP) aims to provide warehousing teams with the best of both OLAP words.

11.7 METADATA REPOSITORY

Although there is a current lack of metadata repository standards, there is a consciousness that the metadata repository should support the documentation of source system data structures, transformation business rules, the extraction and transformation programs that move the data. And data structure definitions of the warehouse or data marts. In addition, the metadata repository should also support aggregate navigation, query statistic collection, and end-uses help for warehouse contents.

Metadata repository products are also referred to as information catalogs and business information directories. Examples of metadata repositories include.

- **Apertus Carleton:** Warehouse Control Center
- **Informatica:** Power Mart Repository
- **Intellidex:** Warehouse Control Center
- **Prism:** Prism Warehouse Directory

11.8 DATA ACCESS AND RETRIEVAL TOOLS

Data warehouse users derive and obtain information these types of tools. Data access and retrieval tools are currently classified into the subcategories below:

Online Analytical Processing (OLAP) Tools

OLAP tools allow users to make ad hoc queries or generate canned queries against the warehouse database. The OLAP category has since divided further into the multidimensional OLAP (MOLAP) and relational OLAP (ROLAP) markets.

MOLAP products run against a multidimensional database (MDDB). These products provide exceptional responses to queries and typically have additional functionality or features, such as budgeting and forecasting capabilities. Some of the tools also have built-in statistical functions. MOLAP tools are better suited to power users in the enterprise.

ROLAP products, in contrast, run directly against warehouses in relational databases (RDBMS). While the products provide slower response time than their MOLAP counterparts, ROLAP products are simpler and easier to use and are therefore suitable to the typical warehouse user. Also, since ROLAP products run directly against relational databases, they can be used directly with large enterprise warehouses.

Examples of OLAP tools include:

Arbor Software: Essbase OLAP

Cognos: Power play

Intranet Business Systems: R/olapXL

Reporting Tools

These tools allow users to produce canned, graphic-intensive, sophisticated reports based on the warehouse data. There are two main classifications of reporting tools: report writers and report servers.

Report writers allow users to create parameterized reports that can be run by users on an as needed basis. These typically require some initial programming to create the report template. Once the template has been defined, however, generating a report can be as easy as clicking a button or two.

Report servers are similar to report writers but have additional capabilities that allow their users to schedule when a report is to be run. This feature is in particularly helpful if the warehouse team prefers to schedule report generation processing during the night, after a successful warehouse load. By scheduling the report run for the evening, the warehouse team effectively removes some of the processing from the daytime, leaving the warehouse free for ad hoc queries from online users. Some report servers also come with automated report distribution capabilities. For example, a report server can e-mail a newly generated report to a specified user or generate a web page that users can access on the enterprise intranet. Report servers can also store copies of reports for easy retrieval by users over a network on an as-needed basis.

Examples of reporting tools include:

- **IQ Software:** IQ/Smart Server
- **Seagate Software:** Crystal Reports

Executive Information Systems (EIS)

EIS systems and other Decision Support Systems (DSS) are packaged applications that run against warehouse data. These provide different executive reporting features, including "what if" or scenario-based analysis capabilities and support for the enterprise budgeting process.

Examples of these tools include:

- **Comshare:** Decision
- **Oracle:** Oracle Financial Analyzer

While there are packages that provide decisional reporting capabilities, there are EIS and DSS development tools that enable the rapid development and maintenance of custom-made decisional systems.

Examples include.

- **Microstrategy:** DSS Executive
- **Oracle:** Express Objects

Data Mining

Data mining tools search for inconspicuous patterns in transaction-grained data to shed new light on the operations of the enterprise. Different data mining products support different data mining algorithms or techniques (e.g., marked basket analysis, clustering), and the selection of a data mining tool is often influenced by the number and type of algorithms supported.

Regardless of the mining techniques, however, the objective of these tools remain the same: crunching though large volumes of data to identify actionable patterns that would otherwise have remained undetected.

Data mining tools work best with transaction-grained data. For this reason, the deployment of data mining tools may result in a dramatic increase in warehouse size. Due to disk costs, the warehousing team may find itself having to make the painful compromise of storing transaction-grained data for only a subset of its customers. Other teams may compromise by storing transaction-grained data for a short time on a first-in-first-out basis (e.g., transaction for all customers, but for the last six months only).

One last important note about data mining: Since these tools infer relationships and patterns in warehouse data, a clean data warehouse will always produce better results than a dirty warehouse. Dirty data may mislead both the data mining tools and their users by producing erroneous conclusions.

Examples of data mining products include:

- **ANGOSS:** Knowledge STUDIO
- **Data Distilleries:** Data Surveyor
- **Hyper Parallel:** Discovery
- **IBM:** Intelligent Miner
- **Integral Solutions:** Clementine
- **Magnify:** Pattern
- **Neo Vista Software:** Decision Series
- **Syllogic:** Syllogic Data Mining Tool

Exception Reporting and Alert Systems

These systems highlight or call an end-user's attention to data of a set of conditions about data that are defined as exceptions. An enterprise typically implements three types of alerts.

- **Operational alerts from individual operational systems.** These have long been used in OLTP applications and are typically used to highlight exceptions relating to transactions in the operational system. However, these types of alerts are limited by the data scope of the OLTP application concerned.
- **Operational alerts from the operational data store.** These alerts require integrated operational data and therefore are possible only on the Operational Data Store. For example, a bank branch manager may wish to be alerted when a bank customer who has missed a loan payment has made a large withdrawal from his deposit account.
- **Decisional alerts from the data warehouse.** These alerts require comparisons with historical values and therefore are possible only on the data warehouse. For example, a sales manager may wish to be alerted when the sales for the current month are found to be at least 8 percent less than sales for the same month last year.

Products that can be used as exception reporting or alert systems include:

- **Compulogic:** Dynamic Query messenger
- **Pine cone systems:** Activator Module (Content Tracker)

Web-Enabled Products

Front-end tools belonging to the above categories gradually been adding web-publishing features. This development is spurred by the growing interest in intranet technology as a cost-effective alternative for sharing and delivering information within the enterprise.

11.9 DATA MODELING TOOLS

Data modeling tools allow users to prepare and maintain an information model of both the source database and the target database. Some of these tools also generate the data structures based on the models that are stored or are able to create models by reverse engineering with existing databases. IT organizations that have enterprise data models will quite likely have documented these models using a data modeling tool. While these tools are nice to have, they are not a prerequisite for a successful data warehouse project.

As an aside, some enterprises make the mistake of adding the enterprise data model to the list of data warehouse planning deliverables. While an enterprise data model is helpful to warehousing, particularly during the source system audit, it is definitely not a prerequisite of the warehousing project. Making the enterprise model a prerequisite of a deliverable of the project will only serve to divert the team's attention from building a warehouse to documenting what data currently exists.

Examples include:

- **Cayenne Software:** Terrain
- **Relational Matters:** Syntagma Designer
- **Sybase:** Power Designer Warehouse Architect

11.10 WAREHOUSE MANAGEMENT TOOLS

These tools assist warehouse administrators in the day-to-day management and administration of the warehouse. Different warehouse management tools support or automate aspects of the warehouse administration and management tasks.

For example, some tools focus on the load process and therefore track the load histories of the warehouse. Other tools track the types of queries that users direct to the warehouse and identify which data are not and therefore are candidates for removal.

Examples include.

- **Pine Cone Systems:** Usage Tracker, Refreshment Tracker
- **Red Brick Systems:** Enterprise Control and Coordination

11.11 SOURCE SYSTEMS

Data warehouses would not be possible without source systems, i.e., the operational systems of the enterprise that serve as the primary source of warehouse data. Although strictly speaking, the source systems are not data warehousing software products, they do influence the selection of these tools or products.

The computing environments of the source systems generally determine the complexity of extracting operational data. As can be expected, heterogeneous computing environments increase the difficulties that a data warehouse team may encounter with data extraction and transformation.

Application packages (e.g., integrated banking or integrated manufacturing and distribution systems) with proprietary database structures will also pose data access problems.

External data sources may also be used. Examples include Bloomberg News, Lundberg, A.C. Nielsen, Dun and Bradstreet, Mail code or Zip code data, Dow Jones news service, Lexis, New York Times Services, and Nexis.

In Summary

Quite a number of technology vendors are supplying warehousing products in more than one category and a clear trend towards the integration of different warehousing products is evidenced by efforts to share metadata across different products and by the many partnerships and alliances formed between warehousing vendors.

Despite this, there is still no clear market leader for an integrated suite of data warehousing products. Warehousing teams are still forced to take on the responsibility of integrating disparate products, tools, and environments or to rely on the services of a solution integrator. Until this situation changes, enterprises should carefully evaluate the form of the tools they eventually select for different aspects of their warehousing initiative. The integration problems posed by the source system data are difficult enough without adding tool integration problems to the project.

CHAPTER 12

WAREHOUSE SCHEMA DESIGN

Dimensional modeling is a term used to refer to a set of data modeling techniques that have gained popularity and acceptance for data warehouse implementations. The acknowledged guru of dimensional modeling is Ralph Kimball, and the most thorough literature currently available on dimensional modeling is his book entitled 'The Data Warehouse, Toolkit. Practical Techniques for Building Dimensional Data Warehouses', published by John Wiley & Sons (ISBN: 0-471-15337-0).

This chapter introduces dimensional modeling as one of the key techniques in data warehousing and is not intended as a replacement for Ralph Kimball's book.

12.1 OLTP SYSTEMS USE NORMALIZED DATA STRUCTURES

Most IT professionals are quite familiar with normalized database structures, since normalization is the standard database design technique for the relational database of Online Transactional Processing (OLTP) systems. Normalized database structures make it possible for operational systems to consistently record hundreds of discrete, individual transactions, with minimal risk of data loss or data error.

Although normalized databases are appropriate for OLTP systems, they quickly create problems when used with decisional systems.

Users Find Normalized Data Structures to Understand

Any IT professional who has asked a business user to review a fully normalized entity relationship diagram has first-hand experience of the problem. Normalized data structures simply do not map to the natural thinking processes of business users. It is unrealistic to expect business users to navigate through such data structures.

If business users are expected to perform queries against the warehouse database on an ad hoc basis and if IT professionals want to remove themselves from the report-creation loop, then users must be provided with data structures that are simple and easy to understand. Normalized data structures do not provide the required level of simplicity and friendliness.

Normalized Data Structures Require Knowledge of SQL

To create even the most basic of queries and reports against a normalized data structure, one requires knowledge of SQL (Structured Query Language) - something that should not be expected of business users, especially decision-makers. Senior executives should not have to learn how to write programming code, and even if they knew how, their time is better spent on non-programming activities.

Unsurprisingly, the use of normalized data structures results in many hours of IT resources devoted to writing reports for operational and decisional managers.

Normalized Data Structures are not Optimized to Support Decisional Queries

By their very nature, decisional queries require the summation of hundreds to thousands of figures stored in perhaps many rows in the database. Such processing on a fully normalized data structure is slow and cumbersome. Consider the sample data structure in Figure 12.1.

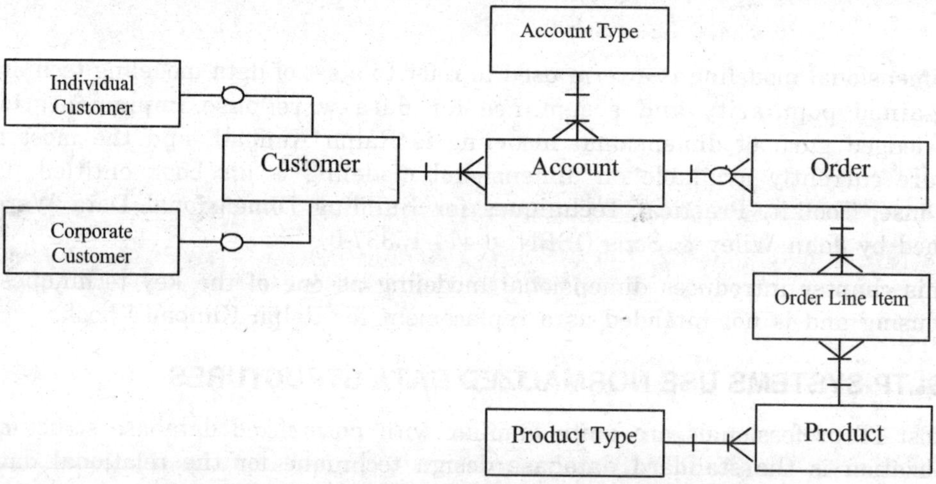

Figure 12.1. Example of a Normalized Data Structure

If a business manager requires a Product Sales per Customer report (see Figure 12.2), the program code must access the Customer, Account, Account Type, Order Line Item, and Product Tables to compute the totals. The WHERE clause of the SWL statement will be straightforward but long; records of the different tables have to be related to one another to produce the correct result.

PRODUCT SALES PER CUSTOMER, Data : March 6, 1998

Customer	Product Name	Sales Amount
Customer A	Product X	1,000
	Product Y	10,000
Customer B	Product X	8,000
.....	....	....

Figure 12.2. Product Sales per Customer Sample Report.

12.2 DIMENSIONAL MODELING FOR DECISIONAL SYSTEMS

Dimensional modeling provides a number of techniques or principles for denormalizing the database structure to create schemas that are suitable for supporting decisional processing. These modeling principles are discussed in the following sections.

Two Types of Tables : Facts and Dimensions

Two types of tables are used in dimensional modeling: Fact tables and Dimensional tables.

Fact Tables

Fact tables are used to record actual facts or measures in the business. Facts are the numeric data items that are of interest to the business.

Below are examples of facts for different industries

- **Retail.** Number of units sold, sales amount
- **Telecommunications.** Length of call in minutes, average number of calls.
- **Banking.** Average daily balance, transaction amount
- **Insurance.** Claims amounts
- **Airline.** Ticket cost, baggage weight

Facts are the numbers that users analyze and summarize to gain a better understanding of the business.

Dimension Tables

Dimension tables, on the other hand, establish the context of the facts. Dimensional tables store fields that describe the facts.

Below are examples of dimensions for the same industries :

- **Retail.** Store name, store zip, product name, product category, day of week.
- **Telecommunications.** Call origin, call destination.
- **Banking.** Customer name, account number, data, branch, account officer.
- **Insurance.** Policy type, insured policy
- **Airline.** Flight number, flight destination, airfare class.

Facts and Dimensions in Reports

When a manager requires a report showing the revenue for Store X, at Month Y, for Product Z, the manager issuing the Store dimension, the Time dimension, and the Product dimension to describe the context of the revenue (fact).

Thus for the sample report in Figure 12.3, sales region and country are dimensional attributes, "2Q, 1997" is a dimensional value. These data items establish the context and lend meaning to the facts in the report-sales targets and sales actual.

For 2Q, 1997

Sales Region	Country	Target (in '000s)	Actuals (in '000s)
Asia	Philippines	14,000	15,050
	Hong Kong	10,000	10,500
Europe	France	4,000	4,050
	Italy	6,000	8,150
North America	United States	1,000	1,500
	Canada	**7,000**	**500**
Africa	Egypt	5,600	6,200

Figure 12.3. Second Quarter Sales Sample Report

12.3 STAR SCHEMA

The multidimensional view of data that is expressed using relational database semantics is provided by the database schema design called start schema. The basic premise of star schemas is that information can be classified into two groups; facts and dimensions. Facts are the core data element being analyzed. For example, units of individual items sold are facts, while dimensions are attributes about the facts. For example, dimensions are the product types purchased and the date of purchase.

Visually, a dimensional schema looks very much like a star, hence the use of the term star schema to describe dimensional models. Fact tables reside at the center of the schema, and their dimensions are typically drawn around it, as shown in Figure 12.4.

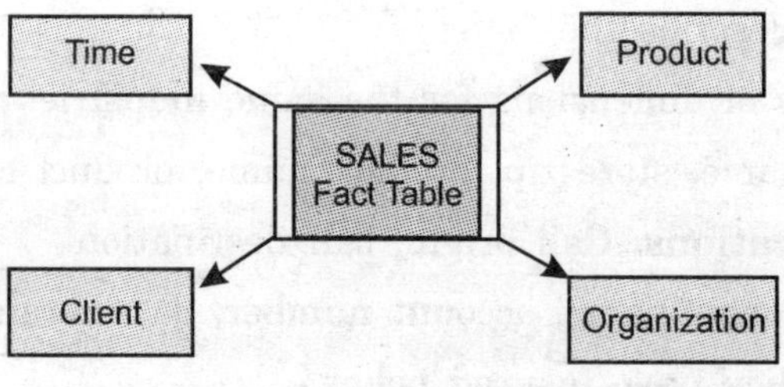

Figure 12.4. Dimensional Star Scheme Example

In Figure 12.4, the dimensions are Client, Time, Product and Organization. The fields in these tables are used to describe the facts in the sales fact table.

Facts are Fully Normalized, Dimensions are Denormalized

One of the key principles of dimensional modeling is the use of fully normalized Fact tables together with fully denormalized Dimension tables. Unlike dimensional schemas, a fully normalized database schema no doubt would implement some of these dimensions as many logical (and physical) tables.

In Figure 12.4 note that because the Dimension tables are denormalized, the schema shows no outlying tables beyond the four dimensional tables. A Fully normalized product dimension, in contrast, may have the additional tables shown in Figure 12.5.

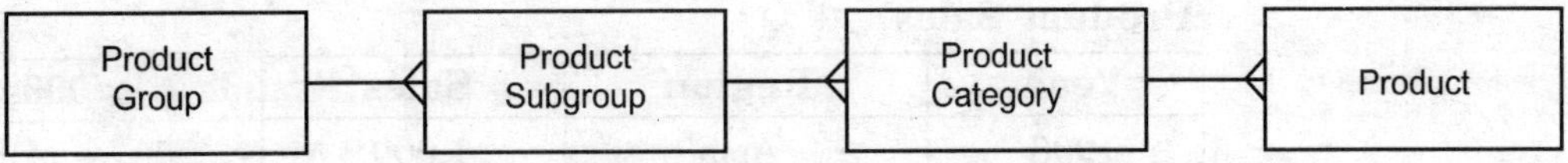

Figure 12.5. Normalized Product Tables

It is the use of these additional normalized tables that decreases the friendliness and navigability of the schema. By denormalizing the dimensions, one makes available to the user all relevant attributes in one table.

12.4 DIMENSIONAL HIERARCHIES AND HIERARCHICAL DRILLING

As a result of denormalization of the dimensions, each dimension will quite likely have hierarchies that imply the grouping and structure.

The easiest example can be found in the Time dimension. As shown in Figure 12.6, the Time dimension has a Day-Month-Quarter-Year hierarchy. Similarly, the Store dimension may have a City-Country-Region-All stores hierarchy. The Product dimension may have a Product-Product category-Product Department-All Products hierarchy.

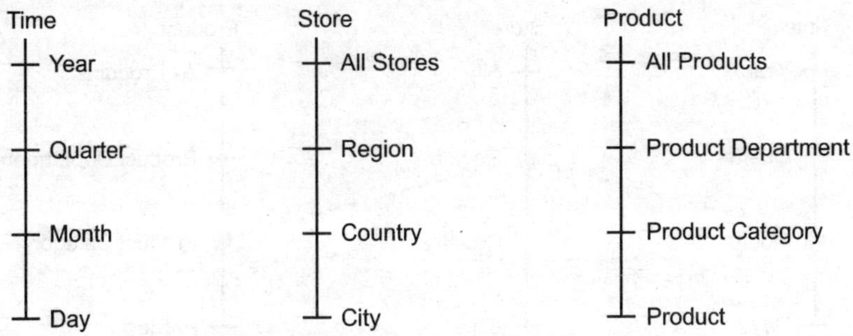

Figure 12.6. Dimensional Hierarchies

When warehouse users drill up and down for detail, they typically drill up and down these dimensional hierarchies to obtain more or less detail, about the business.

For example, a user may initially have a sales report showing the total sales for all regions for the year. Figure 12.7 relates the hierarchies to the sales report.

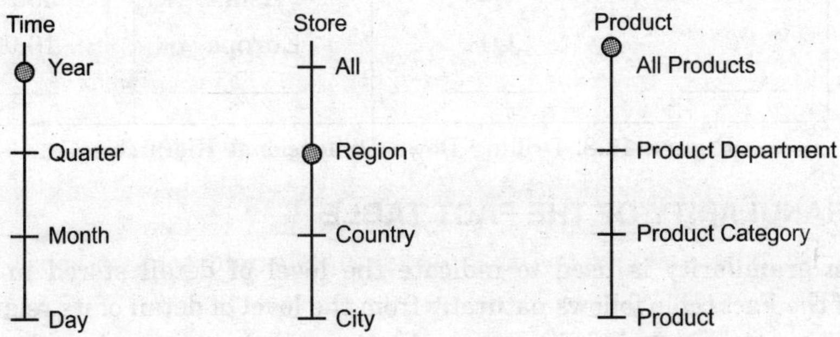

Product Sales

Year	Region	Sales
1996	Asia	1,000
	Europe	50,000
	America	20,000
1997	Asia	1,5000
	______	______

Figure 12.7. Dimensional Hierarchies and the Corresponding Report Sample

For such a report, the business user is at (1) the Year level of the Tim hierarchy; (2) the Region level of the Store hierarchy; and (3) the All Products level of the Product hierarchy.

A drill-down along any of the dimensions can be achieved either by adding a new column or by replacing an existing column in the report. For example, drilling down the Time dimension can be achieved by adding Quarter as a second column in the report, as shown in Figure 12.8.

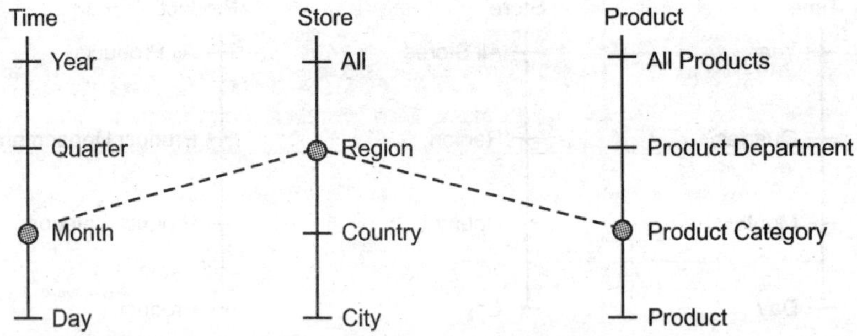

Product Sales

Year	Quarter	Region	Sales
1996	Q1	Asia	200
	Q2	Asia	200
	Q3	Asia	250
	Q4	Asia	350
	Q1	Europe	10,000
______	______	______	______

Figure 12.8. Drilling Down Dimensional Hierarchies

12.5 THE GRANULARITY OF THE FACT TABLE

The term granularity is used to indicate the level of detail stored in the table. The granularity of the Fact table follows naturally from the level of detail of its related dimensions.

For example, if each Time record represents a day, each Product record represents a product, and each Organization record represents one branch, then the grain of a sales Fact table with these dimensions would likely be; sales per product per day per branch.

Proper identification of the granularity of each schema is crucial to the usefulness and cost of the warehouse. Granularity at too high a level severely limits the ability of users to obtain additional detail. For example, if each time record represented an entire year, there will be one sales fact record for each year, and it would not be possible to obtain sales figures on a monthly or daily basis.

In contrast, granularity at too low a level results in an exponential increase in the size requirements of the warehouse. For example, if each time record represented an hour, there will be one sales fact record for each hour of the day (or 8,760 sales fact records for a year with 365 days for each combination of Product, Client, and Organization). If daily sales facts are all that are required, the number of records in the database can be reduced dramatically.

The Fact Table Key Concatenates Dimension Keys

Since the granularity of the fact table determines the level of detail of the dimensions that surround it, it follows that the key of the fact table is actually a concatenation of the keys of each of its dimensions.

Table 12.1. Properties of Fact and Dimension Tables

Property	*Client Table*	*Product Table*	*Time Table*	*Sales Table*
Table Type	Dimension	Dimension	Dimension	Fact
One Record is	One Client	One Product	One Day	Sales per Client per Product per Day
Key	Client Key	Product Key	Time Key	Clint Key + Product Key + Time Key
Sample Fields or Attributes	First Name Last Name Gender City Weight Country	Product Name Color Size Product Class Product Group	Date Month Year Day of Month Day of Week Week Number Weekday Flag Holiday Flag	Amount Sold Quantity Sold

Thus, if the granularity of the sales schema is sale per client per product per day, the sales fact table key is actually the concatenation of the client key, the product key and the time key (Day), as presented in Table 12.1.

12.6 AGGREGATES OR SUMMARIES

Aggregates or Summaries are one of the most powerful concepts in data warehousing. The proper use of aggregates dramatically improves the performance of the data warehouse in terms of query response times, and therefore improves the overall performance and usability of the warehouse.

Computation of Aggregates is Based on Base-Level Schemas

An aggregate is a pre calculated summary stored within the warehouse, usually in a separate schema. Aggregates are typically computed based on records at the most detailed (or base) level (see Figure 12.9). They are used to improve the performance of the warehouse for those queries that require only high-level or summarized data.

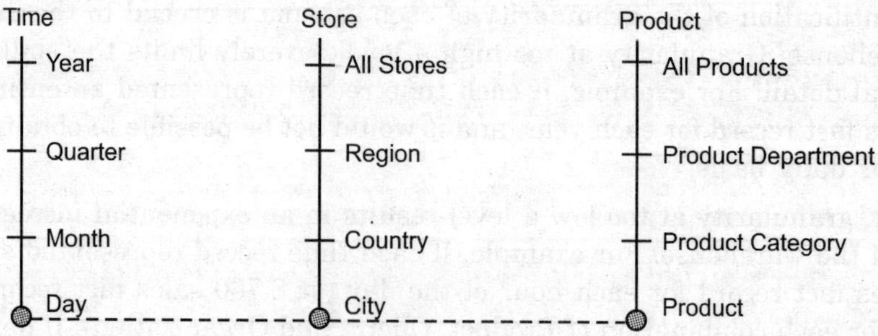

Figure 12.9 Base-Level Schemes Use the Bottom Level of Dimensional Hierarchies

Aggregates are merely summaries of the base-level data higher points along the dimensional hierarchies, as illustrated in Figure 12-10.

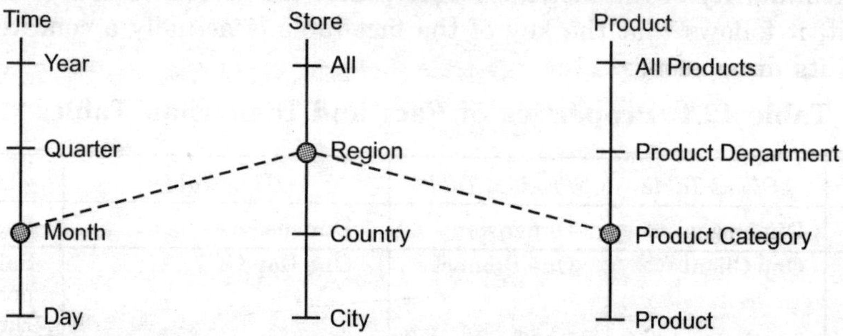

Figure 12.10 Aggregate Schemes are higher along the Dimensional Hierarchies

Rather than running a high-level query against base-level or detailed data, users can run the query against aggregated data. Aggregates provide dramatic improvements in performance because of significantly smaller number of records.

Aggregates have Fewer Records than Do Base-Level Schemas

Consider the schema in Figure 12.11 with the following charactéristics

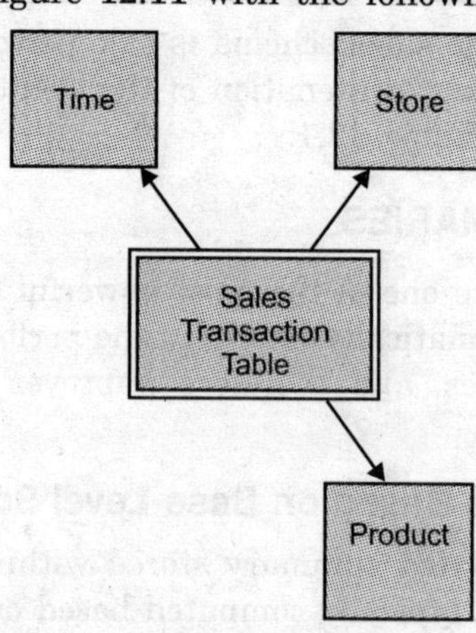

Figure 12.11. Sample Schema

With the assumptions outlined above, it is possible to compute the number of fact records required for different types of queries.

If a Query Involves...	Then it Must Retrieve or Summarize
1 Product, 1 Store, and 1 Week	Only 1 record from the Schema
1 Product, All Stores, 1 Week	10 records from the Schema
1 Brand, 1 Store, 1 Week	100 records from the Schema
1 Brand, All Store, 1 Year	52,000 records from the Schema

If aggregates had been pre-calculated and stored so that each aggregate record provides facts for a brand per store per week, the third query above (1 Brand, 1 Store, 1 Week) would require only 1 record, instead of 100 records. Similarly, the fourth query above (1 Brand, All Stores, 1 Year) would require only 520 records instead of 52,000. The resulting improvements in query response times are obvious.

12.7 DIMENSIONAL ATTRIBUTES

Dimensional attributes play a very critical role in dimensional star schemas. The attribute values are used to establish the context of the facts.

For example, a fact table record may have the following keys: Date, Store, ID, Product ID (with the corresponding Time Store, and Product dimensions). If the key fields have the values "February 16.1998, "101," and "ABC" respectively, then the dimensional attributes in the Time, Store, and Product dimensions can be used to establish the context of the facts in the Fact Record as follows.

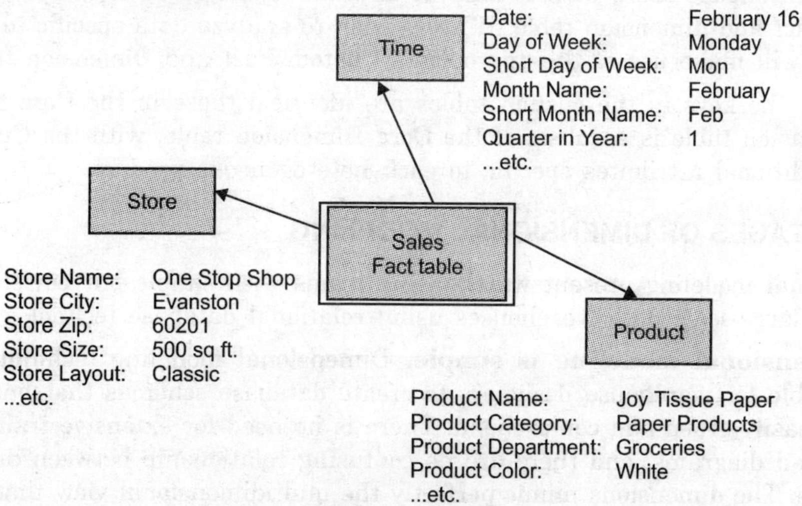

Figure 12.12. For an Example

Form Figure 12.12, it can be quickly understood that one of the sales records in the Fact table refers to the sale of Joy Tissue Paper at the One Stop Shop on the day of February 16.

12.8 MULTIPLE STAR SCHEMAS

A data warehouse will most likely have multiple star schemas, i.e. many Fact tables. Each schema is designed to meet a specific set of information needs. Multiple schemas, each focusing on a different aspect of the business, are natural in a dimensional warehouse.

Equally normal is the use of the same Dimension table in more than one schema. The classic example of this is the Time dimension. The enterprises can reuse the Time dimension in all warehouse schemas, provided that the level of detail is appropriate.

For example, a retail company that has one star schema to track profitability per store may make use of the same Time dimension table in the star schema that tracks profitability by product.

Core and Custom Tables

There are many instances when distinct products within the enterprise are similar enough that these can share the same data structure in the warehouse. For example, banks that offer both current accounts and savings accounts will treat these two types of products differently, but the facts that are stored are fairly similar and can share the same data structure.

Unfortunately, there are also many instances when different products will have different characteristics and different interesting facts. Still within the banking example, a credit card product will have facts that are quite different from the current account or savings account. In this scenario, the bank has heterogeneous products that require the use of Core and Custom tables in the warehouse schema design.

Core Fact and Dimension tables store facts that are common to all types of products, and Custom Fact and Dimension tables store facts that are specific to each distinct heterogeneous product.

Thus, if warehouse users wish to analyze data across all products, they will make use of the Core Fact and dimension table. If users wish to analyze data specific to one type of product, they will make use of the appropriate Custom Fact and Dimension tables.

Note that the keys in the custom tables are identical those in the Core tables. Each Custom Dimension table is a subset of the Core Dimension table, with the Custom tables containing additional attributes specific to each heterogeneous product.

12.9 ADVANTAGES OF DIMENSIONAL MODELING

Dimensional modeling present warehousing teams with simple but powerful concepts for designing large-scale data warehouses using relational database technology.

- **Dimensional modeling is simple.** Dimensional modeling techniques make it possible for warehouse designers to create database schemas that business users can easily grasp and comprehend. There is no need for extensive training on how to read diagrams, and there are no confusing relationship between different data items. The dimensions mimic perfectly the multidimensional view that users have of the business.
- **Dimensional modeling promotes data quality.** By its very nature, the star schema allows warehouse administrators to enforce referential integrity checks on the warehouse. Since the fact record key is a concatenation of the keys of its related dimensions, a fact record is successfully loaded only if the corresponding dimensions records are duly defined and also exist in the database.

  By enforcing foreign key constraints as a form of referential integrity check, warehouse DBAs add a line of defense against corrupted warehouse data.

- **Performance optimization is possible through aggregates.** As the size of the warehouse increases, performance optimization becomes a pressing concern. Users who have to wait hours to get a response to a query will quickly become discouraged with the warehouse. Aggregates are one of the most manageable ways by which query performance can be optimized.
- **Dimensional modeling makes use of relational database technology.** With dimensional modeling, business users are able to work with multidimensional views without having to use multidimensional database (MDDB) structures: Although MDDBs are useful and have their place in the warehousing architecture, they have severe size limitations.

  Dimensional modeling allows IT professionals to rely on highly scalable relational database technology of their large-scale warehousing implementation, without compromising on the usability of the warehouse schema.

In Summary

Dimensional modeling provides a number of techniques or principles for denormalizing the database structure to create schemas that are suitable for supporting decisional processing.

The multidimensional view of data that is expressed using relational database semantics is provided by the database schema design called star schema. The basic premise of star schemas is that information can be classified into two groups: facts and dimensions, in which the fully normalized fact table resides at the center of the star schema and is surrounded by fully denormalized dimensional tables and the key of the fact table is actually a concatenation of the keys of each of its dimensions.

CHAPTER 13

WAREHOUSE METADATA

Metadata, or the information about the enterprise data, is emerging as a critical element in effective data management, especially in the data warehousing arena. Vendors as well as users have began to appreciate the value of metadata. At the same time, the rapid proliferation of data manipulation and management tools has resulted in almost as many different "flavors" and treatments of metadata as there are tools.

Thus, this chapter discusses metadata as one of the most important components of a data warehouse, as well as the infrastructure that enables its storage, management, and integration with other components of a data warehouse. This infrastructure is known as metadata repository, and it is discussed in the examples of several repository implementations, including the repository products from Platinum Technologies, Prism Solution, and R&O.

13.1 METADATA DEFINED

Metadata is one of the most important aspects of data warehousing. It is data about data stored in the warehouse and its users. At a minimum, metadata contains

- The location and description of warehouse system and data components (warehouse objects).
- Names, definition, structure, and content of the data warehouse and end-user views.
- Identification of authoritative data sources (systems of record).
- Integration and transformation rules used to populate the data warehouse these include the mapping method from operational databases into the warehouse, and algorithms used to convert, enhance, or transform data.
- Integration and transformation rules used to deliver data to end-user analytical tools.
- Subscription information for the information delivery to the analysis subscribers
- Data warehouse operational information, which includes a history of warehouse updates, refreshments, snapshots, versions, ownership authorizations, and extract audit trail.

- Metrics used to analyze warehouse usage and performance vis-à-vis end-user usage patterns.
- Security authorizations, access control lists, etc.

13.2 METADATA ARE A FORM OF ABSTRACTION

It is fairly easy to apply abstraction on concrete, tangible items. Information technology professionals do this all the time when they design operational systems. A concrete product is abstracted and described by its properties (i.e., data attributes) - for example, name, color, weight, size, price. A person can also be abstracted and described through his name, age, gender, occupation, etc.

Abstraction complexity increases when the item that is abstracted is not as concrete; however, such abstraction is till routinely performed in operational systems. For example, a banking transaction can be described by the transaction amount, transaction currency, transaction type (e.g., withdrawal) and the date and time when the transaction took place.

Figure 13.1 and Figure 13.2 present two metadata examples for data warehouses; the first example provides sample metadata for warehouse fields. The second provides sample metadata for warehouse dimensions. These metadata are supported by the Warehouse-Designer software product that accompanies this book.

Metada Example for Warehouse Fields

- **Field Name.** The name of the field, as it will be used in the physical table.
- **Caption.** The name of the field, as it should appear to users.
- **Data Type.** The appropriate data type for the field, as supported by the target RDBMS.
- **Index Type.** The type of index to be used on this attribute.
- **Key?** Whether this is a Key field in the Dimension table.
- **Format.** The format of this field.
- **Description.** A description or definition of this field.

Figure 13.1. Metadata Example for Warehouse Fields

In data warehousing, abstraction is applied to the data sources, extraction and transformation rules and programs, data structure, and contents of the data warehouse itself. Since the data warehouse is a repository of data, the results of such an abstraction the metadata can be described as "data about data".

Metada Example for Warehouse Dimension Table

- **Name.** The physical table name to be used in the database.
- **Caption.** The business or logical name of the dimension; used by warehouse users to refer to the dimension.
- **Description.** The standard definition of the dimension.
- **Usage Type.** Indicates if a warehouse object is used as a fact or as a fact or as a dimension.
- **Key Option.** Indicates how keys are to be managed for this dimension. Valid values are Overwrite, Generate New Delhi, and Create Version.
- **Source.** Indicates the primary data source for this dimension. This field is provided for documentation purpose only.
- **Online?** Indicates whether the physical table is actually populated correctly and is available for use by the users of the data warehouse.

Figure 13.2. Metadata Example for Warehouse Dimensions

13.3 IMPORTANCE OF METADATA

Metadata are important to a data warehouse for several reasons. To explain why, we examine the different uses of metadata.

Metadata Establish the Context of the Warehouse Data

Metadata help warehouse administrators and users located and understand data items, both in the source systems and in the warehouse data structures. For example, the data value 02/05/1998 may mean different dates depending on the date convention used. The same set of numbers can be interpreted as February 5, 1998 or as May 2, 1998. If metadata describing the format of this data field were available, the definite and unambiguous meaning of the data item could be easily determined.

In operational systems, software developers and database administrators deal with metadata every day. All technical documentation of source systems are metadata in one form or another. Metadata, however, remain for the most part transparent to the end users of operational systems. They perceive the operational system as a black box and interact only with the user interface.

This practice is in direct contrast to data warehousing, where the users of decisional systems actively browse through the contents of the data warehouse and must first understand the warehouse contents before they can make effective use of the data.

Metadata Facilitate the Analysis Process

Consider the typical process that business analysis follow as part of their work. Enterprise analysis must go through the process of locating data, retrieving data, interpreting and analyzing data to yield information, presenting the information, and then recommending courses of action.

To make the data warehouse useful to enterprise analysis, the metadata must provide warehouse end users with the information they need to easily perform the analysis steps. Thus, metadata should allow users to quickly locate data that are in the warehouse. The metadata should also allow analysts to interpret data correctly by providing information about data formats (as in the above data example) and data definitions.

As a concrete example, when a data item in the warehouse Fact table is labeled "Profit" the user should be able to consult the warehouse metadata to learn how the Profit data item is computed.

Metadata are a Form of Audit Trail for Data Transformation

Metadata document the transformation of source data into warehouse data. Warehouse metadata must be able to explain how a particular piece of warehouse data was derived from the operational systems. All business rules that govern the transformation of data to new values of new formats are also documented as metadata.

This form of audit trail is required if users are to gain confidence in the veracity and quality of warehouse data. It is also essential to the user's understanding of warehouse data to know where they came from.

In addition, some warehousing products use this type of metadata to generate extraction and transformation scripts for use on the warehouse back-end.

Metadata Improve or Maintain Data Quality

Metadata can improve or maintain warehouse data quality through the definition of valid values for individual warehouse data items. Prior to actual loading into the warehouse, the warehouse load images can be reviewed by a data quality tool to check for compliance with valid values for key data items. Data errors are quickly highlighted for correction.

Metadata can even be used, as the basis for any error-correction processing that should be done if a data error is found. Error-correction rules are documented in the metadata repository and executed by program code on an as needed basis.

13.4 TYPES OF METADATA

Although there are still ongoing discussions and debates regarding standards for metadata repositories, it is generally agreed that metadata repository must consider the metadata types described in the next subsections.

Administrative Metadata

Administrative metadata contain descriptions of the source database and their contents, the data warehouse objects and the business rules used to transform data from the sources into the data warehouse.

- **Data sources.** These are descriptions of all data sources used by the warehouse, including information about the data ownership. Each record and each data item is defined to ensure a uniform understanding by all warehousing team members and warehouse users. Any relationships between different data sources (e.g., one provides data to another) are also documented.
- **Source-to-target field mapping.** The mapping of source fields (in operational systems) to target field (in the data warehouse) explains what fields are used to

populate the data warehouse. It also documents the transformations and formatting changes that were applied to the original, raw data to derive the warehouse data.

- **Warehouse schema design.** This model of the data warehouse describes the warehouses servers, databases, database tables, fields, and any hierarchies that may exist in the data. All referential tables, system codes, etc., are also documented.
- **Warehouse back-end data structure.** This is a model of the back-end of the warehouse, including staging tables, load image tables, and nay other temporary data structures that are used during the data transformation process.
- **Warehouse back-end tools or programs.** A definition of each extraction, transformation, and quality assurance program or tool that is used to build or refresh the data warehouse. This definition includes how often the programs are run, in what sequence, what parameters are expected, and the actual source code of the programs (if applicable). If these programs are generated, the name of the tool and the data and time when the programs were generated should also be included.
- **Warehouses architecture.** If the warehouse architecture is one where an enterprise warehouse feeds many departmental or vertical data marts, the warehouses architecture should be documented as well. If the data mart contains a logical subset of the warehouse contents, this subset should also be defined.
- **Business rules and policies.** All applicable business rules and policies are documented. Examples include business formulas for computing costs or profits.
- **Access and security rules.** Rules governing the security and access rights of users should likewise be defined.
- **Units of measure.** All units of measurement and conversion rates used between different units should also be documented. Especially if conversion formulas and rates change over time.

End-user Metadata

End-user metadata help users create their queries and interpret the results. Users may also need to know the definitions of the warehouse data, their descriptions, and any hierarchies that may exist within the various dimensions.

- **Warehouses contents.** Metadata–must described the data structure and contents of the data warehouse in user-friendly terms. The volume of data in various schemas should likewise be presented. Any aliases that are used for data items, are documented as well. Rules used to create summaries and other pre-computed total are also documented.
- **Predefined queries and reports.** Queries and reports that have been predefined and that are readily available to users should be documented to avoid duplication of effort. If a report server is used, the schedule for generating new reports should be made known.
- **Business rules and policies.** All business rules applicable to the warehouse data should be documented in business terms. Any changes to business rules over time should also be documented in the same manner.

- **Hierarchy definitions.** Descriptions of the hierarchies in warehouse dimensions are also documented in end-user metadata. Hierarchy definitions are particularly important to support drilling up and down warehouses dimensions.
- **Status information.** Different rollouts of the data warehouse will be in different stages of development. Status information is required to inform warehouse users of the warehouse status at any point in time. Status information may also vary at the table level. For example, the base-level schemas of the warehouse may already be available and online to users while the aggregates are being computed.
- **Data quality.** Any known data quality problems in the warehouse should be clearly documented for the users. This will prompt users to make careful use of warehouse data.
- A history of all warehouse loads, including data volume, data errors encountered, and load time frame. This should be synchronized with the warehouse status information. The load schedule should also be available—users need to know when new data will be available.
- **Warehouse purging rules.** The rules that determine when data is removed from the warehouse should also be published for the benefit of warehouse end-users. Users need this information to understand when data will become unavailable.

Optimization Metadata

Metadata are maintained to aid in the optimization of the data warehouse design and performance. Examples of such metadata include:

- **Aggregate definitions.** All warehouse aggregates should also be documented in the metadata repository. Warehouse front-end tools with aggregate navigation capabilities rely on this type of metadata to work properly.
- **Collection of query statistics.** It is helpful to track the types of queries that are made against the warehouse. This information serves as an input to the warehouse administrator for database optimization and tuning. It also helps to identify warehouse data that are largely unused.

13.5 METADATA MANAGEMENT

A frequently occurring problem in data warehousing is the inability to communicate to the end user what information resides in the data warehouse and how it can be accessed. The key to providing users and applications with a roadmap to the information stored in the warehouse is the metadata. It can define all data elements and their attributes, data sources and timing, and the rules that govern data use and data transformations. Metadata needs to be collected as the warehouse is designed and built. Since metadata describes the information in the warehouse from multiple viewpoints (input, sources, transformation, access, etc.), it is imperative that the same metadata or its consistent replicas be available to all tools selected for the warehouse implementation, thus enforcing the integrity and accuracy of the warehouse information. The metadata also has to be available to all warehouse users in order to guide them as they use the warehouse. Even though there are a number of tools available to help users understand and use the warehouse, these tools need to be carefully evaluated before any purchasing decision is made. In other words, a well-thought-through strategy for collecting, maintaining, and distributing metadata is needed for a successful data warehouse implementation.

13.6 METADATA AS THE BASIS FOR AUTOMATING WAREHOUSING TASKS

Although metadata have traditionally been used as a form of after-the-fact documentation, there is a clear trend in data warehousing toward metadata taking on a more active role. Almost all the major data warehouse products or tools allow their users to record and maintain metadata about the warehouse, and make use of the metadata as a basis for automating one or more aspects of the back-end warehouse process.

For example:

- **Extraction and transformation.** Users of extraction and transformation tools can specify source-to-target field mappings and enter all business rules that govern the transformation of data from the source to the target. The mapping (which is a form of metadata) serves as the basis for generating scripts that automate the extraction and transformation process.
- **Data quality.** Users of data quality tools can specify valid values for different data items in either the source system, load image, or the warehouse itself. These data quality tools use such metadata as the basis for identifying and correcting data errors.
- **Schema generation.** Similarly, users of Warehouse Designer use the tool to record metadata relating to the data structure of a dimensional data warehouse or data mart into the tool. Warehouse Designer then uses the metadata as the basis for generating the SQL Data Definition Language (DDL) statements that create data warehouse tables, fields, indexes, aggregates, etc.
- **Front-end tools.** Front-end tools also make use of metadata to gain access to the warehouse database. R/OLAPXL (the ROLAP front-end tool) makes use of metadata to display warehouse tables and fields and to redirect queries to summary tables (i.e., aggregate navigation).

13.7 METADATA TRENDS

One of the clearly observable trends in the data warehouse arena is the increase in requirements to incorporate external data within the data warehouse. This is necessary in order to reduce costs and to increase competitiveness and business ability. However, the process of integrating external and internal data into the warehouse faces a number of challenges:

- Inconsistent data formats
- Missing or invalid data
- Different levels of aggregation
- Semantic inconsistency (e.g., different codes may mean different things from different suppliers of data).
- Unknown or questiohable data quality and timeliness

All these issues put an additional burden on the collection and management of the common metadata definitions. Some of this burden is being addressed by standards initiatives like Metadata Coalition's Metadata Interchange Specification, described in Sec. 11.2. But even with the standards in place, the metadata repository implementations will have to be sufficiently robust and flexible to rapidly adopt to handling a new data source, to be able to overcome the semantic differences as well as potential differences in low-level data formats, media types, and communication protocols, to name just a few.

Moreover, as data warehouses are beginning to integrate various data types in addition to traditional alphanumeric data types, the metadata and its repository should be able to handle the new enriched data content as easily as the simple data types before. For example, including text, voice, image, full-motion video, and even Web pages in HTML format into the data warehouse may require a new way of presenting and managing the information about these new data types. But the rich data types mentioned above are not limited to just these new media types. Many organizations are beginning to seriously consider storing, navigating, and otherwise managing data describing the organizational structures. This is especially true when we look at data warehouses dealing with human resources on a large scale (e.g., the entire organization, or an entity like a state, or a whole country). And of course, we can always further complicate the issue by adding time and space dimensions to the data warehouse. Storing and managing temporal and spatial data and data about it is a new challenge for metadata tool vendors and standard bodies alike.

In Summary

Although quite a lot has been written or said about the importance of metadata, there is yet to be a consistent and reliable implementation of warehouse metadata and metadata repositories on an industry-wide scale.

To Address this industry-wide issue, an organization called the Meta Data Coalition was formed to define and support the ongoing evolution of a metadata interchange format. The coalition has released a metadata interchange specification that aims to be the standard for sharing metadata among different types of products. At least 30 warehousing vendors are currently members of this organization.

Until a clear metadata standard is established, enterprises have no choice but to identify the type of metadata required by their respective warehouse initiatives, then acquire the necessary tools to support their metadata requirements.

CHAPTER 14

WAREHOUSING APPLICATIONS

The successful implementation of data warehousing technologies creates new possibilities for enterprises. Applications that previously were not feasible due to the lack of integrated data are now possible. In this chapter, we take a quick look at the different types of enterprises that implement data warehouses and the types of applications that they have deployed.

14.1 THE EARLY ADOPTERS

Among the early adopters of warehousing technologies were the telecommunications, banking, and retail sectors.

Thus, most early warehousing applications can be found in these industries. For example,

- **Telecommunication :** Companies were interested in analyzing (among other things) network utilization, the calling patterns of their clients, and the profitability of their product offerings. Such information was and still is required for formulating, modifying,. and offering different subscription packages with special rates and incentives to different customers.
- **Banks :** Were and still are interested in effectively managing the bank's asset and liability portfolios, analyzing product and customer profitability, and profiling customers and customer profitability, and profiling customers and households as a means of identifying target marketing and cross-selling opportunities.
- **Retail:** The retail sector was interested in sales trends, particularly buying patterns that are influenced by changing seasons, sales promotions, holidays, and competitor activities. With the introduction of customer discount cards, the retail sector was able to attribute previously anonymous purchases to individual customers. Individual buying habits and likes are now used as inputs to formulating sales promotions and guiding direct marketing activities.

14.2 TYPES OF WAREHOUSING APPLICATIONS

Although warehousing found it early use in different industries with different information requirements, it is still possible to categorize the different warehousing applications into the following types and tasks:

Sales and Marketing

- **Performance trend analysis.** Since a data warehouse is designed to store historical data, it is an ideal technology for analyzing performance trends within an organization. Warehouse users can produce reports that compare current performance to historical figures. Their analysis may highlight trends that reveal a major opportunity or confirm a suspected problem. Such performance trend analysis capabilities are crucial to the success of planning activities (e.g., sales forecasting).
- **Cross-selling.** A data warehouse provides an integrated view of the enterprise's many relationships with its cus><Chapter14 | Warehousing Applications><tomers. By obtaining a clearer picture of customers and the services that they avail themselves of, the enterprise can identify opportunities for cross-selling additional products and services to existing customers.
- **Customer profiling and target marketing.** Internal enterprise data can be integrated with census and demographic data to analyze and derive customer profiles. These profiles consider factors such as age, gender, marital status, income brackets, purchasing history, and number of dependents. Through these profiles, the enterprise can, with some accuracy, estimate how appealing customers will find a particular product or product mix. By modeling customers in this manner, the enterprise has better inputs to target marketing efforts.
- **Promotions and product bundling.** The data warehouse allows enterprises to analyze their customers' purchasing histories as an input to promotions and product bundling. This is particularly helpful in the retail sector, where related products from different vendors can be bundled together and offered at a more attractive price. The success of different promotions can be evaluated through the warehouse data as well.
- **Sales tracking and reporting.** Although enterprises have long been able to track and report on their sales performance, the ready availability of data in the warehouse dramatically simplifies this task.

14.3 FINANCIAL ANALYSIS AND MANAGEMENT

- **Risk analysis and management.** Integrated warehouse data allow enterprises to analyze their risk exposure. For example, banks want to effectively manage their mix of assets and liabilities. Loan departments want to manage their risk exposure to sectors or industries that are not performing well. Insurance companies want to identify customer profiles and individual customers who have consistently proven to be unprofitable and to adjust their pricing and product offerings accordingly.
- **Profitability analysis.** If operating costs and revenues are tracked or allocated at a sufficiently detailed level in operational systems, a data warehouse can be used for profitability analysis. Users can slice and dice through warehouse data to produce reports that analyze the enterprise's profitability by customer, agent or salesman, product, time period, geography, organizational unit, and any other business dimension that the user requires.

General Reporting

- **Exception reporting.** Through the use of exception reporting or alert systems, enterprise managers are made aware of important or significant events (e.g., more than x% drop in sales for the current month current year vs. same month, last year). Managers can define the exceptions that are of interest to them. Through exceptions or alerts, enterprise managers learn about business situations before they escalate into major problems. Similarly, managers learn about situations that can be exploited while the window of opportunity is still open.

Customer Care and Service

- **Customer relationship management.** Warehouse data can also be used as the basis for managing the enterprise's relationship with its many customers. Customers will be far from pleased if different groups in the same enterprise ask them for the same information more than once. Customers appreciate enterprises that never forget special instructions, preferences, or requests. Integrated customer data can serve as the basis for improving and growing the enterprise's relationships with each of its customers and are therefore critical to effective customer relationship management.

14.4 SPECIALIZED APPLICATIONS OF WAREHOUSING TECHNOLOGY

Date warehousing technology can be used to develop highly specialized applications, as discussed below.

Call Center Integration

Many organizations, particularly those in the banking, financial services, and telecommunications industries, are looking into Call Center applications to better improve their customer relationships. As with any Operational Data Store or data warehouse implementation, Call Center applications face the daunting task of integrating data from many disparate sources to form an integrated picture of the customer's relationship with the enterprise.

What has not readily been apparent to implementers of call centers is that Operational Data Store and data warehouse technologies are the appropriate IT architecture components to support call center applications. Consider Figure 14.1.

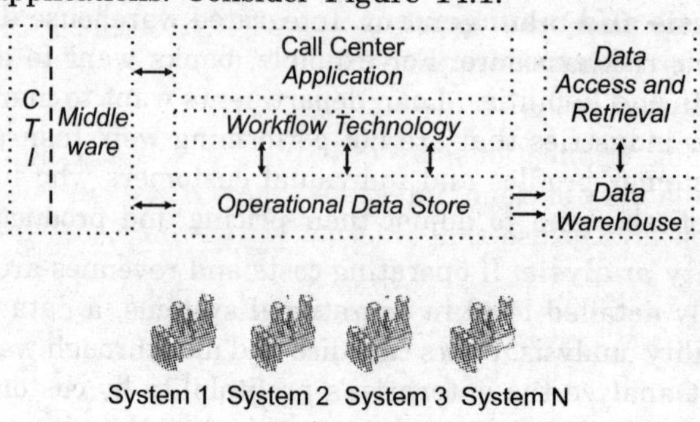

Figure 14.1. Call Center Architecture using Operational Data Store and Data Warehouse Technologies

- Data from multiple sources are integrated into an Operational Data Store provide a current, integrated view of the enterprise operations.
- The Call Centers application uses the Operational Data Store as its primary source of customer information. The Call Center also extends the contents of the Operational Data Store by directly updating the ODS.
- Workflow technologies facilities used in conjunction with the appropriate middleware are integrated with both the Operational Data Store and the Call Center applications.
- At regular intervals, the Operational Data Store feeds the enterprise data warehouse. The data warehouse has its own set of data access and retrieval technologies to provide decisional information and reports.

Credit Bureau Systems

Credit bureaus for the banking, telecommunications, and utility companies can benefit from the use of warehousing technologies for integrating negative customer data from many different enterprises. Data are integrated, then stored in a repository that can be accessed by all authorized users, either directly or through a network connection.

For this process to work smoothly, the credit bureau must set standard formats and definitions for all the data items it will receive. Data providers extract data from their respective operational systems and submit these data, using standard data storage media.

The credit bureau transforms, integrates, de-duplicates, cleans, and loads the data into a warehouse that is designed specifically to meet the querying requirements of both the credit bureau and its customers.

The credit bureau can also use data warehousing technologies to mine and analyze the credit data to produce industry-specific and cross-industry reports. Patterns within the customer database can be identified through statistical analysis (e.g. typical profile of a blacklisted customer) and can be made available to credit bureau customers. Warehouse management and administration modules, such as those that track and analyze queries, can be used as the basis for billing credit bureau customers.

In Summary

The bottom line of any data warehousing investment rests its ability to provide enterprises with genuine business value. Data warehousing technology is merely an enabler; the true values comes from the improvements that enterprises make to decisional and operational business processes-improvement that translate to better customer service, higher-quality products, reduced costs, or faster deliver times.

Data warehousing applications, as described in this chapter, enable enterprises to capitalize on the availability of clean, integrated data; Warehouse users are able to transform data into information and to use that information to contribute to the enterprise's bottom line.

PART V : MAINTENANCE, EVOLUTION AND TRENDS

After the initial data warehouse project is completed, it may seem that the bulk of the work is done. In reality, however, the warehousing team has taken just the first step of a long journey.

This section of the book explores the next steps by considering the following:

- **Warehouse Maintenance and Evolution.** This chapter presents the major considerations for maintaining and evolving the warehouse.
- **Warehousing Trends.** This chapter looks at trends in data warehousing projects.

CHAPTER 15

WAREHOUSE MAINTENANCE AND EVOLUTION

With the data warehouse in production, the warehousing team will face a new set of challenges—the maintenance and evolution of the warehouse.

15.1 REGULAR WAREHOUSE LOADS

New or updated data must be loaded regularly from the source systems into the data warehouse to ensure that the latest data are available to warehouse users. This loading is typically conducted during the evenings, when the operational systems can be taken offline. Each step in the back-end process—extract, transform, quality assure, and load–must be performed for each warehouse load.

New warehouse loads imply the need to calculate and populate aggregate tables with new records. In cases where the data warehouse feeds one or more data marts, the warehouse loading is not complete until the data marts are loaded with the latest data.

15.2 WAREHOUSE STATISTICS COLLECTION

Warehouse usage statistics should be collected on a regular basis to monitor the performance and utilization of the warehouse. The following types of statistics will prove to be insightful:

- **Queries per day.** The number of queries the warehouse responds to, on any given day is categorized into levels of complexity whenever possible. Queries against summary tables also indicate the usefulness of these stored aggregates.
- **Query response times.** It is the time a query takes to execute.
- **Alerts per day.** It refers to the number of alerts or exceptions that are triggered by the warehouse on any given day, if an alert system is in place.
- **Valid users.** It is the number of users who have access to the warehouse.
- **Users per day.** It is the number of users who actually make use of the warehouse on any given day. This number can be compared to the number of valid users.

- **Frequency of use.** It is the number of times a user actually logs on to the data warehouse within a given time frame. This statistics indicates how much the warehouse supports the user's day-to-day activities.
- **Session length.** It is the length of time a user stays online each time he logs on to the data warehouse.
- **Time of day, day of week, day of month.** The statistics of the time of day, day of week, and day of month when each query is executed may highlight periods where there is constant, heavy usage of warehouse data.
- **Subject areas.** This identifies which of the subject areas in the warehouse are more frequently used. This information also serves as a guide for subject areas that are candidates for removal.
- **Warehouse size.** It is the number of records of data for each warehouse table after each warehouse load. This statistics is a useful indicator of the growth rate of the warehouse.
- **Warehouse contents profile.** It is the statistics about the warehouse contents (e.g., total number of customers or accounts, number of employees, number of unique products, etc.). This information provides interesting metrics about the business growth.

15.3 WAREHOUSE USER PROFILES

As more users access the warehouse, the usability of the data access and retrieval tools become critical. The majority of users will not have the patience to learn a whole new set of tools and will simply continue the current and convenient practice of submitting requests to the IT department.

The warehouse team must therefore evaluate the profiles of each of the intended warehouse users. This user evaluation can also be used as input to tool selection and to determine the number of licenses required for each data access and retrieval tool.

In general, there are three types of warehouse end users, and their preferred method for interacting with the data warehouse varies accordingly. These users are:

- **Senior and executive management.** These end users generally prefer to view information through predefined reports with built-in hierarchical drilling capabilities. They prefer reports that use graphical presentation media, such as charts and models, to quickly convey information.
- **Middle management and senior analysts.** These individuals prefer to create their own queries and reports, using the available tools. They create information in an ad hoc style, based on the information needs of senior and executive management. However, their interest is often limited to a specific product group, a specific geographical area, or a specific aspect of the enterprise's performance. The preferred interfaces for users of this type are spreadsheets and front-ends that provide budgeting and forecasting capabilities.
- **Business analyst and IT support.** These individuals are among the heaviest users of warehouse data and are the ones who perform actual data collection and

analysis. They create the charts and reports that are required to present their findings to senior management. They also prefer to work with tools that allow them to create their own queries and reports.

The above categories describe the typical user profiles. The actual preference of individual users may vary, depending on individual IT literacy and working style.

15.4 SECURITY AND ACCESS PROFILES

A data warehouse contains critical information in a readily accessible format. It is therefore important to keep secure not only the warehouse data but also the information that is distilled from the warehouse.

OLTP approaches to security, such as the restriction of access to critical tables, will not work with a data warehouse because of the exploratory fashion by which warehouse data are used. Most analysts will use the warehouse in an ad hoc manner and will not necessarily know at the outset what subject areas they will be exploring or even what range of queries they will be creating. By restricting user access to certain tables, the warehouse security may inadvertently inhibit analysts and other warehouse users from discovering critical and meaningful information.

Initial warehouse rollouts typically require fairly low security because of the small and targeted set of users intended for the initial rollouts. There will be therefore a need to revisit the security and access profiles of users as each rollout is deployed.

When users leave an organization, their corresponding user profiles should be removed to prevent the unauthorized retrieval and use of warehouse data.

Also, if the warehouse data are made available to users over the public internet infrastructure, the appropriate security measures should be put in place.

15.5 DATA QUALITY

Data quality (or the lack thereof) will continue to plague warehousing efforts in the years to come. The enterprise will need to determine how data errors will be handled in the warehouse. There are two general approaches to data quality problems:

- **Only clean data gets in.** Only data that are certified 100 percent correct are loaded into the warehouse. Users are confident that the warehouse contains correct data and can take decisive action based on the information it provides. Unfortunately, data errors may take a long time to identify, and even more to fix, before the completion of a full warehouse load. Also, a vast majority of queries (e.g., who are our top-10 customers? how many product combinations are we selling?) will not be meaningful if a warehouse load is incomplete.
- **Clean as we go.** All data are loaded into the warehouse, but mechanisms are defined and implemented to identify and correct data errors. Although such an approach allows warehouse loads to take place, the quality of the data is suspectable and may result in misleading information and ill-informed decisions. The questionable data quality may also cause problems with user acceptance—users will be less inclined to use the warehouse if they do not believe the information it provides.

It is unrealistic to expect that all data quality errors will be corrected during the course of one warehouse rollout. However, acceptance of this reality does not mean that data quality efforts are for naught and can be abandoned.

Whenever possible, correct the data in the source systems so that cleaner data are provided in the next warehouse load. Provide mechanisms for clearly identifying dirty warehouse data. If users know which parts of the warehouse are suspectable, they will be able to find value in the data that are correct.

It is an unfortunate fact that older enterprises have larger data volumes and, consequently, a larger volume of data errors.

15.6 DATA GROWTH

Initial warehouse deployments may not face space or capacity problems, but as time passes and the warehouse size grows with each new data load, the proper management of data growth expansion proliferation grows in importance.

There are several ways to handle data growth, including:

- **Use of aggregates.** The use of stored aggregates significantly reduces the space required by the data especially if the data are required only at a highly summarized level. The detailed data can be deleted or archived after aggregates have been created. However, the removal of detailed data implies the loss of the ability to drill down for more detail. Also new summaries at other levels may not be derivable from the current portfolio of aggregate schemas.
- **Limiting the time frame.** Although users want the warehouse to store as much data for as long as possible, there may be a need to compromise by limiting the length of historical data in the warehouse.
- **Removing unused data.** Using query statistics gathered over time, it is possible for warehouse administrators to identify rarely used data in the warehouse. These records are ideal candidates for removal since their storage results in costs with very little business value.

15.7 UPDATES TO WAREHOUSE SUBSYSTEMS

As time passes, a number of conditions will necessitate changes to the data structure of the warehouse, its staging areas, its back-end subsystems and consequently, its metadata. We describe some of these conditions in the following subsections.

Source System Evolution

As the source systems evolve, so by necessity does the data warehouse. It is therefore critical that any plans to change the scope, functionality, and availability of the source systems also consider any possible impact on the data warehouse. The CIO is in the best position to ensure that the project efforts are coordinated across multiple projects.

- **Changes in scope.** Scope changes in operational systems typically imply one or more of the following: the availability of new data in an existing system, or removal of previously available data in an existing system, or the migration of currently available data to a new or different computing environment. An example of the latter is the deployment of a new system to replace an existing one.

- **Change in functionality.** There are times when the data structure already existing in the operational systems remains the same but the processing logic and business rules governing the input of future data is changed. Such changes require updates to data integrity rules and metadata used for quality assurance. All quality assurance programs should likewise be updated.
- **Change in availability.** Additional demands on the operational system may affect the availability of the source system (e.g., smaller batch windows). The batch windows may affect the schedule of regular warehouse extractions and may place new efficiency and performance demands on the warehouse extraction and transformation subsystems.

Use of New or Additional External Data

Some data are commercially available for purchase and can be integrated into the data warehouse as the business needs evolve. The use of external data presents its own set of difficulties due to the likelihood of incompatible formats or level of detail.

The use of new or additional external data has the same impact on the warehouse back-end subsystems as changes do to internal data sources.

15.8 DATABASE OPTIMIZATION AND TUNING

As query statistics are collected and user base increases, there will be a need to perform database optimization and tuning tasks to maintain an acceptable level of warehouse performance.

To avoid or control the impact of nasty surprises, the users are to be informed whenever changes are made to the production database. Also any changes to the database should first be tested in a safe environment.

Databases can be tuned through a number of approaches, including but not limited to the following:

- **Use of parallel query options.** Some of the major database management systems offer options that will split up a large query into several smaller queries that can be run in parallel. The results of the smaller queries are then combined and presented to users as a single result set. While such options have costs, their implementation is transparent to users, who notice only the improvements in response time.
- **Indexing strategies.** As very large database (VLDB) implementations are becoming more popular, database vendors are offering indexing options or strategies to improve the response times to queries against very large tables.
- **Dropping of referential integrity checking.** While debates still exist as to whether or not referential integrity checking should be left on during warehouse loading. It is an undeniable fact that when referential integrity is turned off, the loading of warehouse data becomes faster. Some parties reason that since data are checked prior to warehouse loading, there will be no need to enforce referential integrity constraints.

15.9 DATA WAREHOUSE STAFFING

Not all organizations with a data warehouse choose to create a permanent unit to administer and maintain it. Each organization will have to decide if a permanent unit is required to maintain the data warehouse.

A permanent unit has the advantage of focusing the warehouse staff formally on the care and feeding of the data warehouse. A permanent unit also increases the continuity in staff assignments by decreasing the possibility of losing staff to other IT projects or systems in the enterprise.

The use of matrix organizations in place of permanent units has also proven to be effective, provided that roles and responsibilities are clearly defined and that the IT division is not undermanned.

If the warehouse development was partially or completely outsource to third parties because of a shortage of internal IT resources, the enterprise may find it necessary to staff up at the end of the warehouse rollout. As the project draws to a close, the consultants or contractors will be turning over the day-to-day operations of the warehouse to internal IT staff. The lack of internal IT resources may result in haphazard turnovers. Alternatively, the enterprise may have to outsource the maintenance of the warehouse.

15.10 WAREHOUSE STAFF AND USER TRAINING

The enterprise may find it helpful to establish a training program for both technology staff and end users.

User Training

- **Warehousing overview.** Half-day overviews can be prepared for executive or senior management to manage expectations.
- **User roles.** User training should also cover general data warehousing concepts and explain how users are involved during data warehouse planning, design, and construction activities.
- **Warehouse contents and metadata.** Once a data warehouse has been deployed, the user training should focus strongly on the contents of the warehouse. Users must understand the data that are now available to them and must understand also the limitations imposed by the scope of the warehouse. The contents and usage of business metadata should also be explained.
- **Data access and retrieval tools.** User training should also focus on the selected end-user tools. If users find the tools difficult to use, the IT staff will quickly find themselves saddled with the unwelcome task of creating reports and queries for end users.

Warehouse Staff Training

Warehouse staff require training on a number of topics covering the planning, design, implementation, management, and maintenance of data warehouses. Depending on their project roles, the staff will need to specialize or focus on different areas or different aspects of the warehousing life cycle. For example, the metadata administrator needs specialized courses on metadata repository management. Whereas the warehouse DBA needs dimensional modeling training.

15.11 SUBSEQUENT WAREHOUSE ROLLOUTS

The data warehouse is extended continuously. Data warehouse design and construction skills will always be needed as long as end-user requirements and business situations continue to evolve. Each subsequent rollout is designed to extend the functionality and scope of the warehouse.

As new user requirements are studied and subsequent warehouse rollouts get underway, the overall data warehouse architecture is revisited and modified as needed.

Data marts are deployed as needed within the integrating framework of the warehouse. Multiple, unrelated data marts are to be avoided because these will merely create unnecessary data management and administration problems.

15.12 CHARGEBACK SCHEMES

It may be necessary at some point for the IT Department to start charging user groups for warehouse usage, as a way of obtaining continuous funding for the data warehouse initiative.

Note that chargeback schemes will work only if there are reliable mechanisms to track and monitor usage of the warehouse per user. They also put the warehouse to the test—users will have to feel that they are getting their money's worth each time they use the warehouse. Warehouse usage will drop if users feel that the warehouse has no value.

15.13 DISASTER RECOVERY

The challenges of deploying new technology may cause warehouse administrators to place a lower priority on disaster recovery. As time passes and more users come to depend on the data warehouse, however, the warehouse achieves mission-critical status. The appropriate disaster recovery procedures are therefore required to safeguard the continuous availability and reliability of the warehouse.

Ideally, the warehouse team conducts a dry run of the disaster recovery procedure at least once prior to the deployment of the warehouse. Disaster recovery drills on a regular basis will also prove helpful.

Some disasters may require the reinstallation of operating systems and database management systems apart from the reloading or warehouse data and population of aggregate tables. The recovery procedures should consider this possibility.

A final note: Review the disaster recovery plan at the end of each rollout. The plan may have to be updated in light of changes to the architecture, scope, and size of the warehouse.

In Summary

A data warehouse initiative does not stop with one successful warehouse deployment. The warehousing team must sustain the initial momentum by maintaining and evolving the data warehouse.

Unfortunately, maintenance activities remain very much in the background—often unseen and unappreciated until something goes wrong. Many people do not realize that evolving a warehouse can be trickier than the initial deployment. The warehousing team has to meet a new set of information requirements without compromising the performance of the initial deployment and without limiting the warehouse's ability to meet future requirements.

CHAPTER 16

WAREHOUSING TRENDS

This chapter takes a look at trends in the data warehousing industry and their possible implications on future warehousing projects.

16.1 CONTINUED GROWTH OF THE DATA WAREHOUSE INDUSTRY

The data warehousing industry continues to grow in terms of spending, product availability and projects. The number of data warehouse vendors continues to increase, as does the number of available warehousing products. Such a trend, however, may abate in the face of market consolidation, which began in the mid-1990s and continues to this day.

Small companies with compatible products can be seen merging (e.g.. the November 1997 merger of Apertus Technologies and Carleton Corporation) to create larger, more competitive warehouse players. Larger, established corporations have set objectives of becoming end-to-end warehouse solution providers and are acquiring technologies from niche players to fulfill these goals (e.g.. the February 1998 acquisition of Intellidex Systems by Sybase and the March 1998 acquisition of Logic Works by Platinum Technologies).

Partnerships and alliances between vendors continue to be popular. The increasing maturity of the warehousing software market is inevitably turning warehouse software into off-the-shelf packages that can be pieced together. Already companies are positioning groups of products (their own or a combination of products from multiple vendors) as integrated warehousing solutions.

16.2 INCREASED ADOPTION OF WAREHOUSING TECHNOLOGY BY MORE INDUSTRIES

The industries to adopt data warehousing technologies earlier have been the telecommunications, banking, and retail vertical markets. The impetus for their early adoption of warehousing technologies has been attributed largely to government deregulation, and increased competition among industry players–conditions that heightened the need for integrated information.

Over the past few years, however, other industries have begun investing strongly in data warehousing technologies. These include, but are not limited to, companies in financial services, healthcare, insurance, manufacturing, petrochemical, pharmaceutical, transportation and distribution, as well as utilities.

Despite the increasing adoption of warehousing technologies by other industries, however, out research indicates that the telecommunications and banking industries continue to lead in warehouse-related spending, with as much as 15 percent of their technology budgets allocated to warehouse-related purchases and projects.

16.3 INCREASED MATURITY OF DATA MINING TECHNOLOGIES

Data mining tools will continue to mature, and more organizations will adopt this type of warehousing technology. Learning from data mining applications will become more widely available in the trade press and other commercial publications, thereby increasing the chances of data mining success of late adopters.

Data mining initiatives are typically driven by marketing and sales departments and are understandably more popular in large companies with very large databases. Since these tools work best with detailed data at the transaction grain, the popularity of data mining tools will naturally coincide with a boom in very large (terabyte-size) data warehouses. Data mining projects will also underscore further the importance of data quality in warehouse implementations.

16.4 EMERGENCE AND USE OF METADATA INTERCHANGE STANDARDS

There is currently no metadata repository that is a clear industry leader for warehouse implementations. Each product vendor has defined its own set of metadata repository standards as required by its respective products or product suite.

Efforts have long been underway to define an industry-wide set of metadata interchange standards, and a Metadata Interchange Specification is available from the Meta Data Coalition, which has at least 30 vendor companies as members.

16.5 INCREASED AVAILABILITY OF WEB-ENABLED SOLUTIONS

Data warehousing technologies continue to be affected by the increased popularity of intranets and intranet-based solutions. As a result, more and more data access and retrieval tools are becoming web enabled, while more organizations are requiring web-enabled features as a warehousing requirement for their data access and retrieval tools.

Some organizations have started using the Internet as a cost-effective mechanism for providing remote users with access to warehouse data. Understandably, organizations are concerned about the security requirements of such a setup. The warehouse no doubt contains the most integrated, and cleanest data in the entire enterprise. Such highly critical and sensitive data may fall into the wrong hands if the appropriate security measures are not implemented.

16.6 POPULARITY OF WINDOWS NT FOR DATA MART PROJECTS

The Windows NT operating system will continue to gain popularity as a data mart operating system. The operating system is frequently bundled with hardware features that are candidates for base-level or low-end warehousing platforms.

16.7 AVAILABILITY OF WAREHOUSING MODULES FOR APPLICATION PACKAGES

Companies that develop and market major operational application packages will soon be offering warehousing modules as part of their suite of applications. These application packages include SAP, Baan, and PeopleSoft. Companies that offer these application packages are in a position to capitalize on the popularity of data warehousing by creating warehousing modules that make use of data in their applications.

These companies are familiar with the data structures of their respective applications and they can therefore offer configurable warehouse back-ends to extract, transform, quality assure, and load operational data into a separate decisional data structure designed to meet the basic decisional reporting requirements of their customers.

Understandably, each enterprise requires the ability to customize these basic warehousing modules to meet their specific requirements; customization is definitely possible with the right people using the right development tools.

16.8 MORE MERGERS AND ACQUISITIONS AMONG WAREHOUSE PLAYERS

Mergers and acquisitions will continue in the data warehouse market, driven by large corporations acquiring niche specialties, and small companies merging to create a larger warehouse player.

Examples include:

- The acquisition of Stanford technological group by Informix.
- The acquisition of IRI software's OLAP technologies by Oracle Corporation.
- The acquisition of Panorama Software Systems (and their OLAP technology) by Microsoft Corporation.
- The merger of Carleton Corporation and Apertus technologies.
- The acquisition of HP Intelligent Warehouse by Platinum Technologies.
- The acquisition of Intellindex Systems by Sybase Inc., for the former's metadata repository product.
- The acquisition of Logic Works, Inc., by Platinum Technologies.

In Summary

In all respects, the data warehousing industry shows all signs of continued growth at an impressive rate. Enterprises can expect more mature products in almost all software segments, especially with the availability of second- or third-generation products. Improvements in price/performance ratios will continue in the hardware market.

Some vendor consolidation can be expected, although new companies and products will continue to appear. More partnerships and alliances among different vendors can also be expected.

PART VI: ON-LINE ANALYTICAL PROCESSING

The main topics that are covered in this part are:

- **Definition.** It was originally defined by the late Dr. Codd in terms of 12 rules, later extended to the less well-known 18 'features'. All 18 are analyzed, along with preferred 'FASMI' test.
- **Origin.** Despite the recent hype, OLAP products go back much further than many people think. This section reflects on the lessons that can be learned from the 30+ years' of multidimensional analysis.
- **Market Analysis.** A fast way to segment products based on their architectures, plus the OLAP architectural square, used to ensure shortlists are rational.
- **Architecture.** Confusion abounds in discussions about OLAP architectures, with terms like ROLAP, MOLAP, HOLAP and even DOLAP proliferating. This section explains the differences.
- **Multi Dimensional Data Structures.** There is a lot of confusing terminology used to describe multidimensional structures. This section clarifies our use of terms like hypercubes and multicubes.
- **Applications.** Describes the main OLAP applications, and some of the issues that arise with them.

CHAPTER 17

INTRODUCTION

17.1 WHAT IS *OLAP*?

The term, of course, stands for 'On-Line Analytical Processing'. But that is not a definition; it's not even a clear description of what OLAP means. It certainly gives no indication of why you use an OLAP tool, or even what an OLAP tool actually does. And it gives you no help in deciding if a product is an OLAP tool or not.

This problem, started as soon as researching on the OLAP in late 1994, as we needed to decide which products fell into the category. Deciding what is an OLAP has not been easier since then, as more and more vendors claim to have 'OLAP compliant' products, whatever that may mean (often the they don't even know). It is not possible to rely on the vendors' own descriptions and the membership of the long-defunct OLAP council was not a reliable indicator of whether or not a company produces OLAP products. For example, several significant OLAP vendors were never members or resigned, and several members were not OLAP vendors. Membership of the instantly moribund replacement Analytical Solutions Forum was even less of a guide, as it was intended to include non-OLAP vendors.

The **Codd rules** also turned out to be an unsuitable way of detecting 'OLAP compliance', so researchers were forced to create their own definition. It had to be simple, memorable and product-independent, and the resulting definition is the 'FASMI' test. The key thing that all OLAP products have in common is multidimensionality, but that is not the only requirement for an OLAP product.

Here, we wanted to define the characteristics of an OLAP application in a specific way, without dictating how it should be implemented. As research has shown, there are many ways of implementing OLAP compliant applications, and no single piece of technology should be officially required, or even recommended. Of course, we have studied the technologies used in commercial OLAP products and this report provides many such details. We have suggested in which circumstances one approach or another might be preferred, and have also identified areas where we feel that all the products currently fall short of what we regard as a technology ideal.

Here the definition is designed to be short and easy to remember – 12 rules or 18 features are far too many for most people to carry in their heads; it is easy to summarize the OLAP definition in just five key words: ***F****ast* ***A****nalysis of* ***S****hared* ***M****ultidimensional* ***I****nformation* – or, FASMI for short.

*F*ast *A*nalysis of *S*hared *M*ultidimensional *I*nformation

FAST means that the system is targeted to deliver most responses to users within about five seconds, with the simplest analyses taking no more than one second and very few taking more than 20 seconds. Independent research in The Netherlands has shown that end-users assume that a process has failed if results are not received within 30 seconds, and they are apt to hit 'Alt+Ctrl+Delete' unless the system warns them that the report will take longer time. Even if they have been warned that it will take significantly longer time, users are likely to get distracted and lose their chain of thought, so the quality of analysis suffers. This speed is not easy to achieve with large amounts of data, particularly if on-the-fly and *ad hoc* calculations are required. Vendors resort to a wide variety of techniques to achieve this goal, including specialized forms of data storage, extensive pre-calculations and specific hardware requirements, but we do not think any products are yet fully optimized, so we expect this to be an area of developing technology. In particular, the full pre-calculation approach fails with very large, sparse applications as the databases simply get too large, whereas doing everything on-the-fly is much too slow with large databases, even if exotic hardware is used. Even though it may seem miraculous at first if reports that previously took days now take only minutes, users soon get bored of waiting, and the project will be much less successful than if it had delivered a near instantaneous response, even at the cost of less detailed analysis. **The OLAP Survey** has found that slow query response is consistently the most often-cited technical problem with OLAP products, so too many deployments are clearly still failing to pass this test.

ANALYSIS means that the system can cope with any business logic and statistical analysis that is relevant for the application and the user, and keep it easy enough for the target user. Although some pre-programming may be needed, we do not think it acceptable if all application definitions have to be done using a professional 4GL. It is certainly necessary to allow the user to define new *ad hoc* calculations as part of the analysis and to report on the data in any desired way, without having to program, so we exclude products (like Oracle Discoverer) that do not allow adequate end-user oriented calculation flexibility. We do not mind whether this analysis is done in the vendor's own tools or in a linked external product such as a spreadsheet simply that all the required analysis functionality be provided in an intuitive manner for the target users. This could include specific features like time series analysis, cost allocations, currency translation, goal seeking, *ad hoc* multidimensional structural changes, non-procedural modeling, exception alerting, data mining and other application dependent features. These capabilities differ widely between products, depending on their target markets.

SHARED means that the system implements all the security requirements for confidentiality (possibly down to cell level) and, if multiple write access is needed, concurrent update locking at an appropriate level. Not all applications need users to write data back, but for the growing numbers that do, the system should be able to handle multiple updates in a timely, secure manner. This is a major area of weakness in many OLAP products, which tend to assume that all OLAP applications will be read-only, with simplistic security controls. Even products with multi-user read-write often have crude security models; an example is Microsoft OLAP Services.

MULTIDIMENSIONAL is our key requirement. If we had to pick a one-word definition of OLAP, this is it. The system must provide a multidimensional conceptual view of the data, including full support for hierarchies and multiple hierarchies, as this is certainly the most logical way to analyze businesses and organizations. We are not setting up a specific minimum number of dimensions that must be handled as it is too application dependent and most products seem to have enough for their target markets. Again, we do not specify what underlying database technology should be used providing that the user gets a truly multidimensional conceptual view.

INFORMATION is all of the data and derived information needed, wherever it is and however much is relevant for the application. We are measuring the capacity of various products in terms of how much input data they can handle, not how many Gigabytes they take to store it. The capacities of the products differ greatly – the largest OLAP products can hold at least a thousand times as much data as the smallest. There are many considerations here, including data duplication, RAM required, disk space utilization, performance, integration with data warehouses and the like.

We think that the FASMI test is a reasonable and understandable definition of the goals OLAP is meant to achieve. Researches encourage users and vendors to adopt this definition, which we hope will avoid the controversies of previous attempts.

The techniques used to achieve it include many flavors of client/server architecture, time series analysis, object-orientation, optimized proprietary data storage, multithreading and various patented ideas that vendors are so proud of. We have views on these as well, but we would not want any such technologies to become part of the definition of OLAP. Vendors who are covered in this report had every chance to tell us about their technologies, but it is their ability to achieve OLAP goals for their chosen application areas that impressed us most.

17.2 THE CODD RULES AND FEATURES

In 1993, E.F. Codd & Associates published a white paper, commissioned by Arbor Software (now Hyperion Solutions), entitled 'Providing OLAP (On-Line Analytical Processing) to User-Analysts: An IT Mandate'. The late Dr. Codd was very well known as a respected database researcher from the 1960s till the late 1980s and is credited with being the inventor of the relational database model in 1969. Unfortunately, his OLAP rules proved to be controversial due to being vendor-sponsored, rather than mathematically based.

The OLAP white paper included 12 rules, which are now well known. They were followed by another six (much less well known) rules in 1995 and Dr. Codd also restructured the rules into four groups, calling them 'features'. The features are briefly described and evaluated here, but they are now rarely quoted and little used.

Basic Features

1. **Multidimensional Conceptual View** (Original Rule 1). Few would argue with this feature; like Dr. Codd, we believe this to be the central core of OLAP. Dr Codd included 'slice and dice' as part of this requirement.
2. **Intuitive Data Manipulation** (Original Rule 10). Dr. Codd preferred data manipulation to be done through direct actions on cells in the view, without recourse

to menus or multiple actions. One assumes that this is by using a mouse (or equivalent), but Dr. Codd did not actually say so. Many products fail on this, because they do not necessarily support double clicking or drag and drop. The vendors, of course, all claim otherwise. In our view, this feature adds little value to the evaluation process. We think that products should offer a choice of modes (at all times), because not all users like the same approach.

3. **Accessibility: OLAP as a Mediator** (Original Rule 3). In this rule, Dr. Codd essentially described OLAP engines as middleware, sitting between heterogeneous data sources and an OLAP front-end. Most products can achieve this, but often with more data staging and batching than vendors like to admit.
4. **Batch Extraction vs Interpretive** (New). This rule effectively required that products offer *both* their own staging database for OLAP data *as well as* offering live access to external data. We agree with Dr. Codd on this feature and are disappointed that only a minority of OLAP products properly comply with it, and even those products do not often make it easy or automatic. In effect, Dr. Codd was endorsing multidimensional data staging plus partial pre-calculation of large multidimensional databases, with transparent reach-through to underlying detail. Today, this would be regarded as the definition of a hybrid OLAP, which is indeed becoming a popular architecture, so Dr. Codd has proved to be very perceptive in this area.
5. **OLAP Analysis Models** (New). Dr. Codd required that OLAP products should support all four analysis models that he described in his white paper (Categorical, Exegetical, Contemplative and Formulaic). We hesitate to simplify Dr Codd's erudite phraseology, but we would describe these as parameterized static reporting, slicing and dicing with drill down, 'what if?' analysis and goal seeking models, respectively. All OLAP tools in this Report support the first two (but some other claimants do not fully support the second), most support the third to some degree (but probably less than Dr. Codd would have liked) and a few support the fourth to any usable extent. Perhaps Dr. Codd was anticipating data mining in this rule?
6. **Client/Server Architecture** (Original Rule 5). Dr. Codd required not only that the product should be client/server but also that the server component of an OLAP product should be sufficiently intelligent that various clients could be attached with minimum effort and programming for integration. This is a much tougher test than simple client/server, and relatively few products qualify. We would argue that this test is probably tougher than it needs to be, and we prefer not to dictate architectures. However, if you do agree with the feature, then you should be aware that most vendors, who claim compliance, do so wrongly. In effect, this is also an indirect requirement for openness on the desktop. Perhaps Dr. Codd, without ever using the term, was thinking of what the Web would one day deliver? Or perhaps he was anticipating a widely accepted API standard, which still does not really exist. Perhaps, one day, XML for Analysis will fill this gap.
7. **Transparency** (Original Rule 2). This test was also a tough but valid one. Full compliance means that a user of, say, a spreadsheet should be able to get full value from an OLAP engine and not even be aware of where the data ultimately comes

from. To do this, products must allow live access to heterogeneous data sources from a full function spreadsheet add-in, with the OLAP server engine in between. Although all vendors claimed compliance, many did so by outrageously rewriting Dr. Codd's words. Even Dr. Codd's own vendor-sponsored analyses of Essbase and (then) TM/1 ignore part of the test. In fact, there are a few products that do *fully* comply with the test, including Analysis Services, Express, and Holos, but neither Essbase nor iTM1 (because they do not support live, transparent access to external data), in spite of Dr. Codd's apparent endorsement. Most products fail to give either full spreadsheet access or live access to heterogeneous data sources. Like the previous feature, this is a tough test for openness.

8. **Multi-User Support** (Original Rule 8). Dr. Codd recognized that OLAP applications were not all read-only and said that, to be regarded as strategic, OLAP tools must provide concurrent access (retrieval and update), integrity and security. We agree with Dr. Codd, but also note that many OLAP applications are still read-only. Again, all the vendors claim compliance but, on a strict interpretation of Dr. Codd's words, few are justified in so doing.

Special Features

9. **Treatment of Non-Normalized Data** (New). This refers to the integration between an OLAP engine and denormalized source data. Dr. Codd pointed out that any data updates performed in the OLAP environment should not be allowed to alter stored denormalized data in feeder systems. He could also be interpreted as saying that data changes should not be allowed in what are normally regarded as calculated cells within the OLAP database. For example, if Essbase had allowed this, Dr Codd would perhaps have disapproved.

10. **Storing OLAP Results: Keeping them Separate from Source Data** (New). This is really an implementation rather than a product issue, but few would disagree with it. In effect, Dr. Codd was endorsing the widely-held view that read-write OLAP applications should not be implemented directly on live transaction data, and OLAP data changes should be kept distinct from transaction data. The method of data write-back used in Microsoft Analysis Services is the best implementation of this, as it allows the effects of data changes even within the OLAP environment to be kept segregated from the base data.

11. **Extraction of Missing Values** (New). All missing values are cast in the uniform representation defined by the Relational Model Version 2. We interpret this to mean that missing values are to be distinguished from zero values. In fact, in the interests of storing sparse data more compactly, a few OLAP tools such as TM1 do break this rule, without great loss of function.

12. **Treatment of Missing Values** (New). All missing values are to be ignored by the OLAP analyzer regardless of their source. This relates to Feature 11, and is probably an almost inevitable consequence of how multidimensional engines treat all data.

Reporting Features

13. **Flexible Reporting** (Original Rule 11). Dr. Codd required that the dimensions can be laid out in any way that the user requires in reports. We would agree that most products are capable of this in their formal report writers. Dr. Codd did not explicitly state whether he expected the same flexibility in the interactive viewers, perhaps because he was not aware of the distinction between the two. We prefer that it is available, but note that relatively fewer viewers are capable of it. This is one of the reasons that we prefer that analysis and reporting facilities be combined in one module.

14. **Uniform Reporting Performance** (Original Rule 4). Dr. Codd required that reporting performance be not significantly degraded by increasing the number of dimensions or database size. Curiously, nowhere did he mention that the performance must be fast, merely that it be consistent. In fact, our experience suggests that merely increasing the number of dimensions or database size does not affect performance significantly in fully pre-calculated databases, so Dr. Codd could be interpreted as endorsing this approach – which may not be a surprise given that Arbor Software sponsored the paper. However, reports with more content or more on-the-fly calculations usually take longer (in the good products, performance is almost linearly dependent on the number of cells used to produce the report, which may be more than appear in the finished report) and some dimensional layouts will be slower than others, because more disk blocks will have to be read. There are differences between products, but the principal factor that affects performance is the degree to which the calculations are performed in advance and where live calculations are done (client, multidimensional server engine or RDBMS). This is far more important than database size, number of dimensions or report complexity.

15. **Automatic Adjustment of Physical Level** (Supersedes Original Rule 7). Dr. Codd wanted the OLAP system adjust its physical schema automatically to adapt to the type of model, data volumes and sparsity. We agree with him, but are disappointed that most vendors fall far short of this noble ideal. We would like to see more progress in this area and also in the related area of determining the degree to which models should be pre-calculated (a major issue that Dr. Codd ignores). The Panorama technology, acquired by Microsoft in October 1996, broke new ground here, and users can now benefit from it in Microsoft Analysis Services.

Dimension Control

16. **Generic Dimensionality** (Original Rule 6). Dr Codd took the purist view that each dimension must be equivalent in both its structure and operational capabilities. This may not be unconnected with the fact that this is an Essbase characteristic. However, he did allow additional operational capabilities to be granted to selected dimensions (presumably including time), but he insisted that such additional functions should be granted to any dimension. He did not want the basic data structures, formulae or reporting formats to be biased towards any one dimension. This has proven to be one of the most controversial of all the original 12 rules. Technology focused products tend to largely comply with it, so the vendors of such products support it. Application focused products usually make no effort to comply,

and their vendors bitterly attack the rule. With a strictly purist interpretation, few products fully comply. We would suggest that if you are purchasing a tool for general purpose, multiple application use, then you want to consider this rule, but even then with a lower priority. If you are buying a product for a specific application, you may safely ignore the rule.

17. **Unlimited Dimensions & Aggregation Levels** (Original Rule 12). Technically, no product can possibly comply with this feature, because there is no such thing as an unlimited entity on a limited computer. In any case, few applications need more than about eight or ten dimensions, and few hierarchies have more than about six consolidation levels. Dr. Codd suggested that if a maximum must be accepted, it should be at least 15 and preferably 20; we believe that this is too arbitrary and takes no account of usage. You should ensure that any product you buy has limits that are greater than you need, but there are many other limiting factors in OLAP products that are liable to trouble you more than this one. In practice, therefore, you can probably ignore this requirement.
18. **Unrestricted Cross-dimensional Operations** (Original Rule 9). Dr. Codd asserted, and we agree, that all forms of calculation must be allowed across all dimensions, not just the 'measures' dimension. In fact, many products which use only relational storage are weak in this area. Most products, such as Essbase, with a multidimensional database are strong. These types of calculations are important if you are doing complex calculations, not just cross tabulations, and are particularly relevant in applications that analyze profitability.

17.3 THE ORIGINS OF TODAY'S *OLAP* PRODUCTS

The OLAP term dates back to 1993, but the ideas, technology and even some of the products have origins long before then.

APL

Multidimensional analysis, the basis for OLAP, is not new. In fact, it goes back to 1962, with the publication of Ken Iverson's book, *A Programming Language*. The first computer implementation of the APL language was in the late 1960s, by IBM. APL is a mathematically defined language with multidimensional variables and elegant, if rather abstract, processing operators. It was originally intended more as a way of defining multidimensional transformations than as a practical programming language, so it did not pay attention to mundane concepts like files and printers. In the interests of a succinct notation, the operators were Greek symbols. In fact, the resulting programs were so succinct that few could predict what an APL program would do. It became known as a 'Write Only Language' (WOL), because it was easier to rewrite a program that needed maintenance than to fix it.

Unfortunately, this was all long before the days of high-resolution GUI screens and laser printers, so APL's Greek symbols needed special screens, keyboards and printers. Later, English words were sometimes used as substitutes for the Greek operators, but purists took a dim view of this attempted popularization of their elite language. APL also devoured machine resources, partly because early APL systems were interpreted rather than being compiled. This was in the days of very costly, under-powered mainframes, so applications that did APL justice were slow to process and very expensive to run. APL also had a, perhaps undeserved, reputation for being particularly hungry for memory, as arrays were processed in RAM.

However, in spite of these inauspicious beginnings, APL did not go away. It was used in many 1970s and 1980s business applications that had similar functions to today's OLAP systems. Indeed, IBM developed an entire mainframe operating system for APL, called VSPC, and some people regarded it as the personal productivity environment of choice long before the spreadsheet made an appearance. One of these APL-based mainframe products was originally called Frango, and later Fregi. It was developed by IBM in the UK, and was used for interactive, top-down planning. A PC-based descendant of Frango surfaced in the early 1990s as KPS, and the product remains on sale today as the Analyst module in Cognos Planning. This is one of several APL-based products that Cognos has built or acquired since 1999.

However, APL was simply too elitist to catch on with a larger audience, even if the hardware problems were eventually to be solved or become irrelevant. It did make an appearance on PCs in the 1980s (and is still used, sometimes in a revamped form called "J") but it ceased to have any market significance after about 1980. Although it was possible to program multidimensional applications using arrays in other languages, it was too hard for any but professional programmers to do so, and even technical end-users had to wait for a new generation of multidimensional products.

Express

By 1970, a more application-oriented multidimensional product, with academic origins, had made its first appearance: Express. This, in a completely rewritten form and with a modern code-base, became a widely used contemporary OLAP offering, but the original 1970's concepts still lie just below the surface. Even after 30 years, Express remains one of the major OLAP technologies, although Oracle struggled and failed to keep it up-to-date with the many newer client/server products. Oracle announced in late 2000 that it would build OLAP server capabilities into Oracle9*i* starting in mid 2001. The second release of the Oracle9*i* OLAP Option included both a version of the Express engine, called the Analytic Workspace, and a new ROLAP engine. In fact, delays with the new OLAP technology and applications means that Oracle is still selling Express and applications based on it in 2005, some 35 years after Express was first released. This means that the Express engine has lived on well into its fourth decade, and if the OLAP Option eventually becomes successful, the renamed Express engine could be on sale into its fifth decade, making it possibly one of the longest-lived software products ever.

More multidimensional products appeared in the 1980s. Early in the decade, Stratagem appeared, and in its eventual guise of Acumate (now owned by Lucent), this too was still marketed to a limited extent till the mid 1990s. However, although it was a distant cousin of Express, it never had Express' market share, and has been discontinued. Along the way, Stratagem was owned by CA, which was later to acquire two ROLAPs, the former Prodea Beacon and the former Information Advantage Decision Suite, both of which soon died.

System W

Comshare's System W was a different style of multidimensional product. Introduced in 1981, it was the first to have a hypercube approach and was much more oriented to end-user development of financial applications. It brought in many concepts that are still not widely adopted, like full non-procedural rules, full screen multidimensional viewing and data editing, automatic recalculation and (batch) integration with relational data. However, it too was heavy on hardware and was less programmable than the other products of its day, and so was less popular with IT professionals. It is also still used, but is no longer sold and no enhancements are likely. Although it was released on Unix, it was not a true client/server product and was never promoted by the vendor as an OLAP offering.

In the late 1980s, Comshare's DOS One-Up and later, Windows-based Commander Prism (later called Comshare Planning) products used similar concepts to the host-based System W. Hyperion Solution's Essbase product, though not a direct descendant of System W, was also clearly influenced by its financially oriented, fully pre-calculated hypercube approach, which causes database explosion (so a design decision made by Comshare in 1980 lingered on in Essbase until 2004). Ironically, Comshare subsequently licensed Essbase (rather than using any of its own engines) for the engine in some of its modern OLAP products, though this relationship was not to last. Comshare (now Geac) later switched to the Microsoft Analysis Services OLAP engine instead.

Metaphor

Another creative product of the early 1980s was Metaphor. This was aimed at marketing professionals in consumer goods companies. This too introduced many new concepts that became popular only in the 1990s, like client/server computing, multidimensional processing on relational data, workgroup processing and object-oriented development. Unfortunately, the standard PC hardware of the day was not capable of delivering the response and human factors that Metaphor required, so the vendor was forced to create totally proprietary PCs and network technology. Subsequently, Metaphor struggled to get the product to work successfully on non-proprietary hardware and right to the end it never used a standard GUI.

Eventually, Metaphor formed a marketing alliance with IBM, which went to acquire the company. By mid 1994, IBM had decided to integrate Metaphor's unique technology (renamed DIS) with future IBM technology and to disband the subsidiary, although customer protests led to the continuing support for the product. The product continues to be supported for its remaining loyal customers, and IBM relaunched it under the IDS name but hardly promoted it. However, Metaphor's creative concepts have not gone and the former Information Advantage, Brio, Sagent, MicroStrategy and Gentia are examples of vendors covered in The OLAP Report that have obviously been influenced by it.

Another surviving Metaphor tradition is the unprofitability of independent ROLAP vendors: no ROLAP vendor has ever made a cumulative profit, as demonstrated by Metaphor, MicroStrategy, MineShare, WhiteLight, STG, IA and Prodea. The natural market for ROLAPs seems to be just too small, and the deployments too labor intensive, for there to be a sustainable business model for more than one or two ROLAP vendors. MicroStrategy may be the only sizeable long-term ROLAP survivor.

EIS

By the mid 1980s, the term EIS (Executive Information System) had been born. The idea was to provide relevant and timely management information using a new, much simpler user interface than had previously been available. This used what was then a revolutionary concept, a graphical user interface running on DOC PCs, and using touch screens or mouse. For executive use, the PCs were often hidden away in custom cabinets and desks, as few senior executives of the day wanted to be seen as nerdy PC users.

The first explicit EIS product was Pilot's Command Center though there had been EIS applications implemented by IRI and Comshare earlier in the decade. This was a cooperative processing product, an architecture that would now be called client/server. Because of the limited power of mid 1980s PCs, it was very server-centric, but that approach came back into fashion again with products like EUREKA: Strategy and Holos and the Web. Command Center is no longer on sale, but it introduced many concepts that are recognizable in today's OLAP products, including automatic time series handling, multidimensional client/server processing and simplified human factors (suitable for touch screen or mouse use). Some of these concepts were re-implemented in Pilot's Analysis Server product, which is now also in the autumn of its life, as is Pilot, which changed hands again in August 2000, when it was bought by Accrue Software. However, rather unexpectedly, it reappeared as an independent company in mid 2002, though it has kept a low profile since.

Spreadsheets and OLAP

By the late 1980s, the spreadsheet was already becoming dominant in end-user analysis, so the first multidimensional spreadsheet appeared in the form of Compete. This was originally marketed as a very expensive specialist tool, but the vendor could not generate the volumes to stay in business, and Computer Associates acquired it, along with a number of other spreadsheet products including SuperCalc and 20/20. The main effect of CA's acquisition of Compete was that the price was slashed, the copy protection removed and the product was heavily promoted. However, it was still not a success, a trend that was to be repeated with CA's other OLAP acquisitions. For a few years, the old Compete was still occasionally found, bundled into a heavily discounted bargain pack. Later, Compete formed the basis for CA's version 5 of SuperCalc, but the multidimensionality aspect of it was not promoted.

Lotus was the next to attempt to enter the multidimensional spreadsheet market with Improv. Bravely, this was launched on the NeXT machine. This at least guaranteed that it could not take sales away from 1-2-3, but when it was eventually ported to Windows, Excel was already too big a threat to 1-2-3 for Improv's sales to make any difference. Lotus, like CA with Compete, moved Improv down market, but this was still not enough for market success, and new development was soon discontinued. It seems that personal computer users liked their spreadsheets to be supersets of the original 1-2-3, and were not interested in new multidimensional replacements if these were not also fully compatible with their old, macro driven worksheets. Also, the concept of a small multidimensional spreadsheet, sold as a personal productivity application, clearly does not fit in with the real business world. Microsoft went this way, by adding PivotTables to Excel. Although only a small minority of Excel users take advantage of the feature, this is probably the single most widely used multidimensional analysis capability in the world, simply because there are so many users of Excel. Excel 2000 included a more sophisticated version of PivotTables, capable of acting as both a desktop OLAP, and as a client to Microsoft Analysis Services. However, the OLAP features even in Excel 2003 are inferior to those in OLAP add-ins, so there is still a good opportunity for third-party options as well.

By the late 1980s, Sinper had entered the multidimensional spreadsheet world, originally with a proprietary DOS spreadsheet, and then by linking to DOS 1-2-3. It entered the Windows era by turning its (then named) TM/1 product into a multidimensional back-end server for standard Excel and 1-2-3. Slightly later, Arbor did the same thing, although its new Essbase product could then only work in client/server mode, whereas Sinper's could also work on a stand-alone PC. This approach to bringing multidimensionality to spreadsheet users has been far more popular with users. So much so, in fact, that traditional vendors of proprietary front-ends have been forced to follow suit, and products like Express, Holos, Gentia, MineShare, PowerPlay, MetaCube and WhiteLight all proudly offered highly integrated spreadsheet access to their OLAP servers. Ironically, for its first six months, Microsoft OLAP Service was one of the few OLAP servers *not* to have a vendor-developed spreadsheet client, as Microsoft's (very basic) offering only appeared in June 1999 in Excel 2000. However, the (then) OLAP@Work Excel add-in filled the gap, and still (under its new snappy name, Business Query MD for Excel) provides much better exploitation of the server than does Microsoft's own Excel interface. Since then there have been at least ten other third party Excel add-ins developed for Microsoft Analysis Services, all offering capabilities not available even in Excel 2003. However, Business Objects' acquisition of Crystal Decisions has led to the phasing out of BusinessQuery MD for Excel, to be replaced by technology from Crystal.

There was a rush of new OLAP Excel add-ins in 2004 from Business Objects, Cognos, Microsoft, MicroStrategy and Oracle. Perhaps with users disillusioned by disappointing Web capabilities, the vendors rediscovered that many numerate users would rather have their BI data displayed via a flexible Excel-based interface rather than in a dumb Web page or PDF.

ROLAP and DOLAP

A few users demanded multidimensional applications that were much too large to be handled in multidimensional databases, and the relational OLAP tools evolved to meet this need. These presented the usual multidimensional view to users, sometimes even including a spreadsheet front-end, even though all the data was stored in an RDBMS. These have a much higher cost per user, and lower performance than specialized multidimensional tools, but they are a way of providing this popular form of analysis even to data not stored in a multidimensional structure. Most have not survived.

Other vendors expanded into what is sometimes called desktop OLAP: small cubes, generated from large databases, but downloaded to PCs for processing (even though, in Web implementations, the cubes usually reside on the server). These have proved very successful indeed, and the one vendor that sells both a relational query tool and a multidimensional analysis tool (Cognos, with Impromptu and PowerPlay) reports that the latter is much more popular with end-users than is the former.

Now, even the relational database vendors have embraced multidimensional analysis, with Oracle, IBM, Microsoft, the former Informix, CA and Sybase all developing or marketing products in this area. Ironically, having largely ignored multidimensionality for so many years, it seemed for a while that Oracle, Microsoft and IBM might be the new 'OLAP triad', with large OLAP market shares, based on selling multidimensional products they did not invent. In the event, Oracle and IBM failed to achieve this status, but Microsoft is now the largest OLAP vendor.

Lessons

So, what lessons can we draw from this 35-years of history?

- Multidimensionality is here to stay. Even hard to use, expensive, slow and elitist multidimensional products survive in limited niches; when these restrictions are removed, it booms. We are about to see the biggest-ever growth of multidimensional applications.
- End-users will not give up their general-purpose spreadsheets. Even when accessing multidimensional databases, spreadsheets are the most popular client platform, and there are numerous third-party Excel add-ins for Microsoft Analysis Services to fill the gaps in Microsoft's own offering. Most other BI vendors now also offer Excel add-ins as alternative front-ends. Stand-alone multidimensional spreadsheets are not successful unless they can provide full upwards compatibility with traditional spreadsheets, something that Improv and Compete failed to do.
- Most people find it easy to use multidimensional applications, but building and maintaining them takes a particular aptitude – which has stopped them from becoming mass-market products. But, using a combination of simplicity, pricing and bundling, Microsoft now seems determined to prove that it can make OLAP servers almost as widely used as relational databases.
- Multidimensional applications are often quite large and are usually suitable for workgroups, rather than individuals. Although there is a role for pure single-user multidimensional products, the most successful installations are multi-user, client/server applications, with the bulk of the data downloaded from feeder systems once rather than many times. There usually needs to be some IT support for this, even if the application is driven by end-users.
- Simple, cheap OLAP products are much more successful than powerful, complex, expensive products. Buyers generally opt for the lowest cost, simplest product that will meet most of their needs; if necessary, they often compromise their requirements. Projects using complex products also have a higher failure rate, probably because there is more opportunity for things to go wrong.

OLAP Milestones

Year	Event	Comment
1962	Publication of *A Programming Language* by Ken Iverson	First multidimensional language; used Greek symbols for operators. Became available on IBM mainframes in the late 1960s and still used to a limited extent today. APL would not count as a modern OLAP tool, but many of its ideas live on in today's altogether less elitist products, and some applications (e.g. Cognos Planning Analyst and Cognos Consolidation, the former Lex 2000) still use APL internally.
1970	Express available on timesharing (followed by	First multidimensional tool aimed at marketing applications; now owned by Oracle,

	in-house versions later in the 1970s)	and still one of the market leaders (after several rewrites and two changes of ownership). Although the code is much changed, the concepts and the data model are not. The modern version of this engine is now shipping as the MOLAP engine in Oracle9*i* Release 2 OLAP Option.
1982	Comshare System W available on timesharing (and in-house mainframes the following year)	First OLAP tool aimed at financial applications No longer marketed, but still in limited use on IBM mainframes; its Windows descendent is marketed as the planning component of Comshare MPC. The later Essbase product used many of the same concepts, and like System W, suffers from database explosion.
1984	Metaphor launched	First ROLAP. Sales of this Mac cousin were disappointing, partly because of proprietary hardware and high prices (the start-up cost for an eight-workstation system, including 72Mb file server, database server and software was $64,000). But, like Mac users, Metaphor users remained fiercely loyal.
1985	Pilot Command Center launched	First client/server EIS style OLAP; used a time-series approach running on VAX servers and standard PCs as clients.
1990	Cognos PowerPlay launched	This became both the first desktop and the first Windows OLAP and now leads the "desktop" sector. Though we still class this as a desktop OLAP on functional grounds, most customers now implement the much more scalable client/server and Web versions.
1991	IBM acquired Metaphor	The first of many OLAP products to change hands. Metaphor became part of the doomed Apple-IBM Taligent joint venture and was renamed IDS, but there are unlikely to be any remaining sites.
1992	Essbase launched	First well-marketed OLAP product, which went on to become the market leading OLAP server by 1997.
1993	Codd white paper coined the OLAP term	This white paper, commissioned by Arbor Software, brought multidimensional analysis to the attention of many more people than ever before. However, the **Codd OLAP rules** were soon forgotten (unlike his influential and respected relational rules).

1994	MicroStrategy DSS Agent launched	First ROLAP to do without a multidimensional engine, with almost all processing being performed by multi-pass SQL – an appropriate approach for very large databases, or those with very large dimensions, but suffers from a severe performance penalty. The modern MicroStrategy 7*i* has a more conventional three-tier hybrid OLAP architecture.
1995	Holos 4.0 released	First hybrid OLAP, allowing a single application to access both relational and multidimensional databases simultaneously. Many other OLAP tools are now using this approach. Holos was acquired by Crystal Decisions in 1996, but has now been discontinued.
1995	Oracle acquired Express	First important OLAP takeover. Arguably, it was this event that put OLAP on the map, and it almost certainly triggered the entry of the other database vendors. Express has now become a hybrid OLAP and competes with both multidimensional and relational OLAP tools. Oracle soon promised that Express would be fully integrated into the rest of its product line but, almost ten years later, has still failed to deliver on this promise.
1996	Business Objects 4.0 launched	First tool to provide seamless multidimensional and relational reporting from desktop cubes dynamically built from relational data. Early releases had problems, now largely resolved, but Business Objects has always struggled to deliver a true Web version of this desktop OLAP architecture. It is expected finally to achieve this by using the former Crystal Enterprise as the base.
1997	Microsoft announced OLE DB for OLAP	This project was code-named Tensor, and became the 'industry standard' OLAP API before even a single product supporting it shipped. Many third-party products now support this API, which is evolving into the more modern XML for Analysis.
1998	IBM DB2 OLAP Server released	This version of Essbase stored all data in a form of relational star schema, in DB2 or other relational databases, but it was more like a slow MOLAP than a scalable ROLAP. IBM

		later abandoned its "enhancements", and now ships the standard version of Essbase as DB2 OLAP Server. Despite the name, it remains non-integrated with DB2.
1998	Hyperion Solutions formed	Arbor and Hyperion Software 'merged' in the first large consolidation in the OLAP market. Despite the name, this was more of a takeover of Hyperion by Arbor than a merger, and was probably initiated by fears of Microsoft's entry to the OLAP market. Like most other OLAP acquisitions, this went badly. Not until 2002 did the merged company begin to perform competitively.
1999	Microsoft OLAP Services shipped	This project was code-named Plato and then named Decision Support Services in early pre-release versions, before being renamed OLAP Services on release. It used technology acquired from Panorama Software Systems in 1996. This soon became the OLAP server volume market leader through ease of deployment, sophisticated storage architecture (ROLAP/MOLAP/Hybrid), huge third-party support, low prices and the Microsoft marketing machine.
1999	CA starts mopping up failed OLAP servers	CA acquired the former Prodea Beacon, via Platinum, in 1999 and renamed it Decision-Base. In 2000 it also acquired the former IA Eureka, via Sterling. This collection of failed OLAPs seems destined to grow, though the products are soon snuffed-out under CA's hard-nosed ownership, and as The OLAP Survey 2, the remaining CA Cleverpath OLAP customers were very unhappy by 2002. By the **The OLAP Survey 4** in 2004, there seemed to be no remaining users of the product.
2000	Microsoft renames OLAP Services to Analysis Services	Microsoft renamed the second release of its OLAP server for no good reason, thus confusing much of the market. Of course, many references to the two previous names remain within the product.
2000	XML for Analysis announced	This initiative for a multi-vendor, cross-platform, XML-based OLAP API is led by Microsoft (later joined by Hyperion and then SAS Institute). It is, in effect, an XML

		implementation of OLE DB for OLAP. XML for Analysis usage is unlikely to take off until 2006.
2001	Oracle begins shipping the successor to Express	Six years after acquiring Express, which has been in use since 1970, Oracle began shipping Oracle9*i* OLAP, expected eventually to succeed Express. However, the first release of the new generation Oracle OLAP was incomplete and unusable. The full replacement of the technology and applications is not expected until well into 2003, some eight years after Oracle acquired Express.
2001	MicroStrategy abandons Strategy.com	Strategy.com was part of MicroStrategy's grand strategy to become the next Microsoft. Instead, it very nearly bankrupted the company, which finally shut the subsidiary down in late 2001.
2002	Oracle ships integrated OLAP server	Oracle9*i* Release 2 OLAP Option shipped in mid 2002, with a MOLAP server (a modernized Express), called the Analytical Workspace, integrated within the database. This was the closest integration yet between a MOLAP server and an RDBMS. But it is still not a complete solution, lacking competitive front-end tools and applications.
2003	The year of consolidation	Business Objects purchases Crystal Decisions, Hyperion Solutions Brio Software, Cognos Adaytum, and Geac Comshare.
2004	Excel add-ins go mainstream	Business Objects, Cognos, Microsoft, MicroStrategy and Oracle all release new Excel add-ins for accessing OLAP data, while Sage buys one of the leading Analysis Services Excel add-in vendors, IntelligentApps.
2004	Essbase database explosion curbed	Hyperion releases Essbase 7X which included the results of Project Ukraine: the Aggregate Storage Option. This finally cured Essbase's notorious **database explosion** syndrome, making the product suitable for marketing, as well as financial, applications.
2004	Cognos buys its second Frango	Cognos buys Frango, the Swedish consolidation system. Less well known is the fact that Adaytum, which Cognos bought in the previous year, had its origins in IBM's Frango project from the early 1980s.

2005	Microsoft to ship the much-delayed SQL Server 2005?	Originally planned for release in 2003, Microsoft may just manage to ship the major 'Yukon' version before the end of 2005.

17.4 WHAT'S IN A NAME?

Everyone wants to be (or at least look like) a winner, and this is at least as true of the dozens of OLAP vendors, as it would be for any other competitive group – so they all try to be perceived as leaders or pioneers of their chosen niches. They work hard to come up with distinct positioning statements that can make them appear to dominate significant portions of the market. This requires them to define ingeniously subtle variations on common themes, because there aren't enough suitable descriptive words to go round. This self-generated classification system makes the vendors' marketing people feel good, but the results can be very confusing for buyers.

The phrases *business intelligence* and *decision support* crop up most often, but *performance management* seems to have replaced the short-lived EBI or e-BI fashion. *OLAP* is used much less often than might be expected, and the old *EIS* term appears almost to have disappeared. The most popular self-descriptions are *pioneer* and *world/global leading* (or *leader*). Some even claim to be the "only" providers of their type of offering. Ironically, however, few of the largest vendors use grandiose words like these to describe themselves.

However, one change since researchers began monitoring slogans is that vendors have become more cautious in calling themselves "world market leaders": fewer of the obviously small companies now make this outlandish claim (in fact, few of these vendors even make it into our market shares table). Presumably lawyers now check more press releases, particularly in the public companies?

Someone who attempted to classify the products into competing subgroups would have real trouble doing so if their main source of information was vendors' press releases. For example, Brio, Business Objects and Cognos are all direct competitors (and cannot all be the leader of the same segment), but this is hardly apparent from their favored descriptions of themselves.

Another problem is that industry watchers all have their own contrived categories and each refuses to use classifications coined by others. The smaller vendors often try to curry favor with whichever industry analyst they currently regard as most influential and therefore adopt essentially meaningless descriptions like "enterprise business intelligence". Several quite different products that are in no way competitive with each other can therefore apparently fall into the same category, whereas direct competitors might opt for quite different analyst groupings – none of which helps the buyer.

The result is that someone who wishes to select suitable OLAP products cannot even begin the search by using vendors' own classifications of themselves. If, for example, a site wants to implement typical OLAP applications like a management reporting system, a budgeting and planning system or front-end software for a data warehouse, a text search of press releases and Web sites looking for these words is likely to produce a very unreliable list of suppliers.

Company	Self-description
Adaytum	*"the leading provider of enterprise business planning (EBP) solutions"*
AlphaBlox	*"a leading global provider of customer analytics and business planning software that rapidly transforms information into knowledge"*
Applix TM1	*"the leading business intelligence analytical engine that powers a suite of planning, reporting and analysis solutions used by Global 2000 enterprises"*
Brio Software	*"the leading provider of next-generation business intelligence tools that help Global 3000 companies achieve breakthrough business performance"*
Business Objects	*"the world's leading provider of business intelligence (BI) solutions"*
Cartesis	*"a leading provider of world-class strategic financial software"*
Cognos	*"the world leader in business intelligence (BI)"*
Comshare	*"a leading provider of software that helps companies implement and execute strategy"*
CorVu	*"a global provider of Enterprise Business Performance Management, e-Business Intelligence and Balanced Scorecard Solutions"*
Crystal Decisions	*"is one of the world's leading information management software companies"*
Dimensional Insight	*"a pioneer in developing and marketing multi-dimensional data visualization, analysis, and reporting solutions that put you in command of your business"*
Gentia Software	*"a leading supplier of intelligent analytical applications for enterprise performance management and customer relationship management"*
Hummingbird Communications	*"a fully integrated, scalable enterprise business intelligence solution"*
Hyperion Solutions	*"a global leader in business performance management software"*
Longview Solutions	*"a leading provider of fully-integrated financial analysis and decision support solutions"*
MicroStrategy	*"a leading worldwide provider of business intelligence software"*

Oracle Express	*"a powerful, multidimensional OLAP analysis environment"*
ProClarity	*"delivers analytic software and services that accelerate the speed organizations make informed decisions to optimize business performance"*
Sagent Technology	*"provides a complete software platform for business intelligence"*
SAS Institute	*"the market leader in business intelligence and decision support"*
ShowCase	*"provides a complete spectrum of business intelligence (BI) solutions"*
Speedware Corporation	*"a global provider of Internet tools and services, developing innovative solutions for a wide variety of platforms and markets, including business intelligence solutions"*
White Light Systems	*"the leading provider of next-generation analytic applications"*

17.5 MARKET ANALYSIS

Due to the consolidation in the market, it is now less relevant than it once was. There are now fewer significant suppliers, and the mature products have expanded to the extent that they are harder to classify neatly than they once were.

Although there are over many OLAP suppliers, they are not all direct competitors. In fact, they can be grouped into four principal categories, with relatively little overlap between them. It is convenient to show the categories in the form of a square, because this neatly encapsulates the relationships they have with each other. Where there are similarities, they are with vendors on adjacent sides of the square, and not with those on the opposite side.

Vendors can be expected to be quite well informed – though not complimentary – about their direct competitors in the same segment (although they are sometimes alarmingly misinformed), and somewhat less knowledgeable about those in the adjacent sides of the square. They are usually relatively ignorant, and often derisive, about vendors on the opposite side of the square. More surprisingly, the same is often true of hardware suppliers, consultants and systems integrators, whose expertise is usually concentrated on a few products. This means that it can be misleading to assume that someone who clearly has expert knowledge about a couple of OLAP products will be equally well-informed about others, particularly if they are in other different segments.

This is more of a vendor than a product categorization, although in most cases it amounts to the same thing. Even when vendors choose to occupy positions on more than one side of the square (with different products or by unbundling components), their attitudes and style often anchor them to one position. The **architectural differences** between the products are described separately in The OLAP Report.

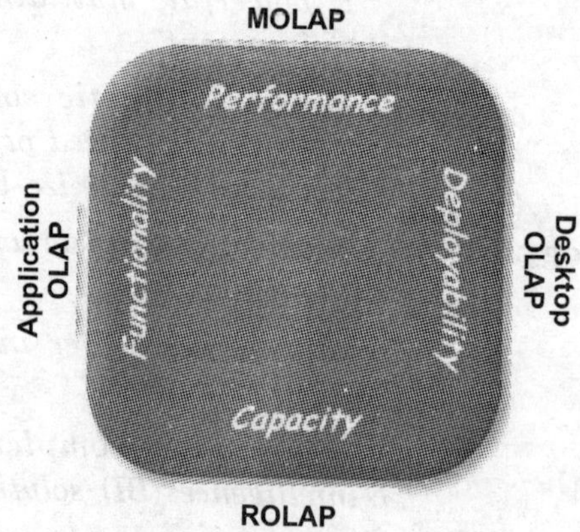

A potential buyer should create a shortlist of OLAP vendors for detailed consideration that fall largely into a *single* one of the four categories. There is something wrong with a shortlist that includes products from opposite sides of the square.

Briefly, the four sectors can be described as:

1. **Application OLAP** is the longest established sector (which existed two decades before the OLAP term was coined), and includes many vendors. Their products are sold either as complete applications, or as very functional, complete toolkits from which complex applications can be built. Nearly all application OLAP products include a multidimensional database, although a few also work as hybrid or relational OLAPs. Sometimes the bundled multidimensional engines are not especially competitive in performance terms, and there is now a tendency for vendors in this sector to use third-party multidimensional engines. The typical strengths include integration and high functionality while the weaknesses may be complexity and high cost per user. Vendors used to include Oracle, Hyperion Solutions, Comshare, Adaytum, formerly Seagate Software, Pilot Software, Gentia Software, SAS Institute, WhiteLight, Sagent, Speedware, Kenan and Information Builders – but many of these have been acquired, and some have disappeared entirely. Numerous specialist vendors build applications on OLAP servers from Hyperion, Microsoft, MicroStrategy and Applix.

   Because many of these vendors and their applications are aimed at particular vertical (e.g., retail, manufacturing, and banking) or horizontal (e.g., budgeting, financial consolidation, sales analysis) markets, there is room for many vendors in this segment as most will not be competing directly with each other. There may be room only for two or three in each narrow niche, however.

2. **MOLAP (Multidimensional Database OLAP)** has been identified since the mid 1990s, although the sector has existed since the late 1980s. It consists of products that can be bought as unbundled, high performance multidimensional or hybrid databases. These products often include multi-user data updating. In some cases, the vendors are specialists, who do nothing else, while others also sell other application components. As these are sold as best of breed solutions, they have to deliver high performance, sophisticated multidimensional calculation functionality

and openness, and are measured in terms of the range of complementary products available from third-parties. Generally speaking, these products do not handle applications as large as those that are possible in the ROLAP products, although this is changing as these products evolve into hybrid OLAPs. There are two specialist MOLAP vendors, Hyperion (Essbase) and Applix (TM1), who provide unbundled high performance, engines, but are open to their users purchasing add-on tools from partners.

Microsoft joined this sector with its OLAP Services module in SQL Server 7.0, which is driving other OLAP technology vendors into the Application OLAP segment; Arbor acquired Hyperion Software to become Hyperion Solutions and Applix is also moving into the applications business. Vendors in this segment are competing directly with each other, and it is unlikely that more than two or three vendors can survive with this strategy in the long term. With SQL Server 2000 Analysis Services, released in September 2000, Microsoft is a formidable competitor in this segment.

3. **DOLAP (Desktop OLAP)** has existed since 1990, but has only become recognized in the mid 1990s. These are client-based OLAP products that are easy to deploy and have a low cost per seat. They normally have good database links, often to both relational as well as multidimensional servers, as well as local PC files. It is not normally necessary to build an application. They usually have very limited functionality and capacity compared to the more specialized OLAP products. Cognos (with PowerPlay) is the leader, but Business Objects, Brio Technology, Crystal Decisions and Hummingbird are also contenders. Oracle is aiming at this sector (and some of its people insist that it is already in it) with Discoverer, although it has far too little functionality for it to be a contender (Discoverer also has less Web functionality than the real desktop OLAPs). It lacks the ability to work off-line or to perform even quite trivial multidimensional calculations, both of which are prerequisites; it is also unable to access OLAP servers, even including Oracle's own Express Server. Crystal Enterprise also aims at this sector, but it too falls short of the full functionality of the mature desktop OLAPs.

   The Web versions of desktop OLAPs include a mid-tier server that replaces some or all of the client functionality. This blurs the distinction between desktop OLAPs and other server based OLAPs, but the differing functionality still distinguishes them.

   Vendors in this sector are direct competitors, and once the market growth slows down, a shake-out seems inevitable. Successful desktop OLAP vendors are characterized by huge numbers of alliances and reseller deals, and many of their sales are made through OEMs and VARs who bundle low cost desktop OLAP products with their applications as a way of delivering integrated multidimensional analysis capabilities. As a result, the leaders in this sector aim to have hundreds of thousands of 'seats', but most users probably only do very simple analyses. There is also a lot of 'shelfware' in the large desktop OLAP sites, because buyers are encouraged to purchase far more seats than they need.

4. **ROLAP (Relational OLAP)** is another sector that has existed since Metaphor in the early 1980s (so none of the current vendors can honestly claim to have invented

it, but that doesn't stop them trying), but it was recognized in 1994. It is by far the smallest of the OLAP sectors, but has had a great deal of publicity thanks to some astute marketing. Despite confident predictions to the contrary, ROLAP products have completely failed to dominate the OLAP market, and not one ROLAP vendor has made a profit to date.

Products in this sector draw all their data and metadata in a standard RDBMS, with none being stored in any external files. They are capable of dealing with very large data volumes, but are complex and expensive to implement, have a slow query performance and are incapable of performing complex financial calculations. In operation, they work more as batch report writers than interactive analysis tools (typically, responses to complex queries are measured in minutes or even hours rather than seconds). They are suitable for read-only reporting applications, and are most often used for sales analysis in the retail, consumer goods, telecom and financial services industries (usually for companies which have very large numbers of customers, products or both, and wish to report on and sometimes analyze sales in detail).

Probably because the niche is so small, no ROLAP products have succeeded in almost 20 years of trying. The pioneer ROLAP, Metaphor, failed to build a sound business and was eventually acquired by IBM, which calls it IDS. Now MicroStrategy dominates what remains of this sector, having defeated Information Advantage in the marketplace. Sterling acquired the failing IA in 1999, and CA acquired Sterling in 2000, and the former IA ROLAP server has, under CA's ownership, effectively disappeared from the market. The former Prodea was acquired by Platinum technology, which was itself acquired by CA in 1999, and the Beacon product (now renamed DecisionBase) has also disappeared from the market. Informix has also failed with its MetaCube product, which it acquired in 1995, but abandoned before the end of 1999. The loss-making WhiteLight also competes in this area, although its architecture is closer to hybrid OLAP, and it positions itself as an applications platform rather than a ROLAP server; it also has a tiny market share. MineShare and Sagent failed to make any inroads at all into the ROLAP market. Even MicroStrategy, the most vociferous promoter of the ROLAP concept, has moved to more of hybrid OLAP architecture with its long-delayed and much improved 7.0 version, which finally shipped in June 2000. Despite being the most successful ROLAP vendor by far, MicroStrategy has also made by far the largest losses ever in the business intelligence industry.

Similarly, customers of hybrid products that allow both ROLAP and MOLAP modes, like Microsoft Analysis Services, Oracle Express and Crystal Holos (now discontinued), almost always choose the MOLAP mode.

17.6 *OLAP* ARCHITECTURES

Much confusion, some of it deliberate, abounds about OLAP architectures, with terms like ROLAP, HOLAP, MOLAP and DOLAP (with more than one definition) proliferating at one stage, though the last of these is used less these days. In fact, there are a number of options for where OLAP data could be stored, and where it could be processed. Most vendors only offer a subset of these, and some then go on to attempt to 'prove' that their approach is the only sensible one. This is, of course, nonsense. However, quite a few products can operate in more than one mode, and vendors of such products tend to be less strident in their architectural arguments.

There are many subtle variations, but in principle, there are only three places where the data can be stored and three where the majority of the multidimensional calculations can be performed. This means that, in theory, there are possible nine basic architectures, although only six make any sense.

Data Staging

Most data in OLAP applications originates in other systems. However, in some applications (such as planning and budgeting), the data might be captured directly by the OLAP application. When the data comes from other applications, it is usually necessary for the active data to be stored in a separate, duplicated form for the OLAP application. This may be referred to as a data warehouse or, more commonly today, as a data mart. For those not familiar with the reasons for this duplication, this is a summary of the main reasons:

- **Performance:** OLAP applications are often large, but are nevertheless used for unpredictable interactive analysis. This requires that the data be accessed very rapidly, which usually dictates that it is kept in a separate, optimized structure which can be accessed without damaging the response from the operational systems.
- **Multiple Data Sources:** Most OLAP applications require data sourced from multiple feeder systems, possibly including external sources and even desktop applications. The process of merging these multiple data feeds can be very complex, because the underlying systems probably use different coding systems and may also have different periodicities. For example, in a multinational company, it is rare for subsidiaries in different countries to use the same coding system for suppliers and customers, and they may well also use different ERP systems, particularly if the group has grown by acquisition.
- **Cleansing Data:** It is depressingly common for transaction systems to be full of erroneous data which needs to be 'cleansed' before it is ready to be analyzed. Apart from the small percentage of accidentally mis-coded data, there will also be examples of optional fields that have not been completed. For example, many companies would like to analyze their business in terms of their customers' vertical markets. This requires that each customer (or even each sale) be assigned an industry code; however, this takes a certain amount of effort on the part of those entering the data, for which they get little return, so they are likely, at the very least, to cut corners. There may even be deliberate distortion of the data if sales people are rewarded more for some sales than others: they will certainly respond to this direct temptation by 'adjusting' (i.e. distorting) the data to their own advantage if they think they can get away with it.
- **Adjusting Data:** There are many reasons why data may need adjusting before it can be used for analysis. In order that this can be done without affecting the transaction systems, the OLAP data needs to be kept separate. Examples of reasons for adjusting the data include:

- Foreign subsidiaries may operate under different accounting conventions or have different year-ends, so the data may need modifying before it can be used.
- The source data may be in multiple currencies that must be translated.
- The management, operational and legal structures of a company may be different.
- The source applications may use different codes for products and customers.
- Inter-company trading effects may need to be eliminated, perhaps to measure true added value at each stage of trading.
- Some data may need obscuring or changing for reasons of confidentiality.
- There may be analysis dimensions that are not part of the operational data such as vertical markets, television advertising regions or demographic characteristics.

- **Timing:** If the data in an OLAP application comes from multiple feeder systems, it is very likely that they are updated on different cycles. At any one time, therefore, the feeder applications may be at different stages of update. For example, the month-end updates may be complete in one system, but not in another and a third system may be updated on a weekly cycle. In order that the analysis is based on consistent data, the data needs to be staged, within a data warehouse or directly in an OLAP database.
- **History:** The majority of OLAP applications include time as a dimension, and many useful results are obtained from time series analysis. But for this to be useful it may be necessary to hold several years' data on-line in this way – something that the operational systems feeding the OLAP application are very unlikely to do. This requires an initial effort to locate the historical data, and usually to adjust it because of changes in organizational and product structures. The resulting data is then held in the OLAP database.
- **Summaries:** Operational data is necessarily very detailed, but most decision-making activities require a much higher level view. In the interests of efficiency, it is usually necessary to store merged, adjusted information at summary level, and this would not be feasible in a transaction processing system.
- **Data Updating:** If the application allows users to alter or input data, it is obviously essential that the application has its own separate database that does not over-write the 'official' operational data.

Storing Active OLAP Data

Given the necessity to store active OLAP data in an efficient, duplicated form, there are essentially three options. Many products can use more than one of these, sometimes simultaneously. Note that 'store' in this context means holding the data in a persistent form (for at least the duration of a session, and often shared between users), not simply for the time required to process a single query.

- **Relational Database:** This is an obvious choice, particularly if the data is sourced from an RDBMS (either because a data warehouse has been implemented using an

RDBMS or because the operational systems themselves hold their data in an RDBMS). In most cases, the data would be stored in a denormalized structure such as a star schema, or one of its variants, such as snowflake; a normalized database would not be appropriate for performance and other reasons. Often, summary data will be held in aggregate tables.

- **Multidimensional Database:** In this case, the active data is stored in a multidimensional database on a server. It may include data extracted and summarized from legacy systems or relational databases and from end-users. In most cases, the database is stored on disk, but some products allow RAM based multidimensional data structures for greater performance. It is usually possible (and sometimes compulsory) for aggregates and other calculated items to be pre-computed and the results stored in some form of array structure. In a few cases, the multidimensional database allows concurrent multi-user read-write access, but this is unusual; many products allow single-write/multi-read access, while the rest are limited to read-only access.
- **Client-based Files:** In this case, relatively small extracts of data are held on client machines. They may be distributed in advance, or created on demand (possibly via the Web). As with multidimensional databases on the server, active data may be held on disk or in RAM, and some products allow only read access.

These three locations have different capacities, and they are arranged in descending order. They also have different performance characteristics, with relational databases being a great deal slower than the other two options.

Processing OLAP Data

Just as there are three possible locations for OLAP data, exactly the same three options are available for processing the data. As will be seen, the multidimensional calculations do not need to occur in the place where the data is stored.

- **SQL:** This is far from being an obvious choice to perform complex multidimensional calculations, even if the live OLAP data is stored in an RDBMS. SQL does not have the ability to perform multidimensional calculations in single statements, and complex multi-pass SQL is necessary to achieve more than the most trivial multidimensional functionality. Nevertheless, this has not stopped vendors from trying. In most cases, they do a limited range of suitable calculations in SQL, with the results then being used as input by a multidimensional engine, which does most of the work, either on the client or in a mid-tier server. There may also be a RAM resident cache which can hold data used in more than one query: this improves response dramatically.
- **Multidimensional Server Engine:** This is an obvious and popular place to perform multidimensional calculations in client/server OLAP applications, and it is used in many products. Performance is usually good, because the engine and the database can be optimized to work together, and the availability of plenty of memory on a server can mean that large scale array calculations can be performed very efficiently.
- **Client Multidimensional Engine:** On the assumption that most users have relatively powerful PCs, many vendors aim to take advantage of this power to

perform some, or most, of the multidimensional calculations. With the expected rise in popularity of thin clients, vendors with this architecture have to move most of the client based processing to new Web application servers.

The OLAP Architectural Matrix

Three places to store multidimensional data, and the same three locations for multidimensional engines: combining these gives nine possible storage/processing options. But some of these are nonsensical: it would be absurd to store data in a multidimensional database, but do multidimensional processing in an RDBMS, so only the six options on or below the diagonal make sense.

Multidimensional data storage options

Multidimensional processing options	*RDBMS*	*Multidimensional databaser server*	*Client files*
Multi-pass SQL	1 Cartesis Magnitude MicroStrategy		
Multidimensional server engine	2 *Crystal Holos (ROLAP mode)* *Hyperion Essbase* Longview Khalix *Speedware Media/MR* *Microsoft Analysis Services* *Oracle Express (ROLAP mode)* Oracle OLAP Option (ROLAP mode) *Pilot Analysis Server* WhiteLight	4 SAS CFO Vision *Crystal Holos* Geac MPC *Hyperion Essbase* *Oracle Express* Oracle OLAP Option AW *Microsoft Analysis Services* PowerPlay Enterprise Server *Pilot Analysis Server* Applix TM1	
Client multidimensional engine	3 Oracle Discoverer	5 Comshare FDC Dimensional Insight Hyperion Enterprise Hyperion Pillar	6 Hyperion Intelligence Business Objects Cognos Power Play Personal Express TM1 Perspectives

The widely used (and misused) nomenclature is not particularly helpful, but roughly speaking:

- Relational OLAP (ROLAP) products are in squares ***1***, ***2*** and ***3***
- MDB (also known as MOLAP) products are in squares ***4*** and ***5***
- Desktop OLAP products are in square ***6***
- Hybrid OLAP products are those that are in **both** squares ***2*** and ***4*** (shown in *italics*)

The fact that several products are in the same square, and therefore have similar architectures, does not mean that they are necessarily very similar products. For instance, DB2 OLAP Server and Eureka are quite different products that just happen to share certain storage and processing characteristics.

Is there an ideal choice?

Each of these options has its own strengths and weaknesses, and there is no single optimum choice. It is perfectly reasonable for sites to use products from more than one of the squares, and even more than one from a single square if they are specialized products used for different applications. As might be expected, the squares containing the most products are also the most widely used architectures, and vice versa. The choice of architecture does affect the performance, capacity, functionality and particularly the scalability of an OLAP solution and this is discussed elsewhere in The OLAP Report.

17.7 DIMENSIONAL DATA STRUCTURES

This is one of the older analyses in The OLAP Report, and it refers to many products that are no longer on the market. For historical accuracy, we have left in these references.

The simplest view of the data for a multidimensional application is that it exists in a large Cartesian space bounded by all the dimensions of the application. Some might call this a data space, emphasizing that it is a logical rather than a physical concept. While it would be perfectly possible to build a product that worked like this, with all the data held in a simple uncompressed array, no large-scale product could be as basic as this.

In fact, as shown in Figure 17.1, multidimensional data is always sparse, and often 'clumpy': that is, data cells are not distributed evenly through the multidimensional space. Pockets of data cells are clustered together in places and time periods when a business event has occurred.

The designers of multidimensional products all know this, and they adopt a variety of technical strategies for dealing with this sparse, but clustered data. They then choose one of two principal ways of presenting this multidimensional data to the user. These are not just viewing options: they also determine how the data is processed, and, in particular, how many calculations are permitted.

Figure 17.1. Data in Multidimensional Applications Tends to be Clustered into Relatively Dense Blocks, with Large Gaps in Between – Rather Like Planets and Stars in Space.

Hypercube

Some large scale products do present a simple, single-cube logical structure, even though they use a different, more sophisticated, underlying model to compress the sparse data. They usually allow data values to be entered for every combination of dimension members, and all parts of the data space have identical dimensionality. In this report, we call this data structure a **hypercube**, without any suggestion that the dimensions are all equal sized or that the number of dimensions is limited to any particular value. We use this term in a specific way, and not as a general term for multidimensional structures with more than three dimensions. However, the use of the term does not mean that data is stored in any particular format, and it can apply equally to both multidimensional databases and relational OLAPs. It is also independent of the degree to which the product pre-calculates the data.

Purveyors of hypercube products emphasize their greater simplicity for the end-user. Of course, the apparently simple hypercube is not how the data is usually stored and there are extensive technical strategies, discussed elsewhere in The OLAP Report, to manage the sparsity efficiently. Essbase (at least up to version 4.1) is an example of a modern product that used the hypercube approach. It is not surprising that Comshare chose to work with Arbor in using Essbase, as Comshare has adopted the hypercube approach in several previous generations of less sophisticated multidimensional products going back to System W in 1981. In turn, Thorn-EMI Computer Software, the company that Arbor's founders previously worked for, adopted the identical approach in FCS-Multi, so Essbase could be described as a third generation hypercube product, with logical (though not technical) roots in the System W family.

Many of the simpler products also use hypercubes and this is particularly true of the ROLAP applications that use a single fact table star schema: it behaves as a hypercube. In practice, therefore, most multidimensional query tools look at one hypercube at a time. Some examples of hypercube products include **Essbase** (and therefore **Analyzer** and

Comshare/Geac Decision), **Executive Viewer**, **CFO Vision**, **BI/Analyze** (the former P^{a}BLO) and **PowerPlay**.

There is a variant of the hypercube that we call the **fringed hypercube**. This is a dense hypercube, with a small number of dimensions, to which additional analysis dimensions can be added for parts of the structure. The most obvious products in this report to have this structure are **Hyperion Enterprise** and Financial Management, **CLIME** and **Comshare (now Geac) FDC**.

Multicubes

The other, much more common, approach is what we call the **multicube** structure. In multicube products, the application designer segments the database into a set of multidimensional structures each of which is composed of a subset of the overall number of dimensions in the database. In this report, we call these smaller structures subcubes; the names used by the various products include variables (Express, Pilot and Acumate), structures (Holos), cubes (TM1 and Microsoft OLAP Services) and indicators (Media). They might be, for example, a set of variables or accounts, each dimensioned by just the dimensions that apply to that variable. Exponents of these systems emphasize their greater versatility and potentially greater efficiency (particularly with sparse data), dismissing hypercubes as simply a subset of their own approach. This dismissal is unfounded, as hypercube products also break up the database into subcubes under the surface, thus achieving many of the efficiencies of multicubes, without the user-visible complexities. The original example of the multicube approach was Express, but most of the newer products also use modern variants of this approach.

Because Express has always used multicubes, this can be regarded as the longest established OLAP structure, predating hypercubes by at least a decade. In fact, the multicube approach goes back even further, to the original multidimensional product, APL from the 1960s, which worked in precisely this way.

ROLAP products can also be multicubes if they can handle multiple base fact tables, each with different dimensionality. Most serious ROLAPs, like those from **Informix**, **CA** and **MicroStrategy**, have this capability. Note that the only large-scale ROLAPs still on sale are MicroStrategy and SAP BW.

It is also possible to identify two main types of multicube: the **block multicube** (as used by **Business Objects**, **Gentia**, **Holos**, Microsoft **Analysis Services** and **TM1**) and the **series multicube** (as used by **Acumate**, **Express**, **Media** and **Pilot**). Note that several of these products have now been discontinued.

Block multicubes use orthogonal dimensions, so there are no special dimensions at the data level. A cube may consist of any number of the defined dimensions, and both measures and time are treated as ordinary dimensions, just like any other. Series multicubes treat each variable as a separate cube (often a time series), with its own set of other dimensions. However, these distinctions are not hard and fast, and the various multicube implementations do not necessarily fall cleanly into one type or the other.

The block multicubes are more flexible, because they make no assumptions about dimensions and allow multiple measures to be handled together, but are often less convenient for reporting, because the multidimensional viewers can usually only look at one block at a time (an example of this can be seen in TM1's implementation of the former OLAP Council's APB-1 benchmark). The series multicubes do not have this restriction. Microsoft Analysis Services, GentiaDB and especially Holos get round the problem by allowing cubes to be joined, thus presenting a single cube view of data that is actually processed and stored physically in multiple cubes. Holos allows views of views, something that not all products support. Essbase transparent partitions are a less sophisticated version of this concept.

Series multicubes are the older form, and only one product (Speedware Media) whose development first started after the early 1980s has used them. The block multicubes came along in the mid 1980s, and now seem to be the most popular choice. There is one other form, the atomic multicube, which was mentioned in the first edition of The OLAP Report, but it appears not to have caught on.

Which is better?

We do not take sides on this matter. We have seen widespread, successful use of both hypercube and both flavors of multicube products by customers in all industries. In general, multicubes are more efficient and versatile, but hypercubes are easier to understand. End-users will relate better to hypercubes because of their higher level view; MIS professionals with multidimensional experience prefer multicubes because of their greater tunability and flexibility. Multicubes are a more efficient way of storing very sparse data and they can reduce the pre-calculation database explosion effect, so large, sophisticated products tend to use multicubes. Pre-built applications also tend to use multicubes so that the data structures can be more finely adjusted to the known application needs.

One relatively recent development is that two products so far have introduced the ability to de-couple the storage, processing and presentation layers. The now discontinued **GentiaDB** and the **Holos compound OLAP architecture** allow data to be stored physically as a multicube, but calculations to be defined as if it were a hypercube. This approach potentially delivers the simplicity of the hypercube, with the more tunable storage of a multicube. Microsoft's **Analysis Services** also has similar concepts, with partitions and virtual cubes.

In Summary

It is easy to understand the OLAP definition in five keywords – Fast Analysis of Shared Multidimensional Information (FASMI). OLAP includes 18 rules, which are categorized into four features: Basic Feature, Special Feature, Reporting Feature, and Dimensional Control. A potential buyer should create a shortlist of OLAP vendors for detailed consideration that fall largely into a single one of the four categories: Application OLAP, MOLAP, DOLAP, ROLAP.

CHAPTER 18

OLAP APPLICATIONS

We define OLAP as Fast Analysis of Shared Multidimensional Information–**FASMI**. There are many applications where this approach is relevant, and this section describes the characteristics of some of them. In an increasing number of cases, specialist OLAP applications have been pre-built and you can buy a solution that only needs limited customizing; in others, a general-purpose OLAP tool can be used. A general-purpose tool will usually be versatile enough to be used for many applications, but there may be much more application development required for each. The overall software costs should be lower, and skills are transferable, but implementation costs may rise and end-users may get less *ad hoc* flexibility if a more technical product is used. In general, it is probably better to have a general-purpose product which can be used for multiple applications, but some applications, such as financial reporting, are sufficiently complex that it may be better to use a pre-built application, and there are several available.

We would advise users never to engineer flexibility out of their applications–the only thing you can predict about the future is that it will not be what you predicted. Try not to hard code any more than you have to.

OLAP applications have been most commonly used in the financial and marketing areas, but as we show here, their uses do extend to other functions. Data rich industries have been the most typical users (consumer goods, retail, financial services and transport) for the obvious reason that they had large quantities of good quality internal and external data available, to which they needed to add value. However, there is also scope to use OLAP technology in other industries. The applications will often be smaller, because of the lower volumes of data available, which can open up a wider choice of products (because some products cannot cope with very large data volumes).

18.1 MARKETING AND SALES ANALYSIS

Most commercial companies require this application, and most products are capable of handling it to some degree. However, large-scale versions of this application occur in three industries, each with its own peculiarities.

- Consumer goods industries often have large numbers of products and outlets, and a high rate of change of both. They usually analyze data monthly, but sometimes it may go down to weekly or, very occasionally, daily. There are usually a number of dimensions, none especially large (rarely over 100,000). Data is often very sparse because of the number of dimensions. Because of the competitiveness of these industries, data is often analyzed using more sophisticated calculations than in other industries. Often, the most suitable technology for these applications is one of the hybrid OLAPs, which combine high analytical functionality with reasonably large data capacity.
- Retailers, thanks to EPOS data and loyalty cards, now have the potential to analyze huge amounts of data. Large retailers could have over 100,000 products (SKUs) and hundreds of branches. They often go down to weekly or daily level, and may sometimes track spending by individual customers. They may even track sales by time of day. The data is not usually very sparse, unless customer level detail is tracked. Relatively low analytical functionality is usually needed. Sometimes, the volumes are so large that a ROLAP solution is required, and this is certainly true of applications where individual private consumers are tracked.
- The financial services industry (insurance, banks etc) is a relatively new user of OLAP technology for sales analysis. With an increasing need for product and customer profitability, these companies are now sometimes analyzing data down to individual customer level, which means that the largest dimension may have millions of members. Because of the need to monitor a wide variety of risk factors, there may be large numbers of attributes and dimensions, often with very flat hierarchies.

Most of the data will usually come from the sales ledger(s), but there may be customer databases and some external data that has to be merged. In some industries (for example, pharmaceuticals and CPG), large volumes of market and even competitor data is readily available and this may need to be incorporated.

Getting the right data may not be easy. For example, most companies have problems with incorrect coding of data, especially if the organization has grown through acquisition, with different coding systems in use in different subsidiaries. If there have been multiple different contracts with a customer, then the same single company may appear as multiple different entities, and it will not be easy to measure the total business done with it. Another complication might come with calculating the correct revenues by product. In many cases, customers or resellers may get discounts based on cumulative business during a period. This discount may appear as a retrospective credit to the account, and it should then be factored against the multiple transactions to which it applies. This work may have been done in the transaction processing systems or a data warehouse; if not, the OLAP tool will have to do it.

There are analyses that are possible along every dimension. Here are a dozen of the questions that could be answered using a good marketing and sales analysis system:

1. Are we on target to achieve the month-end goals, by product and by region?
2. Are our back orders at the right levels to meet next month's goals? Do we have adequate production capacity and stocks to meet anticipated demand?

3. Are new products taking off at the right rate in all areas?
4. Have some new products failed to achieve their expected penetration, and should they be withdrawn?
5. Are all areas achieving the expected product mix, or are some groups failing to sell some otherwise popular products?
6. Is our advertising budget properly allocated? Do we see a rise in sales for products and in areas where we run campaigns?
7. What average discounts are being given, by different sales groups or channels? Should commission structures be altered to reflect this?
8. Is there a correlation between promotions and sales growth? Are the prices out of line with the market? Are some sales groups achieving their monthly or quarterly targets by excessive discounting?
9. Are new product offerings being introduced to established customers?
10. Is the revenue per head the same in all parts of the sales force? Why ?
11. Do outlets with similar demographic characteristics perform in the same way, or are some doing much worse than others? Why?
12. Based on history and known product plans, what are realistic, achievable targets for each product, time period and sales channel?

The benefits of a good marketing and sales analysis system is that results should be more predictable and manageable, opportunities will be spotted more readily and sales forces should be more productive.

18.2 CLICKSTREAM ANALYSIS

This is one of the latest OLAP applications. Commercial Web sites generate gigabytes of data a day that describe every action made by every visitor to the site. No bricks and mortar retailer has the same level of detail available about how visitors browse the offerings, the route they take and even where they abandon transactions. A large site has an almost impossible volume of data to analyze, and a multidimensional framework is possibly the best way of making sense of it. There are many dimensions to this analysis, including where the visitors came from, the time of day, the route they take through the site, whether or not they started/completed a transaction, and any demographic data available about customer visitors.

Unlike a conventional retailer, an e-commerce site has the ability–almost an obligation, it would seem to be redesigned regularly and this should be based, at least in part, on a scientific analysis of how well the site serves its visitors and whether it is achieving its business objectives, rather than a desire merely to reflect the latest design and technology fashions. This means that it is necessary to have detailed information on the popularity and success of each component of a site.

But the Web site should not be viewed in isolation. It is only one facet of an organization's business, and ideally, the Web statistics should be combined with other business data, including product profitability, customer history and financial information. OLAP is an ideal way of bringing these conventional and new forms of data together. This would allow, for instance, Web sites to be targeted not simply to maximize transactions, but to generate profitable business and to appeal to customers likely to create such business. OLAP can also be used to assist in personalizing Web sites.

In the great rush to move business to the Web, many companies have managed to ignore analytics, just as the ERP craze in the mid and late 1990s did. But the sheer volume of data now available, and the shorter times in which to analyze it, make exception and pro-active reporting far more important than before. Failing to do so is an invitation for a quick disaster.

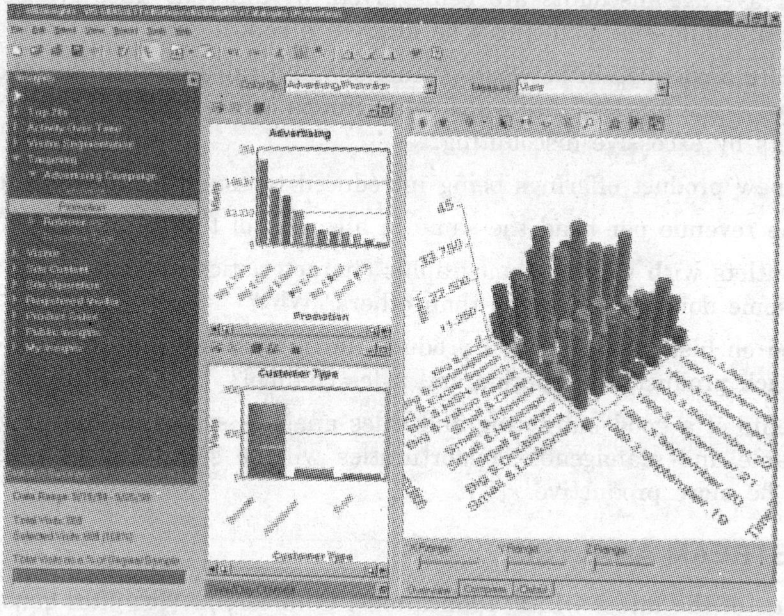

Figure 18.1. An example of a graphically intense clickstream analysis application that uses OLAP invisibly at its core: eBizinsights from Visual Insights. This analysis shows visitor segmentation (browsers, abandoners, buyers) for various promotional activities at hourly intervals. This application automatically builds four standard OLAP server cubes using a total of 24 dimensions for the analyses

Many of the issues with clickstream analysis come long before the OLAP tool. The biggest issue is to correctly identify real user sessions, as opposed to hits. This means eliminating the many crawler bots that are constantly searching and indexing the Web, and then grouping sets of hits that constitute a session. This cannot be done by IP address alone, as Web proxies and NAT (network address translation) mask the true client IP address, so techniques such as session cookies must be used in the many cases where surfers do not identify themselves by other means. Indeed, vendors such as Visual Insights charge much more for upgrades to the data capture and conversion features of their products than they do for the reporting and analysis components, even though the latter are much more visible.

18.3 DATABASE MARKETING

This is a specialized marketing application that is not normally thought of as an OLAP application, but is now taking advantage of multidimensional analysis, combined with other statistical and data mining technologies. The purpose of the application is to determine who are the best customers for targeted promotions for particular products or services based on the disparate information from various different systems.

Database marketing professionals aim to:

- Determine who the preferred customers are, based on their purchase of profitable products. This can be done with brute force data mining techniques (which are slow and can be hard to interpret), or by experienced business users investigating hunches using OLAP cubes (which is quicker and easier).
- Work to build loyalty packages for preferred customers via correct offerings. Once the preferred customers have been identified, look at their product mix and buying profile to see if there are denser clusters of product purchases over particular time periods. Again, this is much easier in a multidimensional environment. These can then form the basis for special offers to increase the loyalty of profitable customers.
- Determine a customer profile and use it to 'clone' the best customers. Look for customers who have some, but not all of the characteristics of the preferred customers, and target appropriate promotional offers at them.

If these goals are met, both parties profit. The customers will have a company that knows what they want and provides it. The company will have loyal customers that generate sufficient revenue and profits to continue a viable business.

Database marketing specialists try to model (using statistical or data mining techniques) which pieces of information are most relevant for determining likelihood of subsequent purchases, and how to weight their importance. In the past, pure marketers have looked for triggers, which works, but only in one dimension. But a well established company may have hundreds of pieces of information about customers, plus years of transaction data, so multidimensional structures are a great way to investigate relationships quickly, and narrow down the data which should be considered for modeling.

Once this is done, the customers can be scored using the weighted combination of variables which compose the model. A measure can then be created, and cubes set up which mix and match across multidimensional variables to determine optimal product mix for customers. The users can determine the best product mix to market to the right customers based on segments created from a combination of the product scores, the several demographic dimensions, and the transactional data in aggregate.

Finally, in a more simplistic setting, the users can break the world into segments based on combinations of dimensions that are relevant to targeting. They can then calculate a return on investment on these combinations to determine which segments have been profitable in the past, and which have not. Mailings can then be made only to those profitable segments. Products like Express allows the users to fine tune the dimensions quickly to build one-off promotions, determine how to structure profitable combinations of dimensions into segments, and rank them in order of desirability.

18.4 BUDGETING

This is a painful saga that every organization has to endure at least once a year. Not only is this balancing act difficult and tedious, but most contributors to the process get little feedback and less satisfaction. It is also the forum for many political games, as sales managers try and manipulate the system to get low targets and cost center managers try and hide pockets of unallocated resources. This is inevitable, and balancing these instinctive pressures against the top down goals of the organization usually means that setting a budget for a large organization involves a number of arduous iterations that can last for many months. We have even come across cases where setting the annual budget took *more* than a year, so before next year's budget had been set, the budgeting department had started work on the following year's budget!

Some companies try the top down approach. This is quick and easy, but often leads to the setting of unachievable budgets. Managers lower down have no commitment to the numbers assigned to them and make no serious effort to adhere to them. Very soon, the budget is discredited and most people ignore it. So, others try the bottom up alternative. This involves almost every manager in the company and is an immense distraction from their normal duties. The resulting 'budget' is usually miles off being acceptable, so orders come down from on high to trim costs and boost revenue. This can take several cycles before the costs and revenues are in balance with the strategic plan. This process can take months and is frustrating to all concerned, but it can lead to good quality, achievable budgets. Doing this with a complex, multi-spreadsheet system is a fraught process, and the remaining mainframe based systems are usually far too inflexible.

Ultimately, budgeting needs to combine the discipline of a top-down budget with the commitment of a bottom-up process, preferably with a minimum of iterations. An OLAP tool can help here by providing the analysis capacity, combined with the actual database, to provide a good, realistic starting point. In order to speed up the process, this could be done as a centrally generated, top down exercise. In order to allow for slippage, this first pass of the budget would be designed to over achieve the required goals. These 'suggested' budget numbers are then provided to the lower level managers to review and alter. Alterations would require justification.

There would have to be some matching of the revenue projections from marketing (which will probably be based on sales by product) and from sales (which will probably be based on sales territories), together with the manufacturing and procurement plans, which need to be in line with expected sales. Again, the OLAP approach allows all the data to be viewed from any perspective, so discrepancies should be identified earlier. It is as dangerous to budget for unachievable sales as it is to go too low, as cost budgets will be authorized based on phantom revenues.

It should also be possible to build the system so that data need not always be entered at the lowest possible level. For example, cost data may run at a standard monthly rate, so it should be possible to enter it at a quarterly or even annual rate, and allow the system to phase it using a standard profile. Many revenue streams might have a standard seasonality, and systems like Cognos Planning and Geac MPC are able to apply this automatically. There are many other calculations that are not just aggregations, because to make the budgeting process as painless as possible, as many lines in the budget schedules as possible should be calculated using standard formulae rather than being entered by hand.

An OLAP based budget will still be painful, but the process should be faster, and the ability to spot out of line items will make it harder for astute managers to hide pockets of costs or get away with unreasonably low revenue budgets. The greater perceived fairness of such a process will make the process more tolerable, even if it is still unpopular. The greater accuracy and reliability of such a budget should reduce the likelihood of having to do a mid year budget revision. But if circumstances change and a re-budget is required, an OLAP based system should make it a faster and less painful process.

18.5 FINANCIAL REPORTING AND CONSOLIDATION

Every medium and large organization has onerous responsibilities for producing financial reports for internal (management) consumption. Publicly quoted companies or public sector bodies also have to produce other, legally required, reports.

Accountants and financial analysts were early adopters of multidimensional software. Even the simplest financial consolidation consists of at least three dimensions. It must have a chart of accounts (general OLAP tools often refer to these as facts or measures, but to accountants they will always be accounts), at least one organization structure plus time. Usually it is necessary to compare different versions of data, such as actual, budget or forecast. This makes the model four dimensional. Often line of business segmentation or product line analysis can add fifth or sixth dimensions. Even back in the 1970s, when consolidation systems were typically run on time-sharing mainframe computers, the dedicated consolidation products typically had a four or more dimensional feel to them. Several of today's OLAP tools can trace their roots directly back to this ancestry and many more have inherited design attributes from these early products.

To address this specific market, certain vendors have developed specialist products. Although they are not generic OLAP tools (typically, they have specific dimensionality), we have included some of them in this report because they could be viewed as conforming to our definition of OLAP (Fast Analysis of Shared Multidimensional Information) and they represent a significant proportion of the market. The market leader in this segment is Hyperion Solutions. Other players include Cartesis, Geac, Longview Khalix, and SAS Institute, but many smaller players also supply pre-built applications for financial reporting. In addition to these specialist products, there is a school of thought that says that these types of problems can be solved by building extra functionality on top of a generic OLAP tool.

There are several factors that distinguish this specialist sector from the general OLAP area. They are:

Special Dimensionality

Normally we would not look favorably on a product that restricted the dimensionality of the models that could be built with it. In this case, however, there are some compelling reasons why this becomes advantageous.

In a financial consolidation certain dimensions possess special attributes. For example the chart of accounts contains detail level and aggregation accounts. The detail level accounts typically will sum to zero for one entity for one time period. This is because this unit of data represents a trial balance (so called because, before the days of computers you did a trial extraction of the balances from the ledger to ensure that they balanced). Since a balanced accounting transaction consists of debits and credits of equal value which are normally posted to one entity within one time period, the resultant array of account values should also sum to zero. This may seem relatively unimportant to non-accountants, but to accountants, this feature is a critical control to ensure that the data is 'in balance'.

Another dimension that possesses special traits is the entity dimension. For an accurate consolidation it is important that entities are aggregated into a consolidation once and only once. The omission or inclusion of an entity twice in the same consolidated numbers would invalidate the whole consolidation.

As well as the special aggregation rules that such dimensions possess, there are certain known attributes that the members of certain dimensions possess. In the case of accounts, it is useful to know:

- Is the account a debit or a credit?
- Is it an asset, liability, income or expense or some other special account, such as an exchange gain or loss account?
- Is it used to track inter-company items (which must be treated specially on consolidation)?

For the entity (or cost center or company) dimension:

- What currency does the company report in?
- Is this a normal company submitting results or an elimination company (which only serves to hold entries used as part of the consolidation)?

By pre-defining these dimensions to understand that this information needs to be captured, not only can the user be spared the trouble of knowing what dimensions to set up, but also certain complex operations, such as currency translation and inter-company eliminations can be completely automated. Variance reporting can also be simplified through the system's knowledge of which items are debits and which are credits.

Controls

Controls are a very important part of any consolidation system. It is crucial that controls are available to ensure that once an entity is in balance it can only be updated by posting balanced journal entries and keeping a comprehensive audit trail of all updates and who posted them. It is important that reports cannot be produced from outdated consolidated data that is no longer consistent with the detail data because of updates. When financial statements are converted from source currency to reporting currency, it is critical that the basis of translation conforms to the generally accepted accounting principles in the country where the data is to be reported. In the case of a multinational company with a sophisticated reporting structure, there may be a need to report in several currencies, potentially on different bases. Although there has been considerable international harmonization of accounting standards for currency translation and other accounting principles in recent years, there are still differences, which can be significant.

Special Transformations of Data

Some non-accountants dismiss consolidation as simple aggregation of numbers. Indeed the basis of a financial consolidation is that the financial statements of more than one company are aggregated so as to produce financial statements that meaningfully present the results of the combined operation. However, there are several reasons why consolidation is a lot more complex than simply adding up the numbers.

Results are often in different currencies. Translating statements from one currency to another is not as simple as multiplying a local currency value by an exchange rate to yield a reporting currency value. Since the balance sheet shows a position at a point in time and the profit and loss account shows activity over a period of time it is normal to multiply the balance sheet by the closing rate for the period and the P&L account by the average rate for the period. Since the trial balance balances in local currency the translation is always going to induce an imbalance in the reporting currency. In simple terms this imbalance is the gain or loss on exchange. This report is not designed to be an accounting primer, but it is important to understand that it is not a trivial task even as described so far. When you also take into account certain non current assets being translated at historic rates and exchange gains and losses being calculated separately for current and non current assets, you can appreciate the complexity of the task.

Transactions between entities within the consolidation must be eliminated (see Figure 18.2).

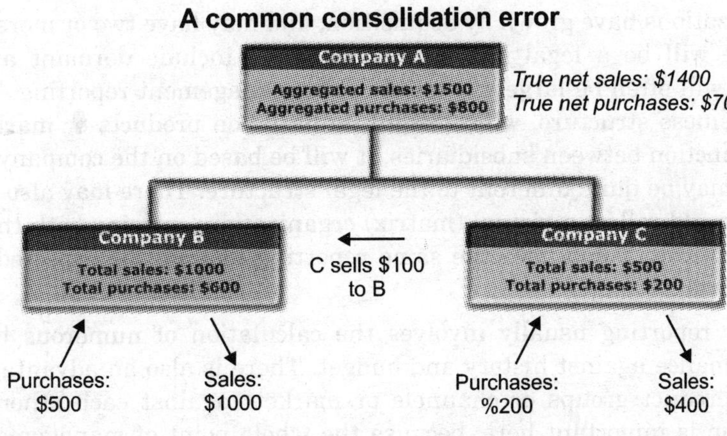

Figure 18.2. Company A owns Companies B and C. Company C sells $100 worth of product to Company B so C's accounts show sales of $500 (including the $100 that it sold to Company B) and purchases of $200. B shows sales of $1000 and purchases of $600 (including $100 that it bought from C). A simple consolidation would show consolidated sales of $1500 and consolidated purchases of $800. But if we consider A (which is purely a holding company and therefore has no sales and purchases itself) both its sales and its purchases from the outside world are overstated by $100. The $100 of sales and purchases become an inter-company elimination. This becomes much more complicated when the parent owns less than 100 percent of subsidiaries and there are many subsidiaries trading in multiple currencies.

Even though we talked about the problems of eliminating inter-company entries on consolidation, the problem does not stop there. How to ensure that the sales of $100 reported by C actually agrees with the corresponding $100 purchase by B? What if C erroneously reports the sales as $90? Consolidation systems have inter-company reconciliation modules which will report any inter-company transactions (usually in total between any two entities) that do not agree, on an exception basis. This is not a trivial task when you consider that the two entities will often be trading in different currencies and translation will typically yield minor rounding differences. Also accountants typically ignore balances which are less than a specified materiality factor. Despite their green eyeshade image, accountants do not like to spend their days chasing pennies!

18.6 MANAGEMENT REPORTING

In most organizations, management reporting is quite distinct from formal financial reporting. It will usually have more emphasis on the P&L and possible cash flow, and less on the balance sheet. It will probably be done more often–usually monthly, rather than annually and quarterly. There will be less detail but more analysis. More users will be interested in viewing and analyzing the results. The emphasis is on faster rather than more accurate reporting and there may be regular changes to the reporting requirements. Users of OLAP based systems consistently report faster and more flexible reporting, with better analysis than the alternative solutions. One popular saying is that "what gets measured, gets managed," so senior management will often use a reporting system to give (subtle or not) direction to subordinates.

Many organizations have grown by acquisition, and may have two or more organizational structures. There will be a legal structure, which will include dormant and non-trading subsidiaries, and will often be largely ignored in the management reporting. There may also be a different business structure, which might be based on products or market sectors, but may blur the distinction between subsidiaries; it will be based on the company's management structure, which may be quite different to the legal structure. There may also be a marketing structure, which could reflect a virtual (matrix) organization, crossing both the legal and the management structures. Sometimes the same reporting tool will be expected to produce all three sets of reports.

Management reporting usually involves the calculation of numerous business ratios, comparing performance against history and budget. There is also an advantage to be gained from comparing product groups or channels or markets against each other. Sophisticated exception detection is important here, because the whole point of management reporting is to manage the business by taking decisions.

The new Microsoft OLAP Services product and the many new client tools and applications being developed for it will certainly drive down 'per seat' prices for general-purpose management reporting applications, so that it will be economically possible to deploy good solutions to many more users. Web deployments should make these easier to administer.

18.7 EIS

EIS is a branch of management reporting. The term became popular in the mid 1980s, when it was defined to mean Executive Information Systems; some people also used the term ESS (Executive Support System). Since then, the original concept has been discredited, as the early systems were very proprietary, expensive, hard to maintain and generally inflexible. Fewer people now use the term, but the acronym has not entirely disappeared; along the way, the letters have been redefined many times. Here are some of the suggestions (you can combine the words in any way you prefer):

Executive	Information	System
Everyone's	Important	Software
Enterprise	Intelligence	Service

With this proliferation of descriptions, the meaning of the term is now irretrievably blurred. In essence, an EIS is a more highly customized, easier to use management reporting system, but it is probably now better recognized as an attempt to provide intuitive ease of use to those managers who do not have either a computer background or much patience. There is no reason why all users of an OLAP based management reporting system should not get consistently fast performance, great ease of use, reliability and flexibility–not just top executives, who will probably use it much less than mid level managers.

The basic philosophy of EIS was that "what gets reported gets managed," so if executives could have fast, easy access to a number of key performance indicators (KPIs) and critical success factors (CSFs), they would be able to manage their organizations better. But there is little evidence that this worked for the buyers, and it certainly did not work for the software vendors who specialized in this field, most of which suffered from a very poor financial performance.

18.8 BALANCED SCORECARD

The balanced scorecard is a 1990s management methodology that in many respects attempts to deliver the benefits that the 1980s executive information systems promised, but rarely produced. The concept was originated by Robert Kaplan and David Norton based on a 1990 study sponsored by the Nolan Norton Institute, the research arm of KPMG. The results were summarized in an article entitled, 'The Balanced Scorecard–Measures That Drive Performance' (Harvard Business Review, Jan/Feb 1992). Other HBR articles and a book (*The Balanced Scorecard*, published by Harvard Business School Press in 1996) followed. Kaplan is still a professor at the Harvard Business School and Norton, who was previously president of the strategy group in Renaissance Worldwide, is now president of the Balanced Scorecard Collaborative.

Renaissance says, "a Balanced Scorecard is a prescriptive framework that focuses on shareholder, customer, internal and learning requirements of a business in order to create a system of linked objectives, measures, targets and initiatives which collectively describe the strategy of an organization and how that strategy can be achieved. A Balanced Management System is a governance system which uses the Balanced Scorecard as the centerpiece in order to communicate an organization's strategy, create strategic linkage, focus business planning, and provide feedback and learning against the company's strategy."

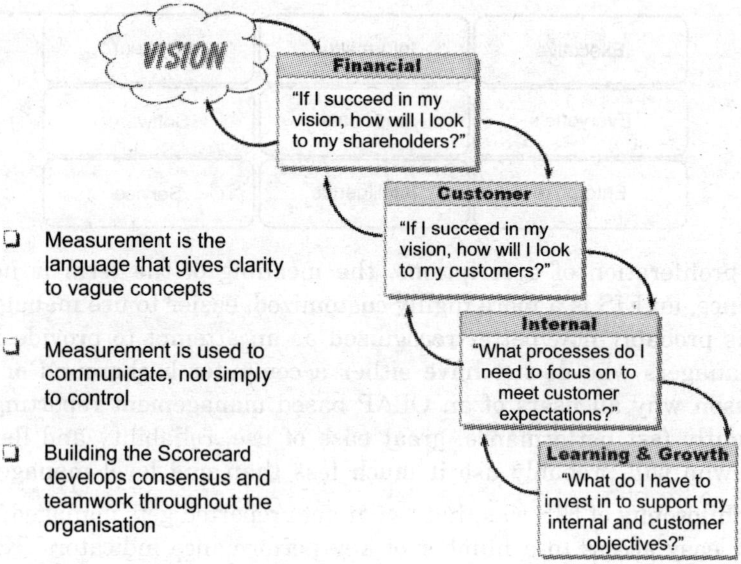

Figure 18.3. The Balanced Scorecard Provides a Framework to Translate Strategy into Operational Terms (source: Renaissance Worldwide)

The basic idea of the balanced scorecard is that traditional historic financial measure is an inadequate way of measuring an organization's performance. It aims to integrate the strategic vision of the organization's executives with the day to day focus of managers. The scorecard should take into account the cause and effect relationships of business actions, including estimates of the response times and significance of the linkages among the scorecard measures. Its aim is to be at least as much forward as backward looking.

The scorecard is composed of four perspectives:

- Financial
- Customer
- Learning and growth
- Internal business process.

For each of these, there should be objectives, measures, targets and initiatives that need to be tracked and reported. Many of the measures are soft and non-financial, rather than just accounting data, and users have a two-way interaction with the system (including entering comments and explanations). The objectives and measures should be selected using a formal top-down process, rather than simply choosing data that is readily available from the operational systems. This is likely to involve a significant amount of management consultancy, both before any software is installed, and continuing afterwards as well; indeed, the software may play a significant part in supporting the consulting activities. For the process to succeed, it must be strongly endorsed by the top executives and all the management team; it cannot just be an initiative sponsored by the IT department (unless it is only to be deployed in IT), and it must not be regarded as just another reporting application.

However, we have noticed that while an increasing number of OLAP vendors are launching balanced scorecard applications, some of them seem to be little more than rebadged

EISs, with no serious attempt to reflect the business processes that Kaplan and Norton advocate. Such applications are unlikely to be any more successful than the many run-of-the-mill executive information systems, but in the process, they are already diluting the meaning of the balanced scorecard term.

18.9 PROFITABILITY ANALYSIS

This is an application, which is growing in importance. Even highly profitable organizations ought to know where the profits are coming from; less profitable organizations have to know where to cut back.

Profitability analysis is important in setting prices (and discounts), deciding on promotional activities, selecting areas for investment or disinvestment and anticipating competitive pressures. Decisions in these areas are made every day by many individuals in large organizations, and their decisions will be less effective if they are not well informed about the differing levels of profitability of the company's products and customers. Profitability figures may be used to bias actions, by basing remuneration on profitability goals rather than revenue or volume.

With deregulation in many industries, privatization and the reduction in trade barriers, large new competitors are more likely to appear than in the past. And, with new technology and the appearance of 'virtual corporations', new small competitors without expensive infrastructures can successfully challenge the giants. In each case, the smart newcomers will challenge the incumbents in their most profitable areas, because this is where the new competitor can afford to offer lower prices or better quality and still be profitable. Often they will focus on added value or better services, because a large incumbent will find it harder to improve these than to cut prices. Thus, once a newcomer has become established in areas that were formerly lucrative, the established player may find it hard to respond efficiently –so the answer is to be proactive, reinforcing the vulnerable areas before they are under attack.

This takes analysis, without knowledge of which customers or products are most profitable, a large supplier may not realize that a pricing umbrella is being created for new competitors to get established. However, in more and more industries, the "direct" labor and material cost of producing a product is becoming a less and less significant part of the total cost. With R&D, marketing, sales, administration and distribution costs, it is often hard to know exactly which costs relate to which product or customer. Many of these costs are relatively fixed, and apportioning them to the right revenue generating activity is hard, and can be arbitrary. Sometimes, it can even be difficult to correctly assign revenues to products, as described above in the marketing and sales application.

One popular way to assign costs to the right products or services is to use activity based costing. This is much more scientific than simply allocating overhead costs in proportion to revenues or floor space. It attempts to measure resources that are consumed by activities, in terms of cost drivers. Typically costs are grouped into cost pools which are then applied to products or customers using cost drivers, which must be measured. Some cost drivers may be clearly based on the volume of activities, others may not be so obvious. They may, for example, be connected with the introduction of new products or suppliers. Others may be connected with the complexity of the organization (the variety of customers, products, suppliers, production facilities, markets etc). There are also infrastructure-sustaining costs that cannot realistically be applied to activities. Even ignoring these, it is likely that the costs of supplying the least profitable customers or products exceeds the revenues they generate. If these are known, the company can make changes to prices or other factors to remedy the situation–possibly by withdrawing from some markets, dropping some products or declining to bid for certain contracts.

There are specialist ABC products on the market and these have many FASMI characteristics. It is also possible to build ABC applications in OLAP tools, although the application functionality may be less than could be achieved through the use of a good specialist tool.

18.10 QUALITY ANALYSIS

Although quality improvement programs are less in vogue than they were in the early 1990s, the need for consistent quality and reliability in goods and services is as important as ever. The measures should be objective and customer rather than producer focused. The systems are just as relevant in service organizations as in the public sector. Indeed, many public sector service organizations have specific service targets.

These systems are used not just to monitor an organization's own output, but also that of its suppliers. There may be for example, service level agreements that affect contract extensions and payments.

Quality systems can often involve multidimensional data if they monitor numeric measures across different production facilities, products or services, time, locations and customers. Many of the measures will be non-financial, but they may be just as important as traditional financial measures in forming a balanced view of the organization. As with financial measures, they may need analyzing over time and across the functions of the organization; many organizations are committed to continuous improvement, which requires that there be formal measures that are quantifiable and tracked over long periods; OLAP tools provide an excellent way of doing this, and of spotting disturbing trends before they become too serious.

In Summary

OLAP has a wide area of applications, which are mainly: Marketing and Sales Analysis, Budgeting, Financial Reporting and Consolidation, EIS etc.

VOLUME II

DATA MINING

Chapter 1: INTRODUCTION

In this chapter, a brief introduction to Data Mining is outlined. The discussion includes the definitions of Data Mining; stages identified in Data Mining Process, Models, and it also address the brief description on Data Mining methods and some of the applications and examples of Data Mining.

CHAPTER 1

INTRODUCTION

1.1 WHAT IS DATA MINING?

The past two decades have seen a dramatic increase in the amount of information or data being stored in electronic format. This accumulation of data has taken place at an explosive rate. It has been estimated that the amount of information in the world doubles every 20 months and the size and number of databases are increasing even faster. The increase in use of electronic data gathering devices such as point-of-sale or remote sensing devices has contributed to this explosion of available data. Figure 1, from the Red Brick company illustrates the data explosion.

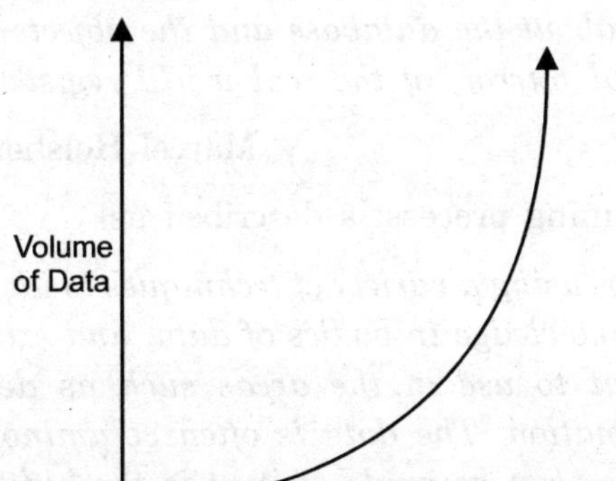

Figure 1.1. The Growing Base of Data

Data storage became easier as the availability of large amount of computing power at low cost i.e. the cost of processing power and storage is falling, made data cheap. There was also the introduction of new machine learning methods for knowledge representation based on logic programming etc. in addition to traditional statistical analysis of data. The new methods tend to be computationally intensive hence a demand for more processing power.

Having concentrated so much attention on the accumulation of data the problem was what to do with this valuable resource? It was recognized that information is at the heart of business operations and that decision-makers could make use of the data stored to gain valuable insight into the business. Database Management systems gave access to the data stored but this was only a small part of what could be gained from the data. Traditional on-line transaction processing systems, OLTPs, are good at putting data into databases quickly, safely and efficiently but are not good at delivering meaningful analysis in return. Analyzing data can provide further knowledge about a business by going beyond the data explicitly stored to derive knowledge about the business. This is where Data Mining or Knowledge Discovery in Databases (KDD) has obvious benefits for any enterprise.

1.2 DEFINITIONS

The term data mining has been stretched beyond its limits to apply to any form of data analysis. Some of the numerous definitions of Data Mining, or Knowledge Discovery in Databases are:

> *Data Mining, or Knowledge Discovery in Databases (KDD) as it is also known, is the nontrivial extraction of implicit, previously unknown, and potentially useful information from data. This encompasses a number of different technical approaches, such as clustering, data summarization, learning classification rules, finding dependency net works, analyzing changes, and detecting anomalies.*
>
> William J Frawley, Gregory Piatetsky-Shapiro and Christopher J Matheus
>
> *Data mining is the search for relationships and global patterns that exist in large databases but are 'hidden' among the vast amount of data, such as a relationship between patient data and their medical diagnosis. These relationships represent valuable knowledge about the database and the objects in the database and, if the database is a faithful mirror, of the real world registered by the database.*
>
> Marcel Holshemier & Arno Siebes (1994)

The analogy with the mining process is described as:

> *Data mining refers to "using a variety of techniques to identify nuggets of information or decision-making knowledge in bodies of data, and extracting these in such a way that they can be put to use in the areas such as decision support, prediction, forecasting and estimation. The data is often voluminous, but as it stands of low value as no direct use can be made of it; it is the hidden information in the data that is useful"*
>
> Clementine User Guide, a data mining toolkit
>
> *Basically data mining is concerned with the analysis of data and the use of software techniques for finding patterns and regularities in sets of data. It is the computer, which is responsible for finding the patterns by identifying the underlying rules and features in the data. The idea is that it is possible to strike gold in unexpected places as the data mining software extracts patterns not previously discernable or so obvious that no one has noticed them before.*

1.3 DATA MINING PROCESS

Data mining analysis tends to work from the data up and the best techniques are those developed with an orientation towards large volumes of data, making use of as much of the collected data as possible to arrive at reliable conclusions and decisions. The analysis process starts with a set of data, uses a methodology to develop an optimal representation of the structure of the data during which time knowledge is acquired. Once knowledge has been acquired this can be extended to larger sets of data working on the assumption that the larger data set has a structure similar to the sample data. Again this is analogous to a mining operation where large amounts of low grade materials are sifted through in order to find something of value.

The figure 1.2, summarizes the some of the stages/processes identified in data mining and knowledge discovery by Usama Fayyad & Evangelos Simoudis, two of leading exponents of this area.

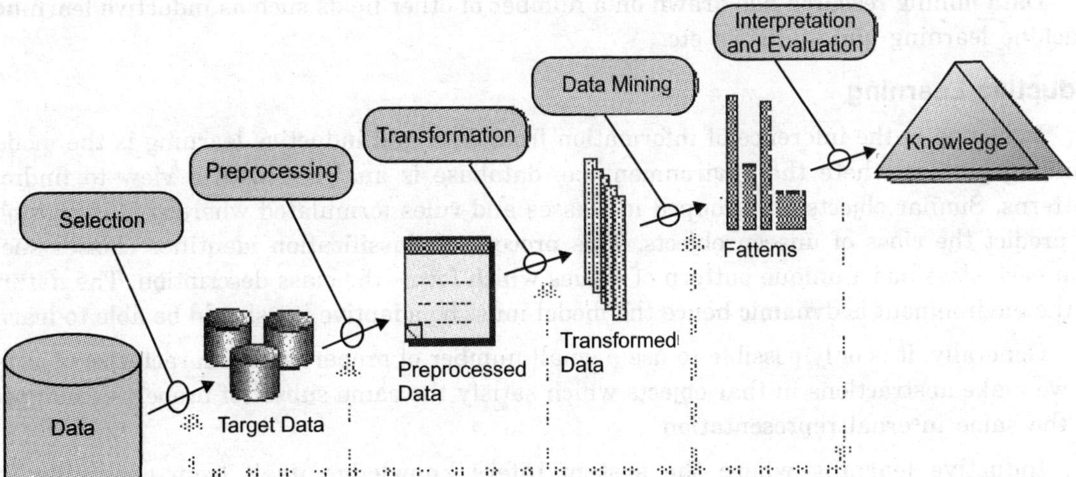

Figure 1.2. Stages/Process Identified in Data Mining

The phases depicted start with the raw data and finish with the extracted knowledge, which was acquired as a result of the following stages:

- *Selection*–selecting or segmenting the data according to some criteria e.g. all those people who own a car; in this way subsets of the data can be determined.
- *Preprocessing*–this is the data cleansing stage where certain information is removed which is deemed unnecessary and may slow down queries, for example unnecessary to note the sex of a patient when studying pregnancy. Also the data is reconfigured to ensure a consistent format as there is a possibility of inconsistent formats because the data is drawn from several sources e.g. sex may recorded as *f* or *m* and also as 1 or 0.

- *Transformation*– the data is not merely transferred across but transformed in that overlays may be added such as the demographic overlays commonly used in market research. The data is made useable and navigable.
- *Data mining*–this stage is concerned with the extraction of patterns from the data. A pattern can be defined as given a set of facts(data) *F*, a language *L*, and some measure of certainty *C*, a pattern is a statement *S* in *L* that describes relationships among a subset *Fs* of *F* with a certainty *C* such that *S* is simpler in some sense than the enumeration of all the facts in *Fs*.
- *Interpretation and evaluation*–the patterns identified by the system are interpreted into knowledge which can then be used to support human decision-making e.g. prediction and classification tasks, summarizing the contents of a database or explaining observed phenomena.

1.4 DATA MINING BACKGROUND

Data mining research has drawn on a number of other fields such as inductive learning, machine learning and statistics etc.

Inductive Learning

Induction is the inference of information from data and inductive learning is the model building process where the environment i.e. database is analyzed with a view to finding patterns. Similar objects are grouped in classes and rules formulated whereby it is possible to predict the class of unseen objects. This process of classification identifies classes such that each class has a unique pattern of values which forms the class description. The nature of the environment is dynamic hence the model must be adaptive i.e. should be able to learn.

Generally, it is only possible to use a small number of properties to characterize objects, so we make abstractions in that objects which satisfy the same subset of properties mapped to the same internal representation.

Inductive learning where the system infers knowledge itself from observing its environment has two main strategies:

- *Supervised learning*–this is learning from examples where a teacher helps the system construct a model by defining classes and supplying examples of each class. The system has to find a description of each class i.e. the common properties in the examples. Once the description has been formulated the description and the class form a classification rule which can be used to predict the class of previously unseen objects. This is similar to discriminate analysis as in statistics.
- *Unsupervised learning*–this is learning from observation and discovery. The data mine system is supplied with objects but no classes are defined so it has to observe the examples and recognize patterns (i.e. class description) by itself. This system results in a set of class descriptions, one for each class discovered in the environment. Again this is similar to cluster analysis as in statistics.

Induction is therefore the extraction of patterns. The quality of the model produced by inductive learning methods is such that the model could be used to predict the outcome of future situations, in other words not only for states encountered but rather for unseen states that could occur. The problem is that most environments have different states, i.e. changes within, and it is not always possible to verify a model by checking it for all possible situations.

Given a set of examples the system can construct multiple models some of which will be simpler than others. The simpler models are more likely to be correct if we adhere to Ockhams Razor, which states that if there are multiple explanations for a particular phenomena it makes sense to choose the simplest because it is more likely to capture the nature of the phenomenon.

Statistics

Statistics has a solid theoretical foundation but the results from statistics can be overwhelming and difficult to interpret, as they require user guidance as to where and how to analyze the data. Data mining however allows the expert's knowledge of the data and the advanced analysis techniques of the computer to work together.

Statistical analysis systems such as SAS and SPSS have been used by analysis to detect unusual patterns and explain patterns using statistical models such as linear models. Statistics have a role to play and data mining will not replace such analysis but rather they can act upon more directed analysis based on the results of data mining. For example statistical induction is something like the average rate of failure of machines.

Machine Learning

Machine learning is the automation of a learning process and learning is tantamount to the construction of rules based on observations of environmental states and transitions. This is a broad field which includes not only learning from examples, but also reinforcement learning, learning with teacher, etc. A learning algorithm takes the data set and its accompanying information as input and returns a statement e.g. a concept representing the results of learning as output. Machine learning examines previous examples and their outcomes and learns how to reproduce these and make generalizations about new cases.

Generally a machine learning system does not use single observations of its environment but an entire finite set called the training set at once. This set contains examples i.e. observations coded in some machine readable form. The training set is finite hence not all concepts can be learned exactly.

Differences between Data Mining and Machine Learning

Knowledge Discovery in Databases (KDD) or Data Mining, and the part of Machine Learning (ML) dealing with learning from examples overlap in the algorithms used and the problems addressed.

The main differences are:

- KDD is concerned with finding understandable knowledge, while ML is concerned with improving performance of an agent. So training a neural network to balance a pole is part of ML, but not of KDD. However, there are efforts to extract knowledge from neural networks which are very relevant for KDD.

- KDD is concerned with very large, real-world databases, while ML typically (but not always) looks at smaller data sets. So efficiency questions are much more important for KDD.
- ML is a broader field which includes not only learning from examples, but also reinforcement learning, learning with teacher, etc.

KDD is that part of ML which is concerned with finding understandable knowledge in large sets of real-world examples. When integrating machine learning techniques into database systems to implement KDD some of the databases require:

- More efficient learning algorithms because realistic databases are normally very large and noisy. It is usual that the database is often designed for purposes different from data mining and so properties or attributes that would simplify the learning task are not present nor can they be requested from the real world. Databases are usually contaminated by errors so the data mining algorithm has to cope with noise whereas ML has laboratory type examples i.e. as near perfect as possible.
- More expressive representations for both data, e.g. tuples in relational databases, which represent instances of a problem domain, and knowledge, e.g. rules in a rule-based system, which can be used to solve users' problems in the domain, and the semantic information contained in the relational schemata.

Practical KDD systems are expected to include three interconnected phases:

- Translation of standard database information into a form suitable for use by learning facilities;
- Using machine learning techniques to produce knowledge bases from databases; and
- Interpreting the knowledge produced to solve users' problems and/or reduce data spaces, data spaces being the number of examples.

1.5 DATA MINING MODELS

IBM has identified two types of model or modes of operation, which may be used to unearth information of interest to the user.

Verification Model

The verification model takes a hypothesis from the user and tests the validity of it against the data. The emphasis is with the user who is responsible for formulating the hypothesis and issuing the query on the data to affirm or negate the hypothesis.

In a marketing division for example with a limited budget for a mailing campaign to launch a new product it is important to identify the section of the population most likely to buy the new product. The user formulates a hypothesis to identify potential customers and the characteristics they share. Historical data about customer purchase and demographic information can then be queried to reveal comparable purchases and the characteristics shared by those purchasers, which in turn can be used to target a mailing campaign. The whole operation can be refined by 'drilling down' so that the hypothesis reduces the 'set' returned each time until the required limit is reached.

The problem with this model is the fact that no new information is created in the retrieval process but rather the queries will always return records to verify or negate the hypothesis. The search process here is iterative in that the output is reviewed, a new set of questions or hypothesis formulated to refine the search and the whole process repeated. The user is discovering the facts about the data using a variety of techniques such as queries, multidimensional analysis and visualization to guide the exploration of the data being inspected.

Discovery Model

The discovery model differs in its emphasis in that it is the system automatically discovering important information hidden in the data. The data is sifted in search of frequently occurring patterns, trends and generalizations about the data without intervention or guidance from the user. The discovery or data mining tools aim to reveal a large number of facts about the data in as short a time as possible.

An example of such a model is a bank database, which is mined to discover the many groups of customers to target for a mailing campaign. The data is searched with no hypothesis in mind other than for the system to group the customers according to the common characteristics found.

1.6 DATA MINING METHODS

Figure 1.3 shows a two-dimensional artificial dataset consisting 23 cases. Each point on the figure presents a person who has been given a loan by a particular bank at some time in the past. The data has been classified into two classes: persons who have defaulted on their loan and persons whose loans are in good status with the bank.

The two primary goals of data mining in practice tend to be prediction and description. *Prediction* involves using some variables or fields in the database to predict unknown or future values of other variables of interest. *Description* focuses on finding human interpretable patterns describing the data. The relative importance of prediction and description for particular data mining applications can vary considerably.

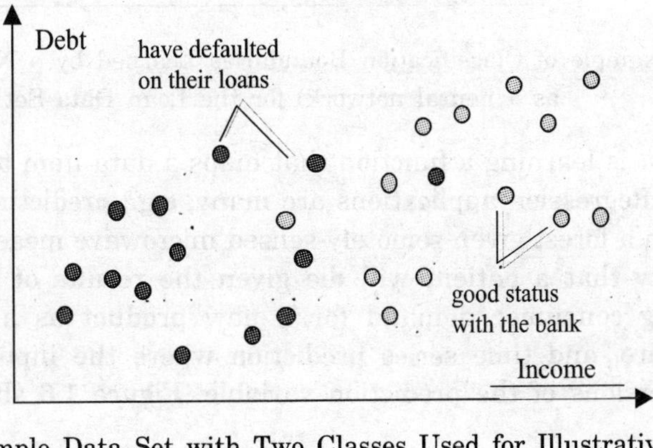

Figure 1.3. A Simple Data Set with Two Classes Used for Illustrative Purpose

- *Classification* is learning a function that maps a data item into one of several predefined classes. Examples of classification methods used as part of knowledge discovery applications include classifying trends in financial markets and automated identification of objects of interest in large image databases. Figure 1.4 and Figure 1.5 show classifications of the loan data into two class regions. Note that it is not possible to separate the classes perfectly using a linear decision boundary. The bank might wish to use the classification regions to automatically decide whether future loan applicants will be given a loan or not.

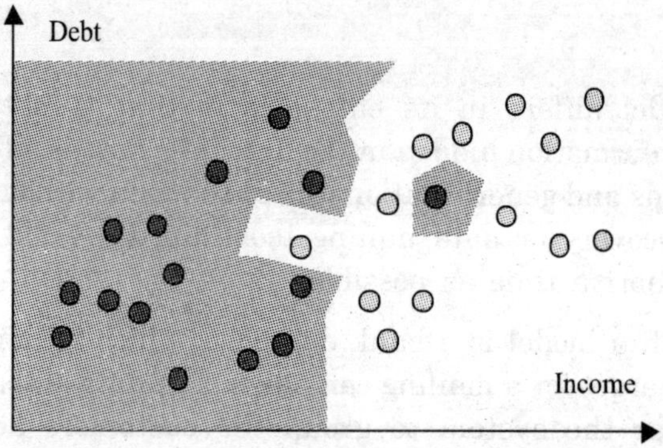

Figure 1.4. Classification Boundaries for a Nearest Neighbor

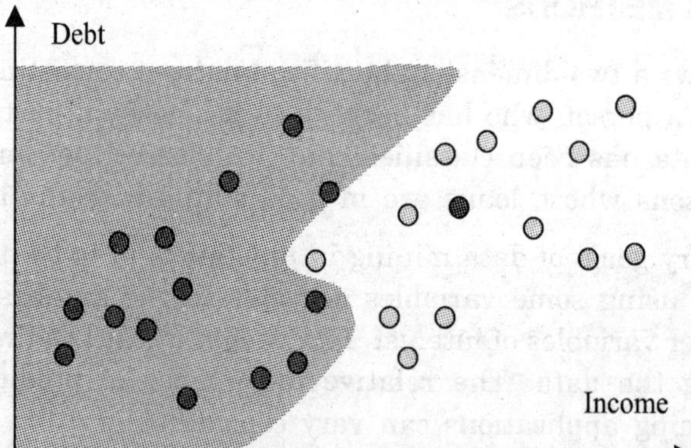

Figure 1.5. An Example of Classification Boundaries Learned by a Non-Linear Classifier (such as a neural network) for the Loan Data Set.

- *Regression* is learning a function that maps a data item to a real-valued prediction variable. Regression applications are many, e.g., predicting the amount of biomass present in a forest given remotely-sensed microwave measurements, estimating the probability that a patient will die given the results of a set of diagnostic tests, predicting consumer demand for a new product as a function of advertising expenditure, and time series prediction where the input variables can be time-lagged versions of the prediction variable. Figure 1.6 shows the result of simple linear regression where "total debt" is fitted as a linear function of "income": the fit is poor since there is only a weak correlation between the two variables.

- *Clustering* is a common descriptive task where one seeks to identify a finite set of categories or clusters to describe the data. The categories may be mutually exclusive and exhaustive, or consist of a richer representation such as hierarchical or overlapping categories. Examples of clustering in a knowledge discovery context include discovering homogeneous sub-populations for consumers in marketing databases and identification of sub-categories of spectra from infrared sky measurements. Figure 1.7 shows a possible clustering of the loan data set into 3 clusters: note that the clusters overlap allowing data points to belong to more than one cluster. The original class labels (denoted by two different colors) have been replaced by "no color" to indicate that the class membership is no longer assumed.

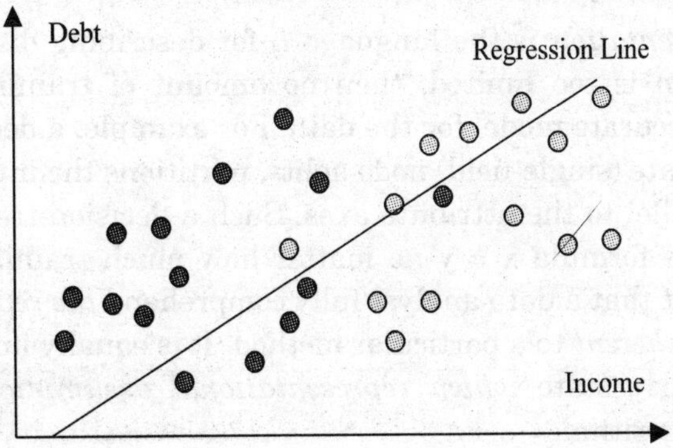

Figure 1.6. A Simple Linear Regression for the Loan Data Set

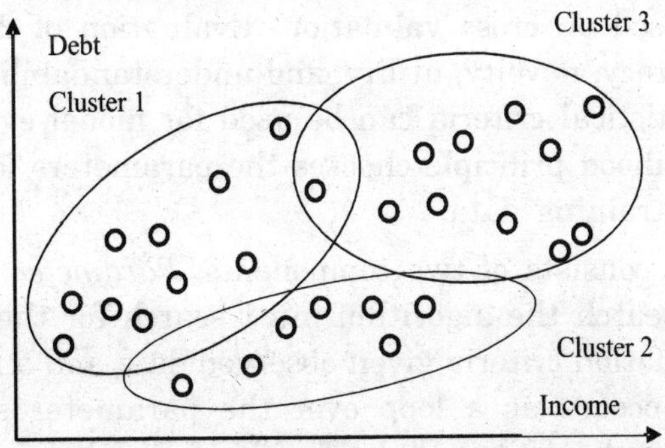

Figure 1.7. A Simple Clustering of the Loan Data Set into Three Clusters

- *Summarization* involves methods for finding a *compact description* for a subset of data. A simple example would be tabulating the mean and standard deviations for all fields. More sophisticated methods involve the derivation of summary rules, multivariate visualization techniques, and the discovery of functional relationships between variables. Summarization techniques are often applied to interactive exploratory data analysis and automated report generation.

- *Dependency Modeling* consists of finding *a model that describes significant dependencies between variables.* Dependency models exist at two levels: the *structural* level of the model specifies (often in graphical form) which variables are locally dependent on each other, whereas the *quantitative* level of the model specifies the strengths of the dependencies using some numerical scale. For example, probabilistic dependency networks use conditional independence to specify the structural aspect of the model and probabilities or correlation to specify the strengths of the dependencies. Probabilistic dependency networks are increasingly finding applications in areas as diverse as the development of probabilistic medical expert systems from databases, information retrieval, and modeling of the human genome.
- *Change and Deviation Detection* focuses on discovering the most significant changes in the data from previously measured values.
- *Model Representation* is the language *L* for describing discoverable patterns. If the representation is too limited, then no amount of training time or examples will produce an accurate model for the data. For example, a decision tree representation, using univariate (single-field) node-splits, partitions the input space into hyperplanes that are parallel to the attribute axes. Such a decision-tree method cannot discover from data the formula x = y no matter how much training data it is given. Thus, it is important that a data analyst fully comprehend *the representational assumptions that may be inherent* to a particular method. It is equally important that an algorithm designer clearly state *which representational assumptions are being made* by a particular algorithm.
- *Model Evaluation* estimates how well a particular pattern (a model and its parameters) meets the criteria of the KDD process. Evaluation of predictive accuracy (validity) is based on cross validation. Evaluation of descriptive quality involves predictive accuracy, novelty, utility, and understandability of the fitted model. Both logical and statistical criteria can be used for model evaluation. For example, the maximum likelihood principle chooses the parameters for the model that yield the best fit to the training data.
- *Search Method* consists of two components: *Parameter Search* and *Model Search*. In parameter search the algorithm must search for the parameters that optimize the model evaluation criteria given observed data and a fixed model representation. Model Search occurs as a loop over the parameter search method: the model representation is changed so that a family of models is considered. For each specific model representation, the parameter search method is instantiated to evaluate the quality of that particular model. Implementations of model search methods tend to use heuristic search techniques since the size of the space of possible models often prohibits exhaustive search and closed form solutions are not easily obtainable.

1.7 DATA MINING PROBLEMS/ISSUES

Data mining systems rely on databases to supply the raw data for input and this raises problems in the databases that tend to be dynamic, incomplete, noisy, and large. Other problems arise as a result of the adequacy and relevance of the information stored.

Limited Information

A database is often designed for purposes different from data mining and sometimes the properties or attributes that would simplify the learning task are not present nor can they be requested from the real world. Inconclusive data causes problems because if some attributes essential to knowledge about the application domain are not present in the data it may be impossible to discover significant knowledge about a given domain. For example cannot diagnose malaria from a patient database if that database does not contain the patient's red blood cell count.

Noise and Missing Values

Databases are usually contaminated by errors so it cannot be assumed that the data they contain is entirely correct. Attributes, which rely on subjective or measurement judgements, can give rise to errors such that some examples may even be mis-classified. Error in either the values of attributes or class information are known as noise. Obviously where possible it is desirable to eliminate noise from the classification information as this affects the overall accuracy of the generated rules.

Missing data can be treated by discovery systems in a number of ways such as;

- Simply disregard missing values
- Omit the corresponding records
- Infer missing values from known values
- Treat missing data as a special value to be included additionally in the attribute domain
- Average over the missing values using Bayesian techniques.

Noisy data in the sense of being imprecise is characteristic of all data collection and typically fit a regular statistical distribution such as Gaussian while wrong values are data entry errors. Statistical methods can treat problems of noisy data, and separate different types of noise.

Uncertainty

Uncertainty refers to the severity of the error and the degree of noise in the data. Data precision is an important consideration in a discovery system.

Size, Updates, and Irrelevant Fields

Databases tend to be large and dynamic in that their contents are ever-changing as information is added, modified or removed. The problem with this from the data mining perspective is how to ensure that the rules are up-to-date and consistent with the most current information. Also the learning system has to be time-sensitive as some data values vary over time and the discovery system is affected by the 'timeliness' of the data.

Another issue is the relevance or irrelevance of the fields in the database to the current focus of discovery, for example post codes are fundamental to any studies trying to establish a geographical connection to an item of interest such as the sales of a product.

1.8 POTENTIAL APPLICATIONS

Data mining has many and varied fields of application some of which are listed below.

Retail/Marketing

- Identify buying patterns from customers
- Find associations among customer demographic characteristics
- Predict response to mailing campaigns
- Market basket analysis

Banking

- Detect patterns of fraudulent credit card use
- Identify 'loyal' customers
- Predict customers likely to change their credit card affiliation
- Determine credit card spending by customer groups
- Find hidden correlations between different financial indicators
- Identify stock trading rules from historical market data

Insurance and Health Care

- Claims analysis - i.e. which medical procedures are claimed together
- Predict which customers will buy new policies
- Identify behavior patterns of risky customers
- Identify fraudulent behavior

Transportation

- Determine the distribution schedules among outlets
- Analyze loading patterns

Medicine

- Characterize patient behavior to predict office visits
- Identify successful medical therapies for different illnesses

1.9 DATA MINING EXAMPLES

Bass Brewers

Bass Brewers is the leading beer producer in the UK and has a 23% of the market. The company has a reputation for great brands and good service but realized the importance of information in order to maintain a lead in the UK beer market.

> *We've been brewing beer since 1777, with increased competition comes a demand to make faster, better informed decisions.*
>
> Mike Fisher, IS director, Bass Brewers

Bass decided to gather the data into a data warehouse on a system so that the users i.e. the decision-makers could have consistent, reliable, online information. Prior to this, users could expect a turn around of 24 hours but with the new system the answers should be returned interactively.

> *For the first time, people will be able to do data mining - ask questions we never dreamt we could get the answers to, look for patterns among the data we could never recognize before.*
>
> Nigel Rowley, Information Infrastructure manager

This commitment to data mining has given Bass a competitive edge when it comes to identifying market trends and taking advantage of this.

Northern Bank

A subsidiary of the National Australia Group, the Northern Bank has a major new application based upon Holos from Holistic Systems now being used in each of the 107 branches in the Province. The new system is designed to deliver financial and sales information such as volumes, margins, revenues, overheads and profits as well as quantities of product held, sold, closed etc.

The application consists of two loosely coupled systems;

- a system to integrate the multiple data sources into a consolidated database,
- another system to deliver that information to the users in a meaningful way.

The Northern is addressing the need to convert data into information as their products need to be measured outlet by outlet, and over a period of time.

> *The new system delivers management information in electronic form to the branch network. The information is now more accessible, paperless and timely. For the first time, all the various income streams are attributed to the branches which generate the business.*
>
> Malcolm Longridge, MIS development team leader, Northern Bank

TSB Group PLC

The TSB Group is also using Holos supplied by Holistic Systems because of

> *its flexibility and its excellent multidimensional functionality, which it provides without the need for a separate multidimensional database*
>
> Andrew Scott, End-User Computing Manager at TSB

The four major applications which have been developed are:

- a company-wide budget and forecasting model, BAF, for the finance department - has 50 potential users taking information out of the Millennium general ledger and enables analysts to study this data using 40 multidimensional models written using Holos;
- a mortgage management information system for middle and senior management in TSB Home loans;
- a suite of actuarial models for TSB Insurance; and
- Business Analysis Project, BAP, used as an EIS type system by TSB Insurance to obtain a better understanding of the company's actual risk exposures for feeding back into the actuarial modeling system.

BeursBase, Amsterdam

BeursBase, a real-time on-line stock/exchange relational data base (RDB) fed with information from the Amsterdam Stock Exchange is now available for general access by institutions or individuals. It will be augmented by data from the European Option Exchange before January 1996. All stock, option and future prices and volumes are being warehoused.

BeursBase has been in operation for about a year and contains approximately 1.8 million stock prices, over half a million quotes and about a million stock trade volumes. The AEX (Amsterdam EOE Index) or the Dutch Dow Jones, based upon the 25 most active securities traded (measured over a year) is refreshed via the database approximately every 30 seconds.

The RDB employs SQL/DS on a VM system and DB2/6000 on an AIX RS/6000 cluster. A parallel edition of DB2/6000 will soon be ready for data mining purposes, data quality measurement, plus a variety of other complex queries.

The project was founded by Martin P. Misseyer, assistant professor on the faculty of economics, business administration and econometrics at Vrije University. BeursBase unique in its kind is characterized by the following features: first BeursBase contains both real time and historical data. Secondly, all data retrieved from ASE are stored, rather than a subset, all broadcasted trade data are stored. Thirdly, the data, BeursBase itself and subsequent applications form the basis for many research, education and public relations activities. A similar data link with the Amsterdam European Option Exchange (EOE) will be established as well.

Delphic Universities

The Delphic universities are a group of 24 universities within the MAC initiative who have adopted Holos for their management information system, MIS, needs. Holos provides complex modeling for IT literate users in the planning departments while also giving the senior management a user-friendly EIS.

> *Real value is added to data by multidimensional manipulation (being able to easily compare many different views of the available information in one report) and by modeling. In both these areas spreadsheets and query-based tools are not able to compete with fully-fledged management information systems such as Holos. These two features turn raw data into useable information.*

Michael O'Hara, chairman of the MIS Application Group at Delphic

Harvard - Holden

Harvard University has developed a centrally operated fund-raising system that allows university institutions to share fund-raising information for the first time.

The new Sybase system, called HOLDEN (Harvard Online Development Network), is expected to maximize the funds generated by the Harvard Development Office from the current donor pool by more precisely targeting existing resources and eliminating wasted efforts and redundancies across the university. Through this streamlining, HOLDEN will allow Harvard to pursue one of the most ambitious fund-raising goals ever set by an American institution to raise $2 billion in five years.

> *Harvard University has enjoyed the nation's premier university endowment since 1636. Sybase technology has allowed us to develop an information system that will preserve this legacy into the twenty-first century*

Jim Conway, director of development computing services, Harvard University

J.P. Morgan

This leading financial company was one of the first to employ data mining/forecasting applications using Information Harvester software on the Convex Examplar and C series.

> *The promise of data mining tools like Information Harvester is that they are able to quickly wade through massive amounts of data to identify relationships or trending information that would not have been available without the tool*

Charles Bonomo, vice president of advanced technology for J.P. Morgan

The flexibility of the Information Harvesting induction algorithm enables it to adapt to any system. The data can be in the form of numbers, dates, codes, categories, text or any combination thereof. Information Harvester is designed to handle faulty, missing and noisy data. Large variations in the values of an individual field do not hamper the analysis. Information Harvester has unique abilities to recognize and ignore irrelevant data fields when searching for patterns. In full-scale parallel-processing versions, Information Harvester can handle millions of rows and thousands of variables.

In Summary

Basically Data Mining is concerned with the analysis of data and the use of software techniques for finding patterns and regularities in sets of data. The stages/processes in data mining and Knowledge discovery includes: Selection, preprocessing, transformation of data, interpretation and evaluation. Data Mining methods are classified by the functions they perform, which include: Classification, Clustering, and Regression etc.

Chapter 2: DATA MINING WITH DECISION TREES

Decision tree is a Classification scheme and is used to find the description of several predefined classes and classify a data item into one of them. The main topics, which are covered in this chapter, are:

- How the Decision Tree Works.
- Construction of Decision Trees.
- Issues in Data Mining with Decision Tree.
- Visualization of Decision tree in CABRO System.
- Strengths and Weaknesses.

CHAPTER 2

DATA MINING WITH DECISION TREES

INTRODUCTION

Decision trees are powerful and popular tools for classification and prediction. The attractiveness of tree-based methods is due in large part to the fact that, in contrast to neural networks, decision trees represent *rules*. Rules can readily be expressed so that we humans can understand them or in a database access language like SQL, the records falling into a particular category may be retrieved.

In some applications, the accuracy of a classification or prediction is the only thing that matters; if a direct mail firm obtains a model that can accurately predict which members of a prospect pool are most likely to respond to a certain solicitation, they may not care how or why the model works. In other situations, the ability to explain the reason for a decision is crucial. In health insurance underwriting, for example, there are legal prohibitions against discrimination based on certain variables. An insurance company could find itself in the position of having to demonstrate to the satisfaction of a court of law that it has not used illegal discriminatory practices in granting or denying coverage. There are a variety of algorithms for building decision trees that share the desirable trait of explicability. Most notably are two methods and systems CART and C4.5 (See5/C5.0) that are gaining popularity and are now available as commercial software.

2.1 HOW A DECISION TREE WORKS

Decision tree is a classifier in the form of a tree structure where each node is either:

- a *leaf node*, indicating a class of instances, or
- a *decision node* that specifies some test to be carried out on a single attribute value, with one branch and sub-tree for each possible outcome of the test.

A decision tree can be used to classify an instance by starting at the root of the tree and moving through it until a leaf node, which provides the classification of the instance.

Example: *Decision making in the London stock market*

Suppose that the major factors affecting the London stock market are:

- what it did yesterday;
- what the New York market is doing today;
- bank interest rate;
- unemployment rate;
- England's prospect at cricket.

Table 2.1 is a small illustrative dataset of six days about the London stock market. The lower part contains data of each day according to five questions, and the second row shows the observed result (Yes (Y) or No (N) for "It rises today"). Figure 2.1 illustrates a typical learned decision tree from the data in Table 2.1.

Table 2.1. Examples of a Small Dataset on the London Stock Market

Instance No.	*1*	*2*	*3*	*4*	*5*	*6*
It rises today	Y	Y	Y	N	N	N
It rose yesterday	Y	Y	N	Y	N	N
NY rises today	Y	N	N	N	N	N
Bank rate high	N	Y	N	Y	N	Y
Unemployment high	N	Y	Y	N	N	N
England is losing	Y	Y	Y	Y	Y	Y

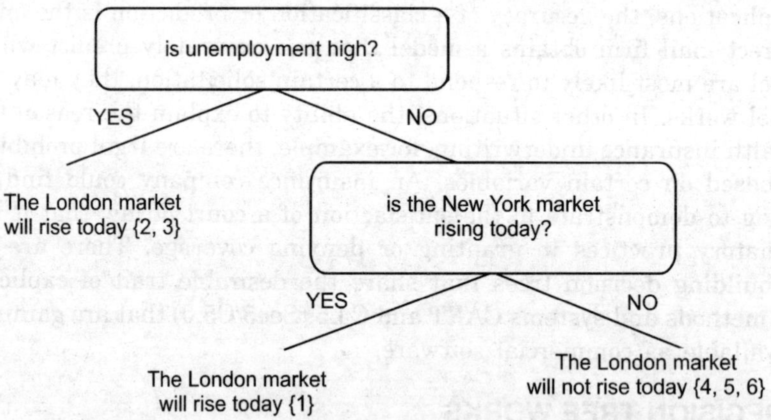

Figure 2.1. A Decision Tree for the London Stock Market

The process of predicting an instance by this decision tree can also be expressed by answering the questions in the following order:

Is unemployment high?

YES: The London market will rise today.

NO: Is the New York market rising today?

YES: The London market will rise today.

NO: The London market will not rise today.

Decision tree induction is a typical inductive approach to learn knowledge on classification. The key requirements to do mining with decision trees are:

- *Attribute-value description*: object or case must be expressible in terms of a fixed collection of properties or attributes.
- *Predefined classes*: The categories to which cases are to be assigned must have been established beforehand (supervised data).
- *Discrete classes*: A case does or does not belong to a particular class, and there must be for more cases than classes.
- *Sufficient data*: Usually hundreds or even thousands of training cases.
- *"Logical" classification model*: Classifier that can only be expressed as decision trees or set of production rules

2.2 CONSTRUCTING DECISION TREES

The Basic Decision Tree Learning Algorithm. Most algorithms that have been developed for learning decision trees are variations on a core algorithm that employs a top-down, greedy search through the space of possible decision trees. Decision tree programs construct a decision tree T from a set of training cases. The original idea of construction of decision trees goes back to the work of Hoveland and Hunt on *concept learning systems* (CLS) in the late 1950s. Table 2.2 briefly describes this CLS scheme that is in fact a recursive top-down divide-and-conquer algorithm. The algorithm consists of five steps.

Table 2.2. CLS Algorithm

1. $T \neg$ the whole training set. Create a T node.
2. If all examples in T are positive, create a 'P' node with T as its parent and stop.
3. If all examples in T are negative, create an 'N' node with T as its parent and stop.
4. Select an attribute X with values $v_1, v_2, \ldots, v_N$ and partition T into subsets $T_1, T_2, \ldots, T_N$ according to their values on X. Create N nodes T_i (i = 1,..., N) with T as their parent and $X = v_i$ as the label of the branch from T to T_i.
5. For each T_i do: $T \neg T_i$ and goto step 2.

We present here the basic algorithm for decision tree learning, corresponding approximately to the ID3 algorithm of Quinlan, and its successors C4.5, See5/C5.0 . To illustrate the operation of ID3, consider the learning task represented by training examples of Table 2.3. Here the target attribute *PlayTennis* (also called class attribute), which can have values *yes* or *no* for different Saturday mornings, is to be predicted based on other attributes of the morning in question.

Table 2.3. Training Examples for the Target Concept *Play Tennis*

Day	*Outlook*	*Temperature*	*Humidity*	*Wind*	*Play Tennis?*
D1	Sunny	Hot	High	Weak	No
D2	Sunny	Hot	High	Strong	No
D3	Overcast	Hot	High	Weak	Yes

(Contd.)

D4	Rain	Mild	High	Weak	Yes
D5	Rain	Cool	Normal	Weak	Yes
D6	Rain	Cool	Normal	Strong	No
D7	Overcast	Cool	Normal	Strong	Yes
D8	Sunny	Mild	High	Weak	No
D9	Sunny	Cool	Normal	Weak	Yes
D10	Rain	Mild	Normal	Weak	Yes
D11	Sunny	Mild	Normal	Strong	Yes
D12	Overcast	Mild	High	Strong	Yes
D13	Overcast	Hot	Normal	Weak	Yes
D14	Rain	Mild	High	Strong	No

Which Attribute is the Best Classifier?

The central choice in the ID3 algorithm selects which attribute to test at each node in the tree, according to the first task in step 4 of the CLS algorithm. We would like to select the attribute that is most useful for classifying examples. What is a good quantitative measure of the worth of an attribute? We will define a statistical property called *information gain* that measures how well a given attribute separates the training examples according to their target classification. ID3 uses this information gain measure to select among the candidate attributes at each step while growing the tree.

Entropy Measures Homogeneity of Examples. In order to define information gain precisely, we begin by defining a measure commonly used in information theory, called entropy, that characterizes the impurity of an arbitrary collection of examples. Given a collection S, containing positive and negative examples of some target concept, the entropy of S relative to this Boolean classification is

$$\text{Entropy}(S) = -p_{\oplus}\log_2 p_{\oplus} - p_{\ominus}\log_2 p_{\ominus} \quad \text{...(2.1)}$$

where $p_{\oplus}$ is the proportion of positive examples in S and p is the proportion of negative examples in S. In all calculations involving entropy we define 0log0 to be 0.

To illustrate, suppose S is a collection of 14 examples of some Boolean concept, including 9 positive and 5 negative examples (we adopt the notation [9+, 5–] to summarize such a sample of data). Then the entropy of S relative to this Boolean classification is

$$\text{Entropy}([9+, 5-]) = -(9/14)\log_2(9/14) - (5/14)\log_2(5/14) = 0.940 \quad \text{...(2.2)}$$

Notice that the entropy is 0 if all members of S belong to the same class. For example, if all members are positive ($p_{\oplus} = 1$), then $p_{\ominus}$ is 0, and $\text{Entropy}(S) = -1 \times \log_2(1) - 0 \times \log_2 0 = -1 \times 0 - 0 \times \log_2 0 = 0$. Note the entropy is 1 when the collection contains an equal number of positive and negative examples. If the collection contains unequal numbers of positive and negative examples, the entropy is between 0 and 1. Figure 2.2 shows the form of the entropy function relative to a Boolean classification, as $p_{\oplus}$ varies between 0 and 1.

One interpretation of entropy from information theory is that it specifies the minimum number of bits of information needed to encode the classification of an arbitrary member of

S (i.e., a member of S drawn at random with uniform probability). For example, if $p_{\oplus}$ is 1, the receiver knows the drawn example will be positive, so no message needs to be sent, and the entropy is 0. On the other hand, if $p_{\oplus}$ is 0.5, one bit is required to indicate whether the drawn example is positive or negative. If $p_{\oplus}$ is 0.8, then a collection of messages can be encoded using on average less than 1 bit per message by assigning shorter codes to collections of positive examples and longer codes to less likely negative examples.

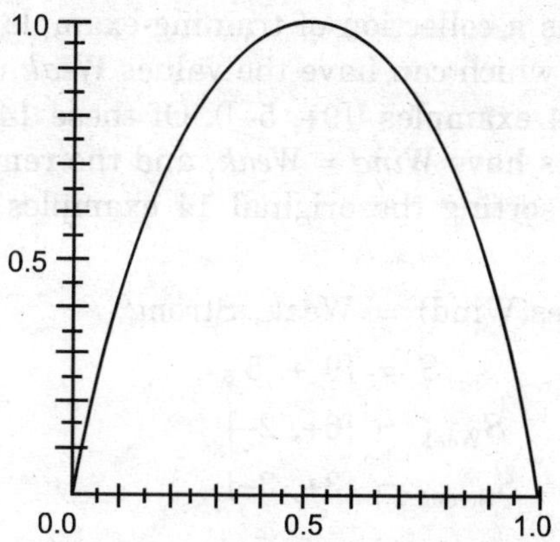

Figure 2.2. The Entropy Function Relative to a Boolean Classification, as the Proportion of Positive Examples p⊕ Varies between 0 and 1.

Thus far we have discussed entropy in the special case where the target classification is Boolean. More generally, if the target attribute can take on c different values, then the entropy of S relative to this c-wise classification is defined as

$$\text{Entropy}(S) = \sum_{i=1}^{c} -p_i \log_2 p_i \quad \text{...(2.3)}$$

where p_i is the proportion of S belonging to class i. Note the logarithm is still base 2 because entropy is a measure of the expected encoding length measured in bits. Note also that if the target attribute can take on c possible values, the entropy can be as large as $\log_2 c$.

Information Gain Measures the Expected Reduction in Entropy. Given entropy as a measure of the impurity in a collection of training examples, we can now define a measure of the effectiveness of an attribute in classifying the training data. The measure we will use, called *information gain*, is simply the expected reduction in entropy caused by partitioning the examples according to this attribute. More precisely, the information gain, *Gain (S, A)* of an attribute A, relative to a collection of examples S, is defined as

$$\text{Gain}(S, A) = \text{Entropy}(S) - \sum_{v \in \text{Values}(A)} \frac{|S_v|}{|S|} \text{Entropy}(S_v) \quad \text{...(2.4)}$$

where *Values* (A) is the set of all possible values for attribute A, and S_v is the subset of S for which attribute A has value v (i.e., $S_v = \{s \in S \mid A(s) = v\}$). Note the first term in Equation (2.4) is just the entropy of the original collection S and the second term is the expected value of the entropy after S is partitioned using attribute A. The expected entropy described by this second term is simply the sum of the entropies of each subset Sv, weighted by the fraction of examples $|S_v|/|S|$ that belong to S_v. *Gain* (S, A) is therefore the expected reduction in entropy caused by knowing the value of attribute A. Put another way, *Gain* (S, A) is the information provided about the target function value, given the value of some other attribute A. The value of *Gain* (S, A) is the number of bits saved when encoding the target value of an arbitrary member of S, by knowing the value of attribute A.

For example, suppose S is a collection of training-example days described in Table 2.3 by attributes including *Wind*, which can have the values *Weak* or *Strong*. As before, assume S is a collection containing 14 examples ([9+, 5–]). Of these 14 examples, 6 of the positive and 2 of the negative examples have *Wind* = *Weak*, and the remainder have *Wind* = *Strong*. The information gain due to sorting the original 14 examples by the attribute *Wind* may then be calculated as

$$\text{Values(Wind)} = \text{Weak, Strong}$$

$$S = [9+, 5-]$$

$$S_{\text{Weak}} \neg [6+, 2-]$$

$$S_{\text{Strong}} \neg [3+, 3-]$$

$$\begin{aligned}\text{Gain (S, Wind)} &= \text{Entropy}\,(S) - \sum_{v \in \{\text{Weak, Strong}\}} \frac{|S_v|}{|S|}\,\text{Entropy}\,(S_v)\\ &= \text{Entropy}(S) - (8/14)\ \text{Entropy}\ (S_{\text{Weak}})\\ &\quad - (6/14)\ \text{Entropy}\ (S_{\text{Strong}})\\ &= 0.940 - (8/14)\ 0.811 - (6/14)1.00\\ &= 0.048\end{aligned}$$

Information gain is precisely the measure used by ID3 to select the best attribute at each step in growing the tree.

An Illustrative Example. Consider the first step through the algorithm, in which the topmost node of the decision tree is created. Which attribute should be tested first in the tree? ID3 determines the information gain for each candidate attribute (i.e., *Outlook, Temperature, Humidity*, and *Wind*), then selects the one with highest information gain. The information gain values for all four attributes are

$$\begin{aligned}Gain(S,\ Outlook) &= 0.246\\ Gain(S,\ Humidity) &= 0.151\\ Gain(S,\ Wind) &= 0.048\\ Gain(S,\ Temperature) &= 0.029\end{aligned}$$

where S denotes the collection of training examples from Table 2.3.

According to the information gain measure, the *Outlook* attribute provides the best prediction of the target attribute, *PlayTennis*, over the training examples. Therefore, *Outlook* is selected as the decision attribute for the root node, and branches are created below the root for each of its possible values (i.e., *Sunny, Overcast,* and *Rain*). The final tree is shown in Figure 2.3.

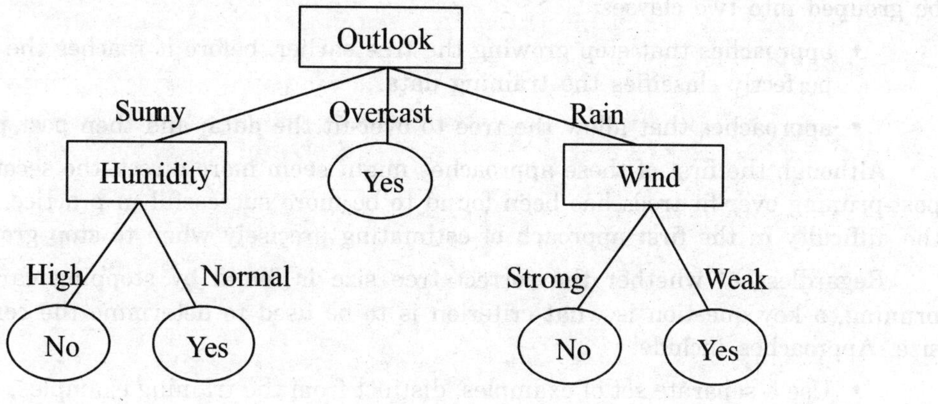

Figure 2.3. A Decision Tree for the Concept *Play Tennis*

The process of selecting a new attribute and partitioning the training examples is now repeated for each non-terminal descendant node, this time using only the training examples associated with that node. Attributes that have been incorporated higher in the tree are excluded, so that any given attribute can appear atmost once along any path through the tree. This process continues for each new leaf node until either of two conditions is met:

1. every attribute has already been included along this path through the tree, or
2. all the training examples associated with this leaf node have the same target attribute value (i.e., their entropy is zero).

2.3 ISSUES IN DATA MINING WITH DECISION TREES

Practical issues in learning decision trees include determining how deeply to grow the decision tree, handling continuous attributes, choosing an appropriate attribute selection measure, handling training data with missing attribute values, handing attributes with differing costs, and improving computational efficiency. Below we discuss each of these issues and extensions to the basic ID3 algorithm that address them. ID3 has itself been extended to address most of these issues, with the resulting system renamed as C4.5 and See5/C5.0.

Avoiding Over-Fitting the Data

The CLS algorithm described in Table 2.2 grows each branch of the tree just deeply enough to perfectly classify the training examples. While this is sometimes a reasonable strategy, in fact it can lead to difficulties when there is noise in the data, or when the number of training examples is too small to produce a representative sample of the true target function. In either of these cases, this simple algorithm can produce trees that *over-fit* the training examples.

Over-fitting is a significant practical difficulty for decision tree learning and many other learning methods. For example, in one experimental study of ID3 involving five different learning tasks with noisy, non-deterministic data, over-fitting was found to decrease the accuracy of learned decision trees by 10-25% on most problems.

There are several approaches to avoid over-fitting in decision tree learning. These can be grouped into two classes:

- approaches that stop growing the tree earlier, before it reaches the point where it perfectly classifies the training data,
- approaches that allow the tree to over-fit the data, and then post prune the tree.

Although the first of these approaches might seem more direct, the second approach of post-pruning over-fit trees has been found to be more successful in practice. This is due to the difficulty in the first approach of estimating precisely when to stop growing the tree.

Regardless of whether the correct tree size is found by stopping early or by post-pruning, a key question is what criterion is to be used to determine the correct final tree size. Approaches include:

- Use a separate set of examples, distinct from the training examples, to evaluate the utility of post-pruning nodes from the tree.
- Use all the available data for training, but apply a statistical test to estimate whether expanding (or pruning) a particular node is likely to produce an improvement beyond the training set. For example, Quinlan uses a chi-square test to estimate whether further expanding a node is likely to improve performance over the entire instance distribution, or only on the current sample of training data.
- Use an explicit measure of the complexity for encoding the training examples and the decision tree, halting growth of the tree when this encoding size is minimized. This approach, based on a heuristic called the Minimum Description Length principle.

The first of the above approaches is the most common and is often referred to as training and validation set approach. We discuss the two main variants of this approach below. In this approach, the available data are separated into two sets of examples: a *training set*, which is used to form the learned hypothesis, and a separate *validation set*, which is used to evaluate the accuracy of this hypothesis over subsequent data and, in particular, to evaluate the impact of pruning this hypothesis.

Reduced error pruning. How exactly might we use a validation set to prevent over-fitting? One approach, called *reduced-error pruning* (Quinlan, 1987), is to consider each of the decision nodes in the tree, to be candidates for pruning. Pruning a decision node consists of removing the sub-tree rooted at that node, making it a leaf node, and assigning it the most common classification of the training examples affiliated with that node. Nodes are removed only if the resulting pruned tree performs no worse than the original over the validation set. This has the effect that any leaf node added due to coincidental regularities in the training set is likely to be pruned because these same coincidences are unlikely to occur in the validation set. Nodes are pruned iteratively, always choosing the node whose removal most increases the decision tree accuracy over the validation set. Pruning of nodes continues until further pruning is harmful (i.e., decreases accuracy of the tree over the validation set).

Rule Post-Pruning

In practice, one quite successful method for finding high accuracy hypotheses is a technique called rule post-pruning. A variant of this pruning method is used by C4.5. Rule post-pruning involves the following steps:

1. Infer the decision tree from the training set, growing the tree until the training data is fit as well as possible and allowing over-fitting to occur.
2. Convert the learned tree into an equivalent set of rules by creating one rule for each path from the root node to a leaf node.
3. Prune (generalize) each rule by removing any preconditions that result in improving its estimated accuracy.
4. Sort the pruned rules by their estimated accuracy, and consider them in this sequence when classifying subsequent instances.

To illustrate, consider again the decision tree in Figure 2.3. In rule post-pruning, one rule is generated for each leaf node in the tree. Each attribute test along the path from the root to the leaf becomes a rule antecedent (precondition) and the classification at the leaf node becomes the rule consequent (post-condition). For example, the leftmost path of the tree in Figure 2.2 is translated into the rule

IF (*Outlook* = *Sunny*) ∧ (*Humidity* = *High*)

THEN *PlayTennis* = *No*

Next, each such rule is pruned by removing any antecedent, or precondition, whose removal does not worsen its estimated accuracy. Given the above rule, for example, rule post-pruning would consider removing the preconditions (*Outlook* = *Sunny*) and (*Humidity* = *High*). It would select whichever of these pruning steps that produce the greatest improvement in estimated rule accuracy, then consider pruning the second precondition as a further pruning step. No pruning step is performed if it reduces the estimated rule accuracy.

Why the decision tree is converted to rules before pruning? There are three main advantages.

- Converting to rules allows distinguishing among the different contexts in which a decision node is used. Because each distinct path through the decision tree node produces a distinct rule, the pruning decision regarding that attribute test can be made differently for each path. In contrast, if the tree itself were pruned, the only two choices would be to remove the decision node completely, or to retain it in its original form.
- Converting to rules removes the distinction between attribute tests that occur near the root of the tree and those that occur near the leaves. Thus, we avoid messy book-keeping issues such as how to reorganize the tree if the root node is pruned while retaining part of the sub-tree below this test.
- Converting to rules improves readability. Rules are often easier for people to understand.

Incorporating Continuous-Valued Attributes

The initial definition of ID3 is restricted to attributes that take on a discrete set of values. First, the target attribute whose value is predicted by the learned tree must be discrete valued. Second, the attributes tested in the decision nodes of the tree must also be discrete valued. This second restriction can easily be removed so that continuous-valued decision attributes can be incorporated into the learned tree. This can be accomplished by dynamically defining new discrete-valued attributes that partition the continuous attribute value into a discrete set of intervals. In particular, for an attribute A that is continuous-valued, the algorithm can dynamically create a new Boolean attribute A_c that is true if $A < c$ and false otherwise. The only question is how to select the best value for the threshold c. As an example, suppose we wish to include the continuous-valued attribute *Temperature* in describing the training example days in Table 2.3. Suppose further that the training examples associated with a particular node in the decision tree have the following values for *Temperature* and the target attribute *PlayTennis*.

Temperature:	40	48	60	72	80	90
PlayTennis:	No	No	Yes	Yes	Yes	No

What threshold-based Boolean attribute should be defined based on *Temperature*? Clearly, we would like to pick a threshold, c, that produces the greatest information gain. By sorting the examples according to the continuous attribute A, then identifying adjacent examples that differ in their target classification, we can generate a set of candidate thresholds midway between the corresponding values of A. It can be shown that the value of c that maximizes information gain must always lie at such a boundary. These candidate thresholds can then be evaluated by computing the information gain associated with each. In the current example, there are two candidate thresholds, corresponding to the values of *Temperature* at which the value of *PlayTennis* changes: (48 + 60)/2 and (80 + 90)/2. The information gain can then be computed for each of the candidate attributes, *Temperature*>54 and *Temperature*>85, and the best can t selected (*Temperature*>54). This dynamically created Boolean attribute can then compete with the other discrete-valued candidate attributes available for growing the decision tree.

Handling Training Examples with Missing Attribute Values

In certain cases, the available data may be missing values for some attributes. For example, in a medical domain in which we wish to predict patient outcome based on various laboratory tests, it may be that the lab test Blood-Test-Result is available only for a subset of the patients. In such cases, it is common to estimate the missing attribute value based on other examples for which this attribute has a known value.

Consider the situation in which *Gain(S, A)* is to be calculated at node n in the decision tree to evaluate whether the attribute A is the best attribute to test at this decision node. Suppose that $< x, c(x)>$ is one of the training examples in S and that the value $A(x)$ is unknown, where $c(x)$ is the class label of x.

One strategy for dealing with the missing attribute value is to assign it the value that is most common among training examples at node n. Alternatively, we might assign it the most common value among examples at node n that have the classification $c(x)$. The elaborated training example using this estimated value for $A(x)$ can then be used directly by the existing decision tree learning algorithm.

A second, more complex procedure is to assign a probability to each of the possible values of A rather than simply assigning the most common value to $A(x)$. These probabilities can be estimated again based on the observed frequencies of the various values for A among the examples at node *n*. For example, given a Boolean attribute *A*, if node n contains six known examples with $A = 1$ and four with $A = 0$, then we would say the probability that $A(x) = 1$ is 0.6, and the probability that $A(x) = 0$ is 0.4. A fractional 0.6 of instance *x* is now distributed down the branch for $A = 1$ and a fractional 0.4 of *x* down the other tree branch. These fractional examples are used for the purpose of computing information *Gain* and can be further subdivided at subsequent branches of the tree if a second missing attribute value must be tested. This same fractioning of examples can also be applied after learning, to classify new instances whose attribute values are unknown. In this case, the classification of the new instance is simply the most probable classification, computed by summing the weights of the instance fragments classified in different ways at the leaf nodes of the tree. This method for handling missing attribute values is used in C4.5.

2.4 VISUALIZATION OF DECISION TREES IN SYSTEM *CABRO*

In this section we briefly describe system CABRO for mining decision trees that focuses on visualization and model selection techniques in decision tree learning.

Though decision trees are a simple notion, it is not easy to understand and analyze large decision trees generated from huge data sets. For example, the widely used program C4.5 produces a decision tree of nearly 18,500 nodes with 2624 leaf nodes from the census bureau database given recently to the KDD community that consists of 199,523 instances described by 40 numeric and symbolic attributes (103 Mbytes). It is extremely difficult for the user to understand and use that big tree in its text form. In such cases, a graphic visualization of discovered decision trees with different ways of accessing and viewing trees is of great support and recently it receives much attention from the KDD researcher and user. System MineSet of Silicon Graphics provides a 3D visualization of decision trees. System CART (Salfort Systems) provides a tree map that can be used to navigate the large decision trees. The interactive visualization system CABRO, associated with a new proposed technique called T2.5D (stands for Tree 2.5 Dimensions) offers an alternative efficient way that allows the user to manipulate graphically and interactively large trees in data mining.

In CABRO, a mining process concerns with *model selection* in which the user try different settings of decision tree induction to attain most appropriate decision trees. To help the user to understand the effects of settings on result trees, the tree visualizer is capable of handling multiple views of different trees at any stage in the induction. There are several modes of view: zoomed, tiny, tightly-coupled, fish-eyed, and T2.5D, in each mode the user can interactively change the layout of the structure to fit the current interests.

The tree visualizer helps the user to understand decision trees by providing different views; each is convenient to use in different situations. The available views are

- *Standard*: The tree is drawn in proportion, the size of a node is up to the length of its label, the parent is vertically located at the middle of its children, and sibling are horizontally aligned.
- *Tightly-coupled*: The window is divided into two panels, one displays the tree in a tiny size, another displays it in a normal size. The first panel is a map to navigate the tree; the second displays the corresponding area of the tree.
- *Fish-eyes*: This view distorts the magnified image so that nodes around the center of interest are displayed at high magnification, and the rest of the tree is progressively compressed.

- *T2.5D*: In this view, Z-order of tree nodes are used to make 3D effects, nodes and links may be overlapped. The focused path of the tree is drawn in the front and by highlighted colors.

The tree visualizer allows the user to customize above views by several operations that include: *zoom*, *collapse/expand*, and *view node content*.

- *Zoom*: The user can zoom in or zoom out the drawn tree.
- *Collapse/expand*: The user can choose to view some parts of the tree by collapsing and expanding paths.
- *View node content*: The user can see the content of a node such as: attribute/value, class, population, etc.

In model selection, the tree visualization has an important role in assisting the user to understand and interpret generated decision trees. Without its help, the user cannot decide to favor which decision trees more than the others. Moreover, if the mining process is set to run interactively, the system allows the user to take part at every step of the induction. He/she can manually choose, which attribute will be used to branch at the considering node. The tree visualizer then can display several hypothetical decision trees side by side to help user to decide which ones are worth to further develop. We can say that an interactive tree visualizer integrated with the system allows the user to use domain knowledge by actively taking part in mining processes.

Very large hierarchical structures are still difficult to navigate and view even with tightly-coupled and fish-eye views. To address the problem, we have been developing a special technique called T2.5D (Tree 2.5 Dimensions). The 3D browsers usually can display more nodes in a compact area of the screen but require currently expensive 3D animation

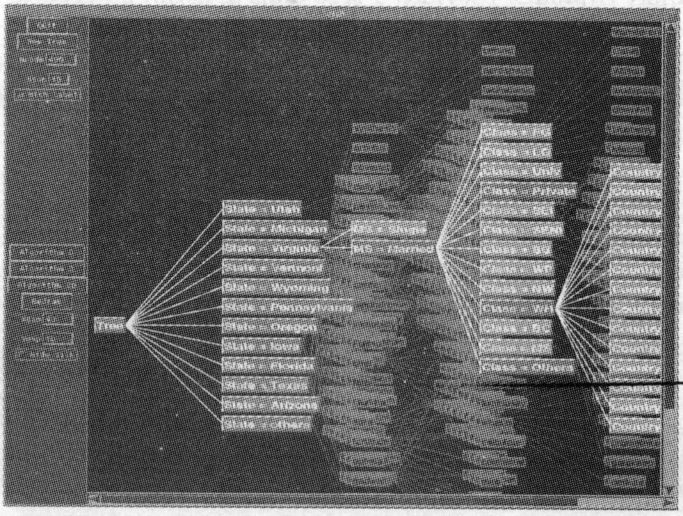

Figure 2.4. T2.5 Visualization of Large Decision Trees.

support and visualized structures are difficult to navigate, while 2D browsers have limitation in display many nodes in one view. The T2.5D technique combines the advantages of both 2D and 3D drawing techniques to provide the user with cheap processing cost, a browser which can display more than 1000 nodes in one view; a large number of them may be partially overlapped but they all are in full size. In T2.5D, a node can be highlighted or dim. The highlighted nodes are that the user currently interested in and they are displayed in 2D to be viewed and navigated with ease. The dim nodes are displayed in 3D and they allow the user to get an idea about overall structure of the hierarchy (Figure 2.4).

2.5 STRENGTHS AND WEAKNESS OF DECISION TREE METHODS

The strengths of decision tree methods

The strengths of decision tree methods are:

- Decision trees are able to generate understandable rules.
- Decision trees perform classification without requiring much computation.
- Decision trees are able to handle both continuous and categorical variables.
- Decision trees provide a clear indication of which fields are most important for prediction or classification.
- **Ability to Generate Understandable Rules.** The ability of decision trees to generate rules that can be translated into comprehensible English or SQL is the greatest strength of this technique. Even when a complex domain or a domain that does decompose easily into rectangular regions causes the decision tree to be large and complex, it is generally fairly easy to follow any one path through the tree. So the explanation for any particular classification or prediction is relatively straightforward.
- **Ability to Perform in Rule-Oriented Domains.** It may sound obvious, but rule induction in general, and decision trees in particular, are an excellent choice in domains where there really are rules to be found. The authors had this fact driven home to them by an experience at Caterpillar. Caterpillar called upon MRJ to help design and oversee some experiments in data mining. One of the areas where we felt that data mining might prove useful was in the automatic approval of warranty repair claims. Many domains, ranging from genetics to industrial processes really do have underlying rules, though these may be quite complex and obscured by noisy data. Decision trees are a natural choice when you suspect the existence of underlying rules.
- **Ease of Calculation at Classification Time.** Although, as we have seen, a decision tree can take many forms, in practice, the algorithms used to produce decision trees generally yield trees with a low branching factor and simple tests at each node. Typical tests include numeric comparisons, set membership, and simple conjunctions. When implemented on a computer, these tests translate into simple Boolean and integer operations that are fast and inexpensive. This is an important point because in a commercial environment, a predictive model is likely to be used to classify many millions or even billions of records.
- **Ability to Handle both Continuous and Categorical Variables.** Decision-tree methods are equally adept at handling continuous and categorical variables. Categorical variables, which pose problems for neural networks and statistical techniques, come ready-made with their own splitting criteria: one branch for each category. Continuous variables are equally easy to split by picking a number somewhere in their range of values.

- **Ability to Clearly Indicate Best Fields.** Decision-tree building algorithms put the field that does the best job of splitting the training records at the root node of the tree.

The Weaknesses of Decision Tree Methods

Decision trees are less appropriate for estimation tasks where the goal is to predict the value of a continuous variable such as income, blood pressure, or interest rate. Decision trees are also problematic for time-series data unless a lot of effort is put into presenting the data in such a way that trends and sequential patterns are made visible.

- **Error-Prone with Too Many Classes.** Some decision-tree algorithms can only deal with binary-valued target classes (yes/no, accept/reject). Others are able to assign records to an arbitrary number of classes, but are error-prone when the number of training examples per class gets small. This can happen rather quickly in a tree with many levels and/or many branches per node.
- **Computationally Expensive to Train.** The process of growing a decision tree is computationally expensive. At each node, each candidate splitting field must be sorted before its best split can be found. In some algorithms, combinations of fields are used and a search must be made for optimal combining weights. Pruning algorithms can also be expensive since many candidate sub-trees must be formed and compared.
- **Trouble with Non-Rectangular Regions.** Most decision-tree algorithms only examine a single field at a time. This leads to rectangular classification boxes that may not correspond well with the actual distribution of records in the decision space.

In Summary

Decision Tree is classification scheme and its structure is in form of tree where each node is either leaf node or decision node. The original idea of construction of decision tree is based on Concept Learning System (CLS)–it is a top-down divide-and-conquer algorithms. Practical issues in learning decision tree includes: Avoiding over- fitting the data, Reduced error pruning, Incorporating continuous- Valued attributes, Handling training examples with missing attributes values. Visualization and model selection in decision tree learning is described by using CABRO system.

Chapter 3: DATA MINING WITH ASSOCIATION RULES

An appeal of market analysis comes from the clarity and utility of its results, is the form of association rule. The discovery of Association rules can help the retailer develop strategies, by gaining insights into matters and it also helps in inventory management, sale promotion strategies, etc. the main topics that are covered in this chapter are:

- Association Rule Analysis.
- Process of Mining Association Rules.
- Strengths and Weaknesses.

CHAPTER 3

DATA MINING WITH ASSOCIATION RULES

3.1 WHEN IS ASSOCIATION RULE ANALYSIS USEFUL?

An appeal of market analysis comes from the clarity and utility of its results, which are in the form of *association rules*. There is an intuitive appeal to a market analysis because it expresses how tangible products and services relate to each other, how they tend to group together. A rule like, "if a customer purchases three way calling, then that customer will also purchase call waiting" is clear. Even better, it suggests a specific course of action, like bundling three-way calling with call waiting into a single service package. While association rules are easy to understand, they are not always useful. The following three rules are examples of real rules generated from real data:

- On Thursdays, grocery store consumers often purchase diapers and beer together.
- Customers who purchase maintenance agreements are very likely to purchase large appliances.
- When a new hardware store opens, one of the most commonly sold items is toilet rings.

These three examples illustrate the three common types of rules produced by association rule analysis: the *useful*, the *trivial*, and the *inexplicable*.

The useful rule contains high quality, actionable information. In fact, once the pattern is found, it is often not hard to justify. The rule about diapers and beer on Thursdays suggests that on Thursday evenings, young couples prepare for the weekend by stocking up on diapers for the infants and beer for dad (who, for the sake of argument, we stereotypically assume is watching football on Sunday with a six-pack). By locating their own brand of diapers near the aisle containing the beer, they can increase sales of a high-margin product. Because the rule is easily understood, it suggests plausible causes, leading to other interventions: placing other baby products within sight of the beer so that customers do not "forget" anything and putting other leisure foods, like potato chips and pretzels, near the baby products.

Trivial results are already known by anyone at all familiar with the business. The second example "Customers who purchase maintenance agreements are very likely to purchase large appliances" is an example of a trivial rule. In fact, we already know that customers purchase maintenance agreements and large appliances at the same time. Why else would they purchase maintenance agreements? The maintenance agreements are advertised with large appliances and are rarely sold separately. This rule, though, was based on analyzing hundreds of thousands of point-of-sale transactions from Sears. Although it is valid and well-supported in the data, it is still useless. Similar results abound: People who buy 2-by-4s also purchase nails; customers who purchase paint buy paint brushes; oil and oil filters are purchased together as are hamburgers and hamburger buns, and charcoal and lighter fluid.

A subtler problem falls into the same category. A seemingly interesting result–like the fact that people who buy the three-way calling option on their local telephone service almost always buy call waiting-may be the result of marketing programs and product bundles. In the case of telephone service options, three-way calling is typically bundled with call waiting, so it is difficult to order it separately. In this case, the analysis is not producing actionable results; it is producing already acted-upon results. Although a danger for any data mining technique, association rule analysis is particularly susceptible to reproducing the success of previous marketing campaigns because of its dependence on un-summarized point-of-sale data–exactly the same data that defines the success of the campaign. *Results from association rule analysis may simply be measuring the success of previous marketing campaigns.*

Inexplicable results seem to have no explanation and do not suggest a course of action. The third pattern ("When a new hardware store opens, one of the most commonly sold items is toilet rings") is intriguing, tempting us with a new fact but providing information that does not give insight into consumer behavior or the merchandise, or suggest further actions. In this case, a large hardware company discovered the pattern for new store openings, but did not figure out how to profit from it. Many items are on sale during the store openings, but the toilet rings stand out. More investigation might give some explanation: Is the discount on toilet rings much larger than for other products? Are they consistently placed in a high-traffic area for store openings but hidden at other times? Is the result an anomaly from a handful of stores? Are they difficult to find at other times? Whatever the cause, it is doubtful that further analysis of just the association rule data can give a credible explanation.

3.2 HOW DOES ASSOCIATION RULE ANALYSIS WORK?

Association rule analysis starts with transactions containing one or more products or service offerings and some rudimentary information about the transaction. For the purpose of analysis, we call the products and service offerings items. Table 3.1 illustrates five transactions in a grocery store that carries five products. These transactions are simplified to include only the items purchased. How to use information like the date and time and whether the customer used cash will be discussed later in this chapter. Each of these transactions gives us information about which products are purchased with which other products. Using this data, we can create a co-occurrence table that tells the number of times, any pair of products was purchased together (see Table 3.2). For instance, by looking at the box where the "Soda" row intersects the "OJ" column, we see that two transactions contain both soda and orange juice. The values along the diagonal (for instance, the value in the "OJ" column and the "OJ" row) represent the number of transactions containing just that item.

Table 3.1. Grocery Point-of-sale Transactions

Customer	*Items*
1	orange juice, soda
2	milk, orange juice, window cleaner
3	orange juice, detergent,
4	orange juice, detergent, soda
5	window cleaner, soda

The co-occurrence table contains some simple patterns:

- OJ and soda are likely to be purchased together than any other two items.
- Detergent is never purchased with window cleaner or milk.
- Milk is never purchased with soda or detergent.

These simple observations are examples of associations and may suggest a formal rule like: "If a customer purchases soda, then the customer also purchases milk". For now, we defer discussion of how we find this rule automatically. Instead, we ask the question: How good is this rule? In the data, two of the five transactions include both soda and orange juice. These two transactions *support* the rule. Another way of expressing this is as a percentage. The support for the rule is two out of five or 40 percent.

Table 3.2. Co-occurrence of Products

Items	*OJ*	*Cleaner*	*Milk*	*Soda*	*Detergent*
OJ	4	1	1	2	1
Window Cleaner	1	2	1	1	0
Milk	1	1	1	0	0
Soda	2	1	0	3	1
Detergent	1	0	0	1	2

Since both the transactions that contain soda also contain orange juice, there is a high degree of *confidence* in the rule as well. In fact, every transaction that contains soda also contains orange juice, so the rule "if soda, then orange juice" has a confidence of 100 percent. We are less confident about the inverse rule, "if orange juice, then soda", because of the four transactions with orange juice, only two also have soda. Its confidence, then, is just 50 percent. More formally, confidence is the ratio of the number of the transactions supporting the rule to the number of transactions where the conditional part of the rule holds. Another way of saying this is that confidence is the ratio of the number of transactions with all the items to the number of transactions with just the "if" items.

3.3 THE BASIC PROCESS OF MINING ASSOCIATION RULES

This basic process for association rules analysis consist of three important concerns

- Choosing the right set of items.

- Generating rules by deciphering the counts in the co-occurrence matrix.
- Overcoming the practical limits imposed by thousands or tens of thousands of items appearing in combinations large enough to be interesting.

Choosing the Right Set of Items. The data used for association rule analysis is typically the detailed transaction data captured at the point of sale. Gathering and using this data is a critical part of applying association rule analysis, depending crucially on the items chosen for analysis. What constitutes a particular item depends on the business need. Within a grocery store where there are tens of thousands of products on the shelves, a frozen pizza might be considered an item for analysis purposes–regardless of its toppings (extra cheese, pepperoni, or mushrooms), its crust (extra thick, whole wheat, or white), or its size. So, the purchase of a large whole wheat vegetarian pizza contains the same "frozen pizza" item as the purchase of a single-serving, pepperoni with extra cheese. A sample of such transactions at this summarized level might look like Table 3.3.

Table 3.3. Transactions with More Summarized Items

	Pizza	*Milk*	*Sugar*	*Apples*	*Coffee*
1	Ö				
2		Ö	Ö		
3	Ö			Ö	Ö
4		Ö			Ö
5	Ö		Ö	Ö	Ö

On the other hand, the manager of frozen foods or a chain of pizza restaurants may be very interested in the particular combinations of toppings that are ordered. He or she might decompose a pizza order into constituent parts, as shown in Table 3.4.

Table 3.4. Transactions with More Detailed Items

	Cheese	*Onions*	*Peppers*	*Mush.*	*Olives*
1	Ö	Ö			Ö
2			Ö		
3	Ö	Ö		Ö	
4		Ö			
5	Ö		Ö	Ö	Ö

At some later point in time, the grocery store may become interested in more detail in its transactions, so the single "frozen pizza" item would no longer be sufficient. Or, the pizza restaurants might broaden their menu choices and become less interested in all the different toppings. The items of interest may change over time. This can pose a problem when trying to use historical data if the transaction data has been summarized.

Choosing the right level of detail is a critical consideration for the analysis. If the transaction data in the grocery store keeps track of every type, brand, and size of frozen pizza-which probably account for several dozen products—then all these items need to map down to the "frozen pizza" item for analysis.

Taxonomies Help to Generalize Items. In the real world, items have product codes and stock-keeping unit codes (SKUs) that fall into hierarchical categories, called taxonomy. When approaching a problem with association rule analysis, what level of the taxonomy is the right one to use? This brings up issues such as

- Are large fries and small fries the same product?
- Is the brand of ice cream more relevant than its flavor?
- Which is more important: the size, style, pattern, or designer of clothing?
- Is the energy-saving option on a large appliance indicative of customer behavior?

The number of combinations to consider grows very fast as the number of items used in the analysis increases. This suggests using items from higher levels of the taxonomy, "frozen desserts" instead of "ice cream". On the other hand, the more specific the items are, the more likely the results are actionable. Knowing what sells with a particular brand of frozen pizza, for instance, can help in managing the relationship with the producer. One compromise is to use more general items initially, then to repeat the rule generation to one in more specific items. As the analysis focuses on more specific items, use only the subset of transactions containing those items.

The complexity of a rule refers to the number of items it contains. The more items in the transactions, the longer it takes to generate rules of a given complexity. So, the desired complexity of the rules also determines how specific or general the items should be in some circumstances, customers do not make large purchases. For instance, customers purchase relatively few items at any one time at a convenience store or through some catalogs, so looking for rules containing four or more items may apply to very few transactions and be a wasted effort. In other cases, like in a supermarket, the average transaction is larger, so more complex rules are useful.

Moving up the taxonomy hierarchy reduces the number of items. Dozens or hundreds of items may be reduced to a single generalized item, often corresponding to a single department or product line. An item like a pint of Ben & Jerry's Cherry Garcia gets generalized to "ice cream" or "frozen desserts " Instead of investigating "orange juice", investigate "fruit juices". Instead of looking at 2 percent milk, map it to "dairy products". Often, the appropriate level of the hierarchy ends up matching a department with a product-line manager, so that using generalized items has the practical effect of finding interdepartmental relationships, because the structure of the organization is likely to hide relationships between departments, these relationships are more likely to be actionable. Generalized items also help find rules with sufficient support. There will be many times as more transactions are to be supported by higher levels of the taxonomy than lower levels.

Just because some items are generalized, it does not mean that all items need to move up to the same level. The appropriate level depends on the item, on its importance for producing actionable results, and on its frequency in the data. For instance, in a department store big-ticket items (like appliances) might stay at a low level in the hierarchy while less expensive items (such as books) might be higher. This hybrid approach is also useful when looking at individual products. Since there are often thousands of products in the data, generalize everything else except for the product or products of interest.

Association rule analysis produces the best results when the items occur in roughly the same number of transactions in the data. This helps to prevent rules from being dominated by the most common items; Taxonomies can help here. Roll up rare items to higher levels in the taxonomy; so they become more frequent. More common items may not have to be rolled up at all.

Generating Rules from All This Data. Calculating the number of times that a given combination of items appears in the transaction data is well and good, but a combination of items is not a rule. Sometimes, just the combination is interesting in itself, as in the diaper, beer, and Thursday example. But in other circumstances, it makes more sense to find an underlying rule. What is a rule? A rule has two parts, a condition and a result, and is usually represented as a statement:

If *condition* then *result*.

If the rule says

If *3-way calling* then *call-waiting*.

we read it as: "if a customer has 3-way calling, then the customer also has call-waiting". In practice, the most actionable rules have just one item as the result. So, a rule likes

If *diapers* and *Thursday*, then *beer* is more useful than

If *Thursday*, then *diapers* and *beer*.

Constructs like the co-occurrence table provide the information about which combination of items occur most commonly in the transactions. For the sake of illustration, let's say the most common combination has three items, A, B, and C. The only rules to consider are those with all three items in the rule and with exactly one item in the result:

If A and B, then C

If A and C, then B

If B and C, then A

What about their confidence level? Confidence is the ratio of the number of transactions with all the items in the rule to the number of transactions with just the items in the condition. What is confidence really saying? Saying that the rule "if B and C then A" has a confidence of 0.33 is equivalent to saying that when B and C appear in a transaction, there is a 33 percent chance that A also appears in it. That is, one time in three A occurs with B and C, and the other two times, A does not.

The most confident rule is the best rule, so we are tempted to choose "if B and C then A". But there is a problem. This rule is actually worse than if just randomly saying that A appears in the transaction. A occurs in 45 percent of the transactions but the rule only gives 33 percent confidence. The rule does worse than just randomly guessing. This suggests another measure called improvement. Improvement tells how much better a rule is at predicting the result than just assuming the result in the first place. It is given by the following formula:

$$\text{improvement} = \frac{\text{p (condition and result)}}{\text{p (condition) p (result)}}$$

When improvement is greater than 1, then the resulting rule is better at predicting the result than random chance. When it is less than 1, it is worse. The rule *"if A then B"* is 1.31 times better at predicting when B is in a transaction than randomly guessing. In this case, as in many cases, the best rule actually contains fewer items than other rules being considered. When improvement is less than 1, negating the result produces a better rule. If the rule

If B and C then A

has a confidence of 0.33, then the rule

If B and C then NOT A

has a confidence of 0.67. Since A appears in 45 percent of the transactions, it does NOT occur in 55 percent of them. Applying the same improvement measure shows that the improvement of this new rule is 1.22 (0.67/0.55). The negative rule is useful. The rule "If A and B then NOT C" has an improvement of 1.33, better than any of the other rules. Rules are generated from the basic probabilities available in the co-occurrence table. Useful rules have an improvement that is greater than 1. When the improvement scores are low, you can increase them by negating the rules. However, you may find that negated rules are not as useful as the original association rules when it comes to acting on the results.

Overcoming Practical Limits. Generating association rules is a multi-step process. The general algorithm is:

- Generate the co-occurrence matrix for single items.
- Generate the co-occurrence matrix for two items. Use this to find rules with two items.
- Generate the co-occurrence matrix for three items. Use this to find rules with three items.
- And so on.

For instance, in the grocery store that sells orange juice, milk, detergent, soda, and window cleaner, the first step calculates the counts for each of these items. During the second step, the following counts are created:

- OJ and milk, OJ and detergent, OJ and soda, OJ and cleaner.
- Milk and detergent, milk and soda, milk and cleaner.
- Detergent and soda, detergent and cleaner.
- Soda and cleaner.

This is a total of 10 counts. The third pass takes all combinations of three items and so on. Of course, each of these stages may require a separate pass through the data or multiple stages can be combined into a single pass by considering different numbers of combinations at the same time.

Although it is not obvious when there are just five items, increasing the number of items in the combinations requires exponentially more computation. This results in exponentially growing run times-and long, long waits when considering combinations with more than three or four items. The solution is *pruning*. Pruning is a technique for reducing the number of items and combinations of items being considered at each step. At each stage, the algorithm throws out a certain number of combinations that do not meet some threshold criterion.

The most common pruning mechanism is called *minimum support pruning*. Recall that support refers to the number of transactions in the database where the rule holds. Minimum support pruning requires that a rule hold on a minimum number of transactions. For instance, if there are 1 million transactions and the minimum support is 1 percent, then only rules supported by 10,000 transactions are of interest. This makes sense, because the purpose of generating these rules is to pursue some sort of action-such as putting own-brand diapers in the same aisle as beer-and the action must affect enough transactions to be worthwhile.

The minimum support constraint has a cascading effect. Say, we are considering a rule with four items in it, like

If A, B, and C, then D.

Using minimum support pruning, this rule has to be true on at least 10,000 transactions in the data. It follows that:

A must appear in at least 10,000 transactions; and,

B must appear in at least 10,000 transactions; and,

C must appear in at least 10,000 transactions; and,

D must appear in at least 10,000 transactions.

In other words, minimum support pruning eliminates items that do not appear in enough transactions! There are two ways to do this. The first way is to eliminate the items from consideration. The second way is to use the taxonomy to generalize the items so the resulting generalized items meet the threshold criterion.

The threshold criterion applies to each step in the algorithm. The minimum threshold also implies that:

A and B must appear together in at least 10,000 transactions; and,

A and C must appear together in at least 10,000 transactions; and,

A and D must appear together in at least 10,000 transactions;

And so on.

Each step of the calculation of the co-occurrence table can eliminate combinations of items that do not meet the threshold, reducing its size and the number of combinations to consider during the next pass. The best choice for minimum support depends on the data and the situation. It is also possible to vary the minimum support as the algorithm progresses. For instance, using different levels at different stages you can find uncommon combinations of common items (by decreasing the support level for successive steps) or relatively common combinations of uncommon items (by increasing the support level). Varying the minimum support helps to find actionable rules, so the rules generated are not all like finding that peanut butter and jelly are often purchased together.

3.4 THE PROBLEM OF LARGE DATASETS

A typical fast-food restaurant that offers several dozen items on its menu, says there are a 100. To use probabilities to generate association rules, counts have to be calculated for each combination of items. The number of combinations of a given size tends to grow exponentially. A combination with three items might be a small fries, cheeseburger, and medium diet Coke. On a menu with 100 items, how many combinations are there with three menu items? There are 161,700! (This is based on the binomial formula from mathematics). On the other hand, a typical supermarket has at least 10,000 different items in stock, and more typically 20,000 or 30,000.

Calculating the support, confidence, and improvement quickly gets out of hand as the number of items in the combinations grows. There are almost 50 million possible combinations of two items in the grocery store and over 100 billion combinations of three items. Although computers are getting faster and cheaper, it is still very expensive to calculate the counts for this number of combinations. Calculating the counts for five or more items is prohibitively expensive. The use of taxonomies reduces the number of items to a manageable size.

The number of transactions is also very large. In the course of a year, a decent-size chain of supermarkets will generate tens of millions of transactions. Each of these transactions consists of one or more items, often several dozen at a time. So, determining if a particular combination of items is present in a particular transaction, it may require a bit of effort multiplied by a million-fold for all the transactions.

3.5 STRENGTHS AND WEAKNESSES OF ASSOCIATION RULES ANALYSIS

The strengths of association rule analysis are:

- It produces clear and understandable results.
- It supports undirected data mining.
- It works on variable-length data.
- The computations it uses are simple to understandable.
- **Results are clearly understood.** The results of association rule analysis are association rules; these are readily expressed as English or as a statement in a query language such as SQL. The expression of patterns in the data as "if-then" rules makes the results easy to understand and facilitates turning the results into action. In some circumstances, merely the set of related items is of interest and rules do not even need to be produced.
- **Association rule analysis is strong for undirected data mining.** Undirected data mining is very important when approaching a large set of data and you do not know where to begin. Association rule analysis is an appropriate technique, when it can be applied, to analyze data and to get a start. Most data mining techniques are not primarily used for undirected data mining. Association rule analysis, on the other hand, is used in this case and provides clear results.
- **Association rule analysis works on variable-length data.** Association rule analysis can handle variable-length data without the need for summarization. Other techniques tend to require records in a fixed format, which is not a natural way to represent items in a transaction. Association rule analysis can handle transactions without any loss of information.
- **Computationally simple.** The computations needed to apply association rule analysis are rather simple, although the number of computations grows very quickly

with the number of transactions and the number of different items in the analysis. Smaller problems can be set up on the desktop using a spreadsheet. This makes the technique more comfortable to use than complex techniques, like genetic algorithms or neural networks.

The weaknesses of association rule analysis are:

- It requires exponentially more computational effort as the problem size grows.
- It has a limited support for attributes on the data.
- It is difficult to determine the right number of items.
- It discounts rare items.
- **Exponential growth as problem size increases.** The computations required to generate association rules grow exponentially with the number of items and the complexity of the rules being considered. The solution is to reduce the number of items by generalizing them. However, more general items are usually less actionable. Methods to control the number of computations, such as minimum support pruning, may eliminate important rules from consideration.
- **Limited support for data attributes.** Association rule analysis is a technique specialized for items in a transaction. Items are assumed to be identical except for one identifying characteristic, such as the product type. When applicable, association rule analysis is very powerful. However, not all problems fit this description. The use of item taxonomies and virtual items helps to make rules more expressive.
- **Determining the right items.** Probably the most difficult problem when applying association rule analysis is determining the right set of items to use in the analysis. By generalizing items up their taxonomy, you can ensure that the frequencies of the items used in the analysis are about the same. Although this generalization process loses some information, virtual items can then be reinserted into the analysis to capture information that spans generalized items.
- **Association rule analysis has trouble with rare items.** Association rule analysis works best when all items have approximately the same frequency in the data. Items that rarely occur are in very few transactions and will be pruned. Modifying minimum support threshold to take into account product value is one way to ensure that expensive items remain in consideration, even though they may be rare in the data. The use of item taxonomies can ensure that rare items are rolled up and included in the analysis in some form.

In Summary

Association Rule is the form of an appeal of market analysis comes from the clarity and utility of its results. The association rule analysis starts with transactions and the basic process for association rules analysis includes three important concerns: Choosing the right set of items, Generating rules and overcoming practical limits.

Chapter 4: AUTOMATIC CLUSTERING DETECTION

Clustering is a method of grouping data into different groups and is used for identifying a finite set of categories or clusters to describe the data. The main topics that are covered in this chapter are:

- K-Mean Method
- Agglomeration Methods
- Evaluating Clusters
- Strengths and Weaknesses.

CHAPTER 4

AUTOMATIC CLUSTERING DETECTION

INTRODUCTION

When human beings try to make sense of complex questions, our natural tendency is to break the subject into smaller pieces, each of which can be explained more simply. Clustering is a technique used for combining observed objects into groups or clusters such that:

- Each group or cluster is homogeneous or compact with respect to certain characteristics. That is, objects in each group are similar to each other.
- Each group should be different from other groups with respect to the same characteristics; that is, objects of one group should be different from the objects of other groups.

4.1 SEARCHING FOR CLUSTERS

For most data mining tasks, we start out with a pre-classified training set and attempt to develop a model capable of predicting how a new record will be classified. In clustering, there is no pre-classified data and no distinction between independent and dependent variables. Instead, we are searching for groups of records—the clusters—that are similar to one another, in the expectation that similar records represent similar customers or suppliers or products that will behave in similar ways.

Automatic cluster detection is rarely used in isolation because finding clusters is not an end in itself. Once clusters have been detected, other methods must be applied in order to figure out what the clusters mean. When clustering is successful, the results can be dramatic: One famous early application of cluster detection led to our current understanding of stellar evolution.

Star Light, Star Bright. Early in this century, astronomers trying to understand the relationship between the luminosity (brightness) of stars and their temperatures, made scatter plots like the one in Figure 4.1. The vertical scale measures luminosity in multiples of the brightness of our own sun. The horizontal scale measures surface temperature in degrees Kelvin (degrees centigrade above absolute, the theoretical coldest possible temperature where molecular motion ceases). As you can see, the stars plotted by astronomers, Hertzsprung and Russell, fall into three clusters. We now understand that these three clusters represent stars in very different phases in the stellar life cycle.

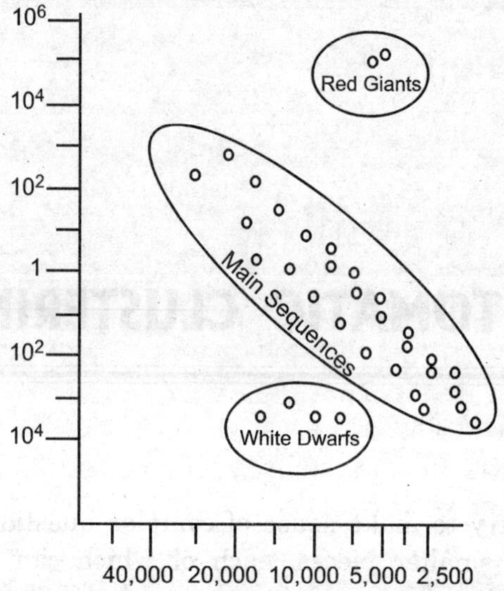

Figure 4.1. The Hertzsprung-Russell Diagram Clusters Stars

The relationship between luminosity and temperature is consistent within each cluster, but the relationship is different in each cluster because a fundamentally different process is generating the heat and light. The 80 percent of stars that fall on the main sequence are generating energy by converting hydrogen to helium through nuclear fusion. This is how all stars spend most of their life.

But after 10 billion years or so, the hydrogen gets used up. Depending on the star's mass, it then begins fusing helium or the fusion stops. In the latter case, the core of the star begins to collapse, generating a great deal of heat in the process. At the same time, the outer layer of gases expands away from the core. A red giant is formed. Eventually, the outer layer of gases is stripped away and the remaining core begins to cool. The star is now a white dwarf. A recent query of the Alta Vista web index using the search terms "HR diagram" and "main sequence" returned many pages of links to current astronomical research based on cluster detection of this kind. This simple, two-variable cluster diagram is being used today to hunt for new kinds of stars like "brown dwarfs" and to understand main sequence stellar evolution.

Fitting the troops. We chose the Hertzsprung-Russell diagram as our introductory example of clustering because with only two variables, it is easy to spot the clusters visually. Even in three dimensions, it is easy to pick out clusters by eye from a scatter plot cube. If all problems had so a few dimensions, there would be no need for automatic cluster detection algorithms. As the number of dimensions (independent variables) increases, our ability to visualize clusters and our intuition about the distance between two points quickly break down.

When we speak of a problem as having many dimensions, we are making a geometric analogy. We consider each of the things that must be measured independently in order to describe something to be a dimension. In other words, if there are N variables, we imagine a space in which the value of each variable represents a distance along the corresponding axis in an N-dimensional space. A single record containing a value for each of the N variables can be thought of as the vector that defines a particular point in that space.

4.2 THE K-MEANS METHOD

The K-means method of cluster detection is the most commonly used in practice. It has many variations, but the form described here was first published by J.B. MacQueen in 1967. For ease of drawing, we illustrate the process using two-dimensional diagrams, but bear in mind that in practice we will usually be working in a space of many more dimensions. That means that instead of points described by a two-element vector (x_1, x_2), we work with points described by an n-element vector $(x_1, x_2, ..., x_n)$. The procedure itself is unchanged.

In the first step, we select K data points to be the seeds. MacQueen's algorithm simply takes the first K records. In cases where the records have some meaningful order, it may be desirable to choose widely spaced records instead. Each of the seeds is an embryonic cluster with only one element. In this example, we use outside information about the data to set the number of clusters to 3.

In the second step, we assign each record to the cluster whose centroid is nearest. In Figure 4.2 we have done the first two steps. Drawing the boundaries between the clusters is easy if you recall that given two points, X and Y, all points that are equidistant from X and Y fall along a line that is half way along the line segment that joins X and Y and perpendicular to it. In Figure 4.2, the initial seeds are joined by dashed lines and the cluster boundaries constructed from them are solid lines. Of course, in three dimensions, these boundaries would be planes and in N dimensions they would be hyper-planes of dimension N–1.

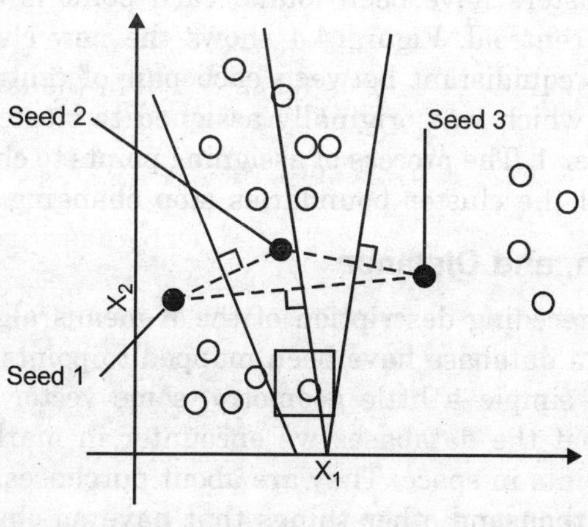

Figure 4.2. The Initial Sets Determine the Initial Cluster Boundaries

As we continue to work through the K-means algorithm, pay particular attention to the fate of the point with the box drawn around it. On the basis of the initial seeds, it is assigned to the cluster controlled by seed number 2 because it is closer to that seed than to either of the others.

At this point, every point has been assigned to one or another of the three clusters centered about the original seeds. The next step is to calculate the centroids of the new clusters. This is simply a matter of averaging the positions of each point in the cluster along each dimension. If there are 200 records assigned to a cluster and we are clustering based on four fields from those records, then geometrically we have 200 points in a 4-dimensional space. The location of each point is described by a vector of the values of the four fields. The vectors have the form (X_1, X_2, X_3, X_4). The value of X_1 for the new centroid is the mean of all 200 X_1s and similarly for X_2, X_3 and X_4.

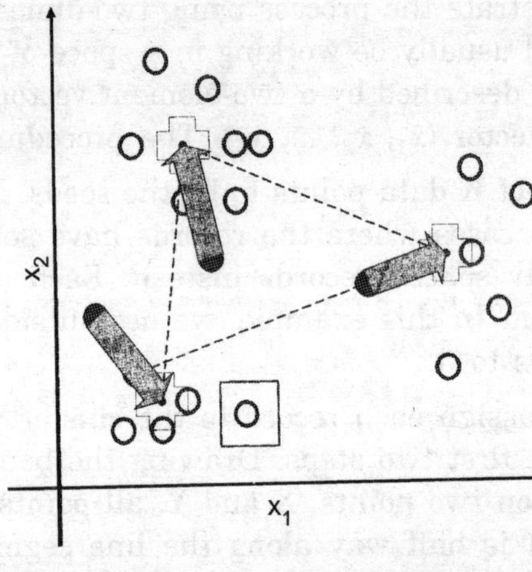

Figure 4.3. Calculating the Centroids of the New Clusters

In Figure 4.3 the new centroids are marked with a cross. The arrows show the motion from the position of the original seeds to the new centroids of the clusters formed from those seeds. Once the new clusters have been found, each point is once again assigned to the cluster with the closest centroid. Figure 4.4 shows the new cluster boundaries–formed as before, by drawing lines equidistant between each pair of centroids. Notice that the point with the box around it, which was originally assigned to cluster number 2, has now been assigned to cluster number 1. The process of assigning points to cluster and then recalculating centroids continues until the cluster boundaries stop changing.

Similarity, Association, and Distance

After reading the preceding description of the K-means algorithm, we hope you agree that once the records in a database have been mapped to points in space, automatic cluster detection is really quite simple–a little geometry, some vector means, and that's all. The problem, of course, is that the databases we encounter in marketing, sales, and customer support are not about points in space. They are about purchases, phone calls, airplane trips, car registrations, and a thousand other things that have no obvious connection to the dots in a cluster diagram. When we speak of clustering records of this sort, we have an intuitive notion that members of a cluster have some kind of *natural association*, that they are more *similar* to each other than to records in another cluster. Since it is difficult to convey intuitive notions to a computer, we must translate the vague concept of association into some sort of numeric measure of the degree of similarity. The most common method, but by no means the only one, is to translate all fields into numeric values so that the records may be treated as points in space. Then, if two points are close in the geometric sense, we assume that they represent similar records in the database. Two main problems with this approach are:

1. Many variable types, including all categorical variables and many numeric variables such as rankings, do not have the right behavior to be treated properly as components of a position vector.
2. In geometry, the contributions of each dimension are of equal importance, but in our databases, a small change in one field may be much more important than a large change in another field.

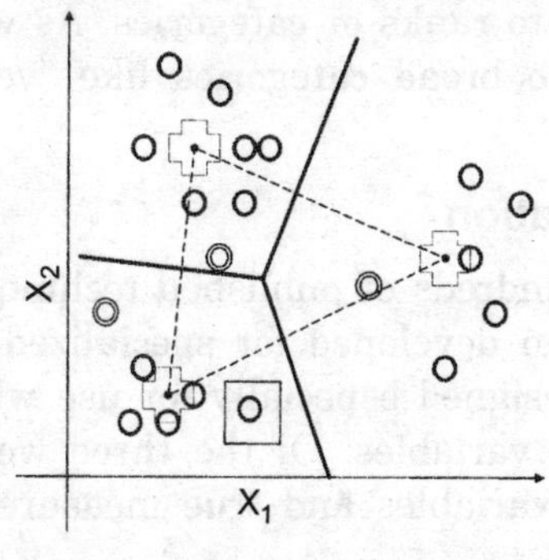

Figure 4.4. At Each Iteration All Cluster Assignments are Reevaluated

A Variety of Variables. Variables can be categorized in various ways–by mathematical properties (continuous, discrete), by storage type (character, integer, floating point), and by other properties (quantitative, qualitative). For this discussion, however, the most important classification is how much the variable can tell us about its placement along the axis that corresponds to it in our geometric model. For this purpose, we can divide variables into four classes, listed here in increasing order of suitability for the geometric model: Categories, Ranks, Intervals, True measures.

Categorical variables only tell us to which of several unordered categories a thing belongs. We can say that this icecream is pistachio while that one is mint-cookie, but we cannot say that one is greater than the other or judge which one is closer to black cherry. In mathematical terms, we can tell that $X \neq Y$, but not whether $X > Y$ or $Y < X$.

Ranks allow us to put things in order, but don't tell us how much bigger one thing is than another. The valedictorian has better grades than the salutatorian, but we don't know by how much. If X, Y, and Z are ranked 1, 2, and 3, we know that $X > Y > Z$, but not whether $(X–Y) > (Y–Z)$.

Intervals allow us to measure the distance between two observations. If we are told that it is 56° in San Francisco and 78° in San Jose, we know that it is 22 degrees warmer at one end of the bay than the other.

True measures are interval variables that measure from a meaningful zero point. This trait is important because it means that the ratio of two values of the variable is meaningful. The Fahrenheit temperature scale used in the United States and the Celsius scale used in most of the rest of the world do not have this property. In neither system does it make sense to say that a 30° day is twice as warm as a 15° day. Similarly, a size 12 dress is not twice as large as a size 6 and gypsum is not twice as hard as talc though they are 2 and 1 on the hardness scale. It does make perfect sense, however, to say that a 50-year-old is twice as old as a 25-year-old or that a 10-pound bag of sugar is twice as heavy as a 5-pound one. Age, weight, length, and volume are examples of true measures.

Geometric distance metrics are well-defined for interval variables and true measures. In order to use categorical variables and rankings, it is necessary to transform them into interval variables. Unfortunately, these transformations add spurious information. If we number ice cream flavors 1 to 28, it will appear that flavors 5 and 6 are closely related while flavors 1 and 28 are far apart. The inverse problem arises when we transform interval variables and true measures into ranks or categories. As we go from age (true measure) to seniority (position on a list) to broad categories like "veteran" and "new hire", we lose information at each step.

Formal Measures of Association

There are dozens if not hundreds of published techniques for measuring the similarity of two records. Some have been developed for specialized applications such as comparing passages of text. Others are designed especially for use with certain types of data such as binary variables or categorical variables. Of the three we present here, the first two are suitable for use with interval variables and true measures while the third is suitable for categorical variables.

The Distance between Two Points. Each field in a record becomes one element in a vector describing a point in space. The distance between two points is used as the measure of association. If two points are close in distance, the corresponding records are considered similar. There are actually a number of metrics that can be used to measure the distance between two points (see aside), but the most common one is the Euclidean distance we all learned in high school. To find the Euclidean distance between X and Y, we first find the differences between the corresponding elements of X and Y (the distance along each axis) and square them.

Distance Metrics. Any function that takes two points and produces a single number describing a relationship between them is a candidate measure of association, but to be a true distance metric, it must meet the following criteria:

$$\text{Distance}(X,Y) = 0 \text{ if and only if } X = Y$$

$$\text{Distance}(X,Y) \geq 0 \text{ for all X and all Y}$$

$$\text{Distance}(X,Y) = \text{Distance}(Y,X)$$

$$\text{Distance}(X,Y) \leq \text{Distance}(X,Z) + \text{Distance}(X,Y)$$

The Angle between Two Vectors. Sometimes we would like to consider two records to be closely associated because of similarities in the way the fields *within* each record are related. We would like to cluster minnows with sardines, cod, and tuna, while clustering kittens with cougars, lions, and tigers even though in a database of body-part lengths, the sardine is closer to the kitten than it is to the tuna.

The solution is to use a different geometric interpretation of the same data. Instead of thinking of X and Y as points in space and measuring the distance between them, we think of them as *vectors* and measure the angle between them. In this context, a vector is the line segment connecting the origin of our coordinate system to the point described by the vector values. A vector has both magnitude (the distance from the origin to the point) and direction. For our purposes, it is the direction that matters.

If we take the values for length of whiskers, length of tail, overall body length, length of teeth, and length of claws for a lion and a house cat and plot them as single points, they will be very far apart. But if the ratios of lengths of these body parts to one another are similar in the two species, than the vectors will be nearly parallel. The angle between vectors provides a measure of association that is not influenced by differences in magnitude between the two things being compared (see Figure 4.5). Actually, the sine of the angle is a better measure since it will range from 0 when the vectors are closest (most nearly parallel) to 1 when they are perpendicular without our having to worry about the actual angles or their signs.

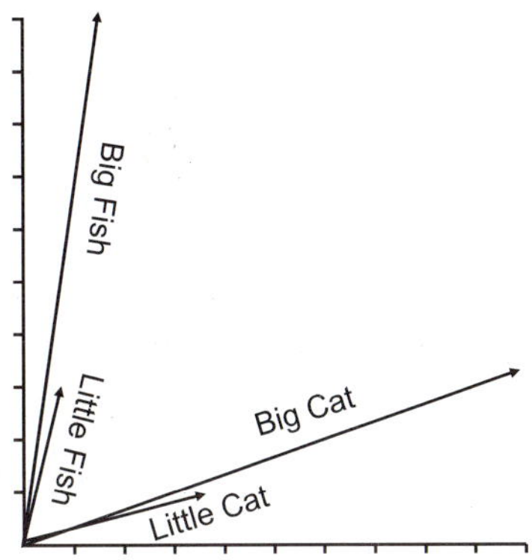

Figure 4.5. The Angle Between Vectors as a Measure of Association

The Number of Features in Common. When the variables in the records we wish to compare are categorical ones, we abandon geometric measures and turn instead to measures based on the degree of overlap between records. As with the geometric measures, there are many variations on this idea. In all variations, we compare two records field by field and count the number of fields that match and the number of fields that don't match. The simplest measure is the ratio of matches to the total number of fields. In its simplest form, this measure counts two null fields as matching with the result that everything we don't know much about ends up in the same cluster. A simple improvement is to not include matches of this sort in the match count. If, on the other hand, the usual degree of overlap is low, you can give extra weight to matches to make sure that even a small overlap is rewarded.

What K-Means

Clusters form some subset of the field variables tend to vary together. If all the variables are truly independent, no clusters will form. At the opposite extreme, if all the variables are dependent on the same thing (in other words, if they are co-linear), then all the records will form a single cluster. In between these extremes, we don't really know how many clusters to expect. If we go looking for a certain number of clusters, we may find them. But that doesn't mean that there aren't other perfectly good clusters lurking in the data where we could find them by trying a different value of K. In his excellent 1973 book, *Cluster Analysis for Applications*, M. Anderberg uses a deck of playing cards to illustrate many aspects of clustering. We have borrowed his idea to illustrate the way that the initial choice of K, the number of cluster seeds, can have a large effect on the kinds of clusters that will be found. In descriptions of K-means and related algorithms, the selection of K is often glossed over. But since, in many cases, there is no a priori reason to select a particular value, we always need to perform automatic cluster detection using one value of K, evaluating the results, then trying again with another value of K.

A♠	A♣	A♦	A♥
K♠	K♣	K♦	K♥
Q♠	Q♣	Q♦	Q♥
J♠	J♣	J♦	J♥
10♠	10♣	10♦	10♥
9♠	9♣	9♦	9♥
8♠	8♣	8♦	8♥
7♠	7♣	7♦	7♥
6♠	6♣	6♦	6♥
5♠	5♣	5♦	5♥
4♠	4♣	4♦	4♥
3♠	3♣	3♦	3♥
2♠	2♣	2♦	2♥

Figure 4.6. K=2 Clustered by Color

A♠	A♣	A♦	A♥
K♠	K♣	K♦	K♥
Q♠	Q♣	Q♦	Q♥
J♠	J♣	J♦	J♥
10♠	10♣	10♦	10♥
9♠	9♣	9♦	9♥
8♠	8♣	8♦	8♥
7♠	7♣	7♦	7♥
6♠	6♣	6♦	6♥
5♠	5♣	5♦	5♥
4♠	4♣	4♦	4♥
3♠	3♣	3♦	3♥
2♠	2♣	2♦	2♥

Figure 4.7. K=2 Clustered by Old Maid Ruless

After each trial, the strength of the resulting clusters can be evaluated by comparing the average distance between records in a cluster with the average distance between clusters, and by other procedures described later in this chapter. But the clusters must also be evaluated on a more subjective basis to determine their usefulness for a given application.

As shown in Figures 4.6, 4.7, 4.8, 4.9, and 4.10, it is easy to create very good clusters from a deck of playing cards using various values for K and various distance measures. In the case of playing cards, the distance measures are dictated by the rules of various games. The distance from Ace to King, for example, might be 1 or 12 depending on the game.

A♠	A♣	A♦	A♥
K♠	K♣	K♦	K♥
Q♠	Q♣	Q♦	Q♥
J♠	J♣	J♦	J♥
10♠	10♣	10♦	10♥
9♠	9♣	9♦	9♥
8♠	8♣	8♦	8♥
7♠	7♣	7♦	7♥
6♠	6♣	6♦	6♥
5♠	5♣	5♦	5♥
4♠	4♣	4♦	4♥
3♠	3♣	3♦	3♥
2♠	2♣	2♦	2♥

Figure 4.8. K=2 Clustered by Rules for War, Beggar My Neighbor, and other Games

A♠	A♣	A♦	A♥
K♠	K♣	K♦	K♥
Q♠	Q♣	Q♦	Q♥
J♠	J♣	J♦	J♥
10♠	10♣	10♦	10♥
9♠	9♣	9♦	9♥
8♠	8♣	8♦	8♥
7♠	7♣	7♦	7♥
6♠	6♣	6♦	6♥
5♠	5♣	5♦	5♥
4♠	4♣	4♦	4♥
3♠	3♣	3♦	3♥
2♠	2♣	2♦	2♥

Figure 4.9. K=3 Clustered by Rules of Hearts

K = N. Even with playing cards, some values of K don't lead to good clusters–at least not with distance measures suggested by the card games known to the authors. There are obvious clustering rules for K = 1, 2, 3, 4, 8, 13, 26, and 52. For these values we can come up with "perfect" clusters where each element of a cluster is equidistant from every other member of the cluster, and equally far away from the members of some other cluster. For other values of K, we have the more familiar situation that some cards do not seem to fit particularly well in any cluster.

A♠	A♣	A♦	A♥
K♠	K♣	K♦	K♥
Q♠	Q♣	Q♦	Q♥
J♠	J♣	J♦	J♥
10♠	10♣	10♦	10♥
9♠	9♣	9♦	9♥
8♠	8♣	8♦	8♥
7♠	7♣	7♦	7♥
6♠	6♣	6♦	6♥
5♠	5♣	5♦	5♥
4♠	4♣	4♦	4♥
3♠	3♣	3♦	3♥
2♠	2♣	2♦	2♥

Figure 4.10. K=4 Clustered by Suit

The Importance of Weights

It is important to differentiate between the notions of *scaling* and *weighting*. They are not the same, but they are often confused. Scaling deals with the problem that different variables are measured in different units. Weighting deals with the problem that we care about some variables more than others.

In geometry, all dimensions are equally important. Two points that differ by 2 in dimensions X and Y and by 1 in dimension Z are the same distance from one another as two other points that differ by 1 in dimension X and by 2 in dimensions Y and Z. We don't even ask what units X, Y, and Z are measured in; it doesn't matter, so long as they are the same.

But what if X is measured in yards, Y is measured in centimeters, and Z is measured in nautical miles? A difference of 1 in Z is now equivalent to a difference of 185,200 in Y or 2,025 in X. Clearly, they must all be converted to a common scale before distances will make any sense. Unfortunately, in commercial data mining there is usually no common scale available because the different units being used are measuring quite different things. If we are looking at plot size, house-hold size, car ownership, and family income, we cannot convert all of them to acres or dollars. On the other hand, it seems bothersome that a difference of 20 acres in plot size is indistinguishable from a change of $20 in income. The solution is to map all the variables to a common range (often 0 to 1 or –1 to 1). That way, at least the ratios of change become comparable—doubling plot size will have the same effect as doubling income. We refer to this re-mapping to a common range as *scaling*. But what if we think that two families with the same income have more in common than two families on the same size plot, and if we want that to be taken into consideration during clustering? That is where weighting comes in.

There are three common ways of scaling variables to bring them all into comparable ranges:

1. Divide each variable by the mean of all the values it takes on.
2. Divide each variable by the range (the difference between the lowest and highest value it takes on) after subtracting the lowest value.
3. Subtract the mean value from each variable and then divide by the standard deviation. This is often called "converting to z scores."

Use Weights to Encode Outside Information. Scaling takes care of the problem that changes in one variable appear more significant than changes in another simply because of differences in the speed with which the units they are measured get incremented. Many books recommend scaling all variables to a normal form with a mean of zero and a variance of one. That way, all fields contribute equally when the distance between two records is computed. We suggest going further. The whole point of automatic cluster detection is to find clusters that make sense to you. If, for your purposes, whether people have children is much more important than the number of credit cards they carry, there is no reason not to bias the outcome of the clustering by multiplying the number of children field by a higher weight than the number of credit cards field.

After scaling to get rid of bias that is due to the units, you should use weights to introduce bias based on your knowledge of the business context. Of course, if you want to evaluate the effects of different weighting strategies, you will have to add yet another outer loop to the clustering process. In fact, choosing weights is one of the optimization problems that can be addressed with genetic algorithms.

Variations on the K-Means Method

The basic K-means algorithm has many variations. It is likely that the commercial software tools you find to do automatic clustering will incorporate some of these variations. Among the differences you are likely to encounter are:

- Alternate methods of choosing the initial seeds
- Alternate methods of computing the next centroid
- Using probability density rather than distance to associate records with clusters.

Of these, only the last is important enough to merit further discussion here.

Gaussian Mixture Models. The K-means method as we have described it has some drawbacks.

- It does not do well with overlapping clusters.
- The clusters are easily pulled off center by outliers.
- Each record is either in or out of a cluster; there is no notion of some records being more or less likely than others to really belong to the cluster to which they have been assigned.

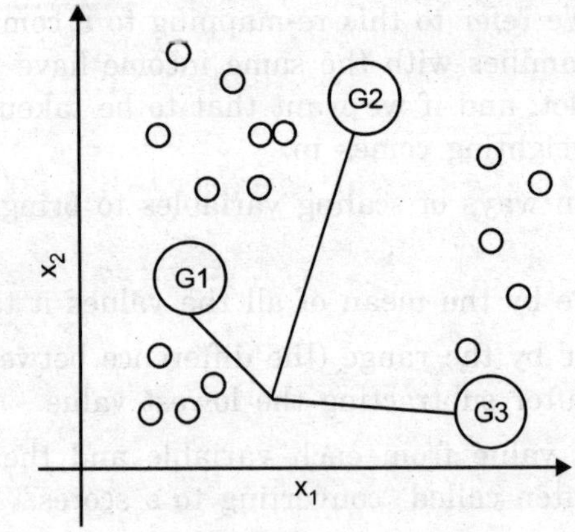

Figure 4.11. In the Estimation Step, Each Gaussian is Assigned Some Responsibility for Each Point. Thicker Indicate Greater Responsibility.

Gaussian mixture models are a probabilistic variant of K-means. Their name comes from the Gaussian distribution, a probability distribution often assumed for high-dimensional problems. As before, we start by choosing K seeds. This time, however, we regard the seeds as means of Gaussian distributions. We then iterate over two steps called the estimation step and the maximization step. In the estimation step, we calculate the responsibility that each Gaussian has for each data point (see Figure 4.11). Each Gaussian has strong responsibility for points that are close to it and weak responsibility for points that are distant. The responsibilities will be used as weights in the next step. In the maximization step, the mean of each Gaussian is moved towards the centroid of the entire data set, weighted by the responsibilities as illustrated in Figure 4.12.

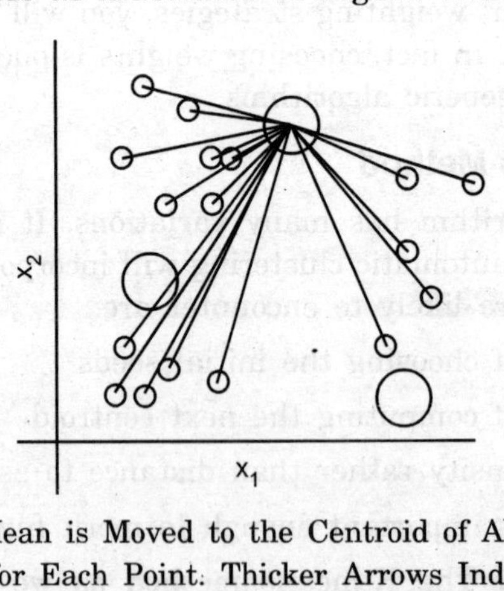

Figure 4.12. Each Gaussian Mean is Moved to the Centroid of All the Data Points Weighted by the Responsibilities for Each Point. Thicker Arrows Indicate Higher Weights

These steps are repeated until the Gaussians are no longer moving. The Gaussians themselves can grow as well as move, but since the distribution must always integrate to one, a Gaussian gets weaker as it gets bigger. Responsibility is calculated in such a way that a given point may get equal responsibility from a nearby Gaussian with low variance and from a more distant one with higher variance. This is called a "mixture model" because the probability at each data point is the sum of a mixture of several distributions. At the end of the process, each point is tied to the various clusters with higher or lower probability. This is sometimes called *soft clustering*.

4.3 AGGLOMERATIVE METHODS

In the K-means approach to clustering, we start out with a fixed number of clusters and gather all records into them. There is another class of methods that works by agglomeration. In these methods, we start out with each data point forming its own cluster and gradually merge clusters until all points have been gathered together in one big cluster. Towards the beginning of the process, the clusters are very small and very pure–the members of each cluster are few, but very closely related. Towards the end of the process, the clusters are large and less well-defined. The entire history is preserved so that you can choose the level of clustering that works best for your application.

The Agglomerative Algorithm

The first step is to create a *similarity matrix*. The similarity matrix is a table of all the pair-wise distances or degrees of association between points. As before, we can use any of a large number of measures of association between records, including the Euclidean distance, the angle between vectors, and the ratio of matching to non-matching categorical fields. The issues raised by the choice of distance measures are exactly the same as previously discussed in relation to the K-means approach.

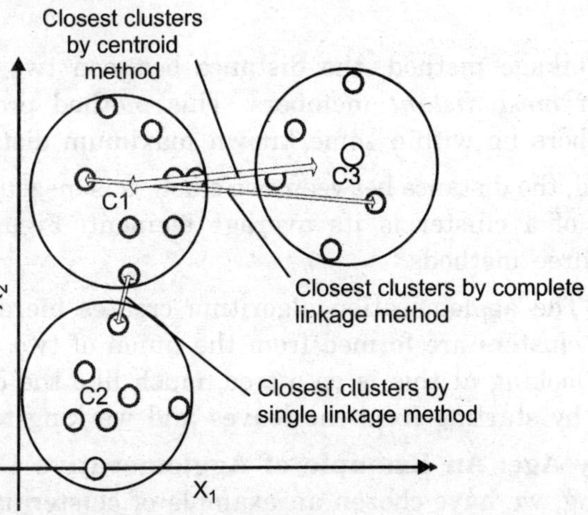

Figure 4.13. Three Methods of Measuring the Distance Between Clusters

At first glance you might think that if we have N data points we will need to make N2 measurements to create the distance table, but if we assume that our association measure is a true distance metric, we actually only need half of that because all true distance metrics follow the rule that Distance (X,Y) = Distance(Y,X). In the vocabulary of mathematics, the similarity matrix is lower triangular. At the beginning of the process there are N rows in the table, one for each record.

Next, we find the smallest value in the similarity matrix. This identifies the two clusters that are most similar to one another. We merge these two clusters and update the similarity matrix by replacing the two rows that described the parent cluster with a new row that describes the distance between the merged cluster and the remaining clusters. There are now N–1 clusters and N–1 rows in the similarity matrix.

We repeat the merge step N–1 times, after which all records belong to the same large cluster. At each iteration we make a record of which clusters were merged and how far apart they were. This information will be helpful in deciding which level of clustering to make use of.

Distance between Clusters. We need to say a little more about how to measure distance between clusters. On the first trip through the merge step, the clusters to be merged consist of single records so the distance between clusters is the same as the distance between records, a subject we may already have said too much about. But on the second and subsequent trips around the loop, we need to update the similarity matrix with the distances from the new, multi-record cluster to all the others. How do we measure this distance? As usual, there is a choice of approaches. Three common ones are:

- Single linkage
- Complete linkage
- Comparison of centroids

In the single linkage method, the distance between two clusters is given by the distance between their *closest* members. This method produces clusters with the property that every member of a cluster is more closely related to at least one member of its cluster than to any point outside it.

In the complete linkage method, the distance between two clusters is given by the distance between their *most distant* members. This method produces clusters with the property that all members lie within some known maximum distance of one another.

In the third method, the distance between two clusters is measured between the centroids of each. The centroid of a cluster is its average element. Figure 4.13 gives a pictorial representation of all three methods.

Clusters and Trees. The agglomeration algorithm creates hierarchical clusters. At each level in the hierarchy, clusters are formed from the union of two clusters at the next level down. Another way of looking at this is as a tree, much like the decision trees except that cluster trees are built by starting from the leaves and working towards the root.

Clustering People by Age: An Example of Agglomerative Clustering. To illustrate agglomerative clustering, we have chosen an example of clustering in one dimension using the single linkage measure for distance between clusters. These choices should enable you to follow the algorithm through all its iterations in your head without having to worry about squares and square roots.

The data consists of the ages of people at a family gathering. Our goal is to cluster the participants by age. Our metric for the distance between two people is simply the difference in their ages. Our metric for the distance between two clusters of people is the difference in age between the oldest member of the younger cluster and the youngest member of the older cluster. (The one-dimensional version of the single linkage measure.)

Because the distances are so easy to calculate, we dispense with the similarity matrix. Our procedure is to sort the participants by age, then begin clustering by first merging clusters that are 1 year apart, then 2 years, and so on until there is only one big cluster. Figure 4.14 shows the state of the clusters after six iterations, with three clusters remaining. This is the level of clustering that seems the most useful. The algorithm appears to have clustered the population into three generations.

4.4 EVALUATING CLUSTERS

When using the K-means approach to cluster detection, we need a way to determine what value of K finds the best clusters. Similarly, when using a hierarchical approach, we need a test for which level in the hierarchy contains the best clusters. But what does it mean to say that a cluster is good?

In general terms, we want clusters whose members have a high degree of similarity–or in geometric terms, are close to each other–and we want the clusters themselves to be widely spaced.

A standard measure of the within-cluster similarity is the variance—the sum of the squared differences of each element from the mean, so we might simply look for the solutions that produce the clusters with the lowest variance. But for hierarchical clustering, this does not make sense since we always start out with clusters of one that have no variance at all.

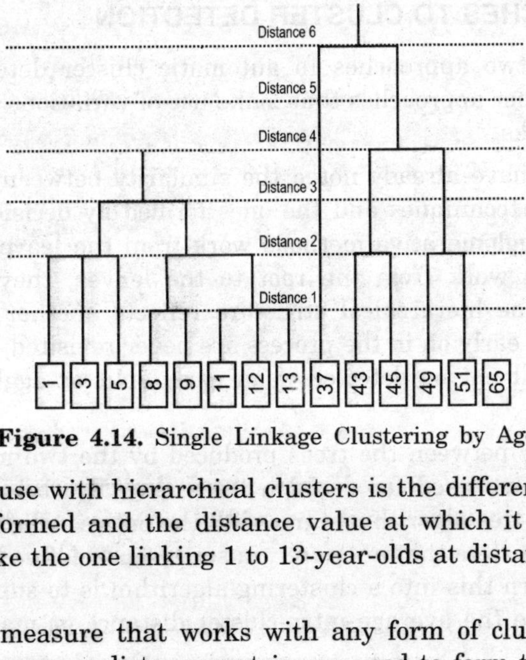

Figure 4.14. Single Linkage Clustering by Age

A good measure to use with hierarchical clusters is the difference between the distance value at which it was formed and the distance value at which it is merged into the next level. Strong clusters, like the one linking 1 to 13-year-olds at distance 3 in Figure 4.14, last a long time.

A general-purpose measure that works with any form of cluster detection is to take whatever similarity measure or distance metric you used to form the clusters and use it to compare the average distance within clusters to the average distance between clusters. This can be done for each cluster individually and for the entire collection of clusters.

If you find that there are one or two good clusters along with a number of weaker ones, you may be able to improve your results by removing all members of the strong clusters. You will want to isolate the strong clusters for further analysis anyway, and removing their strong pull may allow new clusters to be detected in the records left behind.

Inside the Cluster. Once you have found a strong cluster, you will want to analyzc what makes it special. What is it about the records in this cluster that causes them to be lumped together? Even more importantly, is it possible to find rules and patterns within this cluster now that the noise from the rest of the database has been eliminated?

The easiest way to approach the first question is to take the mean of each variable within the cluster and compare it to the mean of the same variable in the parent population. Rank order the variables by the magnitude of the difference. Looking at the variables that show the largest difference between the cluster and the rest of the database will go a long way towards explaining what makes the cluster special. As for the second question, that is what all the other data mining techniques are for!

Outside the Cluster. Clustering can be useful even when only a single cluster is found. When screening for a very rare defect, there may not be enough examples to train a directed data mining model to detect it. One example is testing electric motors at the factory where they are made. Cluster detection methods can be used on a sample containing only good motors to determine the shape and size of the "normal" cluster. When a motor comes along that falls outside the cluster for any reason, it is suspect. This approach has been used in medicine to detect the presence of abnormal cells in tissue samples.

4.5 OTHER APPROACHES TO CLUSTER DETECTION

In addition to the two approaches to automatic cluster detection described in this chapter, there are two other approaches that make use of variations of techniques of decision trees and neural networks.

Divisive Methods. We have already noted the similarity between the tree formed by the agglomerative clustering techniques and the ones formed by decision tree algorithms such as C4.5. Although the agglomerative methods work from the leaves to the root, while the decision tree algorithms work from the root to the leaves, they both create a similar hierarchical structure. The hierarchical structure reflects another similarity between the methods. Decisions made early on in the process are never revisited, which means that some fairly simple clusters will not be detected if an early split or agglomeration destroys the structure.

Seeing the similarity between the trees produced by the two methods, it is natural to ask whether the algorithms used for decision trees may also be used for clustering. The answer is yes. A decision tree algorithm starts with the entire collection of records and looks for a way to spit it into clusters that are *purer*, in some sense defined by a diversity function. All that is required to turn this into a clustering algorithm is to supply a diversity function chosen to either minimize the average intra-cluster distance or maximize the inter-cluster distances.

Self-Organizing Maps. Self-organizing maps are a variant of neural networks that have been used for many years in applications such as feature detection in two-dimensional images. More recently, they have been applied successfully for more general clustering applications. There is a discussion of self-organizing neural networks.

4.6 STRENGTHS AND WEAKNESSES OF AUTOMATIC CLUSTER DETECTION

The main strengths of automatic cluster detection are:

- Automatic cluster detection is an unsupervised knowledge discovery
- Automatic cluster detection works well with categorical, numeric, and textual data
- Easy to apply.
- **Automatic Cluster Detection is Unsupervised.** The chief strength of automatic cluster detection is that it is undirected. This means that it can be applied even when you have no prior knowledge of the internal structure of a database. Automatic cluster detection can be used to uncover hidden structure that can be used to improve the performance of more directed techniques.
- **Clustering can be Performed on Diverse Data Types.** By choosing different distance measures, automatic clustering can be applied to almost any kind of data. It is as easy to find clusters in collections of new stories or insurance claims as in astronomical or financial data.
- **Automatic Cluster Detection is Easy to Apply.** Most cluster detection techniques require very little massaging of the input data and there is no need to identify particular fields as inputs and others as outputs.

The main weaknesses of automatic cluster detection are:

- It can be difficult to choose the right distance measures and weights.
- Sensitivity to initial parameters.
- It can be hard to interpret the resulting clusters.
- **Difficulty with Weights and Measures.** The performance of automatic cluster detection algorithms is highly dependent on the choice of a distance metric or other similarity measure. It is sometimes quite difficult to devise distance metrics for data that contains a mixture of variable types. It can also be difficult to determine a proper weighting scheme for disparate variable types.
- **Sensitivity to Initial Parameters.** In the K-means method, the original choice of a value for K determines the number of clusters that will be found. If this number does not match the natural structure of the data, the technique will not obtain good results.
- **Difficulty Interpreting Results.** A strength of automatic cluster detection is that it is an unsupervised knowledge discovery technique. The flip side is that when you don't know what you are looking for, you may not recognize it when you find it! The clusters you discover are not guaranteed to have any practical value.

In Summary

Clustering is a technique for combining observed objects into groups or clusters. The most commonly used Cluster detection is K-means method. And this algorithm has a many variations: alternate methods of choosing the initial seeds, alternating methods of computing the next centroid, and using probability density rather than distance to associate records with record.

Chapter 5: DATA MINING WITH NEURAL NETWORKS

Neural Networks are a paradigm for computing and the appeal of neural network is that they bridge between digital computer and the neural connections in the human brain by modeling. The main topics that are covered in this chapter are:

- Neural Network Topologies
- Neural Network Models
- Iterative Process
- Strengths and Weaknesses

CHAPTER 5

DATA MINING WITH NEURAL NETWORKS

INTRODUCTION

Artificial neural networks are popular because they have a proven track record in many data mining and decision-support applications. They have been applied across a broad range of industries, from identifying financial series to diagnosing medical conditions, from identifying clusters of valuable customers to identifying fraudulent credit card transactions, from recognizing numbers written on checks to predicting the failure rates of engines.

Whereas people are good at generalizing from experience, computers usually excel at following explicit instructions over and over. The appeal of neural networks is that they bridge this gap by modeling, on a digital computer, the neural connections in human brains. When used in well-defined domains, their ability to generalize and learn from data mimics our own ability to learn from experience. This ability is useful for data mining and it also makes neural networks an exciting area for research, promising new and better results in the future.

5.1 NEURAL NETWORKS FOR DATA MINING

A neural processing element receives inputs from other connected processing elements. These input signals or values pass through weighted connections, which either amplify or diminish the signals. Inside the neural processing element, all of these input signals are summed together to give the total input to the unit. This total input value is then passed through a mathematical function to produce an output or decision value ranging from 0 to 1. Notice that this is a real valued (analog) output, not a digital 0/1 output. If the input signal matches the connection weights exactly, then the output is close to 1. If the input signal totally mismatches the connection weights then the output is close to 0. Varying degrees of similarity are represented by the intermediate values. Now, of course, we can force the neural processing element to make a binary (1/0) decision, but by using analog values ranging between 0.0 and 1.0 as the outputs, we are retaining more information to pass on to the next layer of neural processing units. In a very real sense, neural networks are analog computers.

Each neural processing element acts as a simple pattern recognition machine. It checks the input signals against its memory traces (connection weights) and produces an output signal that corresponds to the degree of match between those patterns. In typical neural networks, there are hundreds of neural processing elements whose pattern recognition and decision making abilities are harnessed together to solve problems.

5.2 NEURAL NETWORK TOPOLOGIES

The arrangement of neural processing units and their interconnections can have a profound impact on the processing capabilities of the neural networks. In general, all neural networks have some set of processing units that receive inputs from the outside world, which we refer to appropriately as the "input units." Many neural networks also have one or more layers of "hidden" processing units that receive inputs only from other processing units. A layer or "slab" of processing units receives a vector of data or the outputs of a previous layer of units and processes them in parallel. The set of processing units that represents the final result of the neural network computation is designated as the "output units". There are three major connection topologies that define how data flows between the input, hidden, and output processing units. These main categories feed forward, limited recurrent, and fully recurrent networks are described in detail in the next sections.

Feed-Forward Networks

Feed-forward networks are used in situations when we can bring all of the information to bear on a problem at once, and we can present it to the neural network. It is like a pop quiz, where the teacher walks in, writes a set of facts on the board, and says, "OK, tell me the answer." You must take the data, process it, and "jump to a conclusion." In this type of neural network, the data flows through the network in one direction, and the answer is based solely on the current set of inputs.

In Figure 5.1, we see a typical feed-forward neural network topology. Data enters the neural network through the input units on the left. The input values are assigned to the input units as the unit activation values. The output values of the units are modulated by the connection weights, either being magnified if the connection weight is positive and greater than 1.0, or being diminished if the connection weight is between 0.0 and 1.0. If the connection weight is negative, the signal is magnified or diminished in the opposite direction.

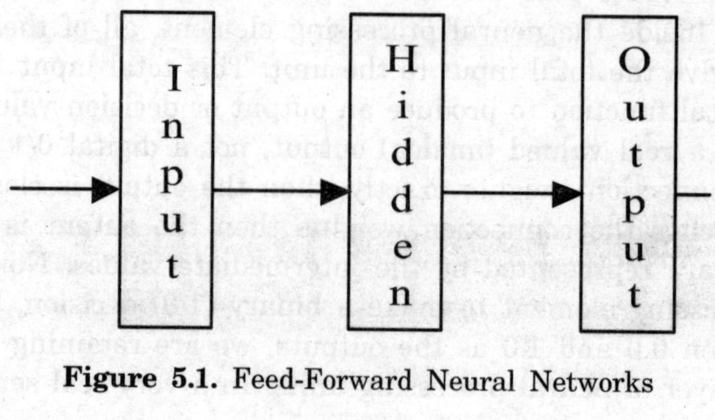

Figure 5.1. Feed-Forward Neural Networks

Each processing unit combines all of the input signals corning into the unit along with a threshold value. This total input signal is then passed through an activation function to determine the actual output of the processing unit, which in turn becomes the input to another layer of units in a multi-layer network. The most typical activation function used in neural networks is the S-shaped or sigmoid (also called the logistic) function. This function converts an input value to an output ranging from 0 to 1. The effect of the threshold weights is to shift the curve right or left, thereby making the output value higher or lower, depending on the sign of the threshold weight. As shown in Figure 5.1, the data flows from the input layer through zero, one, or more succeeding hidden layers and then to the output layer. In most networks, the units from one layer are fully connected to the units in the next layer. However, this is not a requirement of feed-forward neural networks. In some cases, especially when the neural network connections and weights are constructed from a rule or predicate form, there could be less connection weights than in a fully connected network. There are also techniques for pruning unnecessary weights from a neural network after it is trained. In general, the less weights there are, the faster the network will be able to process data and the better it will generalize to unseen inputs. It is important to remember that "feed-forward" is a definition of connection topology and data flow. It does not imply any specific type of activation function or training paradigm.

Limited Recurrent Networks

Recurrent networks are used in situations when we have current information to give the network, but the sequence of inputs is important, and we need the neural network to somehow store a record of the prior inputs and factor them in with the current data to produce an answer. In recurrent networks, information about past inputs is fed back into and mixed with the inputs through recurrent or feedback connections for hidden or output units. In this way, the neural network contains a memory of the past inputs via the activations (see Figure 5.2).

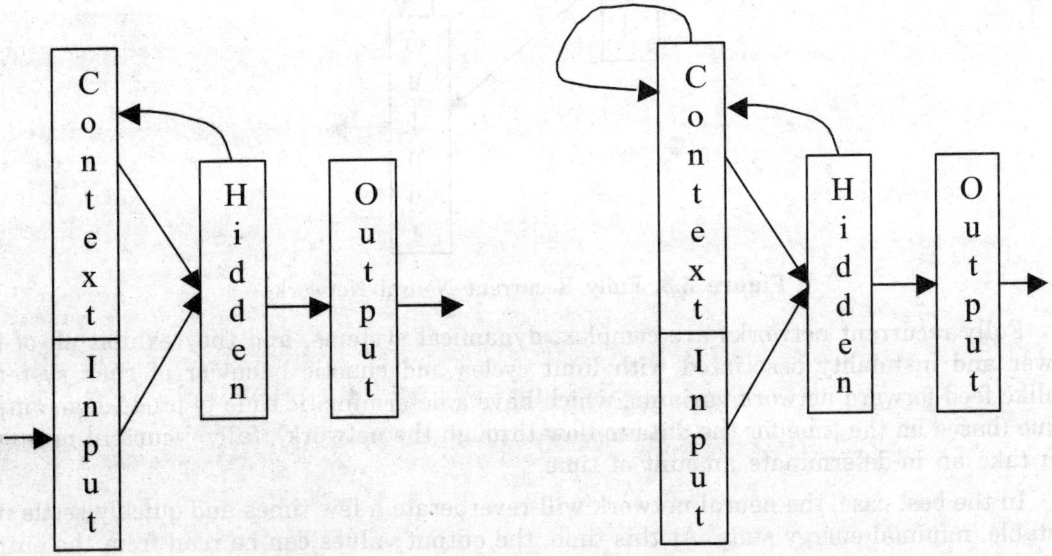

Figure 5.2. Partial Recurrent Neural Networks

Two major architectures for limited recurrent networks are widely used. Elman (1990) suggested allowing feedback from the hidden units to a set of additional inputs called context units. Earlier, Jordan (1986) described a network with feedback from the output units back to a set of context units. This form of recurrence is a compromise between the simplicity of a feed-forward network and the complexity of a fully recurrent neural network because it still allows the popular back propagation training algorithm (described in the following) to be used.

Fully Recurrent Networks

Fully recurrent networks, as their name suggests, provide two-way connections between all processors in the neural network. A subset of the units is designated as the input processors, and they are assigned or clamped to the specified input values. The data then flows to all adjacent connected units and circulates back and forth until the activation of the units stabilizes. Figure 5.3 shows the input units feeding into both the hidden units (if any) and the output units. The activations of the hidden and output units then are recomputed until the neural network stabilizes. At this point, the output values can be read from the output layer of processing units.

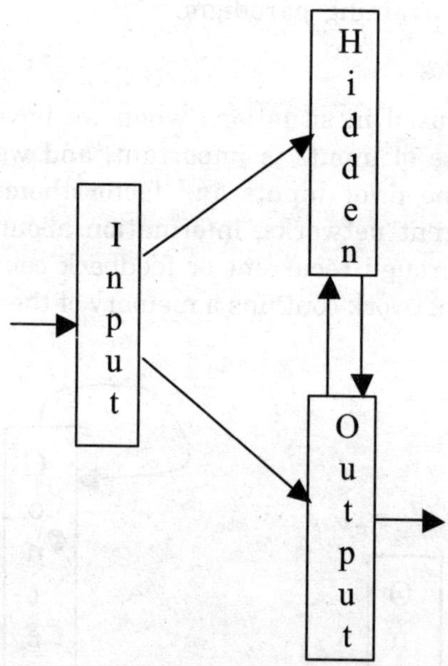

Figure 5.3. Fully Recurrent Neural Networks

Fully recurrent networks are complex, dynamical systems, and they exhibit all of the power and instability associated with limit cycles and chaotic behavior of such systems. Unlike feed-forward network variants, which have a deterministic time to produce an output value (based on the time for the data to flow through the network), fully recurrent networks can take an in-determinate amount of time.

In the best case, the neural network will reverberate a few times and quickly settle into a stable, minimal energy state. At this time, the output values can be read from the output units. In less optimal circumstances, the network might cycle quite a few times before it settles into an answer. In worst cases, the network will fall into a limit cycle, visiting the same set of answer states over and over without ever settling down. Another possibility is that the network will enter a chaotic pattern and never visit the same output state.

By placing some constraints on the connection weights, we can ensure that the network will enter a stable state. The connections between units must be symmetrical. Fully recurrent networks are used primarily for optimization problems and as associative memories. A nice attribute with optimization problems is that depending on the time available, you can choose to get the recurrent network's current answer or wait a longer time for it to settle into a better one. This behavior is similar to the performance of people in certain tasks.

5.3 NEURAL NETWORK MODELS

The combination of topology, learning paradigm (supervised or non-supervised learning), and learning algorithm defines a neural network model. There is a wide selection of popular neural network models. For data mining, perhaps the back propagation network and the Kohonen feature map are the most popular. However, there are many different types of neural networks in use. Some are optimized for fast training, a few others for fast recall of stored memories, and the next for computing the best possible answer regardless of training or recall time. But the best model for a given application or data mining function depends on the data and the function required.

The discussion that follows is intended to provide an intuitive understanding of the differences between the major types of neural networks. No details of the mathematics behind these models are provided.

Back Propagation Networks

A back propagation neural network uses a feed-forward topology, supervised learning, and the (what else) back propagation learning algorithm. This algorithm was responsible in large part for the reemergence of neural networks in the mid 1980s.

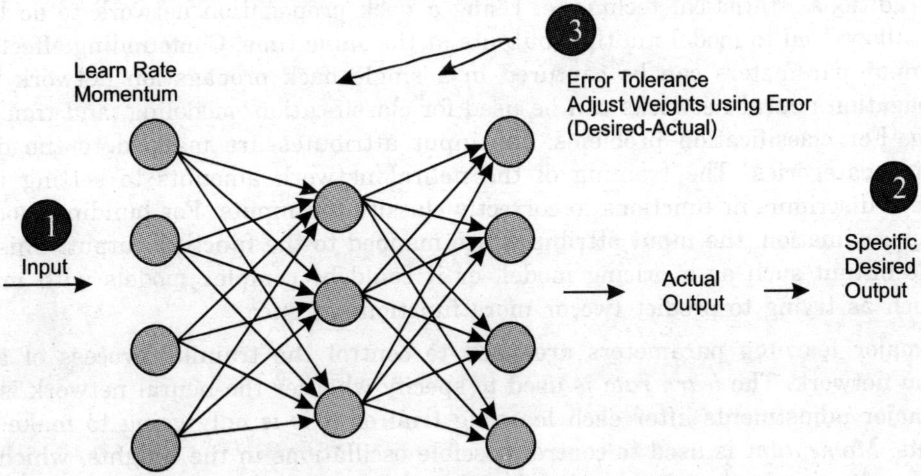

Figure 5.4. Back Propagation Networks

Back propagation is a general purpose learning algorithm. It is powerful but also expensive in terms of computational requirements for training. A back propagation network with a single hidden layer of processing elements can model any continuous function to any degree of accuracy (given enough processing elements in the hidden layer). There are literally hundreds of variations of back propagation in the neural network literature, and all claim to be superior to "basic" back propagation in one way or the other. Indeed, since back propagation is based on a relatively simple form of optimization known as gradient descent, mathematically astute observers soon proposed modifications using more powerful techniques such as conjugate gradient and Newton's methods. However, "basic" back propagation is still the most widely used variant. Its two primary virtues are that it is simple and easy to understand, and it works for a wide range of problems.

The basic back propagation algorithm consists of three steps (see Figure 5.4). The input pattern is presented to the input layer of the network. These inputs are propagated through the network until they reach the output units. This forward pass produces the actual or predicted output pattern. Because back propagation is a supervised learning algorithm, the desired outputs are given as part of the training vector. The actual network outputs are subtracted from the desired outputs and an error signal is produced. This error signal is then the basis for the back propagation step, whereby the errors are passed back through the neural network by computing the contribution of each hidden processing unit and deriving the corresponding adjustment needed to produce the correct output. The connection weights are then adjusted and the neural network has just "learned" from an experience.

As mentioned earlier, back propagation is a powerful and flexible tool for data modeling and analysis. Suppose you want to do linear regression. A back propagation network with no hidden units can be easily used to build a regression model relating multiple input parameters to multiple outputs or dependent variables. This type of back propagation network actually uses an algorithm called the *delta rule*, first proposed by Widrow and Hoff (1960).

Adding a single layer of hidden units turns the linear neural network into a nonlinear one, capable of performing multivariate logistic regression, but with some distinct advantages over the traditional statistical technique. Using a back propagation network to do logistic regression allows you to model multiple outputs at the same time. Confounding effects from multiple input parameters can be captured in a single back propagation network model. Back propagation neural networks can be used for classification, modeling, and time-series forecasting. For classification problems, the input attributes are mapped to the desired classification categories. The training of the neural network amounts to setting up the correct set of discriminant functions to correctly classify the inputs. For building models or function approximation, the input attributes are mapped to the function output. This could be a single output such as a pricing model, or it could be complex models with multiple outputs such as trying to predict two or more functions at once.

Two major learning parameters are used to control the training process of a back propagation network. The *learn rate* is used to specify whether the neural network is going to make major adjustments after each learning trial or if it is only going to make minor adjustments. *Momentum* is used to control possible oscillations in the weights, which could be caused by alternately signed error signals. While most commercial back propagation tools provide anywhere from 1 to 10 or more parameters for you to set, these two will usually produce the most impact on the neural network training time and performance.

Kohonen Feature Maps

Kohonen feature maps are feed-forward networks that use an unsupervised training algorithm, and through a process called self-organization, configure the output units into a topological or spatial map. Kohonen (1988) was one of the few researchers who continued working on neural networks and associative memory even after they lost their cachet as a research topic in the 1960s. His work was reevaluated during the late 1980s, and the utility of the self-organizing feature map was recognized. Kohonen has presented several enhancements to this model, including a supervised learning variant known as *Learning Vector Quantization* (LVQ).

A feature map neural network consists of two layers of processing units an input layer fully connected to a competitive output layer. There are no hidden units. When an input pattern is presented to the feature map, the units in the output layer compete with each other for the right to be declared the winner. The winning output unit is typically the unit whose incoming connection weights are the closest to the input pattern (in terms of Euclidean distance). Thus the input is presented and each output unit computes its closeness or match score to the input pattern. The output that is deemed closest to the input pattern is declared the winner and so earns the right to have its connection weights adjusted. The connection weights are moved in the direction of the input pattern by a factor determined by a learning rate parameter. This is the basic nature of competitive neural networks.

The Kohonen feature map creates a topological mapping by adjusting not only the winner's weights, but also adjusting the weights of the adjacent output units in close proximity or in the neighborhood of the winner. So not only does the winner get adjusted, but the whole neighborhood of output units gets moved closer to the input pattern. Starting from randomized weight values, the output units slowly align themselves such that when an input pattern is presented, a neighborhood of units responds to the input pattern. As training progresses, the size of the neighborhood radiating out from the winning unit is decreased. Initially large numbers of output units will be updated, and later on smaller and smaller numbers are updated until at the end of training only the winning unit is adjusted. Similarly, the learning rate will decrease as training progresses, and in some implementations, the learn rate decays with the distance from the winning output unit.

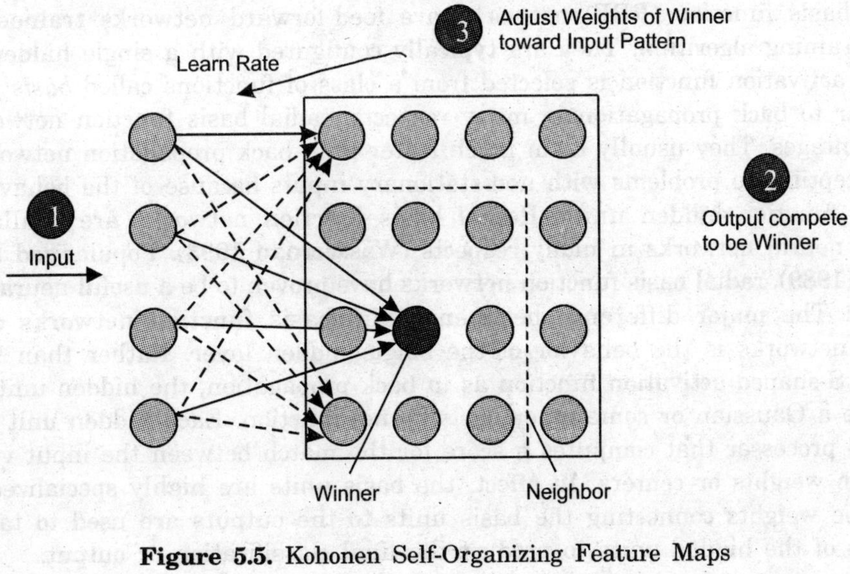

Figure 5.5. Kohonen Self-Organizing Feature Maps

Looking at the feature map from the perspective of the connection weights, the Kohonen map has performed a process called vector quantization or code book generation in the engineering literature. The connection weights represent a typical or prototype input pattern for the subset of inputs that fall into that cluster. The process of taking a set of high dimensional data and reducing it to a set of clusters is called segmentation. The high-dimensional input space is reduced to a two-dimensional map. If the index of the winning output unit is used, it essentially partitions the input patterns into a set of categories or clusters.

From a data mining perspective, two sets of useful information are available from a trained feature map. Similar customers, products, or behaviors are automatically clustered together or segmented so that marketing messages can be targeted at homogeneous groups. The information in the connection weights of each cluster defines the typical attributes of an item that falls into that segment. This information lends itself to immediate use for evaluating what the clusters mean. When combined with appropriate visualization tools and/or analysis of both the population and segment statistics, the makeup of the segments identified by the feature map can be analyzed and turned into valuable business intelligence.

Recurrent Back Propagation

Recurrent back propagation is, as the name suggests, a back propagation network with feedback or recurrent connections. Typically, the feedback is limited to either the hidden layer units or the output units. In either configuration, adding feedback from the activation of outputs from the prior pattern introduces a kind of memory to the process. Thus adding recurrent connections to a back propagation network enhances its ability to learn temporal sequences without fundamentally changing the training process. Recurrent back propagation networks will, in general, perform better than regular back propagation networks on time-series prediction problems.

Radial Basis Function

Radial basis function (RBF) networks are feed-forward networks trained using a supervised training algorithm. They are typically configured with a single hidden layer of units whose activation function is selected from a class of functions called *basis functions*. While similar to back propagation in many respects, radial basis function networks have several advantages. They usually train much faster than back propagation networks. They are less susceptible to problems with non-stationary inputs because of the behavior of the radial basis function hidden units. Radial basis function networks are similar to the probabilistic neural networks in many respects (Wasserrnan 1993). Popularized by Moody and Darken (1989), radial basis function networks have proven to be a useful neural network architecture. The major difference between radial basis function networks and back propagation networks is the behavior of the single hidden layer. Rather than using the sigmoidal or S-shaped activation function as in back propagation, the hidden units in RBF networks use a Gaussian or some other basis kernel function. Each hidden unit acts as a locally tuned processor that computes a score for the match between the input vector and its connection weights or centers. In effect, the basis units are highly specialized pattern detectors. The weights connecting the basis units to the outputs are used to take linear combinations of the hidden units to product the final classification or output.

• •

Remember that in a back propagation network, all weights in all of the layers are adjusted at the same time. In radial basis function networks, however, the weights in the hidden layer basis units are usually set before the second layer of weights is adjusted. As the input moves away from the connection weights, the activation value falls off. This behavior leads to the use of the term "center" for the first-layer weights. These center weights can be computed using Kohonen feature maps, statistical methods such as K-Means clustering, or some other means. In any case, they are then used to set the areas of sensitivity for the RBF hidden units, which then remain fixed. Once the hidden layer weights are set, a second phase of training is used to adjust the output weights. This process typically uses the standard back propagation training rule.

In its simplest form, all hidden units in the RBF network have the same width or degree of sensitivity to inputs. However, in portions of the input space where there are few patterns, it is sometime desirable to have hidden units with a wide area of reception. Likewise, in portions of the input space, which are crowded, it might be desirable to have very highly tuned processors with narrow reception fields. Computing these individual widths increases the performance of the RBF network at the expense of a more complicated training process.

Adaptive Resonance Theory

Adaptive resonance theory (ART) networks are a family of recurrent networks that can be used for clustering. Based on the work of researcher Stephen Grossberg (1987), the ART models are designed to be biologically plausible. Input patterns are presented to the network, and an output unit is declared a winner in a process similar to the Kohonen feature maps. However, the feedback connections from the winner output encode the expected input pattern template. If the actual input pattern does not match the expected connection weights to a sufficient degree, then the winner output is shut off, and the next closest output unit is declared as the winner. This process continues until one of the output unit's expectation is satisfied to within the required tolerance. If none of the output units wins, then a new output unit is committed with the initial expected pattern set to the current input pattern.

The ART family of networks has been expanded through the addition of fuzzy logic, which allows real-valued inputs, and through the ARTMAP architecture, which allows supervised training. The ARTMAP architecture uses back-to-back ART networks, one to classify the input patterns and one to encode the matching output patterns. The MAP part of ARTMAP is a field of units (or indexes, depending on the implementation) that serves as an index between the input ART network and the output ART network. While the details of the training algorithm are quite complex, the basic operation for recall is surprisingly simple. The input pattern is presented to the input ART network, which comes up with a winner output. This winner output is mapped to a corresponding output unit in the output ART network. The expected pattern is read out of the output ART network, which provides the overall output or prediction pattern.

Probabilistic Neural Networks

Probabilistic neural networks (PNN) feature a feed-forward architecture and supervised training algorithm similar to back propagation (Specht, 1990). Instead of adjusting the input layer weights using the generalized delta rule, each training input pattern is used as the connection weights to a new hidden unit. In effect, each input pattern is incorporated into the PNN architecture. This technique is extremely fast, since only one pass through the network is required to set the input connection weights. Additional passes might be used to adjust the output weights to fine-tune the network outputs.

Several researchers have recognized that adding a hidden unit for each input pattern might be overkill. Various clustering schemes have been proposed to cut down on the number of hidden units when input patterns are close in input space and can be represented by a single hidden unit. Probabilistic neural networks offer several advantages over back propagation networks (Wasserman, 1993). Training is much faster, usually a single pass. Given enough input data, the PNN will converge to a Bayesian (optimum) classifier. Probabilistic neural networks allow true incremental learning where new training data can be added at any time without requiring retraining of the entire network. And because of the statistical basis for the PNN, it can give an indication of the amount of evidence it has for basing its decision.

Table 5.1. Neural Network Models and Their Functions

Model	*Training Paradigm*	*Topology*	*Primary Functions*
Adaptive resonance theory	Unsupervised	Recurrent	Clustering
ARTMAP	Supervised	Recurrent	Classification
Back propagation	Supervised	Feed-forward	Classification, modeling, time-series
Radial basis function networks	Supervised	Feed-forward	Classification, modeling, time-series
Probabilistic neural networks	Supervised	Feed-forward	Classification
Kohonen feature map	Unsupervised	Feed-forward	Clustering
Learning vector quantization	Supervised	Feed-forward	Classification
Recurrent back propagation	Supervised	Limited recurrent	Modeling, time-series
Temporal difference learning	Reinforcement	Feed-forward	Time-sereis

Key Issues in Selecting Models and Architecture

Selecting which neural network model to be used for a particular application is straightforward if you use the following process. First, select the function you want to perform. This can include clustering, classification, modeling, or time-series approximation. Then look at the input data with which you have to train the network. If the data is all binary, or if it contains real-valued inputs, that might disqualify some of the network architectures. Next you should determine how much data you have and how fast you need to train the network. This might suggest using probabilistic neural networks or radial basis function networks rather than a back propagation network. Table 5.1 can be used to aid in this selection process. Most commercial neural network tools should support at least one variant of these algorithms.

Our definition of architecture is the number of inputs, hidden, and output units. So in my view, you might select a back propagation model, but explore several different architectures having different numbers of hidden layers, and/or hidden units.

Data Type and Quantity. In some cases, whether the data is all binary or contains some real numbers that might help to determine which neural network model to be used. The standard ART network (called ART l) works only with binary data and is probably preferable to Kohonen maps for clustering if the data is all binary. If the input data has real values, then fuzzy ART or Kohonen maps should be used.

Training Requirements. (Online or batch learning) In general, whenever we want online learning, then training speed becomes the overriding factor in determining which neural network model to use. Back propagation and recurrent back propagation train quite slowly and so are almost never used in real-time or online learning situations. ART and radial basis function networks, however, train quite fast, usually in a few passes over the data.

Functional Requirements. Based on the function required, some models can be disqualified. For example, ART and Kohonen feature maps are clustering algorithms. They cannot be used for modeling or time-series forecasting. If you need to do clustering, then back propagation could be used, but it will be much slower training than using ART of Kohonen maps.

5.4 ITERATIVE DEVELOPMENT PROCESS

Despite all your selections, it is quite possible that the first or second time that you try to train it, the neural network will not be able to meet your acceptance criteria. When this happens you are then in a troubleshooting mode. What can be wrong and how can you fix it?

The major steps of the interactive development process are data selection and representation, neural network model selection, architecture specification, training parameter selection, and choosing an appropriate acceptance criteria. If any of these decisions are off the mark, the neural network might not be able to learn what you are trying to teach it. In the following sections, I describe the major decision points and the recovery options when things go wrong during training.

Network Convergence Issues

How do you know that you are in trouble while training a neural network model? The first hint is that it takes a long, long time for the network to train, and you are monitoring the classification accuracy or the prediction accuracy of the neural network. If you are plotting the RMS error, you will see that it falls quickly and then stays flat, or that it oscillates up and down. Either of these two conditions might mean that the network is trapped in a local minima, while the objective is to reach the global minima.

There are two primary ways around this problem. First, you can add some random noise to the neural network weights in order to try to break it free from the local minima. The other option is to reset the network weights to new random values and start training all over again. This might not be enough to get the neural network to converge on a solution. Any of the design decisions you made might be negatively impacting the ability of the neural network to learn the function you are trying to teach.

Model Selection

It is sometimes best to revisit your major choices in the same order as your original decisions. Did you select an inappropriate neural network model for the function you are trying to perform? If so, picking a neural network model that can perform the function is the solution. If not, it is most likely a simple matter of adding more hidden units or another layer of hidden units. In practice, one layer of hidden units usually will suffice. Two layers are required only if you have added a large number of hidden units and the network still has not converged. If you do not provide enough hidden units, the neural network will not have the computational power to learn some complex nonlinear functions.

Other factors besides the neural network architecture could be at work. Maybe the data has a strong temporal or time element embedded in it. Often a recurrent back propagation or a radial basis function network will perform better than regular back propagation. If the inputs are non-stationary, that is they change slowly over time, then radial basis function networks are definitely going to work best.

Data Representation

If a neural network does not converge to a solution, and if you are sure that your model architecture is appropriate for the problem, then the next thing is to reevaluate your data representation decisions. In some cases, a key input parameter is not being scaled or coded in a manner that lets the neural network learn its importance to the function at hand. One example is a continuous variable, which has a large range in the original domain and is scaled down to a 0 to 1 value for presentation to the neural network. Perhaps a thermometer coding with one unit for each magnitude of 10 is in order. This would change the representation of the input parameter from a single input to 5, 6, or 7, depending on the range of the value.

A more serious problem is a key parameter missing from the training data. In some ways, this is the most difficult problem to detect. You can easily spend much time playing around with the data representation trying to get the network to converge. Unfortunately, this is one area where experience is required to know what a normal training process feels like and what one that is doomed to failure feels like. It is also important to have a domain expert involved who can provide ideas when things are not working. A domain expert might recognize an important parameter missing from the training data.

Model Architectures

In some cases, we have done everything right, but the network just won't converge. It could be that the problem is just too complex for the architecture you have specified. By adding additional hidden units, and even another hidden layer, you are enhancing the computational abilities of the neural network. Each new connection weight is another free variable, which can be adjusted. That is why it is good practice to start out with an abundant supply of hidden units when you first start working on a problem. Once you are sure that the neural network can learn the function, you can start reducing the number of hidden units until the generalization performance meets your requirements. But beware. Too much of a good thing can be bad, too!

If some additional hidden units are good, is adding a few more better? In most cases, no! Giving the neural network more hidden units (and the associated connection weights) can actually make it too easy for the network. In some cases, the neural network will simply learn to memorize the training patterns. The neural network has optimized to the training set's particular patterns and has not extracted the important relationships in the data. You could have saved yourself time and money by just using a lookup table. The whole point is to get the neural network to detect key features in the data in order to generalize when presented with patterns it has not seen before. There is nothing worse than a fat, lazy neural network. By keeping the hidden layers as thin as possible, you usually get the best results.

Avoiding Over-Training

While training a neural network, it is important to understand when to stop. It is natural to think that if 100 epochs are good, then 1000 epochs will be much better. However, this intuitive idea of "more practice is better" doesn't hold with neural networks. If the same training patterns or examples are given to the neural network over and over, and the weights are adjusted to match the desired outputs, we are essentially telling the network to memorize the patterns, rather than to extract the essence of the relationships. What happens is that the neural network performs extremely well on the training data. However, when it is presented with patterns it hasn't seen before, it cannot generalize and does not perform well. What is the problem? It is called over-training.

Over-training a neural network is similar to when an athlete practices and practices for an event on his home court, and when the actual competition starts he or she is faced with an unfamiliar arena and circumstances, it might be impossible for him or her to react and perform at the same levels as during training.

It is important to remember that we are not trying to get the neural network to make as best predictions as it can on the training data. We are trying to optimize its performance on the testing and validation data. Most commercial neural network tools provide the means to switch automatically between training and testing data. The idea is to check the network performance on the testing data while you are training.

Automating the Process

What has been described in the preceding sections is the manual process of building a neural network model. It requires some degree of skill and experience with neural networks and model building in order to be successful. Having to tweak many parameters and make somewhat arbitrary decisions concerning the neural network architecture does not seem like a great advantage to some application developers. Because of this, researchers have worked in a variety of ways to minimize these problems.

Perhaps the first attempt was to automate the selection of the appropriate number of hidden layers and hidden units in the neural network. This was approached in a number of ways: a priori attempts to compute the required architecture by looking at the data, building arbitrary large networks and then pruning out nodes and connections until the smallest network that could do the job is produced, and starting with a small network and then growing it up until it can perform the task appropriately.

Genetic algorithms are often used to optimize functions using parallel search methods based on the biological theory of nature. If we view the selection of the number of hidden layers and hidden units as an optimization problem, genetic algorithms can be used to find the optimum architecture.

The idea of pruning nodes and weights from neural networks in order to improve their generalization capabilities has been explored by several research groups (Sietsma and Dow, 1988). A network with an arbitrarily large number of hidden units is created and trained to perform some processing function. Then the weights connected to a node are analyzed to see if they contribute to the accurate prediction of the output pattern. If the weights are extremely small, or if they do not impact the prediction error when they are removed, then that node and its weights are pruned or removed from the network. This process continues until the removal of any additional node causes a decrease in the performance on the test set.

Several researchers have also explored the opposite approach to pruning. That is, a small neural network is created, and additional hidden nodes and weights are added incrementally. The network prediction error is monitored, and as long as performance on the test data is improving, additional hidden units are added. The cascade correlation network allocates a whole set of potential new network nodes. These new nodes compete with each other and the one that reduces the prediction error the most is added to the network. Perhaps the highest level of automation of the neural network data mining process will come with the use of intelligent agents.

5.5 STRENGTHS AND WEAKNESSES OF ARTIFICIAL NEURAL NETWORKS

Strengths of Artificial Neural Networks

- **Neural Networks are Versatile.** Neural networks provide a very general way of approaching problems. When the output of the network is continuous, such as the appraised value of a home, then it is performing prediction. When the output has discrete values, then it is doing classification. A simple re-arrangement of the neurons and the network becomes adept at detecting clusters.

  The fact that neural networks are so versatile definitely accounts for their popularity. The effort needed to learn how to use them and to learn how to massage data is not wasted, since the knowledge can be applied wherever neural networks would be appropriate.

- **Neural Networks can Produce Good Results in Complicated Domains.** Neural networks produce good results. Across a large number of industries and a large number of applications, neural networks have proven themselves over and over again. These results come in complicated domains, such as analyzing time series and detecting fraud, that are not easily amenable to other techniques. The largest neural network in production use is probably the system that AT&T uses for reading numbers on checks. This neural network has hundreds of thousands of units organized into seven layers.

As compared to standard statistics or to decision-tree approaches, neural networks are much more powerful. They incorporate non-linear combinations of features into their results, not limiting themselves to rectangular regions of the solution space. They are able to take advantage of all the possible combinations of features to arrive at the best solution.

- **Neural Networks can Handle Categorical and Continuous Data Types.** Although the data has to be massaged, neural networks have proven themselves using both categorical and continuous data, both for inputs and outputs. Categorical data can be handled in two different ways, either by using a single unit with each category given a subset of the range from 0 to 1 or by using a separate unit for each category. Continuous data is easily mapped into the necessary range.
- **Neural Networks are Available in Many Off-the-Shelf Packages.** Because of the versatility of neural networks and their track record of good results, many software vendors provide off-the-shelf tools for neural networks. The competition between vendors makes these packages easy to use and ensures that advances in the theory of neural networks are brought to market.

Weaknesses of Artificial Neural Networks

- **All Inputs and Outputs Must be Massaged to [0.1].** The inputs to a neural network must be massaged to be in a particular range, usually between 0 and 1. This requires additional transforms and manipulations of the input data that require additional time, CPU power, and disk space. In addition, the choice of transform can effect the results of the network. Fortunately tools try to make this massaging process as simple as possible. Good tools provide histograms for seeing categorical values and automatically transform numeric values into the range. Still, skewed distributions with a few outliers can result in poor neural network performance. The requirement to massage the data is actually a mixed blessing. It requires analyzing the training set to verify the data values and their ranges. Since data quality is the number one issue in data mining, this additional perusal of the data can actually forestall problems later in the analysis.
- **Neural Networks cannot Explain Results.** This is the biggest criticism directed at neural networks. In domains where explaining rules may be critical, such as denying loan applications, neural networks are not the tool of choice. They are the tool of choice when acting on the results is more important than understanding them. Even though neural networks cannot produce explicit rules, sensitivity analysis does enable them to explain which inputs are more important than others. This analysis can be performed inside the network, by using the errors generated from back propagation, or it can be performed externally by poking the network with specific inputs.

- **Neural Networks may Converge on an Inferior Solution.** Neural networks usually converge on some solution for any given training set. Unfortunately, there is no guarantee that this solution provides the best model of the data. Use the test set to determine when a model provides good enough performance to be used on unknown data.

In Summary

Neural networks are the different paradigm for computing and this act as a bridge between digital computer and the neural connections in human brain. There are three major connections topologies that define how data flows between the input, hidden and output processing units of networks. These main categories are Feed forward, Limited recurrent and fully recurrent networks.

The key issues in selecting models and architecture includes: data type and quantity, Training requirements, functional requirements.